from Seed to Fruit

Global Trends, Fruitful Practices, and Emerging Issues among Muslims

EDITED BY
J. DUDLEY WOODBERRY

From Seed to Fruit:
Global Trends, Fruitful Practices, and Emerging Issues among Muslims
Copyright © 2008 by J. Dudley Woodberry

Unless otherwise indicated, all biblical quotations are taken from the Holy Bible, New Revised Standard Version Bible, copyright © 1989 National Council of the Churches of Christ in the United States of America. Used by permission. All rights reserved.

Cover and text: Hugh Pindur
Copyediting: Jennifer Orona
Editorial Manager: Naomi Bradley
Editorial Assistant: Johanna Deming

Published by William Carey Library
1605 E. Elizabeth St.
Pasadena, CA USA 91104
www.missionbooks.org

William Carey Library is a ministry of the
U.S. Center for World Mission, Pasadena, California
www.uscwm.org

Library of Congress Cataloging-in-Publication Data

From seed to fruit : global trends, fruitful practices, and emerging issues among Muslims / edited by J. Dudley Woodberry.
    p. cm.
ISBN 978-0-87808-003-8 (pbk.)
1. Missions to Muslims. I. Woodberry, John Dudley, 1934-
BV2625.F75 2008
266.0088'297--dc22
            2008014501

Contents

Foreword: The Vision

RICK LOVE

Revelation 5:9 provided the inspiration for the Global Trends and Fruitful Practices Consultation. In this heavenly scene, the Lamb of God is worshipped:

> *You are worthy to take the scroll and to open its seals, because you were slain, and with your blood you purchased for God members of every tribe and language and people and nation (TNIV).*

During our gathering in Southeast Asia, we experienced a foretaste of the multi-ethnic diversity of this harvest. What a privilege it was to gather with almost 500 brothers and sisters from around the globe. We analyzed Global Trends, discerned Fruitful Practices, enjoyed stimulating fellowship, and celebrated what God is doing around the world.

Revelation 5:9 not only inspires us but also guides us into the future. The Lamb of God has purchased people from every tribe and language and people and nation. Because of this, we know that there will be followers of Jesus from every Muslim ethnic group worshipping around the throne of God. The cross of Christ secures this future harvest. We do not know when this vision will be fulfilled, but we have a cross-centered *certainty* that it will be!

This rock-solid certainty of the harvest is based on the cross of Christ. Because of this, there should be no place for triumphalism or superiority in our lives. We are saved by the cross, and our service should be marked by the cross. If we follow the Lamb who was slain, our lives should reflect his meekness and gentleness. Our cross-centered certainty should be matched by a cross-centered *humility*.

The cross also guarantees the rich diversity of the future harvest: the Lamb of God has purchased men and women from every language, tribe, people, and nation. Revelation 5:9 specifically describes cultural *diversity* as part of God's plan. This Consultation previewed the diversity of the future. As followers of Jesus from many cultures and countries, we gathered together to learn from one another. Our goal was to become more fruitful in offering the Gospel of peace to Muslims.

Our time of celebration on the last night of the Consultation was one of the highlights for me. The joyful multi-colored throng of culturally diverse people leading us in worship on stage was a foretaste of heaven. This is where Revelation 5:9 leads us—to worship. Back at the heavenly scene, the worship of the Lamb continues (Revelation 5:10) by saying that we are a kingdom of priests. The ultimate goal of our gathering and laboring is *doxology*!

Acknowledgements: Laborers United by a Vision

"We are laborers together with God" (*1 Corinthians 3:9,* KJV).

The present volume was far more of a team project than possibly anything on this topic before. First there was the vision by emerging leaders shortly after the turn of the millennium to see, by the grace of God, effective efforts to plant Jesus-fellowships among all Muslim people groups. Most of the people are unnamed, leaving the glory to God and not wanting to cause difficulties for their callings around the world.

The thousands who became involved in the subsequent surveys, discussions, case studies, and testimonies again are unnamed, but this book would not have been possible without them. The same can be said of the many involved in the analysis since the Consultation in Southeast Asia in the spring of 2007.

However, there are some behind the scenes whom we must mention. Jennifer Orona served as the administrator and copyeditor of the entire book with competence and grace, despite other pressing duties and severe sickness in her family. I offer special thanks to Darrell and Linda Dorr, who, through the editorial process, offered wise counsel and helpful proofreading. Sherry Charis served well as the copyeditor of the Fruitful Practices section, which involved mountains of information following the Consultation.

Additionally, a number of people pitched in at difficult times, such as Chris and Jaime Hantla, Minh Ha Nguyen, the Knowledge Stewardship Team, and others.

Then there are our families—my wife Roberta in my case—who have had to live without the level of help and companionship they deserve.

Finally, there is praise to God—the Lord of the Harvest—who inspires and empowers us and is worthy of all our honor and praise.

J. Dudley Woodberry
July 1, 2008

Introduction: From Seed to Fruit

"I appointed you to go and bear fruit, fruit that will last."
John 15:16

A picture of the seeds spilling out of a pomegranate was chosen for the cover of this book, not only because of its striking appearance, but because through the ages the pomegranate has become a symbol of new life—a major reason for the compiling of these studies.

Biblical metaphors from nature have been chosen as an integrating theme because they express the mystery of the interplay between the divine and the human, as in Paul's description, "I planted, Apollos watered but God gave the growth" (1 Corinthians 3:6). We see the same in the sower, the seed, the soil, and the sun in the Parable of the Sower (Luke 8:4–15), which provides imagery throughout the book. Like all analogies, it is possible to read into this picture more than is intended, in this case for people made in the image of God to feel that they are depersonalized when they are portrayed as grain to be harvested. But such was far from the mind of the original Sower and must also be far from the thoughts of those of us who seek to follow in his footsteps.

THE SHOULDERS ON WHICH WE STAND

A century ago, the first General Conference for work among Muslims met in Cairo (April 4–9, 1906), with sixty-two appointed delegates representing twenty-nine mission societies and sixty official visitors. They looked at the state of Islam throughout the world, the scope of Christian ministries among Muslims, and the practices employed among them—all themes of the present publication.[1] The chairman was Samuel Zwemer, through whom, as a boy, I received my own call to ministry. He also co-edited with Annie Van Sommer *Our Moslem Sisters*,[2] the papers presented on work among women.

The Muslim world had a prominent place in the World Missionary Conference in Edinburgh in 1910, but a conference in Lucknow, January 23–28, 1911, was devoted entirely to the Muslim world. The conference surveyed the Muslim world more completely than the 1906 conference, addressed the equipping of Christian workers, and work among women—again, themes of the present volume.[3]

The focus on people groups more than nations became prominent at the Lausanne Congress on World Evangelization in 1974. Then at Glen Eyrie in Colorado Springs in 1978, the North American Lausanne Committee sponsored a conference on the Muslim world. In preparation for this, papers were written on the comparative status of Christianity and Islam throughout the world. But with few Muslim background believers or worshipping fellowships comprised of them to draw from, authors of papers on practices had to draw largely on insights from anthropology, church growth, and contextualization among other people groups, coupled with Scripture, to suggest practices that might be fruitful. These papers were published in *The Gospel and Islam*, edited by Don M. McCurry.[4]

These insights and the focus on Muslim unreached people groups (MUPGs) continued with the Muslim Track of the Lausanne Committee in a series of consultations in Pattaya in Thailand, Zeist in Holland, and Manila in the Philippines. Concurrently, there began to be considerable growth in the number of Muslims who followed Jesus.

The Present Volume

In the light of that growth, for the past few years, practitioners from more than a dozen Christian organizations have been sharing the practices that God has been blessing in raising groups of Jesus-followers and collecting data on Muslim people

---

[1]   J. Christy Wilson, *Apostle to Islam: A Biography of Samuel M. Zwemer* (Grand Rapids, MI: Baker Book House, 1952), 171–173; S.M. Zwemer et al., eds., *The Mohammedan World of Today* (New York: Fleming H. Revell, 1906).

[2]   New York: Fleming H. Revell, 1907.

[3]   Wilson, *Apostle to Islam*, 173–176; the papers published in E.M. Wherry, et al., *Islam and Mission* (New York: Fleming H. Revell, 1912).

[4]   Monrovia, CA: MARC/World Vision International, 1979.

groups and their access to Christian witness. These surveys were then discussed with a group of practitioners in Southeast Asia in the spring of 2007.

What was new about this consultation was that it included both a larger number of practitioners whom God had used to plant Jesus-fellowships in the Muslim world and a sufficient number of executives of organizations who could make decisions concerning future activity. The results of the deliberations at the Consultation were analyzed in the subsequent months and compiled in this volume. Also, an attempt has been made to include men and women writers from the North and the Global South—including in the editing of the volume, though the sensitivity of the material, coupled with ministry commitments and communication problems, ultimately precluded the latter. In the following, we will highlight some of the fresh insights that have been developed in the subsequent chapters.

GLOBAL TRENDS

Three major sources of demographic analysis of Muslim people groups (MPGs) and their access to the gospel witness were integrated. These were the *World Christian Encyclopedia*,[5] the Church Planting Progress Indicators of the International Mission Board (Southern Baptist), and the Joshua Project. Field practitioners then compared this data with their current surveys of each region and updated the data. The results are on the CD accompanying this Compendium. Besides updating the data on Muslim people groups, the researchers found a substantial increase in the number of Muslims who have decided to follow Christ—more in the last forty years than in the previous centuries since the rise of Islam. Many of these have not chosen to join existing churches, however.

In chapter one, Patrick Johnstone surveys the world and the relative status of Muslims and Christians, noting the trend of major Christian—especially Evangelical—growth pointing into the future. He introduces the designation Affinity Bloc to refer to the largest cluster of people groups in which the Gospel can spread without encountering significant barriers of understanding and acceptance (e.g., Arab peoples, Malay peoples). He in turn divides these Affinity Blocs into People Clusters (e.g., Kurds, Berbers). Both designations are helpful for assisting with inter-ministry cooperation. Details can be found on the CD accompanying this volume.

---

5   David B. Barrett, et al., eds. (New York: Oxford University Press, 2001).

In chapter two Jeff Liverman looks at the unreached, or unengaged, Muslim people groups—approximately 247 of which, at the time, were 100,000 or more. He looks at the criteria for evaluating them and the task that lies ahead.

Andrea and Leith Gray in chapter three join many others in the field of Scripture translation by moving from considering the end goal to be just a printed Bible in the language of a people. Instead, the goal is to facilitate people being transformed by the Gospel, with the printed Bible being one of the Scripture-based tools. Seven factors are identified that God has been using to impact Muslims with the Scriptures—such as the intended audience, oral communication strategies, and relevance of the message.

In chapter four, Greg Livingstone, in his typically provocative way, shows the potential and problems of expecting witnesses from the Global South to complete the task of engaging the rest of the Muslim world. He then offers promising examples from Africa of local leadership and funding of Christians to live in Muslim contexts.

Sue Eenigenberg, in chapter five, calls attention to the major role women have had in mission history, the unique roles they can play in ministries among Muslims, and encourages respect for women as co-laborers.

Since this is a time of "first fruits" of the harvest, Jim Haney, in chapter six, notes issues that call for our attention as we work toward future harvests—such as improving our information on people groups, monitoring engagement, giving attention to the types of people sent, and learning from Muslim background believers (MBBs).

FRUITFUL PRACTICES

For the Fruitful Practices track, 280 practitioners of thirty-seven nationalities and from fifty-six different organizations gathered. They were from teams that had planted 738 fellowships, and they evaluated ninety-four practices that had been gathered from surveys of 5,800 field workers. The evaluation of the practices took place in small group discussions in which case studies were shared and the extent to which fruitful practices were practiced and considered important was determined. Individual accounts were also recorded and transcribed. In the following months, this material was analyzed and given to key practitioners who wrote the chapters in this compendium.

With respect to the contexts in which Jesus-fellowships are developing, 40 percent of them had experienced social upheaval or natural disasters—an observation previously made in church growth studies. Also, Muslims are following Jesus throughout the spectrum of types of contextualization—from those in traditional churches using non-indigenous language to secret believers. A majority of the fellowships are in what is called the C3 to C5 range—that is, from those using the Muslims' language and non-religious indigenous cultural forms and calling themselves Christians to "Messianic Muslims" who have accepted Jesus as Lord and Savior but remain legally and socially in the Muslim community.

Don Allen in chapter seven sets the tone for the Fruitful Practices approach—learning what God is doing so that we can cooperate with him. In the subsequent four chapters, each team of authors discusses ten or so fruitful practices, indicating the extent to which the practitioners practiced them and considered them important.

In chapter eight, on witnessing, by David Greenlee and Pam Wilson, some practices might have been expected, such as communicating in the heart language of the people, as opposed to the trade language. Subsequent analysis, however, suggested a far greater importance for this than might have been expected because teams that did use the heart language saw significantly more churches planted. Other observations were against conventional wisdom, such as a believer from the Sahel who said the best time to share your faith with women is not when it can be one-on-one, when they may be uncomfortable, but at parties and other gatherings where they feed on each other's questions.

John Becker and Erik Simuyu in chapter nine, on discipling, as one would expect, bring out the importance of modeling the Christian life, but then, perhaps unexpectedly, note that discipling often begins before conversion (belonging before believing in some contexts).

Chapter ten on planting reproducing fellowships or churches by Eric and Laura Adams emphasizes working within relational networks with pre-existing trust bonds and allowing Muslim background believers to discern the interpretation of Scripture in their context and under the guidance of the Holy Spirit. They also raise the problem of identity in relation to the Muslim community and any traditional churches in the area.

"The Equipping of Leaders," chapter eleven by Debora Viveza and Dwight Samuel, emphasizes choosing local leaders on the basis of character over credentials (e.g., level of literacy is not a primary qualification) and mentoring leaders intentionally, through practical experience, and locally to the extent possible.

In "The Gathering of Teams of Laborers," chapter twelve, Andrew and Rachel Chard bring out some interesting results from our sample. Teams of eight or more adults had a greater probability of planting at least one fellowship, and teams of at least twelve adults had a greater probability of planting multiple fellowships. Also, teams with at least one member with high language skill who also incorporated the learning preference of the people (oral or written) had a greater probability of planting multiple fellowships.

EMERGING ISSUES IN FRUITFUL PRACTICES

Some issues arose in the Fruitful Practices track that called for more attention. Muslims are following Jesus and choosing to identify with any one of a spectrum of fellowships, yet there has been some tension between Christian workers as to the legitimacy of what has been termed 'insider movements'—that is, Muslims who accept Jesus as Savior and Lord but retain their Muslim legal and social identity. Therefore, John and Anna Travis wrote chapter thirteen on "Factors Affecting the Identity That Jesus-followers Choose" with contributions by Phil Parshall, since the authors had differing perspectives but were irenic. The context, attitudes toward Islam and traditional Christians, and understandings of what is the best way to attract families and neighbors to Christ are among the influences.

"Factors That Facilitate Fellowships Becoming Movements," chapter fourteen, by David Garrison and Seneca Garrison, develops the five elements in every church planting movement—effective ways of initiating a Gospel witness, an effective Gospel witness, immediate and basic discipleship, effective fellowship formation, and ongoing leadership development.

Jack Colgate in chapter fifteen writes on "Bible Storying and Oral Use of the Scriptures" since 75 percent of the people at the Consultation work with people who have an oral learning preference. Annie Ward suggests in a sidebar that, even for literate groups, oral story presentations should often be given before the written Word so that people are better able to share with others. Some Muslims are already familiar with many biblical characters, so stories can be built on what they know.

Chapter sixteen, on "Expatriates Empowering Indigenous Leaders," is written by practitioners from North Africa, Central Asia, and the Middle East—Abraham Durán, Michael Schuler, and Moses Sy. After stating that the expatriates must decrease and the local leaders must increase, they note different ways that this is handled. In some cases, the expatriate models servant leadership but turns over responsibility as quickly as possible to the identified leaders. In other cases, expatriates do "shadow pastoring," coaching a local leader but not attending the gatherings. For this to work well, there must be a "man or woman of peace," an influential member of the community who acts as a bridge to the community.

In chapter seventeen J. R. Meydan and Ramsay Harris deal with the dilemma of Muslim background believers and funding. While recognizing the value of humanitarian aid, community development, relief work, and the importance of generosity, the authors point out specific issues in work among Muslims and give a number of sobering case studies of the problems that unwise funding has caused. The authors end with a helpful suggested code of financial ethics to stimulate further discussion.

A significant proportion of the people whom the practitioners live among could be described as folk Muslims—that is, Muslims whose faith and practice are mixed with many pre-Islamic elements and often occult practices. Therefore, in chapter eighteen, Caleb Chul-Soo Kim outlines a common folk Islamic worldview and the felt needs that it expresses. John and Anna Travis then describe their ministry of power encounters and a holistic approach to healing prayer, which addresses elements of the occult and inner hurts that hinder faith and often continue in new disciples.

In chapter nineteen, Don Allen and Abraham Durán deal with the question of how those who feel called to ministry among Muslims can start preparing themselves for serving in a team. The necessary qualifications include communion with Christ, character, living in community, biblical and professional knowledge, and cross-cultural skills.

Emerging Issues in Global Trends

Some issues have developed or been intensified by current trends today. As previously noted, 40 percent of the participants in the Consultation indicated that there had been a social upheaval or natural disaster in the last three years that affected their people group. These include the rise of Islamism, often in a militant form. Moussa Bongoyok, who was born in a Muslim family, has seen the spread of Islamism through his previously folk-Islamic part of Africa. Therefore, in chapter twenty, he speaks of the increased receptivity to the Gospel that has been observed in places where there has been a rise in Islamism and an alternative Christian presence as well—as in places such as Iran.

Since 9/11, there has been a polarization between some Muslims and Christians and a demonization of each other that has affected Christian witness. Joseph Cumming, in chapter twenty-one, shows that this is contrary to the character of our Lord and gives some amazing accounts of how God has enabled him to give a respectful witness in what would appear to be the most unlikely contexts.

In these troubled times, many Christians have felt that they needed to concentrate on peacemaking or planting churches but not both because either might hinder the other. However, the same Lord who charged us to "make disciples of all peoples" (Matthew 28:19) also said, "Blessed are the peacemakers" (Matthew 5:9). David Shenk and Ahmed Haile in chapter twenty-two have recounted some noteworthy examples of how a focus on peacemaking with Muslims also resulted in church formation.

Patrick Lai and Rick Love in chapter twenty-three tackle the problem of negotiating the tension between the secular and the apostolic roles that many practitioners must have in today's world, and how to honor commitments to the community one serves in the field and the sending community. With a study of the apostolic tent maker model of Paul and traditional rabbis with other jobs, the authors seek to develop an integrated identity that has integrity and credibility.

Nik Ripken, in the final chapter on "Recapturing the Role of Suffering," takes a different perspective than is common in the West, suggesting that rescuing brothers and sisters from persecution may not be compatible with planting fellowships. He counsels that we accept that persecution is normal and prepare ourselves and others for it, but strive to create a safe context for people to believe and experience Pentecost before the persecution.

Our Audiences, Including Muslim Friends

Some will read this book as a whole. Others will sample parts of it. For the latter, we have repeated some material and what certain abbreviations designate (such as MBB for Muslim background believers). But we also realize that this book will have three audiences—cross-cultural workers in the Church for which it is intended, but also Muslims and the media. This creates certain challenges in writing. Christians want to see how the present research relates to previous literature on church growth, church planting, and church-planting movements. But much of this material and the words used to convey it can be very offensive to our Muslim friends. Therefore there has been an attempt, though perhaps unsuccessful, to lean away from more militant, triumphalistic, and patronizing terms toward more sensitive, loving ones.

Both Islam and Christianity are missionary religions, however; so we both need to bear witness of our faith, but in a gracious way. The Qur'an says:

> *Invite to the Way of your Lord with wisdom and good exhortation*
> *(An-Nahl [16]:125).*

> *Dispute not with the People of the Book except in the best way*
> *(al-Ankabut [29]:46).*

The Bible in turn says:

> *Always be prepared to give an answer to anyone who calls you to*
> *account for the hope that is in you with gentleness and respect*
> *(1 Peter 3:15).*

Therefore, we have a common challenge.

A Seed That 'Dies'

The last chapter on suffering and even martyrdom is a reminder that unless a seed "falls into the ground and dies, it remains a single seed. But if it dies it brings forth much fruit" (John 12:24). In the following pages, we can see more fully the means God is using to transform that seed into fruit.

Part 1

Global Trends: Soils, Seed, Sowers, and First Fruits

EDITED BY JIM HANEY, SCOTT HOLSTE, AND MIKE BARNETT

Chapter 1

Look at the Fields: Survey of the Task

PATRICK JOHNSTONE

"Look at the fields! They are ripe for harvest."
John 4:35, NIV

INTRODUCTION

This Consultation is a very special event for me for several reasons. First, it is the first major gathering of its kind organized by mission agencies. Previous conferences on world evangelization in the twentieth century were initiated by evangelistic or Christian organizations with relatively little input invited from the very mission agencies most involved in doing the job. This Consultation is one in which the workers meeting together are engaged on the frontiers of implementing the command of Jesus in the Great Commission.

Secondly, this Consultation is a successor to the earlier significant Glen Eyrie Conference in 1978 in the United States on "The Gospel and Islam." Some of those who were there then are with us here. The major thrust of that earlier Consultation was on how to effectively share Christ among Muslims. A generation later, we meet to explore how better to plant churches or fellowships of followers of Jesus among Muslims. Praise God: we have moved on to a new level of engagement—not primarily evangelism, but church planting.

Just as the farmer went forth to sow his seed and found different soils and responses to his sowing, we live in a world today where there are measures of success and failure. We need to understand the degree to which we have been effective in the scattering of this precious seed. This chapter seeks to communicate this mix—encouragement with what God is doing and challenge about the task before us in the twenty-first century.

We have before us the challenge of formulating goals, for thinking strategically about our task, and working practically to accomplish our strategies. We want to establish accountability mechanisms to ensure we remain on target. I want to paint the broad picture to show how far we have come, and I want us to look to the future as well so that we can project into the future what are likely developments and how we could be prepared for effective twenty-first-century ministry.

I will be drawing on much hard work and research by many to do this, and in my projections I want to look ahead to the time when we hope to see effective church planting among all Muslim people groups (MPGs).

GOOD NEWS OR BAD NEWS?

In *The Clash of Civilizations and the Remaking of World Order*,[6] the scenario painted by Samuel Huntington is one in which Islam becomes the dominant world religion at the expense of Christianity. He seriously underestimated the growth of Christianity in the non-Western world, as do many Westerners. Subsequently, Philip Jenkins corrected Huntington in his book, *The Next Christendom: The Coming of Global Christianity*,[7] showing how Christianity was not about to succumb to the rise of Islam in the world. However, even he seriously underestimated the nature of the growth of the evangelical stream of Christianity, which far outstrips Islam in winning new followers of Christ.

So there exist two religious belief systems convinced of their unique rightness and with a clear eschatology of end-times—the Islamist wing of the Muslims and the evangelical stream of Christianity. These two movements are the major contenders for the souls of humankind in the first half of our new century. Later, I want to elaborate a little on the growth of both and the implications for us as we seek to bring the Gospel to Muslims.

---

[6]   New York: Simon & Schuster, 1996, 109–20.
[7]   Oxford: Oxford University Press, 2002, 5–6.

The bad news is that we face an enormous challenge in the twenty-first century if we are to see churches planted in every part of the Muslim world. It will be a tearful, painful, costly harvest, but the good news is that we are blessed with the promises of God, the presence of Jesus, the power of the Holy Spirit, and the ministry of intercession as "means" incomparably more powerful[8] than any opposing plans or actions.[9] The further good news is that since the rise of Islamism and the 1978 revolution in Iran, more Muslims have turned to Christ than in any time since the advent of Islam. Is it possible that the very advent of a radical Islamism could ultimately prove to be making the greatest cleft ever in the wall of Islam?

THE SPREAD OF ISLAM AND CHALLENGES

Islam is a missionary faith with a clear command from its scriptures to spread throughout the world.

From Islam's early years, conflict has been a means for achieving this. The massive expansion of the rule of Islam in the first century of its existence was largely through conquest. In later centuries, traders also became a vital means for Islam's expansion. During this time, large Christian populations in conquered lands were usually permitted to continue to exercise their faith in a state of *dhimmitude*.[10] As Muslim political and economic power waned after 1500, any expansion came largely through trade and migrations. By the twentieth century, migration became the dominant means for the spread of this faith, but not to the exclusion of the other two means—such as in the spread of Islam in the African Sahel, India, and parts of Indonesia.

Saudi Arabia has given vast sums of its oil wealth to promote its own variety of austere Wahhabi Islam. Saudi Arabia has successfully done this through mosque-building, aid programs, the provision of scholarships for Islamic studies, and in the West, and through political agendas and finance markets. In doing so, Saudi Arabia also prepared a seedbed for Islamism of the more extreme form.

Osama bin Laden's declaration of war against the "infidel" West in 1998 preceded the infamous 9/11 event, which has so powerfully defined the course

---

[8] See 2 Corinthians 10:3–5.

[9] See Psalm 2.

[10] Second-class, but protected, non-Muslim subjects of a Muslim state.

of this century so far. The result has been the polarization of the Muslim world and the specter of a global war.

Our Founder, the Prince of Peace, gave a very different order for world take-over in the Great Commission. In his plan, the meek would inherit the earth. Sadly, the whole nature of Christianity morphed into a militant Christendom after the conversion of the Roman Emperor Constantine in the fourth century. Muslims today have too many grounds for believing that Christian nations remain "crusaders"—politically, economically, and militarily. How can Westerners be bearers of the character and demeanor of our Founder rather than bearers of the heavy legacy of our dysfunctional national histories and the negative interactions with the world of Islam?

This has enormous impact on our role as church planters. I note a few:

» The rise of Islamism has been devastating for many indigenous Christian minorities and more dangerous for the survival of Jesus-centered believers. They are often in considerably more danger than the foreigner.
» Islamism has widened the cultural chasm between Muslims and non-Muslims in many multicultural societies, making "Islamic space" that excludes non-Muslims and openly hinders any form of cultural assimilation into host countries. So any form of outreach becomes more sensitive.
» Westerners, and especially missionaries from the United States and the United Kingdom, face particular additional challenges in serving in many parts of the Muslim world. Koreans, Indians, and Indonesians, and, to a lesser extent, Chinese and Filipinos do not carry the same historical and cultural baggage—the latter having their own restive Muslim minorities. We need to wisely involve this globalization of the world's mission force.
» I have often admired the almost brazen fearlessness of Nigerians and Indonesians in sharing the Gospel with Muslims. When we witness the growing use of suicide bombers by militant Islamists, how can we be any less dedicated to the point of laying down our lives for the sake of securing their eternal salvation?
» The successes of the Gospel.

THE RISE OF EVANGELICAL CHRISTIANITY

Now I want to switch tracks and look at evangelical[11] Christianity and its astonishing rise since 1960. Then I will return to the growth of Islam and compare and contrast their respective growths.

A careful reading of mission history will reveal that we owe a great debt to William Carey's passionate challenge to Protestant churches to engage in mission. Still, with the abundant Gospel sowing of the modern missionary movement, there may have been only three million Jesus-followers by as late as 1887, according to B. Broomhall in his *The Evangelisation of the World: a Missionary Band, a Record of Consecration, and an Appeal*.[12] Gospel sowing continued into the twentieth century, but after the 1910 Edinburgh Missionary Conference, the following half-century (1910–1960) found the seed falling upon an increasingly hardened soil marked by modern liberal theology. Compared to the years after 1960, few people chose to follow Christ during this time.

After 1960, two major factors stimulated an upturn in response—the rapid ending of Western colonial empires and the impact of people of God such as Billy Graham. The former freed the Gospel from its imperial shackles, and the latter united and encouraged cooperation among Evangelicals for world evangelization and made the evangelical movement credible.

The two lines on the next graph tell an amazing story. A revived evangelical movement in Europe, North America, and the Pacific grew in the midst of massive declines among non-Evangelicals, but it was in Africa, Asia, and Latin America where the massive growth occurred.

---

[11] Evangelicals generally believe the Lord Jesus to be the sole source of salvation through faith in him, have personal faith and conversion with regeneration by the Holy Spirit, recognize the Bible as the inspired Word of God and that it is the essential basis for faith and Christian living, and are committed to biblical witness, evangelism, and missions that bring others to faith in Christ.

[12] London: Morgan & Scott, 1889.

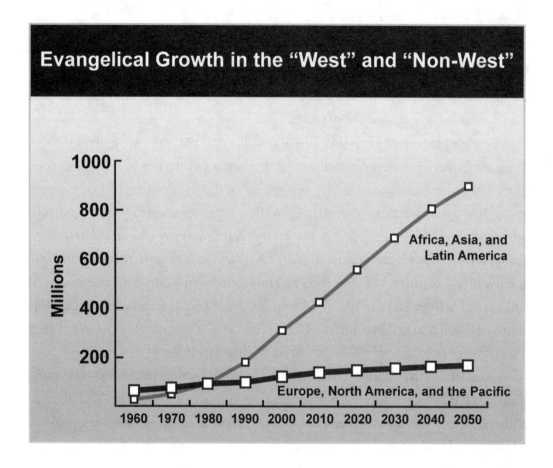

Fig.1.1

The following diagram shows the top twenty countries for evangelical populations in 1960 and 2000 while projecting the growth of Evangelicals well into the twenty-first century.

Evangelical Populations - The World's Top 20 Countries

1960		2000		2050	
Country	**mil**	**Country**	**mil**	**Country**	**mil**
United States	43.7	United States	99.8	China	240.9
United Kingdom	3.6	China	76.0	United States	138.1
South Africa	2.6	Nigeria	27.9	Nigeria	76.3
India	2.4	India	22.1	India	75.5
Brazil	2.4	Brazil	21.4	Ethiopia	58.1
Nigeria	2.2	Ethiopia	12.3	Brazil	51.3
Germany	2.1	Philippines	12.3	Uganda	41.6
Australia	1.9	Kenya	10.8	Philippines	34.0
Canada	1.6	Uganda	10.2	Congo, DRC	28.8
Kenya	1.4	Congo, DRC	10.0	Mexico	18.7
Congo, DRC	1.3	Indonesia	8.6	Indonesia	16.9
Indonesia	1.3	South Africa	7.8	Tanzania	15.9
China	1.2	Korea, South	7.3	Kenya	13.6
Korea, South	0.9	Mexico	6.6	Angola	12.5
Egypt	0.9	Tanzania	5.7	Sudan	10.9
Uganda	0.9	United Kingdom	5.0	Guatemala	9.5
Netherlands	0.8	Canada	3.3	Ghana	8.7
Romania	0.8	Sudan	3.1	Peru	8.3
Mexico	0.8	Ghana	3.0	Colombia	8.3
Philippines	0.7	Zimbabwe	3.0	Argentina	7.9

Africa	
Asia	
Latin America	
West	

Decline in Order	
Rise in Order	
New to Top 20	
No Change	

Fig.1.2

What does this diagram show us?

» The top twenty countries in 1960 are overwhelmingly Western, and even more, Anglophone. The United States is dominant in numbers and influence.

» The second top twenty shows the rise of African and Asian nations with huge increases in their evangelical populations. The United States retains its dominant position, but all other Western nations have fallen in ranking or dropped off the list entirely. This decline is less from absolute decline in numbers than from the fact that non-European nations have seen such growth and displaced the Western nations from this list. Ten of the twenty top nations

» are African.

» The 2050 list is, of course, a long-term prediction based on present trends and probable scenarios. One will immediately note that the United States has been replaced by China as having the world's largest number of Evangelicals of any country. Another noteworthy possibility is of the increase in Latin American Evangelicals during the coming decades in the twenty-first century.

If the trend becomes reality, by 2050 evangelical Christianity will be the most global of all religious movements. Secondly, the dominance of China in its numbers of Evangelicals will be reflected in almost every area of Christian activity—theology, missions, and leadership. This, combined with China's increased wealth, will mean that the post-modern secular worldview of the West may well be of less influence than the evangelical Christian Chinese worldview. Thirdly, the United States will be the only Western nation in the top twenty by 2050. Finally, Europe, in 1900, had more than half of the world's Evangelicals, but by 2050 Europe will have the lowest percentage of Evangelicals of any continent, with only 2.3 percent. On the other hand, Muslims by then will be around 11 percent or more in Europe.

The Growth of Islam and Its Implications for Evangelicals

We now return to Islam and look to the future. Islam is now the majority religion of fifty countries. Many think of Islam as being predominantly Arab, but Arabs are only around 20 percent of the total population of Muslims. In fact, there are far higher numbers of Muslims in South and Southeast Asia. The cultural diversity is evident in the mosques that have been built across the world.

The oft-repeated statement, "Islam is the fastest growing religion in the world" has both a ring of truth about it and is seemingly self-evident to Westerners with highly visible and growing Muslim minority communities in their midst. It certainly bolsters the self-confidence of many Muslims in the demise of Christianity and its own assumption of final global dominance. Their growth and confidence is such that few governments with their democratic mindset and value of "tolerance" know how to cope with their Muslim communities and with the radicalization of locally-born young Muslims. Nor do they understand how to cope with Evangelicals. Yet how true is this comment about Islam's growth?

I have carefully evaluated every country of the world and the religious trends and likely developments over the period 1900 to 2050, and I have paid special attention to both Evangelicals and Muslims. Here are some of the results.

» Muslim population growth is very significant. Over the period 1900 to 2050, the world population will have grown nearly six-fold, but the number of Muslims will have grown more than twelve-fold and increased in population from 0.2 billion to 2.5 billion.

» The Christian percentage will be likely little different in 2050 from what it was in 1900, but Islam will have grown significantly. What this graph does not show is that the massive decline in the West of Christianity and its influence on the worldview of the majority is more than compensated for with the growth of vital Christianity in the non-Western world.

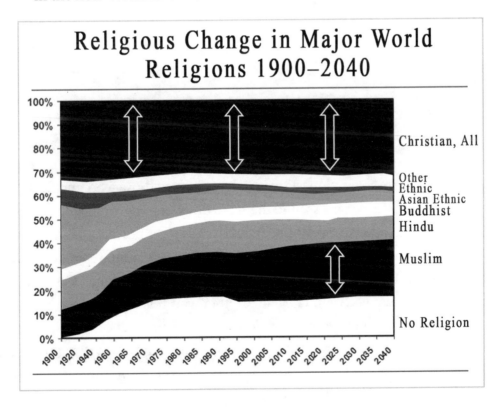

Fig.1.3

» What is the nature of Muslim growth? The world population growth rate is dropping quickly, but the world's population is unlikely to reach a measure of stabilization for another fifty or so years. Some religious movements are growing more slowly than global population growth. Muslims and Protestants are growing at about the same rate. The startling fact is that Evangelicals far outstrip the growth of Muslims, and Evangelicals' growth occurs primarily when adults and young people choose to follow Christ. On the other hand, almost all of Muslim growth is through birth rate. Conversion to Islam through marriage and conversion by conviction or persuasion likely accounts for no more than 10 percent of the growth of Islam.

Muslim Background Believers (MBBs)

The major contest for souls in the twenty-first century will be that between the two newly resurgent religious movements—Muslims and evangelical Christians. If my analysis is reasonably correct, I assess that during the 1990s, for every non-Muslim who chose to follow Islam, four non-Christians chose to follow Christ among Evangelicals.

GOD IS WORKING IN AMAZING WAYS IN ANSWER TO PRAYER.

The next big question is, "How many Muslims are finding new life in Christ? "Also, an even more solemn question is, "How many of those who find the pressures too hard, the Christians around them too unwelcoming, or the replacement for the close-knit societal and family network such large hurdles that they leave their new faith in Christ and return to Islam?" It is very hard to separate out fact from fiction or propaganda by both Muslim and Christian spokespersons as to how many have changed their allegiance either way. It is difficult to know how many Jesus-centered believers there are who have come out or remain within Islam to one degree or another. We may never know until Christ returns just how many there are, but one day we may be surprised at the number of disciples of Jesus who rise from Muslim graves.

God is working in amazing ways in answer to prayer. He is giving visions, dreams, and miracles to many. The significant increase in the number of MBBs and even MBB churches in the last twenty years parallels the rise of Islamism. However, with greater levels of emigration to non-Muslim countries by Muslims, turmoil in predominantly Muslim countries, strife between Sunni and Shi'i factions (sometimes fueled by Western interventions), and the kind of jihad promoted by militant Islamists, how will future trends challenge our representation of Christ amidst Muslims?

CHURCH PLANTING AMONG MUSLIM PEOPLES— THE PEOPLE LISTS

One goal for many of us is to see every Muslim unreached people group (MUPG) equal to or greater than 100,000 in population engaged by church planters by the close of the year 2012. I move on to statistics and maps, but let us remember that we are speaking of real men, women, and children for whom the Lord Jesus died and rose again.

Our goal propels us into listing Muslim people groups and finding out how many of these are still unengaged. This is no simple task for a whole range of reasons. We have enough of a problem in defining the 239 countries and territories of the world. However, it is much harder with the thousands of people groups in the world today when various ministries define people groups differently.

Here we are specifically concerned with church planting, so our lists reflect this—those peoples for whom a separate cross-cultural church-planting movement has been or will be necessary. These lists also reflect the rapidly changing world where whole cultures are being changed by globalization, wars, migrations, separations, and amalgamations. So a static list with 100 percent accuracy will be impossible to attain! We need to work together to constantly improve our lists as vital tools and make them servants to achieving our goals and not masters!

We are privileged today. For the first time since Jesus commissioned us to make disciples of all peoples, we now have a reasonably complete listing of all the world's peoples. This was published for the first time only in 2001 when David Barrett et al. published the second edition of the *World Christian*

Encyclopedia.[13] We owe a great debt of gratitude to them for this Herculean task. The other two active global lists are those of the International Mission Board (IMB) of the Southern Baptist Convention and of the Joshua Project, and both are derived from the original *World Christian Encyclopedia* listing. One of the great attainments in writing this chapter has been to stimulate a remarkable level of fellowship and cooperation to draw on the strengths of each version of people lists, expose areas of weakness, and reveal omissions or duplicates. So now we have a confluence list pulled together by these list-holders and orchestrated by Chris Maynard.[14] The confluence list is a means for all in our midst to be able to link up with the primary list holders for information or input for improvement.

We have a total list with approximately 1,000 Muslim unreached people groups. This list is rather overwhelming and complicated. We can easily be distracted by any discrepancies between lists or about apparently incorrect information in people groups with which we are most familiar. We can make better sense of the present lists by realizing that there are multiple levels of interlinking or relationships between them. We need to focus also on the bigger picture so that we better understand the situation for individual MUPGs. Here are four levels, the last being the vital goal listing for engagement.

Affinity Blocs

Over the last few years, I have classified people groups into a pragmatic two-tier hierarchy of fifteen Affinity Blocs and 251 or more People Clusters. The basic principle is that the categorization is not strictly "scientific," but rather what could be most helpful for practical purposes of mobilization and engagement. We therefore retain the flexibility to make adjustments to people groups listed within the clusters, or even create new clusters that best suit our ministries on the ground. We expect developments to be more affected by those closest to the action and therefore field-driven.[15]

---

[13]   New York: Oxford University Press, 2001, 552–3. See also David B. Barrett et al., "Missiometrics 2007: Creating Your Own Analysis of Global Data," *International Bulletin of Missionary Research* 31, no. 1 (January 2007): 32.

[14]   For more on this topic, please see the sixth chapter of this volume, along with the resource CD.

[15]   For more on the topic of Affinity Blocs, please see Patrick Johnstone, "Affinity Blocs and People Clusters: An Approach Toward Strategic Insight and Mission Partnership," *Mission Frontiers*, March–April 2007, 8–15, http://www. missionfrontiers.org/archive.htm.

An Affinity Bloc is the largest people grouping that includes all peoples with a closer relatedness of language, history, and culture, and is usually indigenous to a geographical location. The map below shows the Affinity Blocs in the world today.

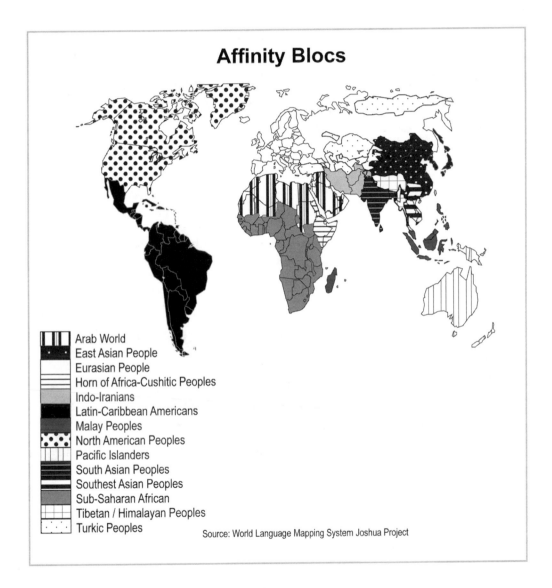

Fig.1.4

"Affinity" does not imply compatibility or mutual attraction between the constituent peoples of an Affinity Bloc. Their associations may also be due to military conquest, colonial exploitation, social oppression, and inter-ethnic strife. The variously shaded areas represent the homelands of the people groups and are formed by consolidating their language areas. Many people groups have migrated from their original homelands in recent years. They are still considered part of the original Affinity Bloc if they continue to retain their language and cultural origins, but because they do not really have a specific home area, they cannot be shown on such a map.

Of these fifteen Affinity Blocs, five are composed almost entirely of Muslim people groups—Arab World, Horn of Africa-Cushitic Peoples, Turkic Peoples, Indo-Iranians, and the Malay Peoples. Two have a large number of Muslim people groups—Sub-Saharan African and South Asian Peoples.

For our Consultation and our ongoing efforts, this level is useful for strategic planning and consultation. We have been assigning Affinity Bloc codes to our people group lists.

People Clusters

Every Affinity Bloc can be broken down into a number of People Clusters where there are more and closer commonalities. Peoples often comprise a cluster with a common name that is widely recognizable. An example of this is the Kurdish people cluster. In this example, there are thirteen distinct people groups that regard themselves as Kurdish, but they are scattered in identifiable communities in thirty-five countries.

A People Cluster is a smaller grouping within an Affinity Bloc, often with a common name or identity, but separated from one another by political boundaries, language, or migration patterns.

The following map shows the Arab World Affinity Bloc and the People Clusters within it.

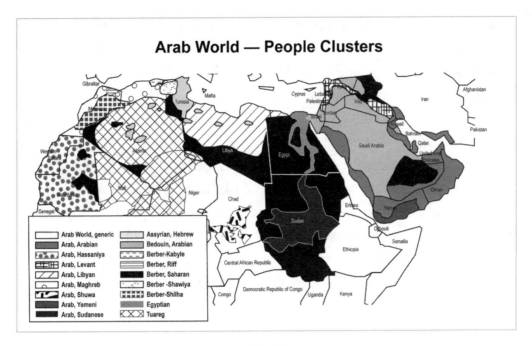

Fig.1.5

The People Cluster level is of major significance in developing partnerships, deployment, use of specialist ministries, and publicity. It is far easier to explain about ministry to the Kurds, Somalis, Pashtuns, or Berbers than by using the less-well-known individual tribal or clan names.

The Resource CD accompanying this volume contains a listing of all Affinity Blocs, People Clusters within Affinity Blocs, and people groups within People Clusters. One should also note that as peoples migrate to new places, Affinity Blocs and People Clusters are likely scattered beyond their traditional homelands.

People Groups

A people group is a significantly large sociological (predominantly ethno-linguistic) grouping of individuals who perceive themselves to have a common affinity with one another. From the viewpoint of evangelization, this is the largest possible group within which the Gospel can spread without encountering significant barriers of understanding or acceptance. It is the most helpful unit to use when considering church planting.

I need to make a careful observation at this point about the two active lists drawn upon most heavily for our listing. The Joshua Project list has nearly 16,000 people groups, and the IMB's Church Planting Progress Indicators (CPPI) lists nearly 12,000. The major discrepancy is caused by the handling of the largely Hindu castes in South Asia—should we recognize castes as people groups for church planting or not, and if so, do we thereby condone and even help perpetuate the present caste system?

The Resource CD contains the various Muslim people group listings and has broken them out by Affinity Bloc, People Cluster, and People Group. The Joshua Project list also includes the concept of people groups across countries as well as people groups within countries. Only the CPPI has engagement information, but it is our desire that every organization confirm and engage people groups on the list as new information is discovered that will sharpen the accuracy of the list. For now, the list of Muslim unreached people groups equal to or greater than 100,000 in population is 247. However, there are several points I need to make:

» There has been a large amount of work done by many to try to ensure we have a list of unengaged people groups, so we are reasonably confident that the other 429 "engaged, but unreached" Muslim unreached people groups are engaged by at least one agency. Many of these other 429 are highly under-engaged, and the larger ones will need considerable cross-cultural input to cover every key access point to begin to claim that the people group is fully engaged.

» What remains? We have this list of 247 people groups where we do not have enough evidence to say that they are being reached, but it can be a statement of our ignorance rather than firm on-the-ground information. The first task in seeking to engage these peoples is to make absolutely sure that this people group is a valid candidate for engagement—there are many reasons why it may not be:

  » The people group may be sufficiently integrated or undifferentiated in a wider people group—for instance, Bedouin groups in the Arab World or Crimean Tatars in Turkey.

  » The people group may represent a historical reality, but they have not retained a distinct culture to make a specific church-planting effort necessary. This is especially true of some migrant communities.

» The people group may later prove to have other Christian groups or denominations that have engaged them.

» The people group may already have a sizeable Christian community that we have not taken into account. One such group is the Malayali from India working in Middle Eastern countries.

» This list of 247 is a vital core to our goal-setting, but checking off each one will be a painstaking process—either to prove that a specific new engagement is not required or to actually commit teams to engage them. In this way, we avoid the frustration of finding that a number of entries are no longer valid for engagement.

The best way to facilitate this process is through people cluster and people groups across countries partnering and networking so that local knowledge may be discovered to establish the facts and to ensure every segment of the people group is engaged and discipled.

Two Levels of People Grouping Valid for Our Thinking— People Groups across Countries

Many larger and some smaller Muslim peoples are artificially divided by national boundaries—Kurds in Turkey, Iraq, Iran, Syria, and other large Kurdish communities on nearly every continent. This is important for strategic planning—language acquisition, accessibility, and Bible translation may better be carried out in one country but with the view of eventually ministering in a presently closed heartland of the people. The way the church was planted in Afghanistan is a case in point—much was based on the original work in the refugee camps in Pakistan. We may find that our criterion of 100,000 populations for Muslim unreached people groups actually excludes some people groups of 100,000 or more that have been divided in this way.

Two Levels of People Grouping Valid for Our Thinking— People Groups in Countries

Both source lists and our goal listing use this category for goal-setting. Some of these peoples are large and complex, and may require that we work in multiple church and agency partnerships to see both the engagement of a Muslim unreached people group and the launching of a church-planting movement.

CONCLUSION

We face a huge challenge, but Islam is not too hard for God. Never before in history have we had such an opportunity to share the redeeming love of Jesus with Muslims than now; never before have we had such understanding of the need or the tools or workforce that we have to actually lead Muslims to Jesus and launch church-planting movements.

Let us go forth in faith and with firm resolve to finish the task set for us by Jesus!

Chapter 2

Unplowed Ground: Engaging the Unreached

JEFF LIVERMAN

> *"Break up your unplowed ground ...*
> *until he comes and showers righteousness upon you."*
> Hosea 10:12, NIV

By God's grace, Christ's ambassadors have taken tremendous strides in recent years to make the Gospel available to the world's unreached people groups. Nevertheless, huge swaths of humanity remain unaffected by this message. In spite of our best efforts, many have yet to hear the Gospel presented to them in a meaningful way—even once!

In an effort to ensure that all Muslims have an opportunity to hear the Good News, a group of mission leaders began to consult with one another in 2004. These leaders began to ask the following crucial questions:

» What does it mean to "engage" a people?
» From what vantage point would we determine if all Muslim peoples are engaged?
» Which people groups are currently unengaged with such efforts? Who are these peoples and are Gospel messengers positioned to present the Gospel message in the most fruitful way?

We will now examine each of the above questions in turn.

Effective Engagement[16]

First, how shall we define "engaged"?

If we are to be fruitful in establishing communities of Jesus-followers, I am convinced our efforts must be based on the initial and fundamentally sound step of engagement. In order to accurately and meaningfully determine whether such engagement is underway, we must first arrive at a meaningful definition for what it means to "engage" an unreached people group.

As we look at engagement, we need to address the quality of mission activity among a people. It is not adequate that an effort merely include "evangelistic activity." To consider a people to be engaged, there must be activity that is strategic and will most likely produce fruit that remains and multiplies. So perhaps the term should be "effective engagement," or at least we must all understand that this is what we are pursuing.

In the codification process, we are concerned primarily about two things—distinguishing which groups have or have not heard from the preacher (per Romans 10) and describing that distinction in such a way as to increase the likelihood that the people in the recipient society hear and receive the Gospel as good news indeed. It should be noted that the question of engagement does not encompass the full cycle of church planting, but engagement does seek to establish a minimum benchmark that, when met, will help set the stage for thriving church planting and church-planting movements.

A Closer Look at the Criteria

I suggest that four essential elements constitute effective engagement: apostolic effort in residence, commitment to work in the local language and culture, commitment to long-term ministry, and sowing in a manner consistent with the goal of seeing a church-planting movement. When all four of these elements are in place, effective engagement is achieved.

---

[16] Jeff Liverman, "What Does It Mean to Effectively 'Engage' a People?" *Mission Frontiers*, November–December 2006, 10–12, http://www.missionfrontiers.org/archive.htm (accessed February 4, 2008).

Apostolic Effort in Residence

Taking the Gospel from where it is to where it is not is the essence of the apostolic task. This may be accomplished through any number of means: by teams or individuals, by Westerners, by workers from the "Global South," or by catalyzing people groups that live in proximity to the Unengaged People Group (UPG). The primary consideration in this criterion is that Gospel messengers live among those upon whom their efforts are focused. Thus, short-term or what Ralph Winter calls "amateur" or "drive-by"[17] workers who blitz in and are gone in a few months do not sufficiently meet this criterion.

Commitment to Work in the Local Language and Culture

Essential to the task of sharing the Gospel is the issue of effective communication. In order for the message of hope to be communicated effectively, it must be communicated in the language of the recipient culture. Lamin Sanneh notes, "Translatability is the source of the success of Christianity across cultures."[18] This requires the significant commitment and work necessary to acculturate oneself and one's message to whatever degree possible (without falling into syncretism) in order to make the Gospel understandable and attractive in the recipient culture.

FOUR ESSENTIAL ELEMENTS FOR EFFECTIVE ENGAGEMENT

1. *Apostolic effort in residence;*
2. *Commitment to work in the local language and culture;*
3. *Commitment to long-term ministry; and*
4. *Sowing in a manner consistent with the goal of seeing a church-planting movement emerge.*

---

17   Ralph D. Winter, "The Editorial of Ralph D. Winter," *Mission Frontiers*, March—April 1996, 3, http://www.mission-frontiers.org/archive.htm (accessed February 2, 2008).

18   Lamin Sanneh, *Translating the Message: The Missionary Impact on Culture* (Maryknoll, NY: Orbis Books, 1989), 51.

Commitment to Long-term Ministry

The apostolic effort must persevere for as long as it takes in order to see the Gospel understood and received by enough individuals in the recipient society. Too often, our desire for quick results causes us to neglect forging the deep and demanding long-term relationships necessary to establish the kind of trust essential to church planting. Too many have drawn the target around what they have been able to achieve through short-term efforts. They "meet" that insufficient target and then move on. Instead, we should commit to and demonstrate a willingness to follow "most fruitful practices" for as long as it takes to realize our objectives.

Sowing in a Manner Consistent with the Goal of Seeing a Church-Planting Movement (CPM) Emerge

Clearly this criterion suggests that an evaluation of means must occur. We are looking for the employment of methods that take into consideration cultural sensitivities, linguistic peculiarities, and political realities. Additionally, there must be a strategic and active proclamation in place—what David Garrison refers to as "over sowing."[19] No single method meets this criterion, and "over sowing" is necessary because of the many soils upon which the seed is scattered. We should carefully note which methods have borne fruit and which have led to minimal or disastrous results.

A PROPER PERSPECTIVE

A clear and concise understanding of engagement answers only one of our questions. We must also address the issue of evaluation, or vantage point. From what perspective will we view the state of the Gospel? Who can accurately evaluate whether a people is engaged? How will this evaluation be established? It is critical to establish whose perspective is to be solicited when considering the application of the criteria for engagement. Whose voice will shape the outcome of our analysis?

These are not insignificant questions, for whatever perspective we use will inevitably exert considerable influence over how the state of the Gospel will appear. Permit me a couple of illustrations.

---

[19] David Garrison, *Church Planting Movements—How God Is Redeeming a Lost World* (Bangalore, India: WIGTake Resources, 2004), 177.

The Zwemer–Mott Perspective at Edinburgh 1910

The 1910 perspective was arguably based on nineteenth-century research. Although much work has been done to modify this research, today's lists of Muslim peoples still carry some of the vestiges of colonial influence. This is a real problem since much of the data we see and hear today about Muslims was originally gathered and codified during the pre-Zwemer era of mission to Muslims. If we were to rely on this data, we would end up with information that may be interesting to the average church member but is inaccurate according to the facts faced on the ground by today's cross-cultural workers in residence.

Evaluation from a Former Missionary or a Group of Former Missionaries

As much as we may wish to respect and honor those who have gone before us, we must recognize that our predecessors' perspectives may no longer be up-to-date. If we rely on their knowledge alone, we are in danger of failing to see today's vantage point on the state of the Gospel. The Muslim world is changing at a rapid pace. I respectfully submit that anyone who has not been completely immersed among a given people group within the past five years has probably lost his or her ability to effectively discern the state of the Gospel among them.

It is our opinion that the best vantage point from which to determine the state of the Gospel among a particular people is the one held by the current cross-cultural workers, or "field practitioners." We describe a "field practitioner" as someone who is in residence among a given people group, knows the local language(s) and culture (with a broad understanding of how members of that group think, feel, and act), and is involved in face-to-face relationships (thus, having intimate knowledge of who is hearing, how people are responding, and what is and is not working).

Thus, in order to make a preliminary assessment of which people groups are engaged and which are not, the data must be shaped by a clear understanding of engagement (and other key terms) from the vantage point of current field practitioners (wherever possible).

THE UNENGAGED: A FIRST LOOK

In order to answer the third question regarding the current status of engagement among unreached Muslim peoples, each of the agencies represented by the gathering in 2004 was asked to gather data from their field practitioners about the state of the Gospel in their respective countries of service. We analyzed only the data representing those people groups with populations of 100,000 or more. The sidebar shows an example of a survey circulated by one of the agencies.

SURVEY

1. About you:
   a. Where are you presently based? (Name city, town, or, if a large city, name of section):
   b. How long have you been on the field?
   c. How long have you been where you are now?

2. Here is a list of the People Groups in _____, as identified by the Joshua Project. Please mark X by the groups that you are presently working with. (Please mark only those groups with whom you are presently ACTIVELY sharing the good news. Do not mark those groups whom you may be aspiring to work among).

3. Please could you also share your insight for each of the groups with which you are engaging, using the form(s) below. Please discard any blank forms that are not needed, or copy and paste new forms if necessary.

   People Group (PG) name:
   Population of PG:
   Number of agency teams:
   Number of agency team members:
   What is the CP phase for your work among this PG:
   Number of (God's) teams:
   Number of (God's) team workers:

4. We would also like to ask if you could verify or suggest approximate populations for any of the other people groups in _____? Here is the data that we have. Please indicate if you would estimate a different population size, and what level of confidence you would have (high/med/low):

{List of Muslim People Groups}

5. We would finally like to ask for your reflections on the use of people group terminology.
    a. Do you subscribe to the "Homogeneous Unit Principle" as it is known? _____ (Y/N)
    b. If no, please state the reason: _____
    c. Are you working in an area where traditional ethno-linguistic distinctions are blurred (as in an urban setting)? _____ (Y/N)
    d. Are you working in an area where political realities make it unwise and/or unfruitful to distinguish ethnicity of those you work among?_____(Y/N)

6. Please add any comments you think might be helpful to us as we look at the state of the Gospel in your area:

The goal of this agency was to understand how current field practitioners viewed ethno-linguistic realities in their areas and how that compared with the information on existing lists of data.

Analysis of the survey results revealed some surprises.

1. Many of the field practitioners voiced considerable disagreement with the data as presented in the people group list that was circulated. The field practitioners pointed to many "inaccuracies" in the people group data that much of the Western Church currently uses. The field practitioners said that the existing lists of people groups are outdated and often do not reflect current ethno-linguistic realities.

2. The Muslim world has seen a substantial increase in the number of people now calling Jesus "Lord"! Reports suggest that more Muslims have chosen to identify themselves as followers of Christ in the past forty years than in the previous 1,000 years combined.

3. As remarkable as the progress among Muslims has been during the past forty years, there remains a large number of Muslim people groups who have not been effectively engaged according to our definition. We estimated that approximately 247 Muslim people groups (with a population of at least 100,000) fit into this lamentable category.

4. The results indicated a high concentration of unengaged Muslim people groups in Sudan and India. We now realize just how sparse Kingdom resources are among Muslim people groups in these countries.

"How shall they hear unless ..."

What action is called for? Where do we go from here? Our research has helped us uncover additional issues that need to be addressed:

1. In order to continue and strengthen our ability to determine the state of the Gospel, we must systematically repair and refine our people group lists. Only then will we be able to identify the Kingdom voids, where few if any church-planting resources are engaging unreached peoples, and then direct resources to fill those voids.

2. Kingdom resources must be focused on Sudan and India in particular. High concentrations of unengaged peoples can be found in these two countries. India, with its complex mosaic of ethnic and social factors, poses one of the greatest challenges to missions today.

3. Our efforts to mobilize and deploy resident disciple-makers must be redoubled, and emphasis must be placed on directing these resources to the unengaged.

4. The Global South provides huge potential for new workers. Relying only on Western resources and workers clearly will not provide a sufficient number of pioneers to go where Muslims are not yet engaged. The task is immense, but so are God's resources. We should make special efforts to involve and partner with these new global resources the Church has at the ready.

5. We need to implement innovative strategies, while not abandoning proven missiological principles. Effective missions in the future will likely involve strategies such as the strategic use of the Internet and other technologies, the mobilizing of itinerant evangelists, and the utilization of "commuter apostles." But, with each successive wave of creativity and innovation, the fundamentals of effective missions should not be lost in the excitement and rush to try the "next best thing."

6. We must consider the ultimate goal—effective church planting among all Muslim people groups. What will it take to monitor effective church planting among all Muslim people groups? Chris Maynard, a member of a research task force, suggests some practical considerations.

Toward an Effective Church-planting Registry

By Chris Maynard

What will it take to monitor effective church planting among all Muslim Unreached People Groups?

1. *Ensure we have a useful list of MPGs.* This is the base requirement, and it is within reach. We have made a good start. The run up to the consultation saw good cooperation between our research group and those who manage people group lists. They gave us tremendous help to pull together a reasonable list of MPGs over 100,000 very quickly. We also saw signs that we can stimulate better interaction between the data managers of the various lists and between them and the experts in the field. This is of value to the whole Body of Christ. We need to build on this cooperation to improve the quality of the data, and we need to extend the list below 100,000.

2. *Move on to a Church-planting Registry.* A list of MPGs does not in itself tell us where effective church planting is taking place. That requires us to register church-planting efforts *against* the MPG list.

3. *Define what information we need in a register.* We need to be clear about what questions we will be "asking" the registry, and how those answers will change our decisions—presumably decisions about future research and deployment.

    a. *Understand the key stages of church planting* that we need to register. These should ideally be well defined, unambiguous, well accepted, and easy to recognize on the field. There will always be gray areas, but a clear definition will save a lot of trouble collecting and understanding the data.

b. *Define any other key aspects of the real world* that we need to capture. There was some discussion at the Consultation about the difference in "effective" engagement of a people of ten million when compared with a people of a 100,000. An effective engagement of a large people group may require "breadth" as well as "depth." Being at an advanced stage of church planting in one town may not be considered effective.

4. *Design a process for keeping it up-to-date.* The implications of a register are weighty. The information must be secure, and yet those who manage it must be able to verify it and accurately record changes in the situation. This will not just be a one-off exercise. We must ensure at the outset that we have a system that can be sustained and kept up-to-date.

5. *Define limits of publication.* If the register is not available to partners, then there is no positive value to its existence. But if its availability compromises our church-planting efforts, then it would have a negative effect on the work. Care must be taken to get the best of both worlds. We need to think this through very carefully from the beginning. There is experience in handling this type of situation, and there are techniques we can use.

May God grant us the wisdom and compassion to more fully understand what remains of the task before us and what steps must be taken to see the Great Commission accomplished in our generation.

Chapter 3

The Imperishable Seed: Toward Effective Sharing of Scripture

ANDREA AND LEITH GRAY

"This is the meaning of the parable: The seed is the word of God."
Luke 8:11, TNIV

INTRODUCTION

What does it mean for a people group to have access to the Scriptures? In the past, we might have said that a people group has access to the Scriptures when a printed New Testament has been published in their language. But what if the printed New Testament sits in warehouses because both the general Muslim population and the local church consider it to be foreign propaganda? What if tens of thousands of New Testaments *are* distributed to illiterate villagers who accept these books politely and place them on a shelf, never to be opened? What if the format and terminology of the published New Testament reflect the preferences of the Christian minority in a country, but are alien or even offensive to the Muslim community? In these situations, does the Muslim people group truly have access to the Word of God?

In recent years, many people involved in Scripture translation and promotion around the world have been moving away from considering the end goal of their ministry to be the publication or even the distribution of a printed New Testament. Instead, the goal is a community transformed by the Gospel, with a printed New Testament being one of many possible Scripture-based tools that can lead to and support such transformation. In other words, the focus is shifting from Scripture access to Scripture engagement.

As we consider how God has been using the Scriptures to impact communities in the Muslim world in recent years, certain factors seem to emerge again and again. These factors have been consolidated into seven issues below. An examination of these seven issues will help in identifying whether a given people group truly has access to the Scriptures. The discussion that follows is a resource for both church planters and Bible translators who seek, by the leading of the Holy Spirit, to present Muslim people groups with the best possible opportunity to engage with and be transformed by the Word of God.

Issue #1:
Intended Audience

One of the first things Bible translators and church planters working in a particular language group must do is determine the intended audience for the Scripture materials they hope to produce or use. This seems like a simple task, but when there is both a Muslim and a Christian community in a given language group, the situation is more complicated.

A senior executive in a major Bible translation agency once observed that, throughout the world, the primary consumers of Bibles are Christians. This is true everywhere except in the Muslim world, where, in addition to Christian readers, there are large numbers of Muslims who want to read the Bible and learn about the prophets and about Jesus, since the Qur'an itself commends these books and persons. In addition, there are Muslim followers of Jesus, unconnected to traditional churches, who want the Scriptures in their own language in order to grow in their faith.

David Zeidan, formerly of Operation Mobilization, describes how centuries of conflict and mutual prejudice have led to a cultural gap between the ancient Orthodox and Catholic churches on the one hand and the Muslim majority in most Middle Eastern countries on the other. There is a further cultural gap between the Protestant churches started by missionaries in the nineteenth and twentieth centuries and the ancient Christian community. Moreover, in some Middle Eastern countries, there is a subset of Protestants called Evangelicals (this is not so much a theological distinction as in the West, but more of a socio-cultural distinction). Zeidan describes four different categories of expatriates that result from these conflicts and disparities: "foreigners using conventional methods," "Evangelicals working for Western missions," "foreigners using contextualized approaches" with minority groups, and "foreigners using contextualized approaches" with the dominant majority group.[20] Each group has different reasons and goals for translating the Scriptures.

Since human nature leads us to associate with those most like ourselves, Protestant missionaries often choose Protestants for their language helpers and cultural guides. While this tendency allows the missionary some much-needed fellowship, it often leaves him or her uninformed of the worldview, customs, and linguistic preferences of the Muslim majority. We need to keep the cultural gap in mind when seeking out people to work on a translation committee. When Protestants from the local community are involved in the translation and/or distribution of Scripture materials, they will often need cross-cultural training to help them understand the Muslims they hope to reach with the Gospel.

In describing the history of Bible translation in Africa, Dapila Fabian points out that even though the mission of most Christian churches is to spread the Gospel of Jesus Christ to all, "little reference has been made to the 'un-churched' or non-Christians for that matter, and little attention has been paid to whether the translation is intelligible to non-Christians or not."[21] Fabian advocates working with non-Christians on translation projects and makes suggestions for revising the set of criteria (such as Christian theological training) that has traditionally been used for selecting Bible translators.

---

[20]   David Zeidan, "The Problem of Alienation—Nibbling at the Fringes or Going for the Centre?" www.angel fire.com/az/rescon/alienation.html (accessed August 28, 2007).

[21]   Dapila N. Fabian, "The Muslim Bible Translator in the Context of Today's African Christianity—A Dilemma for Missions." http://academic.sun.ac.za/as/cbta/Bible%20in%20Africa_Sept2005/Table%20of%20conts%20The%20Bible%20in%20Africa_Papers.htm (accessed August 28, 2007).

> ### SEVEN ISSUES TO EXAMINE FOR
> ### EFFECTIVE SHARING OF SCRIPTURE
>
> 1. *Intended Audience*
> 2. *Distinctives of the Local Language*
> 3. *Oral Communication Strategies*
> 4. *Presentation*
> 5. *Context and Background Information*
> 6. *Relevance of the Message*
> 7. *Distribution*

Tim James presents three case studies of teams that have worked closely with Muslims at all stages of the Bible translation process. James presents both the challenges and advantages of working with Muslims, and states that "in 20 years (of working with Muslim colleagues), I have had no cause for complaint or mistrust or concern because of their being Muslims, and their work and commitment to the scripture translation projects has been exemplary."[22] Furthermore, "my own experience of my Muslim colleagues is that they respect the exegetical input of those they see as being knowledgeable about the Biblical texts and Biblical languages."[23]

The call for a translation of the Bible that Muslims could call their own is not a new phenomenon. "At the Bhamdun conference in 1954, at least two Muslims were candid in their criticism of the Arabic version of the Bible, and one of them preferred to read the New Testament in English. *He pleaded for an Arabic version that the Muslims could enjoy*."[24]

Those who desire to see Muslim communities being impacted by the message of Jesus will find it useful to examine some of the literature on what are often called 'insider movements' or 'C5 movements'. A good summary of this topic is provided in Travis and Travis.[25]

---

[22] Tim James, "Working with Colleagues from Other Faith Traditions," *International Journal of Frontier Missions* 23, no. 2 (2006): 61.

[23] James, "Working with Colleagues from Other Traditions," 63.

[24] Tim Matheny, *Reaching the Arabs: A Felt Need Approach* (Pasadena, CA: William Carey Library, 1981), 70, italics mine.

[25] John Travis and Anna Travis, "Appropriate Approaches in Muslim Contexts," in *Appropriate Christianity*, ed. Charles H. Kraft (Pasadena, CA: William Carey Library, 2005), 403. See also chapter 13 in this volume.

ISSUE #2:

DISTINCTIVES OF THE LOCAL LANGUAGE

In many parts of the Muslim world, languages are characterized by a phenomenon that linguists call *diglossia*. Diglossia can be described as a situation in which people have two or more languages, each of which covers certain functions. One language (the high language) is used for writing and formal public speaking, and another (the low language) is used for speaking about everyday topics. The low language (essentially the mother tongue) is the variety best understood by the community, but the high language is more prestigious. In such situations, people usually feel strongly that the Scriptures must be presented as a printed book, in a high, formal language that is not necessarily understood.

What should the translation team do when the language the people understand best is not acceptable for printed Scriptures? The first step is to find out *from Muslims in the language community* what forms they would find most acceptable for learning biblical truths. Audio or video presentations of Scripture, oral or written poetry, and posting Scripture on the Internet are suitable options in most diglossic situations.

FIND OUT FROM MUSLIMS IN THE LANGUAGE COMMUNITY WHAT FORMS THEY WOULD FIND MOST ACCEPTABLE FOR LEARNING BIBLICAL TRUTHS.

In addition to diglossia, another important aspect of language to consider is ecclesiastical terminology and names. Christian religious terms are often borrowed directly from other languages, such as Syriac or Greek. In many cases, missionaries or local church leaders have rejected local names and terms derived from Arabic. For example, some of the well-known prophets have ancient Arabized names that differ from the traditional Christian names for the prophets. Shortly after deciding to follow Jesus, a friend from a Muslim family came to us with her Bible, saying, "Please tell me the Arabic names for these prophets." Interestingly, she did not say 'Islamic names'. To her, the names used by Christians are foreign names.

The issue of choosing appropriate biblical key terms for Muslim audiences has been treated extensively in missiological literature. Brown[26] has dealt with the exegesis and translation of the term 'Son of God' for Muslim audiences. John Travis[27] and Brad Williams[28] also address the issue from their experience in translation in South Asia and West Africa, respectively.

Brown and Samuel[29] have also dealt with the key term 'Lord', a problem that Travis identifies as needing careful consideration in Muslim language translations. Travis points out that boundary-marking terms such as 'church', 'Christian', and 'baptism' are particularly important for a translator to think about carefully because the choice of terminology can lead the Muslim to say either, "This is for me," or "This is only for ethnic Christians and foreigners."

---

[26] Rick Brown, "Explaining the Biblical Term 'Son(s) of God' in Muslim Contexts," *International Journal of Frontier Missions* 22, no. 3 (2005): 91–96; and Rick Brown, "Translating the Biblical Term 'Son(s) of God' in Muslim Contexts," *International Journal of Frontier Missions* 22, no. 4 (2005): 135–45.

[27] John Travis, "Producing and Using Meaningful Translations of the Taurat, Zabur and Injil," *International Journal of Frontier Missions* 23, no. 2 (2006): 73–77.

[28] Brad Williams, "The Emmaus–Medina Intertextual Connection: Contextualizing the Presentation of God's Word," *International Journal of Frontier Missions* 23, no. 2 (2006): 67–72.

[29] Rick Brown and Christopher Samuel, "The meanings of κυριος 'Lord' in the New Testament" (unpublished paper, 2002).

A Practical Application—One Way of Applying the Principles of This Chapter

By Kevin Higgins

Henki is from a people group that is 100 percent non-Christian. He became a follower of Jesus through the combined impact of faithful witness by several believers, a dramatic dream and vision, and meditation upon a highly contextualized translation of a Harmony of the Gospels (the four Gospels combined to make one story) in the national language of his country. He and a growing number of leaders have continued to use the Harmony in basic discipleship. Unfortunately, although there was a New Testament available in their mother tongue, it was slightly unnatural grammatically, and used ecclesiastical terminology, and they felt they could not use it. However, the style and language of the Harmony have inspired Henki and a team of indigenous translators to work on a new, highly contextualized translation of the entire New Testament for the Muslim majority audience, in their mother tongue. They have received training and ongoing mentoring in this effort from a well-known translation organization, and the results in the process of evangelism, discipleship, and church multiplication have been dramatic. Families have come to faith and churches have been planted even in the translation checking process as those involved go from village to village to check comprehension.

ISSUE #3:
ORAL COMMUNICATION STRATEGIES

Most Muslim societies can be classified as oral cultures. They prefer to communicate through story, song, poetry, proverbs, and dialogue. Therefore, a non-print translation is likely to speak more naturally and powerfully to the ordinary members of the community who are either non-literate or who simply prefer oral communication.

Some of the strategies that are particularly successful in Muslim areas include the following:

» Chronological Bible storying;
» Dramatized audio Bible stories;
» Scripture portions in the "new media" such as Internet, mobile phone, and video clips; and
» Poetry, proverbs, and chanting.

Chronological Bible Storying[30]
Chronological Bible Storying (CBS) is a method of evangelism and discipleship in which the storyteller tells selected Scripture stories in chronological order. Ordinarily, a CBS session includes a time of dialogue after the story, and questions are used to guide listeners to discover the meaning and significance of the biblical story. CBS can be considered a method rather than a product, since CBS in its true form requires a human storyteller to be physically present.

There are many advantages to CBS:

» The storying approach uses language in the same way local people use it, with appropriate idioms and discourse elements.
» Because the stories are told chronologically, starting with Genesis, the listener is given much of the Old Testament background information needed to understand the New Testament.
» The CBS approach can be especially powerful when it includes stories that respond to felt needs of the community.

---

30   For a form of this, see chapter 15.

» Stories can be easily "carried" into areas that prohibit proselytizing. When told properly, they sound like local stories, not foreign stories, and are therefore more acceptable. Local believers can witness in a low-key way by reciting stories. This allows them a lower profile than they would have if they were using a printed book or even cassettes.

Dramatized Audio Bible Stories

Many translation teams have chosen to present the message of the Bible in recorded dramatized form, using the insights of CBS. Typically, a project will consist of three series: 1) a series of biographical portions from the Old Testament, 2) the full Gospel of Luke, and 3) the Acts of the Apostles and selections from the Epistles. The Scripture portions selected are designed to move people from a position of little knowledge of and a negative attitude toward the Gospel toward more knowledge and an accepting attitude. The Old Testament series draws on the interest people already have in Old Testament characters because of their mention in the Qur'an. People become more receptive to biblical truths as they hear them presented over and over again in different stories. Local music, poetry, and proverbs are used to effectively communicate the message, and the openings and closings of the stories focus on felt needs of the community. The goal is to move people toward a greater understanding of the biblical message, to repentance and faith in Christ, and to see them gain maturity in Christ, as shown in Figure 3.1.[31]

---

[31]   Rick Brown, "Selecting and Using Scripture Portions Effectively in Frontier Missions," *International Journal of Frontier Missions* 18, no. 4 (2002): 10–25.

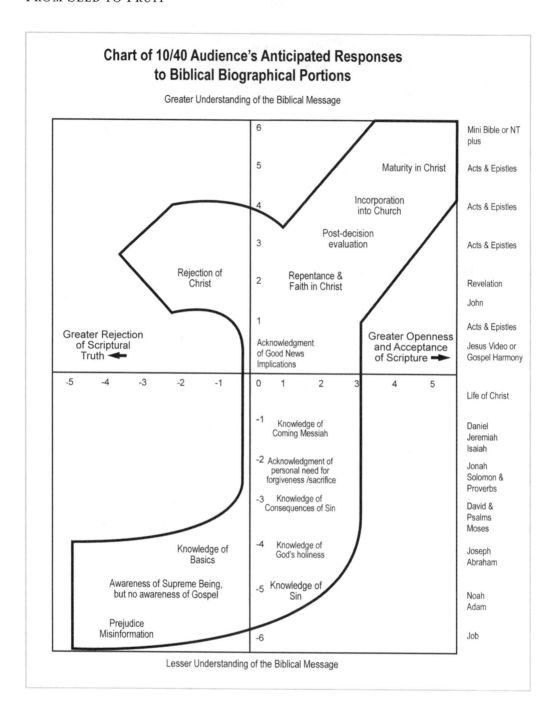

Fig.3.1

There are some factors that enhance the acceptability of dramatized Bible stories:

» They are seen as being more documentary in nature rather than propaganda—preachy messages are avoided.
» The style is culturally appropriate for the genre.
» They are entertaining and engaging.

The New Media: Internet, Mobile Phone, and Video

Consider the importance of what are called "new media" in the Middle East: between 2000 and 2007, the growth rate for Internet use was 491.4 percent. Furthermore, as of March 2007, 10 percent of the population had access to the Internet.[32] Mobile phone usage is widespread, with about one in five people owning mobile phones. Satellite television is considered a household necessity for even the poorest families, along with drinking water and electricity.

What are the implications of these new media for how we present the message of Jesus to people in Muslim societies? Will we see Psalms of David set to music and passed from one mobile phone to another? Will we see the parables of Jesus presented as streaming video on an Internet site? Those concerned with sharing the message of Jesus with Muslims need to remain informed of the developments in communications technology and the way people in the local culture are using it.

Poetry and Chanting

Poetry speaks to the hearts of people. It simultaneously reflects and shapes a people's worldview. Therefore, when we consider how the message of Jesus might reshape a community's worldview at the deepest levels, poetry should not be ignored. Short passages of Scripture can be translated as poetry, particularly those passages that were most likely composed originally as poetry such as the Psalms, and the songs of Mary and Zechariah at the beginning of Luke. Another way of incorporating poetry into the Bible story is to have a poet summarize certain passages as poetry or to compose a poem based on some of the key themes of the story.

---

[32] Internet World Stats, "Internet Usage in the Middle East," http://www.internetworldstats.com/stats5.htm (accessed March 14, 2007).

Issue #4:
Presentation

Muslim readers (or listeners) are more likely to approve of a translation that does not seem to alienate them from their community. Factors that can influence acceptability of a translation are the physical layout, script, and endorsements. Color is very important. Bibles in the Middle East traditionally have had black covers. For Muslims, black is the color of Hell. Green, on the other hand, is the color of Paradise, and has positive connotations for Muslims. Muslims we know, both seekers and believers, have reacted more positively to an edition of the Bible with a green cover than to an edition of the same translation with a navy blue cover. A decorative frame around the Scripture text, and arabesque designs on the cover rather than a cross are other features that have enhanced the acceptability of some Bible translations.

Endorsements by Muslim religious leaders go a long way in making a translation acceptable to the community. A commentary on the Gospel of John that was prepared by an Arab believer from a Muslim background includes an introduction by respected Muslim scholars. This approach has had a positive impact on sales of the book and on the receptiveness of people who receive it as a gift.

Does God's revelation have to be called "The Bible"?

Sometimes, a community might have a negative attitude toward the Scriptures because of a belief that they have been corrupted. Or the community might not accept that a holy book can be written in their mother tongue. In such instances, the translation team might want to consider an approach that exposes people to the Scriptures without actually calling it "the Bible," "the New Testament," and so on. Instead, the project might use titles such as "Stories of the Prophets," "The Biography of Jesus," and "Selections from the Psalms of David." It may be useful to identify the source of the stories in a low-key way, saying for example, "from the books of the prophets" or "from the Noble Injeel." This will make it clear that the stories are not from the Qur'an but are from other Scriptures.

ISSUE #5:
CONTEXT AND BACKGROUND INFORMATION

Anyone who has worked in another culture knows that cross-cultural communication is difficult under the best of circumstances. That is because the two conversation partners do not share the same set of cultural knowledge. When modern-day people approach the Bible, they are interacting with a message that was crafted at least 2,000 years ago in a very different cultural environment, so the amount of shared background information is often quite low, making it difficult for the reader or listener to fully understand the text. How can Christian workers help compensate for this lack of background information?

MUSLIM COMMUNITIES SHARE MANY CULTURAL PRACTICES AND VALUES WITH OLD TESTAMENT CULTURE. HONOR AND SHAME, HOSPITALITY, GENEROSITY, AND FAMILY AND COMMUNITY SOLIDARITY ARE JUST SOME OF THESE.

Muslim communities share many cultural practices and values with Old Testament culture. Honor and shame, hospitality, generosity, and family and community solidarity are just some of these. When Old Testament materials are presented first, the audience is introduced to the background behind important biblical key terms and concepts in a context that is less challenging to their worldview. For example, the background for the key term "Son of God" occurs in 2 Samuel 7 and Psalm 2, and the background for the term "Son of Man" occurs in Daniel 7. It will also be easier for the audience to accept Jesus' death if they see how this was prophesied in Isaiah 53.

Background Information

Harriet Hill conducted a study among the Adioukrou people to determine whether contextual information makes a difference in comprehension of the Bible. The results of 271 interviews of both clergy and lay people showed that the scores for comprehension were doubled when background information was provided either in footnotes or in the text itself.[33]

---

[33] Harriet Hill, *The Bible at Cultural Crossroads: From Translation to Communication* (Manchester, UK: St. Jerome Publishing, 2006), 61–68.

In a printed translation, background information can be placed in footnotes, explanatory articles, glossaries, and simple charts and maps. In a dramatized Bible story, the narrator can provide background information, or a character from the narrative frame can interrupt the story to ask for essential information.

Sometimes the interruption in a dramatized story can provide background information for a passage that is itself background for a later passage. For example, in one translation of the story of David, a character from the narrative frame interrupts the account of Samuel anointing Saul to ask, "Why did they wipe oil on his head?" The narrator answers, "It was the custom that God, when he wanted to put a king over the sons of Jacob, would say to them, 'Anoint him with oil.'" This explanation not only helps the audience better understand the story of David but also gives the background of the term 'Messiah' (anointed one), an important key term in the Gospels.

Do We Do Windows?

By Leith Gray

Bible translation is like cleaning a dirty window. In many languages, the Bible translation is very inadequate. Perhaps it is in print where illiteracy is high, or it uses inappropriate terminology or theological terms. It is as if the audience has to look through a very dirty window to see what is on the other side. They might be able to discern that there is a person standing there, but they will not be able to see the whole picture clearly. Paul-Gordon Chandler relates the story of Mazhar Mallouhi, who, as a young Muslim man, read a traditional Arabic translation twenty-seven times in the New Testament and thirteen times in the Old Testament before coming to faith! Even then, he needed lots of help from Christians to make sense of the text. Although some highly motivated seekers are willing to persevere until they have scrubbed away the dirt and are able to see clearly through the window, how much better if we offer people a clear view in the first place!

ISSUE #6:
RELEVANCE OF THE MESSAGE

One way to emphasize that the biblical message is relevant to people in a particular culture is to portray them using the Bible to address their felt needs. In one series of dramatized Bible stories of this sort recorded for an unreached Muslim people group, each story begins with a brief drama in a modern-day setting. The characters raise an important issue, and then the narrator, who is portrayed as a well-respected and honorable figure in the community, relates a Bible story related to the issue, beginning with some background information to set the scene.

Tim Matheny maintains that Muslims will not be interested in the Gospel message unless they can see how it meets their felt needs.

He identified eighteen categories of felt needs for transitional Arabs (Arabs in the midst of the transition from a traditional way of life to a way of life that characterizes industrial societies), a few of which are listed here:

> » Need to reconcile modern thought with religion;
> » Need for community;
> » Need for honor;
> » Need for protection from the evil eye and spirits;
> » Need for blessing; and
> » Need for freedom from sickness.[34]

"There is evidence that the emotional needs met by the animistic rituals are still felt needs. It is reasonable to assume that although modernizing Arabs have dropped some traditional animistic practices, the emotional felt needs still exist and are not being met."[35] It has been our experience that even Muslims who believe in Jesus still look for freedom from sickness, curses, the evil eye, *jinn*, and demons as they did in the past. If they do not discover that these needs can be met in Jesus Christ, they revert to the old ways of dealing with those needs, even while professing a biblical faith in other areas of their lives.

---

34   Matheny, *Reaching the Arabs: A Felt Need Approach*, 147–52.
35   Matheny, *Reaching the Arabs: A Felt Need Approach*, 153.

ALL THAT I COMMANDED
BY TED BERGMAN

The Great Commission not only says to go to all peoples, it also says to begin "teaching them to observe all that I commanded you" (Matthew 28:19–20, NASB). The word "all" appears twice. So, how well are we progressing in our goal to make the message accessible to every Muslim people group?

We have data on the number of languages that people speak. We know how many of these languages have the Scriptures, which ones have work in progress and which ones are not likely to need a translation. Regardless of Scripture translation among these people groups, how many truly have access to the Bible, the New Testament, or a portion of it?

Jesus commanded us to teach people to obey all his teachings, so we cannot simply proclaim Scripture and count our task done. If we are teaching Scripture "effectively," that means people are engaging Scripture—and being engaged by Scripture—in such a way that they become more like Jesus. It is hard to measure how well people are obeying everything Jesus taught, but since that is the goal, we need to estimate how well we are facilitating it. We want to go beyond just "counting products" and proclamation.

This information can be estimated for peoples where we have workers, but so far we do not have a system to collect this data. To do so goes beyond the capabilities of any single agency. In order to accomplish this, we need a high level of commitment, organization, and inter-agency cooperation.

Unless we know the progress toward our ultimate goal, how can we prioritize our work? How can we direct new missionaries to priority work? Our goal of reaching all people groups is not accomplished without effective teaching of all that God has commanded us.

ISSUE #7:

DISTRIBUTION

If the translation team has worked hard to overcome the challenges presented by the above six issues, it would be a shame for the translation to be rejected because they did not think through a distribution strategy carefully. This is especially important in Muslim contexts. Whenever it is possible, it is important to obtain the advice of Muslims in the community regarding acceptable and effective methods of distribution.

Even a translation that is acceptable in every other regard can be rejected if it is distributed in the wrong way. In Central Asia, for example, radio has been used so much for government propaganda that people regard any other messages in that medium as propaganda. The identity of the distributor is also important. In one country, non-Christian vendors can be found in a major market openly hawking audio stories of biblical prophets. However, if a foreigner were to distribute the same materials, it would raise suspicions about the materials.

Before embarking on a large-scale project of distribution, Christian workers need to discover how non-Christians view such efforts. One Arab newspaper recently wrote disparagingly about the mass distribution of Bibles and video discs to Muslims in European cities. This led to criticism of the particular translation of the Bible being distributed, which was considered to be Western Christian propaganda.

While it is important to work hard to ensure that Muslims feel a sense of ownership of the Bible in their language, this does not mean that churches should be overlooked in the distribution process. Some Muslims who have had a dream about Jesus will go to a church in order to find out more. Muslims are more likely to go to an Orthodox or a Catholic church than a Protestant church, and unfortunately, these traditional churches are not always represented in translation teams or included in distribution efforts. At some ancient church buildings, non-Christians come in large numbers to pray for healing or to make vows. Such seekers are at a point where they are open to the message of the Scriptures. Church workers could have ready Scripture portions that deal with the most common felt needs of visitors and seekers.

In order for local Christians to be most effective in the distribution effort, open-minded local Christian leaders will need training to understand the validity of decisions on theological terms, the rationale for using the ancient Arabic names for the prophets, and even why the cover is green or other seemingly small, but emotionally-charged, characteristics of the translation. The power of personal relationships over time is invaluable, but formal training workshops for local Christians can also be quite effective.

Conclusion

How many Muslim people groups truly have access to the Word of God? As can be seen from this chapter, the answer is not as simple as counting the number of printed New Testaments that have been translated and distributed. The seven issues outlined above should help those communicating the Gospel message to evaluate their own situations and determine steps to move forward.

Chapter 4

Laborers from the Global South: Partnering in the Task

GREG LIVINGSTONE

"The harvest is plentiful, but the laborers are few;
pray therefore the Lord of the harvest to
send out laborers into his harvest."
Matthew 9:37–38, RSV

INTRODUCTION

Our Consultation on Global Trends and Fruitful Practices revealed few surprises. We are at best only up to "station two" on the climb up the mountain of the Muslim world. As Churchill coined, "We are not at the beginning of the end, but only the end of the beginning" in the effort to see ambassadors for Christ significantly engage all Muslim peoples.

Secondly, "business as usual" at its utmost holds little promise of reaching the goal of "a church for every Muslim people."

The Fruitful Practices section deals with the *qualitative* issues: how to be more effective *once contact with Muslims is established*. This section, "Global Trends," attempts to find God's answers to the *quantitative* problem. How can sufficient numbers of appropriately motivated and gifted persons, such as the Twelve who were with Christ and sent out into the nations, gain residence conducive to making disciples among the remaining Muslim peoples presently without a church, or church planters among them?

WHAT IS CLEAR

» Even with local churches forming their own teams and perked-up interest in the West to do something for Muslim peoples, there is no possibility that the existing agencies and churches in the West will be able to recruit, place, and oversee the quantity of new pioneer church planters needed to engage the many unengaged and under-engaged Muslim peoples in the world today.

» Many countries with large Muslim populations are making it difficult for Americans, British, and Germans to obtain long-term residence.

» Muslim governments, with or without sophisticated technology, are able to detect the presence of "missionaries." To them "a rose by any other name" still has thorns!

» Even those who hold recognized jobs (tentmakers) or favor "Business as Mission," who learn the language and spend time talking about religion with local people, are often considered to be missionaries.

More than 2,000 Muslim people groups are largely blocked by governmental or social restrictions from considering the claims of Christ Jesus. Where a commitment to Islam is more than a veneer, congregations of Muslims consciously obedient to the Savior are still few. In West Malaysia, for example, a relatively free country with a Muslim majority, in five years I never met a Malay Muslim who had ever met a Malay follower of Christ Jesus. There is only one validated functioning community of MBBs (Muslim background believers), and this community is led by an ordained Chinese pastor.

Secondly, and equally puzzling, is how disappointingly short of the early Church of Acts 2 and 4 are most house churches or fellowships of MBBs or MBs (Muslim believers in Jesus) of being a lighthouse to their people in any country.

At best, for the most part, the elder-less gatherings tend to be too weak to even be considered congregations, although there are some outstanding exceptions.

Thirdly, we know there has been a significant increase in the number of would-be disciple-makers taking up residence among Muslims from Mauritania to Mindanao since 1975. The organizations at our Consultation represent upwards of 10,000 workers from more than twenty organizations engaging Muslim people groups.

Our rejoicing, however, must be somewhat muted when we ask how many of those 10,000 are long-term? How many can and regularly do make the Gospel understandable in the heart language of the Muslims they are seeking to enlighten?

What potential and actual pioneer church-planting efforts can and will be accomplished by Africans, Asians, and Latinos among Muslims?

In any case, we know that there are still not even close to a sufficient number of "sent ones" making disciples among the 1.4 billion Muslims in the world today. Twenty percent of the world's population goes to bed nightly without awareness of the Creator's sacrifice of atonement for their eternal blessedness.

This particular chapter considers the participation of the Global South. What potential and actual pioneer church-planting efforts can and will be accomplished by Africans, Asians, and Latinos among Muslims? There are some exciting cross-cultural initiatives within and into Muslim people groups by Global South workers. It is our hope that these initiatives will arise and make real progress in engaging Muslim people groups.

The enthusiasts looking to the "Global South" to complete the Great Commission among Muslims differ on which of the strategies below is the priority:

» Existing mission agencies and churches send out members in the traditional manner from the rapidly expanding churches of Latin America, Africa, and Asia to unengaged (or under-engaged) Muslim unreached people groups (MUPGs).

» Agencies work in catalyzing believers who live most proximate to unengaged Muslim peoples to birth new sending entities.

» Agencies work in equipping MBBs who have the potential to stay within their societies as yeast to trigger a people-movement to Christ among their own people. Then, these are able to go beyond to proximate MUPGs who are totally unengaged.

There are both enthusiasts and mild skeptics of the proposal that the great increase in the number of Evangelicals in the Global South will translate into a great increase in pioneer church planters among unengaged Muslims. Is the Lord of the Harvest shifting his "thrusting out" from the West to the countries of the Global South? What is the evidence?

Philip Jenkins' *The New Faces of Christianity: Believing the Bible in the Global South* maintains that believers in the Global South expect to see God break into human affairs and work in unusual and miraculous ways.[36] Perhaps emerging mission leaders in the Global South will confidently rely on their experience of the Lord's supernatural intervention to such a degree that the power of the living, resurrected Christ will be the convincing element to Muslims. After all, they want to see God at work, not simply discussed. While workers from the West may tend to rely on wealth, power, and the latest technology, less wealthy workers from the Global South may be better positioned to demonstrate how God works for the poor.

Even if Jenkins may be too optimistic, it is evident that churches in Latin America, Africa, and Asia are beginning to realize that the worldwide evangelical community expects them to have a significant role in evangelizing the Muslims of the world, especially among Muslims within or proximate to their national borders!

Missionaries report that the Spirit of God is speaking and motivating some church and mission leaders in the Global South to find ways to get more involved in "reaching Muslim peoples without a church." There are some (though not carefully documented) encouraging initiatives.

---

[36] Oxford: Oxford University Press, 2006, 16–17.

What Is Not Clear

» What has already been accomplished among previously unengaged Muslim peoples (not simply a plan on paper or talked about) by African, Latino, and Asian pioneer church planters before or after the year 2000?

» Which of those ventures were sparked or birthed by Western agencies and their resources? Which came into being by African, Asian, or Latin American agencies or churches without any Western resources?

» What are the Global South leaders requesting from the West? For example, how does the Global South prefer the West to partner with them to engage MUPGs that today do not have a viable church-planting effort in their midst?

» What do Global South mission and church leaders say about the roles Westerners and other outsiders should be filling in Global South initiatives to engage Muslim people groups?

» What is the best manner to evaluate the reality or accuracy of what has been written or spoken?

We also know that to simply "leave it to local believers" is naïve. Perhaps 99 percent of all the Christian believers in residence, in the workplace, or in schools near Muslims choose not to attempt witnessing to their fellow citizens who are Muslims. Even if good salaries were available to Christian or tribal background believers, possibly only in India and Indonesia could a sufficient number be mobilized who would actually spend 30 hours per week witnessing face-to-face with Muslims!

For example, I asked my teammate of the 1960s, K.P. Yohannan, Director of Gospel For Asia (GFA), how many of the 4,000 Asians they underwrite financially were *majoring* in church planting among Muslims? He was not sure. He had heard that their *one* team with Muslims in Assam had quit Muslim work after one team member was stabbed. GFA hopes their many Bible schools will produce pioneer church planters among Muslims. History might predict otherwise.

The truth of the matter is that a significant proportion of God's people have an "allergic reaction" to Muslims, a reaction understandable from history.

As a student of history, I am not judgmental of Christians living in Muslim majority countries. They have suffered humiliation and deprivation as second-class citizens for centuries.

No wonder that countless, well-meaning, so-called training events by Western missionaries challenging local Christians in the Middle East, Pakistan, India, Bangladesh, Malaysia, and Indonesia to "reach their own people" (whom Muslims are not) have resulted in a silent or defensive response!

But then, from where should such change agents come? From where is the Lord of the Harvest seeking to recruit the next wave of disciple-makers to Muslims? How should we respond to the well-iterated facts that the vast majority of Evangelicals now live in Africa, Latin America, and Asia? Is God shifting his recruiting grounds, and if he is, how will this shift impact the sharing of the Good News within the Global South, home to many of the world's unreached people groups, and throughout the world?

CAN WE IMAGINE A MAJOR SHIFT IN THE NEXT DECADES SO THAT THE VAST MAJORITY OF THE NEXT GENERATION OF PIONEERS AMONG MUSLIMS WILL BE COMING FROM BRAZIL, COLOMBIA, NIGERIA, KENYA, GHANA, INDIA, INDONESIA, THE PHILIPPINES, OR CHINA?

Ben Naja, a veteran of Muslim work in Sub-Saharan Africa, has asked the question, "How many times in the last century has 'final' been postulated?" He says:

» "By 2010, non-Western Evangelicals will be seven times more numerous than those in the West."
» "In the year 2025, four out of five missionaries will come from the Global South."
» "The work of the harvest will largely be done by them."[37]

---

[37] *Releasing the Workers of the Eleventh Hour* (Pasadena, CA: William Carey Library, 2007).

Can we imagine a major shift in the next decades so that the vast majority of the next generation of pioneers among Muslims will be coming from Brazil, Colombia, Nigeria, Kenya, Ghana, India, Indonesia, the Philippines, or China? Has not Korea reportedly already surpassed the United Kingdom in the number of missionaries working in the 10/40 Window between West Africa and East Asia?

What are we to think of the mind-boggling vision of the *Back to Jerusalem* movement of mainland China? Can anyone seriously envision 100,000 rural Chinese farmer-missionaries actually coming out of China and taking up residence among Buddhists, Hindus, and Muslims across Asia, Eastern Europe, and the Middle East? If so, how will they be financed?

Consider tentmaking or business as mission. This is not exactly a new idea. William Carey started with an indigo factory. The Jesuits found employment under the Mongols of North India in the 1600s. We are told that the Philippines has millions working outside their country, including as many as 100,000 in the Arab Gulf alone. However, even if these numbers are close to being accurate, what percentage of those Filipinos feel led to jeopardize their opportunity to send money home by attempting to win Arab Muslims to Christ?

WHAT WE DO NOT KNOW

1. How many who can obtain work in a Muslim country will become effective disciple-makers? Michael Griffiths commonly asks, "How many men or women can do two things well?" How many examples actually exist of someone finding a job or starting a business in a Muslim context that has in fact led to a group of Muslims forming a community of Christ followers?

2. How many Africans, Asians, or Latin Americans have sufficient skills, experience, or business acumen to start a profitable business in a Muslim country? What if they have never done this in their own country? How does this fact affect their chances of success?

3. Should someone who has never started a business try it for the first time in a Muslim country? I am thinking of several efforts to export rugs or some other local product to the West that failed because buyers could not be found.

4. Why are we attempting to make business people or social workers out of people who are called to be evangelists?

5. Though we must always consider the impact of our actions on others, why is planned expulsion unthinkable? To what degree were the apostle Paul and his teammates assuming expulsion was likely sooner or later? Where did the earliest apostolic missionaries establish residence for fifteen to twenty years?

6. What about children? Followers of Christ are commanded to care for their families (1 Timothy 5:8), but what does this mean in cross-cultural settings? We have few examples in the New Testament of missionaries traveling and living in other cultures with their children.[38] Still, we know that both Paul and Peter traveled with and discipled younger believers such as Timothy and John Mark. For many followers of Christ today, opportunities for children in areas such as education are a key factor in their decision to move to a different country, and also affect which countries they will be willing to live in. What are the implications for building church-planting movements if this is the case?

7. Apostolic church planting among Muslims is risky and dangerous. Many start well but do not persevere long enough to make real progress. Those who follow the call of the Lord are not promised an easy life. Jesus says,

---

[38]   Peter, for example, was probably married (Matthew 8:14 mentions his mother-in-law), but we do not know if his wife was still living, or if he had any children.

Behold, I send you out as sheep in the midst of wolves; therefore, be shrewd as serpents, and innocent as doves. But beware of men; for they will deliver you up to the courts and scourge you in their synagogues; and you shall even be brought before governors and kings for my sake, as a testimony to them and to the Gentiles. But when they deliver you up, do no become anxious about how or what you will speak; for it shall be given you in that hour what you are to speak. For it is not you who speak, but it is the Spirit of your Father who speaks in you. And brother will deliver up brother to death, and a father his child; and children will rise up against parents, and cause them to be put to death. And you will be hated by all on account of my name, but it is the one who has endured to the end who will be saved. But whenever they persecute you in this city, flee to the next ...
(Matthew 10:16–23, NASV).

Is the current generation up to the challenge? Certainly not without the sustaining presence and power of the Holy Spirit. So far, only a small percentage of believers from the Global South have become Great Commission Christians, and only a tiny percentage of them have been willing and able to take up and maintain residence within a Muslim people group. The survey below is one example of a tool that can be used to learn more about past and current work among Muslims.

A Survey of the History of Partners and Their Work among Muslims Since 1960

By Greg Livingstone

Please provide information as directed in the survey below. If you need more space, feel free to attach additional pages in order to help us share what we have attempted among Muslims since 1960.

1. What was the name of your agency in 1960?

2. What is the name of your agency today?

3. What is your name?

4. What is your e-mail address?

5. What is your telephone number?

6. In what countries has/is your organization ministered/ministering among Muslims? (Give countries, dates of entry, dates of withdrawal/ turnover, locations, people groups, etc.)

7. What has been your agency's experience in not being able (for what-ever reasons) to keep people in a Muslim city/area long enough to learn the language and culture well and to gain significant relation-ships of trust? (Please give examples but not names.)
    (Example: One Canadian couple entered Libya in 1992, and they moved to Bahrain a year later. In 1999, a Dutch couple left after a year because of poor health.)

8. To what degree have you utilized citizens of the country—CBBs or MBBs, in your agency-related ministries to Muslims?
(Example: A small group of churches in Chad has sent 11 TBB families to 11 Muslim villages to do farming.)

9. What comments can you make to explain language and culture opportunities?
(Example: If there is a trade language, do they tend to use it? If none, are they forced to learn the local dialects? Are MBBs better suited for choosing vocabulary to express their new faith than CBBs who bring church clichés with them?)

10. In what cities or country has your agency seen MBBs regenerated?

11. Give a rough percentage estimate for each of the following:
Percentage of MBBs who have disappeared?
Percentage of MBBs who have joined a CBB church?
Percentage of MBBs who have become part of an MBB fellowship?
(Example: Probably about half of those who professed Christ have disappeared; almost all were originally part of an MBB house church, but maybe 20% found the CBB churches more exciting and chose to be extracted.)

12. What lessons has your agency learned that you would like to share with others?

ON A MORE POSITIVE NOTE

The Lord of the Harvest is not bewildered by modern-day obstacles in the Muslim world. He will answer our petitions to raise up laborers for his harvest among Muslims. History demonstrates that our great God can and will use those who make themselves available.

Despite disappointments with many existing Christians in Muslim countries, there is a fresh, even if sporadic, impetus to find ways to help Great Commission Christians of countries with large evangelical populations to launch new sending initiatives.

Ben Naja's success in seeing one small denomination in Chad manage to see more than twenty farmer couples obtain an invitation to move into Muslim villages is heralded as a wave of the future to increase Christian presence among Muslims. In Naja's scheme, outside funding is limited to seed money. This seed money enables a couple to take up residence as farmers "where Christ is not named." Naja maintains that there are five areas in which nearby mission entities may have an advantage over the Western models of mission: 1) local leadership and structures, 2) local self-funding, 3) proximate sending, 4) in-place sending, and 5) overseas employment.[39] Let us examine each in more detail, then look at possible gaps and challenges in this model.

Local Leadership and Structures

Leaders in Latin America, Africa, and Asia need opportunities to try things their way. The Nigerian Evangelical Missions Association (NEMA) sends out workers without guaranteed income. That may seem cruel or irresponsible to Western mission leaders, but it may be closer to the model of the Lord Jesus and Paul than today's Western mission model. Many Nigerian believers who have a heart for sharing Christ among others have obtained job transfers to move into new areas untouched by the Gospel. These teachers, government workers, bank workers, and other skilled professionals have planted many churches among unreached people groups through this strategy. The example of NEMA is exciting; however, Western models of funding missions have spread far and wide, and infected the kind of strategy that NEMA seeks to implement.

Local Self-Funding

Naja urges us to find ways to help Africans avoid dependence on outside funding.

The opposite view is that funding from the church and agencies in the West and wealthy Asia to underwrite workers from the Global South is logical: "We have the money, you have the people, so let's 'partner' together." Does that not seem consistent with 2 Corinthians 8:13–14, where those with abundance are encouraged to share with those in want?

---

[39]   *Releasing the Workers of the Eleventh Hour.*

Is it really a foregone conclusion that whoever controls the purse strings controls the direction and the decisions? Is it inconceivable that there could be times when funds are rightly held back when the local workers have diverted funding toward accumulating their own properties?

FIVE AREAS TO CONSIDER

1. *Local leadership and structures;*
2. *Local self-funding;*
3. *Proximate sending;*
4. *In-place sending; and*
5. *Overseas employment.*

It is easy, of course, to insist that, instead of foreign funding, obtaining locally sustainable resources should be encouraged. Who can fault such a goal? Perhaps when the accountability is as effective as certain projects in Bangladesh, one-time provisions from outside will become the sustaining method of the future.

Years ago, George Verwer decided he would prefer seeing a great increase in proclamation to the goal of "self-sufficiency." Operation Mobilization (OM) created a method of supporting several thousand evangelists in India by starting bookstores in the United Kingdom, operated largely by volunteers. The profits then went to publish literature in India. When the Indian workers sold that literature, they then had money to maintain themselves.

Proximate Sending

Tim Lewis and Bob Goldmann assert that pioneer workers in the Global South often have the advantage of "proximity" with their Muslim neighbors. They point out "the Gospel-spreading advantages that come from being close to [Muslims] in various dimensions—geography, linguistics, culture, socioeconomics, worldview, lifestyle, standard of living, etc." They argue that it is only sensible to give priority to helping mission-concerned believers in Africa and Asia to design approaches to the Muslim peoples who are proximate to them.[40]

In-Place Sending

"In-place sending" is of course ideal when courageous exceptions to the fearful mute are discovered. In-place sending is when workers are trained to take the Gospel cross-culturally into an unreached people group without quitting their jobs or moving their residence because they already live and/or work near or among an unreached people group. *Nicodemus Ministries* in North India deploys this strategy in Agra and Bihar by helping local people become effective in sharing their faith in their own neighborhoods. This tends to work better for witnesses from non-Muslim backgrounds as they are not considered traitors to Islam.

Overseas Employment

Overseas employment is another low-cost sending strategy that is an exception to giving priority to proximate peoples. This strategy takes advantage of existing trends of Evangelicals leaving their own country to work in a Muslim region. For example, more than eight million Filipinos work in more than 180 countries, with one million sent out in 2005 alone. Likewise, the Chinese diaspora is assuming greater significance.

These dual-vocation workers, in theory, have a salary or a business that either fully or partially covers their expenses. This is especially needful for the pioneer workers coming from countries where their monthly cost of living in a Muslim area might be five times the income of the pastor of their sending church, as is the case in China, the Philippines, India, and Sri Lanka.

Tentmaking advocates would maintain that those obviously earning their living in the presence of their Muslim friends are generally more credible because they are working "just like everyone else." Presumably, they are then less vulnerable to the accusation that they are being paid by foreigners to preach the Gospel. Also, if they are sent to a Muslim people in their region (e.g., Filipinos to Sumatra), it may be easier for the less-skilled or less-educated to find gainful

---

[40] "Saul's Armor and David's Sling: Innovative Sending in the Global South," *Mission Frontiers 29*, no. 3 (May–June 2007): 20.

employment than if they are sent to distant areas where they do not know the language and culture, or where only those with highly technical skills can obtain a visa.

Gaps in Tentmaking by Foreigners

» Foreigners may be overworked with little time to socialize with Muslims.

» Foreigners, if they are considered to be lower-class (e.g., as some Asians are viewed by local people in Saudi Arabia), may be barred from social contact with Muslims.

» Many who move to other countries work in groups that are close but not within unreached people groups. Examples include Filipino oil-rig workers in Libya, taxi drivers in the Arab Gulf, Chinese construction workers in Sudan, and so on. Because they do not live within these people groups, they have few opportunities to socialize or make friends with Muslims. In addition, foreign workers may have little opportunity to learn the local language.

» Many foreign workers have dependents back home who would be horrified if they lost their well-paying jobs due to participation in evangelism. "Honoring their father and mother" is seen as a biblical reason to leave Muslims alone, unless the Muslims themselves ask for information about the Christian faith.

Gospel Implantation

Being proximate in culture or skin color does not necessarily mean that one will be an effective evangelist or disciple-maker. It makes little difference how close one lives to Muslims when the Gospel presentation offered may be repugnant to the Muslim.

Unless otherwise guided, even near-culture workers tend to start churches similar to their own without consideration of how they may be perceived by those they hope to reach. Too often they are focused on a building and meetings, missing the kind of community reflected in the early Church in Acts 2 and 4. How will the messengers learn to establish a community of faith that is natural to the new context rather than seeming foreign to the new believers?

CONCLUSION

Without necessarily doing less of what they are doing fruitfully, Western agencies need to consider how they can also increase their deployment of significant resources to help catalyze pioneer efforts of proximate workers, even though these new sending entities would probably not be related to their organizations. Doing so might release more of our "Northern workers" to Muslim peoples where there are no Global South sending agencies or churches.

Chapter 5

Sister Laborers:
Partnering in the Task

SUE EENIGENBURG

"She said, 'Please let me glean and gather among the sheaves.'"
Ruth 2:7

"The twelve were with him, and also some women ...
These women were helping to support them out of their own means."
Luke 8:1–3, TNIV

April, 1906. Cairo, Egypt. Listen to this plea from missionary women at the
First Missionary Conference on behalf of the Muslim world:

> We, the women missionaries assembled at the Cairo Conference, would
> send this appeal on behalf of the women of Moslem lands...

> While we have heard with deep thankfulness of many signs of God's
> blessing on the efforts already put forth, yet, we have been appalled at
> the reports which have been sent in to the conference from all parts of
> the Moslem world, showing us only too plainly that, as yet, but a fringe
> of this great work has been touched.

The same story has come back from India, Persia, Arabia, Africa and other Mohammedan lands, making evident that the conditions of women under Islam is everywhere the same and that there is no hope of effectually remedying the spiritual, moral and physical ills which they suffer, except to take them the message of the Saviour, and that there is no chance of their hearing, unless we give ourselves to the work. No one else will do it. This lays a heavy responsibility on all Christian women.

The number of women is so vast that any adequate effort to meet the need must be on a scale far wider than has ever yet been attempted. We do not suggest new organizations, but that every church and board of missions at present working in Moslem lands should take up their own women's branch of work with an altogether new ideal before them, determining to reach the whole world of Moslem women in this generation. Each part of the women's work already being carried on needs to be widely extended. (We need) trained and consecrated women doctors; trained and consecrated women teachers; groups of women workers in the villages; ...with love in their hearts to seek and to save the lost.[41]

One hundred years have passed since this impassioned plea, and we have seen much happen. Many more missionary women have gone out to unreached Muslim people groups. A wealth of resources for missionary women is available now compared to even what was around when I first went overseas twenty years ago. At least four multi-organizational training consultations have been held for women ministering in the Muslim world. One regional conference, sponsored by several like-minded organizations, took place in Spain for seventy missionary women who work with North African Muslims. Some women have pioneered new areas and others have been able to stay in countries to minister where men have been expelled. Rebecca Lewis recognized this as she wrote, "Women with strange ideas are not as threatening to governments as men. This amazing fact should not be overlooked when discussing strategies for the Muslim world."[42]

---

41   J. A. Lepsius, et al., *Methods of Mission Work among Moslems* (New York: Fleming H. Revell Co., 1906), 21–22.

42   Rebecca Lewis, "Strategizing for Church Planting Movements in the Muslim world," *International Journal of Frontier Missions* 21, no. 2 (Summer 2004): 76. See W.K. Eddy, "Islam in Syria and Palestine," in *The Mohammedan World of To-day: Being Papers Read at the First Missionary Conference on Behalf of the Mohammedan World Held at Cairo April 4th–9th, 1906* (New York: Fleming H. Revell, 1906), 76.

Whereas the call for missionary women 100 years ago was mainly to Western countries, today Muslim women are hearing the Gospel from missionaries from Latin America, the Philippines, Africa, Korea, China, Indonesia, Malaysia, India, and their own Muslim countries. Women can now hear the Gospel message via television and radio. Even more exciting is that in some areas, MBB (Muslim background believer) women are mentoring and leading others. Churches have been planted among MBBs around the world. Praise God! And yet, the task remains unfinished, and after 100 years it is necessary to present another call. It is the call for women, not just the missionary women but the MBB women, to press on in fulfilling their strategic roles in the church-planting process. For church planting to be effective, women must be a part of the process.

In determining the significance and variety of the roles that women have in church planting for the future, it might be beneficial to look to the past. As we look at the important roles of women in the early church plants, we see women with the same vital roles today. The roles of missionary women are critical; however, the roles of MBB women are crucial to church planting in the twenty-first century. Let us take a look at the roles women have had in the Bible as well as their contributions today in church planting.

PROCLAMATION

New Testament women were told to be witnesses and received the Holy Spirit (Luke 24:33, 46–49; Acts 1:8, 12–15; 2:4, 17–21).

Missionary women creatively witness to Muslim friends. In Europe, a dance night is held for women in which refugees wear their national dress. As missionaries, Muslims, and MBBs mingle, the Gospel is shared and questions are answered. In other countries, missionary women visit homes, lead aerobics classes, teach English, hold craft classes, and conduct Bible studies to share the Gospel.

An MBB woman, Oumi, leaves her city to share the Gospel in villages. She says: "I became a Christian thanks to foreigners who came to Senegal to share God's Word. They left their comfortable lives and came here to see a Senegalese woman come to know Christ. So, I'm going to where other women are. I'm not going to wait for them to come to me."[43]

---

[43]   Kay Marshall Strom and Michele Rickett, *Daughters of Hope* (Downers Grove, IL InterVarsity Press, 2003), 84.

PRAYER

New Testament women were in the upper room praying with the disciples (Acts 1:14).

Missionary women pray boldly for the salvation of Muslim women. In one Middle Eastern country, they meet regularly to learn how to pray more intentionally and deeply for their Muslim friends.

At an Iranian church plant in Asia Minor, there is one lady who came to the city as a strict Muslim, with thick veil, prayer beads, and Qur'an. A friend invited her to come to an Iranian service. She heard Scripture in her own language and people joyfully singing hymns and praying from their hearts. After some time, she was convinced that Jesus was who he claimed to be, and she accepted him. What a dramatic change in this woman! She began to learn the hymns and read the Bible, and to hear her prayers is a beautiful experience. Today, she visits with other women in the church and is a strong and vibrant witness. However, it is her prayer life that has been the greatest help in the growth of the church.

PERSECUTION

New Testament women were persecuted and put in prison for their faith (Acts 8:3; 9:2; 22:4).

Missionary women have been harassed, questioned, deported, imprisoned, and killed. One woman in North Africa was held at the airport, and then was denied entry back into the country. Her husband and children were left to pack up their home and move.

One Egyptian woman faced pressure from her family and threats of death from her father. She asked fellow believers to pray, and she experienced God's protection. Her family searched her purse and her room to get rid of any Christian materials. One night, her father said he had had enough. He was getting up to hurt her when the doorbell rang. When those guests left, the doorbell rang again. Guests came throughout the evening, and by the time the last guests left, her father's wrath had cooled. No more was said, at least for awhile. Through facing these events, she learned that God is faithful and that other members of the Body of Christ were upholding her with prayer and fasting.

Roles of Women in the Bible and Today

- *Proclamation;*
- *Prayer;*
- *Persecution;*
- *Kind acts;*
- *Hospitality;*
- *Serving;*
- *Mentoring; and*
- *Raising children.*

Kind Acts

In the New Testament, older widows were to be cared for by the church if they had been the wife of one husband, doing good works, raising children, being hospitable, washing the feet of the saints, and assisting those in distress (1 Timothy 5:9–10). It is interesting to note the many different roles that women have often balanced in their homes, churches, and communities.

Missionary women, one a doctor and the other a nurse, opened up a clinic in a Muslim village in East Asia to meet physical needs, but also to plant a church.

Two single, middle-aged MBB Iranian women have great influence in churches in their country. Though they are not visible in the weekly, larger gathering they attend, they visit people in their homes, share and encourage, and are interested in meeting the physical as well as the spiritual needs of people.

Hospitality

Mary, mother of John Mark, hosted a prayer meeting in her home (Acts 12:12–13).

Missionary women host churches in their homes. In Central Asia, Asia Minor, East Asia, and around the world, women open their homes for Bible studies and gatherings.

Tanina in North Africa came to know the Lord through radio and corresponding with Rebecca, an North African Berber who had immigrated to France when she was twelve. Rebecca took the time to answer Tanina's questions, and after six months of correspondence, she made a trip to visit her. Rebecca spent one month with Tanina. She patiently answered Tanina's questions. She discipled Tanina and her mother. She prayed with them that they would continue to be able to learn through the radio program and committed herself to continue answering any questions they had. Tanina was soon married to a man twenty-five years older than her, a man who already had one wife and several children in Paris. He lives there for six months and with Tanina in North Africa for six months each year. When her husband is in North Africa, Tanina listens to the radio in secret. When her husband is gone, a small group of women meet regularly in her house and listen to the radio with her. Her mother is one of these women. Tanina reads the Bible to these women and teaches them the things she learned from Rebecca.[44]

SERVING

Phoebe was a servant of the church in Cenchrea and a helper to many (Romans 16:1–2). Paul encouraged the Romans to receive her in a manner worthy of the saints and to help her in whatever she needed. It is likely that she carried the letter to the Romans.

Missionary women serve in church plants. They cook meals, serve tea, distribute literature, disciple, teach, work with children, train, do evangelistic outreaches, travel to other areas, translate material, lead worship, and do whatever is needed to help plant churches.

In their host European country, MBB refugee women have served on the leadership team, led the worship team and worship portion of the Sunday service, facilitated mixed-group Bible studies, led the weekly ladies' Bible study, organized and taught Sunday School for the children, cooked for Wednesday night meetings and other events, led the youth group, handled aspects of a Bible correspondence course, led prayer times, given testimonies of their new lives in Christ in front of the church body, greeted and visited newcomers, shown great hospitality, and participated in evangelistic outreach.

---

[44] Strom and Rickett, *Daughters of Hope*, chapter 11.

MENTORING

Older women in the church were to mentor and teach the younger women in areas related to their behavior, roles, and work (Titus 2:3–5).

More experienced missionary women mentor those newer to their areas of service. Missionary women soon learn that the needs of Muslim women can be very similar to their own needs—security, love, and significance. However, there are some differences in how these needs present themselves. In a world of evil spirits and the evil eye, for example, fear reigns. When one word of gossip or slander reaches the ears of a young woman's family, it can mean life or death. When divorce can occur over lack of offspring or bringing displeasure in any area, Muslim women can live in much uncertainty. The needs of Muslims vary from one culture to another, as do their strengths. They love their children, they seek to help their society and families, and they persevere through tremendous obstacles.

Sharing Christ with Muslim women is often done in the home setting. As women drink tea and share life's struggles, Jesus is proclaimed as the one who can help, not only in this life but in the one to come. Discipling takes place holistically, not in discussing theories or debating issues. Women learn how Jesus can help them and how they can serve him each day of their lives. As missionary women proclaim, disciple, and gather women in the church-planting process, MBB women are being mentored and may soon be ready to begin the same process with their friends and family. Some mentoring takes place naturally, but intentional mentoring is essential for MBB women so that they are effectively equipped for their church-planting roles.

Naomi and Aida have known the Lord for more than twenty years. They have grown in grace and truth. Aida is an evangelist and several of her female family members have come to faith. Two of Naomi's five children are serving the Lord in different countries. When a small fellowship was started, these women were the oldest believers in the body. They are well respected by the men and share in the work of the church. They take turns teaching Sunday school and serving communion, including leading the sharing time before communion. They have translated music into their mother tongue for the body to sing. They take turns with other members in leading worship. As the workers were growing in the Lord, they did not use any specific materials except the Bible. The workers were always careful about making everything they did transferable. They both have a burden to reach their people group with the Gospel as well as disciple believing women in the countryside. This is difficult logistically for them to do, but whenever they get the chance to minister, the Lord uses them greatly to encourage younger believing women. Naomi and Aida have a very healthy view of the difference between religion and what is essential for a relationship with Christ. This is what they pass on to others who are seeking.

RAISING CHILDREN

Lois and Eunice raised children in sincere faith and scriptural truth (2 Timothy 1:5; 3:15).

Missionary mothers seek to raise their children to love the Lord and serve him. Many moms "home school," help their children with homework from national schools, or simply care for the day-to-day needs of their children. They wipe noses, discipline, nurture, and minister to their families. They remember that their children are also their disciples.

Rebecca Lewis writes:

When we were in Morocco, I noticed an interesting phenomenon. While many men who had become believers reverted to Islam at the time of marriage, those who remained believers almost always had a believing mother standing behind them. In the more oppressive Muslim societies, the women seek power and security through their sons, who serve both as protection and as support once their husbands die. It follows that believing wives, while not necessarily able to win their husbands to the Lord, will have the power to win their sons, even if secretly.

The women in many Islamic countries feel tremendous insecurities due to easy divorce, the husband's control over the children of divorce, and infidelity. Some would argue this makes them more likely to hide their faith, which is true. But it also makes them people searching for the kind of relationship with God, and the power and joy it brings, that only Jesus the Messiah can give them. They and their children can become the foundation of tomorrow's house-church movement within Islam.

The women of Islam could very well be the gateway of the Gospel into Islamic networks.[45]

It is clearly evident that the roles and ministries of women in the church-planting process are vital and must be utilized. It is not enough just to reach the heads of households; we must also intentionally reach the ones with true and lasting influence in the home.

WHAT CAN WE DO TO FACILITATE THE ROLES THAT MBB WOMEN CAN HAVE IN THE CHURCH-PLANTING PROCESS?

However, though women have had these roles and progress has been made, something has to change in order to be more effective. What can we do to facilitate the roles that MBB women can have in the church-planting process? May I suggest one action point for each of these areas that, if implemented, could dramatically increase our church-planting efforts?

PROCLAMATION: ENCOURAGE WOMEN TO SHARE THEIR STORIES

Every believer has a story of God's grace in her life. Women need to have open doors to share that story. They can begin to proclaim in small groups of believers, and soon with groups of believers and Muslims together. In time, with care and sensitivity, they can share with their families. Silence cannot remain a viable option. Women must be able to share their stories as soon as possible.

PERSECUTION: ENCOURAGE WOMEN THAT THEY CAN CONQUER FEAR THROUGH FAITH

Most choose not to proclaim because they are afraid. Fear of loss, harassment, rejection, and persecution keep many from proclaiming the Gospel. Faith must be developed by knowing God, continuing to focus on eternity, and choosing to walk by faith. We must get those who are fearful in touch with those who have gained victory. Could we not have sisters who have learned how to persevere

---

45 "Strategizing for Church Planting Movements in the Muslim world," *International Journal of Frontier Missions* (Summer 2004), 76.

through persecution and do not give in to fear who will minister to those who continue to live in fear? They can come alongside and share their experience—verbally or through written means—with those who are struggling. Missionaries and national believers themselves must model boldness and enduring strength in the midst of persecution. Fear can only be conquered through faith.

PRAYER: ENCOURAGE WOMEN TO OVERCOME RITUAL PROHIBITIONS

For years, Muslim women have been taught that they cannot pray or handle a holy book during their monthly cycle. They must go through a certain ritual before they can come before God, and even then they are not certain he will hear them; many go to tombs of dead saints or religious leaders for help. Fear of going to the bathroom, where evil spirits lurk, keeps them trapped. They must be encouraged to pray as they enter and boldly trust God to protect them. Our Korean partners, known worldwide for their fervent prayers, can have a remarkable impact on the prayer life of MBB women as they interact. We must teach, train, and encourage our sisters to pray at any and all times. As their prayer lives are revolutionized, so will be our church plants.

KIND DEEDS: ENCOURAGE WOMEN TO PROMPTLY START USING THEIR GIFTS

It is not just the leader or the woman with the strongest personality or gifting who does everything, but everyone must be involved with reaching out to others through deeds of kindness. It can be easy in some Muslim cultures to sit back and let one person do everything. From the beginning of every church plant, each person must have a role to play. One mistake is waiting too long to get people involved because we think they may not be ready or need to mature first. Being kind is something everyone can do and is less threatening than leading a study or worship. Kind deeds, though seemingly simple, have a powerful effect on the community. As believers share their faith by producing good works befitting that faith, more lives will be touched because others see faith in action and not just in words.

HOSPITALITY: ENCOURAGE WOMEN TO USE HOSPITALITY AS MINISTRY

Many times in the Muslim world, hospitality is the cornerstone of the community. However, at times hospitality may not be done for the good of the guest but for the honor of the host. Hospitality must be done as an expression of the Gospel, and it will as a result make church planting more effective.

Fran Love speaks of hospitality well when she says,

> By hospitality I mean more than just serving tea. I mean the very essence of church as the household of God, where often the home is the church. It means welcoming women into a circle, building relationships, exposing them to the body before they themselves are believers; welcoming them as seekers and loving them before they know Christ's love; inviting them to pray, to search Scripture, to read Scripture, to comment on Scripture, and to participate in community life together even before they know Christ as their Savior. Hospitality provides a safe and warm environment for women where they can seek God together. It also gives them an opportunity to begin to exercise gifts that build the Body of Christ, the church. In this safe environment some learn how to teach, to lead, to care for others, and reach out to other friends and family members. Hospitality first brings women together into a place of healing and then sends them out as Christ's ambassadors to the world.[46]

SERVING: ENCOURAGE WOMEN BY RESPECTING THEM AS CO-LABORERS

In many Muslim countries, women are not viewed as having much to contribute. Their voice can be easily discounted. We need, like the Apostle Paul in a patriarchal structure, to plant the seed that will transform culture: "there is no longer male and female; for all of you are one in Christ Jesus" (Galatians 3:28). In our desire to adapt to the different countries where we work, this view of women may affect how missionary men interact with them. We must intentionally and proactively fight against this. Seeking to be culturally appropriate is good, but not when it goes against what Scripture teaches. Women, MBB and

---

[46]   Fran Love, e-mail to author, November 6, 2007.

missionary, are valuable co-workers and must be respected and treated as such. To give them less-than-equal standing in the Body of Christ is sin.

When churches bless and encourage women in their roles, listen to them, and utilize them and their roles, these churches will thrive. It will be the one place in their city where they know they are welcomed and valued as members, as joint heirs in the Kingdom of God.

WHEN CHURCHES BLESS AND ENCOURAGE WOMEN IN THEIR ROLES, LISTEN TO THEM, AND UTILIZE THEM AND THEIR ROLES, THESE CHURCHES WILL THRIVE.

MENTORING: ENCOURAGE WOMEN TO ACQUIRE TRAINING

In previous women's consultations held in the United States, it was difficult to find MBB women and get them there. We also were not sure what their expertise was and how they could help the group the most. So they were invited to give testimonies of how they came to faith. This was a tremendous blessing, but sorely lacking in utilizing their greatest assets.

Holding regional consultations, sponsored by a multi-organizational task force and led by MBB and missionary women working together, would be much more effective not only in effectively training everyone but in partnering together. They would be less expensive, more easily accessible, and led by those with a fuller understanding of the culture in which they minister.

RAISING CHILDREN: ENCOURAGE MOTHERS TO LEAD THE YOUNGER GENERATION TO CHRIST

In many of the cultures where we work, children are not seen as having the ability to make decisions. Children are given much freedom when they are small, and when they reach a certain age, that freedom is taken away as they are seen more as adults and as able to think more clearly. We must educate MBBs, especially mothers, by teaching them that children can choose to trust Jesus at an early age and that they can be discipled and coached as they grow up as believers. In their homes, mothers can teach their children. In our church plants, we must not just baby-sit the children. We must teach them and their parents that

Jesus wants the children to come to him and that they are able to respond to him (Matthew 19:14; Mark 10:14; Luke 18:16).

Today, more than 100 years after the meeting in Cairo, we call on churches and mission agencies worldwide to continue to send well-equipped women missionaries. We also call on all church planters, men and women, to labor together in planting churches as they did in the early church. We call on MBB women to come alongside, in increasing numbers, to work with us and to help guide us into more effective church planting. We must facilitate the roles of women in church planting by implementing these actions for the glory of God as churches are planted among every unreached Muslim people group.

Chapter 6

First Fruits and Future Harvests

Jim Haney

"Greet my beloved Epaenetus,
who was the first fruits in Asia for Christ."
Romans 16:5

Introduction

If we are to make progress toward implementing effective church planting among all Muslim people groups, we need to consider our mutual task prayerfully and thoughtfully. Our task is overwhelming, and we are tempted to dive in, think through the challenges, formulate strategies, and deploy our forces with vigor. Is not that what we have always done? Before we go further in our appraisal of how we might follow God in building his Kingdom, let us take a look at our foundation.

About God and His People

There is an overriding spiritual reality that supersedes all that overwhelms us in our world—God is love. Let us begin with that reality so that we are not confused or become grieved like others who have no hope (1 Thessalonians 4:13).

Sin separates us from God.

> Then the LORD God said, "See, the man has become like one of us, knowing good and evil; and now, he might reach out his hand and take also from the tree of life, and eat, and live forever—therefore the LORD God sent him forth from the garden of Eden, to till the ground from which he was taken" (Genesis 3:22–23).

God loves us in spite of our sin.

> In this is love, not that we loved God but that he loved us and sent his Son to be the atoning sacrifice for our sins (1 John 4:10).

God wants us—all of us—to be with him; he wants us in his presence.

> They sing a new song: "You are worthy to take the scroll and to open its seals, for you were slaughtered and by your blood you ransomed for God saints from every tribe and language and people and nation" (Revelation 5:9).

GOD IS LOVE

Sin separates us from God.
God loves us in spite of our sin.
God wants us in his presence.
He invites all people to rest in him.

He invites all people—every tribe, language, people, and nation—to rest in him.

> Come to me, all you that are weary and are carrying heavy burdens, and I will give you rest (Matthew 11:28).

FIRST FRUITS AND FUTURE HARVESTS

Ask yourself the question, "Is your *Gospel*, the Gospel of abiding rest?" If not, how would you describe your *Gospel* or the *Gospel* of your organization? Do Muslims understand it? Do they want it? Without abiding in the Vine—resting in It—how can Jesus flow through us and fill us so that in his time, he can produce fruit in us—it is the fruit that people want from the vine; it is the grain they want from the seed.

It should be obvious to us by now that there is nothing wrong with the imperishable seed, which is the Word of God. We are also happy to report that today the seed is falling on fallow ground upon which it has never fallen, at least in our generation, and we are eager to sow abundantly because we cannot know how the various soils will receive it. We want to see the germinating in the soil. We have established that there are sowers beyond ourselves—men, women, new believers, the poor and persecuted, those who are willing to give and support, and harvest forces that are emerging from unanticipated corners of the world.

Who better to reach the corners than the redeemed already living there? There are many branches on the Vine, and each has potential to bear fruit if that which brings the fruit is unhindered.

How are you doing as a sower? Have you already made up your mind as to which places the seed will grow and which it will not? Perhaps there are fallow fields that remain so because the fields are in tough places, surrounded by hedges. The sower sows because he wants to see the fruit of his sowing.

What will God do in our day? Perhaps we may cast the seed onto new pathways and find that some of it is carried from there to new places before it is totally consumed. Perhaps we may cast the seed onto rocks and find that some of it takes root in the shaded clefts before the hot sun destroys it all. Perhaps we may cast the seed amongst the thorns only to find that the fires of change sweep through, burn the obstacles away, and allow the seed to grow.

Are we not seeing these phenomena already? It seems that God has wonderful ways to defy our thinking and manifests himself in unimaginable breakthroughs for his glory. Have you not had these experiences in your ministry? If not, I hope you will.

The seed is growing today in unexpected places. It is growing in places that even ten years ago we thought it could never grow because all that we could see were resistant and hardened soils.

The state of the Gospel is strong—it is the power of God for the salvation of everyone who believes (Romans 1:6). As we spread the seed, which is the Word of God, it will take root; it will grow, mature, and multiply, and it will accomplish its purpose (Isaiah 55:11). Let us take a brief look back at some of the milestones in the advance of the Gospel to appreciate how God has prepared us to sow his seed throughout the world today. Then, we will move to some examples of first fruits that have appeared.

GOD HAS PREPARED US FOR THIS TIME

Warren Larson, Director of the Zwemer Center for Muslim Studies at Columbia International University, writes:

> One hundred years ago a new era dawned as to the attitude of Christian mission among Muslims. The different atmosphere was sensed at the *Cairo Conference* (1906), but it came to fruition four years later at the *World Missionary Conference in Edinburgh* (1910).[47] At Edinburgh, when Samuel Zwemer challenged those taking part in the Conference to carry the Gospel to the Muslim world, he called for a new level of commitment to learn about Islam and to share Christ boldly.[48]

For another fifty years, the movement lagged, as already discussed by Patrick Johnstone, until the 1950s and 1960s, when a war-weary world turned to Christ in significant numbers. With renewed zeal for the lost, followers of Jesus shared their faith with family, friends, and neighbors. In the 1970s, a bold new emphasis on world evangelization came in the historic *International Congress of World Evangelization*. The Congress was held in Lausanne, Switzerland, July

---

[47] Interestingly enough, those attending are reported to have given God praise for the gains made since 1810 in evangelism, Bible translation, mobilizing church support, and training indigenous leaders.

[48] Warren Larson, editorial on "Then and Now: New Challenges and New Breakthroughs," *Understanding Muslims: Journal of the Zwemer Center for Muslim Studies,* Columbia International University, March 16, 2007, http://www.ciu.edu/muslimstudies/journal/modules/smartsection/item.php?itemid=3.

16–25, 1974, and involved more than 2,300 participants who determined to "let the earth hear his voice."[49]

Four years later, the *North American Conference on Muslim Evangelization*[50] convened to focus on evangelizing the Muslim world. *The Gospel and Islam: a 1978 Compendium*, edited by Don M. McCurry, captures for us much of what was reported and discussed at this pivotal event.

In the *Compendium*, McCurry and others shared their excitement for new trends in Christian movements among Muslims. As much as they were excited about these trends, significant global hindrances to the spread of the Gospel alarmed them, and the alarms are still sounding today—the ongoing Arab–Israeli conflict, oil politics, demonstrations, bombings and terrorism, and government takeovers by Islamic fundamentalists, to name a few.[51] It's easy to blame Muslims for all the hindrances to the spread of the Gospel among them, but similar forces are at work within non-Muslim powers, including the Church, which for the most part seems unsure about how to respond to Islam, whether as a global force or as the new Muslim family that just moved into the neighborhood!

How did global realities impact those attending the Glen Eyrie Conference? It impacted them the same way it should impact us today—it both humbled them and fired their urgency for renewed commitment to sharing Christ with Muslims. In the keynote address, however, W. Stanley Mooneyham voiced a further concern—a deep concern that I want to raise again in this writing and something that you may feel as well—"'business as usual' cannot be our stance before a rapidly and radically changing Islam. A ripening harvest, that God is bringing, will not allow us the luxury of delaying the reaping until it suits our convenience."[52]

Since 1978, the number of adherents to Islam has doubled to 1.4 billion. However, we are excited that new harvests are coming from once fallow fields and new branches are producing first fruits from the Vine.

[49] The Lausanne Movement, http://www.lausanne.org/lausanne-1974/lausanne-1974.html (accessed February 13, 2008).

[50] The Conference was sponsored by the North American Lausanne Committee and World Vision International. It was held in Glen Eyrie, Colorado Springs, Colorado, from October 15 to 21, 1978. The conference was a time of thinking through the issues of the day related to Islam, and at the time was marked by a mood of penitence and humility.

[51] Don McCurry, "A Time for New Beginnings," in *The Gospel and Islam: a 1978 Compendium*, ed. Don McCurry (Monrovia, CA: MARC, 1979), 13.

[52] W. Stanley Mooneyham, "Keynote Address," in *The Gospel and Islam: a 1978 Compendium*, ed. Don McCurry (Monrovia, CA: MARC, 1979), 23.

FIRST FRUITS

Accompanying this compendium is a CD that provides listings of people groups by Affinity Bloc, People Cluster, country, language, and other data categories. Parts of this CD were distributed in the Consultation in Southeast Asia in the spring of 2007 to those involved in the Global Trends sessions. The listings are integrated in such a way that information provided by the International Mission Board (CPPI),[53] *World Christian Encyclopedia*,[54] and Joshua Project (JP)[55] may shed light on the state of the Gospel among the Muslim peoples of the world. None of the listings is perfect, and it is unlikely that they will ever be so, but as we move ahead with the mission of sharing Christ with the peoples who will one day be represented around God's throne, it is imperative that we put this information before our partners so that we can:

» Improve people group listings;
» Maintain up-to-date information about people groups;
» Monitor and verify engagement; and
» Monitor and verify effective church planting.

Today, it is exciting to see increases in followers of Jesus among many Muslim people groups. Additionally, we are seeing the first fruits among Muslim people groups where previously we had not seen the seed taking root.

While it would be lengthy to list all Muslim people groups here, January 2008 reports from the CPPI and JP show remarkably similar results, as shown in the following diagram.[56]

---

[53] Church Planting Progress Indicators.

[54] David B. Barrett and George Thomas Kurian, eds., 2nd ed. (Oxford: Oxford University Press, 2001).

[55] See www.joshuaproject.net/peoples.

[56] Download the "Complete List of People Groups Excel Spreadsheet—xls," http://www.peoplegroups.org/Downloads. aspx, (accessed January 15, 2008) and "All Peoples-by-Country (single file)," http://www.joshuaproject.net/download. php, (accessed February 13, 2008). Note that the populations reported do not reflect the total number of Muslims in the world today. The populations are the populations of all Muslim people groups, and most of these people groups are not 100 percent Muslim. Additionally, there are Muslims in non-Muslim people groups that are not reported here.

Population of All Muslim People Groups and Evangelical Totals Within These People Groups						
	Population (CPPI)	Population (JP)	Evangelicals (CPPI)	Evangelicals (JP)	% of Population Evangelical (CPPI)	% of Population Evangelical (JP)
Grand Total	1,426,085,471	1,462,819,077	8,270,479	8,295,048	0.5799%	0.5671%

Fig.6.1

From this diagram, we may infer that there are at least eight million Evangelicals living within Muslim people groups today—known to those who have inventoried the harvest[57]—and that they are an extreme minority. Although there are certainly estimates that are higher than this and more assessments are underway, the percentage of Evangelicals in these people groups is just over .5 percent, or one Evangelical for every 200 non-Evangelicals.

As we partner together, we are especially burdened for the unengaged peoples of the world. At the time of our Consultation in Southeast Asia in the spring of 2007, we estimated that there were 247 unengaged, Muslim unreached people groups of at least 100,000 in population in the world today. Nearly a year later and at the time of this writing, the people group list, which is dynamic, has changed slightly, and the number is down to 229. Ongoing feedback is an important part of the process, and we are encouraged with new reports of engagement each month. With this in mind, we must remember that engagement is only a beginning and local believers need our prayers as they witness and develop churches.

---

[57] How many could there really be? Sources have diverging views about the number of Evangelicals living within Muslim people groups, and sources reveal high estimates or low estimates depending on the accuracy of their data, their research biases, and their intention for reporting. There are reports of large movements of Muslims to Christ. A few of these have been assessed by external teams, and certainly these movements show that many are coming to Christ in church-planting movements and other kinds of movements to Christ. Because of the difficulties these believers face in living their new faith in Christ, we may never know how many followers of Jesus there are. However, the Vine Keeper, our Lord, knows it all and his is the harvest, and may he receive all the glory. In the meantime, we do our best to make assessments so that we can be good stewards of the work to which he has entrusted us.

THE PRECIOUS FRUIT OF OUR DAY—
MUSLIM BACKGROUND BELIEVERS

Before moving on to outline some future consideration about future harvests, let us take some time to consider that it is the Holy Spirit that produces fruit in our lives as we abide in him, and our best opportunity to share Christ with Muslim people groups is to be in places where the fruit of the Spirit can draw others to Christ. Our Lord had time upon his entry to Jericho to heal the road-side blind man, and he had time to show kindness to Zacchaeus, even though his agenda was pretty full that week! His words were an overflow of his love. Today as the first fruits of faith are found among Muslims, God is letting us see his unfolding harvest so that we can say with him, "Today, salvation has come to them because they too are sons of Ibrahim" (cf. Luke 19:9).

TODAY AS THE FIRST FRUITS OF FAITH ARE FOUND AMONG MUSLIMS, GOD IS LETTING US SEE HIS UNFOLDING HARVEST SO THAT WE CAN SAY WITH HIM, "TODAY, SALVATION HAS COME TO THEM BECAUSE THEY TOO ARE SONS OF IBRAHIM."

What kinds of breakthroughs are drawing Muslims to Christ?

» Abdul from Asia—"A missionary stopped his rickshaw and offered me a ride."[58]
» Rajib Ali Nozad from Teheran—"A Christian boldly witnessed to me, and I had a vision and I remember these words—'God is and Jesus is true. Of that rest assured and come.' Immediately the vision went away, and all at once, the dejection, gloom and resentment fled from me. A new happiness, joy and tranquility took their place. I was in truth, a new creature, with a new life!"[59]

---

[58]   Jim Haney, "Abdul's Testimony," from an interview during a church-planting movement assessment, Asia, 2002.
[59]   William McElwee Miller, *Ten Muslims Meet Christ* (William B. Eerdman's Publishing Company, 1969), 55–67; and Colin Melbourne, "Nozad: New Born in Christ," from a testimony (paraphrased in modern English), http://www.born-again-christian.info/nozad.htm (accessed February 10, 2008).

» A North African—"When I was in prison I had a dream. In the dream I saw thousands of believers pouring through the streets of my city, openly proclaiming their faith. Even though I was tortured with electricity, this dream told me that one day it would be good."[60]

» A South African—"A believer shared Christ with me, but I was afraid. After a while, I came back to him and said, 'I'm interested in joining your party.'"[61]

» Church-planting movements (CPMs)—Recently, one assessment team reported the following regarding a CPM among an isolated nomadic people group:

A highly significant movement is underway among a nomadic, Muslim people group of herders. There is a genuine turning to Christ as Lord and Savior, as is evident in the testimonies of those interviewed. This turning to Christ is peculiar to only one people group, as yet, within the people cluster. At present the movement exists within the nomadic and not the settled part of the group. Persecution of any who announce their profession of faith in Christ is certain, sudden, and often deadly. The family of the person who makes this choice is the first to take steps to threaten and to do everything they can to force their relative back into Islam. The certain consequences for these followers of Christ are:

» The immediate loss of his cattle forever.
» The sending of his wife and his children home to her family.
» Persecution with beatings that often result in death.

60 J. Dudley Woodberry and Russell G. Shubin, "Why I Chose Jesus," *Mission Frontiers* (March 2001): 31.
61 Tabitha Frizzell, "Christ Draws Young Muslims, in Spite of the Dangers" IMB News Stories, (August 21, 2002). The person was too afraid to say the word "Christian" in a crowd after hearing the Gospel, so he used the word "party" instead of saying that he wanted to become a Christian. Later, he accepted Christ beside the ocean.

Few of the followers of Christ flee, for most stay to continue their bold witness among family and friends. They simply move to a safer section of the nomadic trek and become committed witnesses for Christ. Because this people group learns best by oral strategies, Chronological Bible Storying has been effective among them. The movement is healthy and continues to add new believers into new fellowships every day.[62]

There is more to share about first fruits, but this book is not big enough to contain all that is happening. Pray that the fruit will remain and that it will mature.

FUTURE HARVESTS

The Global Trends track discussed the future of both Christianity and Islam. Models of the future cannot anticipate all of the variables we might encounter or that may affect future harvests, so I will not attempt that here. Global systems are interlinked and have a momentum of their own, and in the few years, dynamic forces will continue to affect global systems, sometimes dramatically.

Hopefully, our cooperation will be one of the forces that makes a dramatic impact on the world as we go about making disciples of all nations. Through a severe mercy of God, our understanding and power are limited so that we must act in faith, but through faith we realize that the one who possesses all authority has sent us and that he is with us until the end of the age.

A look at our world today might leave even the most faithful fainthearted and find us like those who looked out at the Promised Land with Moses long ago—the longer they thought about the results of their survey of the land, the smaller became their God and the larger became the Amorites who lived in the hills. They rebelled and began to think about all that it would take to win the day instead of trusting God for their mission. Things went from bad to worse when they devised their own plans: they were defeated and ran from the Amorites, who attacked the faithful like bees (Deuteronomy 1).

---

[62] Jim Slack, consultant for Field Services and Assessments, Global Research Department, Office of Overseas Operations, International Mission Board; and see chapter 24 on "Recapturing the Role of Suffering."

With this in mind, let us provide some suggestions for our cooperation to move us forward to future harvests.[63]

1. Set aside a special time for confession and renewed submission to God.
2. Consider the strategic misses that we are making by maintaining "business as usual" while Islam and other global forces are rapidly and radically changing.
3. Be clear and consistent about:
    a. Our cooperation so that we work with those who have a common vision.
    b. Our "Gospel."
        i.   Contextualization—Show sensitivity to Muslim views while listening to the opinions of Muslim background believers who seek to engage and reach their peoples. Appreciate that it may take time for MBB fruitful practices to emerge—do not let non-MBB practices get in the way of their processes. Challenge boundary terms used by partners that may unnecessarily create barriers to understanding and acceptance.
        ii. Challenge syncretism by discussing potential syncretistic elements as they arise.
        iii. Conversion—Understand that conversion and Christian growth are most often incremental and process-oriented rather than instantaneous.
    c. The peoples we seek to engage and congregate.
        i.   Sharpen people group research through dialogue with practitioners and researchers.
        ii. Share engagement information.
        iii. Share effective church-planting information—do not forget the transferable principles behind the fruitful practices.

---

63   These were suggested by various members of the Global Trends track during the Consultation in Southeast Asia in the spring of 2007 and as contained in presentation materials, chapter materials, and discussion questions.

4. Think carefully about the kind of missionaries and missionary teams that are needed today. Specifically, consider team composition—single/married, long-term/short-term, residential/non-residential, foreign/local/mixed, supported locally/supported from afar, and so forth. Report results to leadership. Critically and clinically, evaluate experimental strategies.

5. Consider responses to Muslim threats and deeds.

6. Search out like-minded partners in all continents with Westerners taking a genuine supportive role in Global South initiatives.

7. Evaluate Scripture engagement from the client side in addition to the provider side. Consider Scripture impact along with Scripture engagement.

8. Considering that many MBB men within Muslim people groups are not sharing their new faith with their wives and children, we should explore ways to promote the eight suggestions made by Sue Eenigenburg so that MBB women may be more active in church planting.

CONCLUSION

Pray, trust, and obey. God loves Muslims, and it is hard to imagine Muslims coming to Christ through even the best efforts unless Muslims feel the love of the one who bears the Gospel and can see Christ manifested in the life of the witness. New threats have surfaced since 1978, but God remains fixed on his Covenant with humans and the promise of Revelation 5:9. New opportunities have come since 1978, and Muslim people groups, once thought to be impenetrable, are responding to the imperishable seed from Great Commission initiatives throughout the world.

Part 2

Fruitful Practices: Sowing, Watering, Gathering, and Reproducing

EDITED BY DON ALLEN

Chapter 7

Eyes to See, Ears to Hear

DON ALLEN

"Blessed are your eyes, for they see, and your ears, for they hear ...
Hear then the parable of the sower."
Matthew 13:16, 18

Picture yourself, a foreigner, in a crowded guesthouse in a Central Asian city. Accepting your invitation to dinner is a Jesus follower from your home country, widely respected for his love for and good relations with Muslims. As he sips hot chai, he glances about the room, which reeks of musty clothing and cigarettes. Your own eyes are smarting, and not just from the smoke.

"Tell me the secret," you plead, despairingly, "What is happening here?"

He looks startled.

"What do you mean?" he asks.

"How is it possible that your Muslim friends are becoming followers of Isa, and forming communities of faith in the Messiah? My friends and I have been here three years since we left our home country to serve God, and we haven't seen a single new community of *Isa* come together like this. Not one!"

He looks a bit puzzled as he settles back into his chair, resting his cup on the slight rise of his stomach. "Tell me your approach," he says.

Your cup clatters on its saucer.

"My friends and I have established a successful business. It brings jobs to our neighborhood." You tick off your carefully rehearsed points on your fingers. "We are well respected in the community. In fact, people look up to us and recognize that we are God-fearing people! Our neighbors regularly drop in for tea and conversation.

"I just don't get it! We seem to be doing everything *you're* doing. Your town is so close and so similar to ours, I can't blame it on culture differences." Resting your forearms on your knees, your eyes meet his. "What are you doing that we're not doing?"

"Hm." He ponders the question. "Tell me about your language learning."

"Language isn't the problem, either." You shuffle your chair to one side as an old man stumbles past you, pulling a bottle from inside his coat. "Everyone in our team is fluent in Russian, and each of us shares the good news about *Isa* with everyone we meet."

Your guest sips his chai as he listens; his eyes follow the old man weaving his way toward the door.

"Well, for the first few years living here, our story was much like yours," your companion says. "We felt we were stumbling around in the dark, even though we, too, were fluent in Russian. And like you, we spent countless hours with our local friends, actively sharing with them about our life experience with *Isa*. But nothing happened. Then about three years ago, everything changed for us ..."

"Really? How?" The questions tumble out of your mouth. "A spontaneous work of God? Someone with a special gift in convincing people?"

He smiles, shaking his head *no*.

"Then what? A special program?"

"Not exactly." He laughs.

"What changed?"

He leans toward you and tells you his story.

"Seeing and Hearing" How God Blesses Muslims

So what was the problem when "you" tried unsuccessfully to share with your local friends about the love of Jesus? Did you fail to take good notes in your previous seminary classes back home? Should you have followed your supervisor's philosophy of ministry more closely? Did you lack the spiritual maturity of your countryman who witnessed so much fruit in a neighboring town? Did you simply need to pray more effectively?

Such questions are asked because people like you and I often invest a lot of effort living in another culture and sharing about how a community can be transformed when *Isa* comes to occupy a central place in it without seeing the fruit of that labor. Thank God for selfless servants who persevere for years in such conditions! Certainly, this demands authentic sacrifice. But this offers no relief for those who want to see this transformation take place quickly. And when fruit is not forthcoming, you may receive one of two admonitions: a) work harder at following the advice given you back home or b) love Jesus more. Both imply that you are spiritually inept.

Many frustrated workers reject what they learned back home; in desperation, they use a "scattershot" approach, trying everything under the sun. But this approach may still not lead to people coming together into communities that focus on *Isa's* teaching and lifestyle, whatever the projects and methods used. We often call this "reinventing the wheel." As one prominent thinker on this topic acknowledges, "Some people say we need twenty years of experience. But often twenty years' experience is really just *one* year, repeated twenty times, with no better results after the twentieth year than the first!"

Recently, a new generation of worker-observers has discovered an encouraging alternative. As they examine common practices among colleagues living in the Muslim world, certain patterns emerge in places where Jesus-centered communities do blossom. So as we labor to make disciples, there may be some patterns that are more effective than others. We call them "Fruitful Practices"[64] because they are principles and activities that have resulted in such communities. Imagine the potential for new fruitfulness around you, if you knew that some practices were more helpful than others!

Fruitful Practices enable us to *delight in seeing and hearing* how God is building a people for himself among all the nations of the world, including Muslims, and empower us to join him in his work. We echo the Psalmist, who declares, "Great are the works of the Lord, studied by all who delight in them"

---

[64]   The designation "Fruitful Practices" has been a modification of the business term "Best Practices" to convey that the results, like fruit, are dependent on factors beyond our control, such as the sun. The witness, like the farmer, has a role to play, but there are also divine factors beyond our control. According to Melissie Rumizen, "Best Practices, processes, and techniques are those that have produced outstanding results in another situation and that could be adapted for your situation. Like all knowledge, it is contextual. A best practice is what is best for you." Also see Carla O'Dell and C. Jackson Grayson, *If Only We Knew What We Know: The Transfer of Internal Knowledge and Best Practices* (New York: Free Press/Simon Schuster, 1998).

(Psalm 111:2). We study his works so we can labor alongside him in this awe-inspiring process of sowing, reaping, and bearing much fruit for eternity.

There are both a divine dimension
(what God is doing)
and a human dimension
(studying his works so we can join him).
This is what Fruitful Practices are all about.

Discovering Fruitful Patterns

What is our method of studying and applying the common practices that most often lead to reproducing communities that are focused on the person of Jesus in the Muslim world? Here is what we did:

Research

We asked questions across various regions and contexts throughout the Muslim world. Rather than hypothesizing about which practices are most fruitful, we surveyed and interviewed effective teams from thirteen organizations representing more than 5,800 workers in the Muslim world.

Analysis

We examined questionnaires, interviews, and case studies for common patterns of attitudes and activities among people working cross-culturally. We compiled a list of the practices that were common among those teams that had witnessed the emergence of at least one Jesus-centered fellowship. This working document was issued as a "Primer" to the participants of a larger consultation that brought together many more individuals walking the way of Jesus in another culture.

During the Consultation, we conducted an additional survey in each of the four major areas of discussion:

» Witnessing
» Discipling
» Gathering Fellowships
» Gathering Teams of Ministry

In each of the surveys, we asked participants to respond to each practice in two ways:

» "My team does this fruitful practice (yes/no)."
» "How important is this practice to fruitfulness in church planting (unimportant/somewhat important/very important)."

We compared these responses to the ministry profile of each participant, as it pertains to their particular focus, the place where they live and other similar factors, in order to discern their individual level of fruitfulness.

Finally, we conducted 100 recorded interviews and collected notes from twenty-five discussion groups that met daily throughout the five-day consultation. The results from all our research tools gave us more than 300 responses from individuals experienced in planting fellowships representing over thirty organizations, two-thirds of which have witnessed the emergence of at least one Christ-centered community in the Muslim world. We combined and analyzed the list, the surveys, interviews, and the small group notes.

Benchmark

This book represents the first stage of analysis of the Consultation material. Where do we go from here? We believe we must continually evaluate our plans, goals, attitudes, and activities against the standard of Fruitful Practices. Our approach differs significantly from those who use a *deductive* method of ministry (following the anecdotes and practices of a particular leader, seminary, or missiological theory.) We believe the inductive approach promises to be more fruitful (discovering how God is currently operating to bless the nations by inviting them into his Kingdom among Muslims so we can better partner with him in sowing and reaping.)

COOPERATING WITH GOD

This process is our imperfect attempt to understand the *mystery of ministry*. As noted above, all true ministry involves God's part and our part. 1 Corinthians 3:5–7 vividly describes this dynamic: "What then is Apollos? What is Paul? Servants through whom you came to believe … I planted, Apollos watered, but God gave the growth. So then neither the one who plants nor the one who waters is anything, but only God who gives the growth." We cannot transform people. That is God's part. But we can share faithfully God's Good News of Jesus and demonstrate his love. That is our part.

Fruitful Practices enlighten us as we endeavor to do our part. They show us how God works through certain principles, practices, and innovation to accomplish his purposes. *They point us in a direction that has great potential* to bear fruit for his glory.

PEOPLE FACTORS

Differences among individuals within our team—such as personality, skill set, gifting, and personal holiness—can affect fruitfulness. How does team unity affect fruitfulness? What happens if there are no gifted language learners in the team? We can explore such questions thanks to the data from our surveys, interviews, and focus group discussions.

Differences among Muslim people groups also affect our ability to bear fruit. There are some key questions we must ask:

» Are they literate or oral?
» Are they urban or rural?
» Are they a minority group oppressed by the majority, or do they enjoy social equality?

The challenge is to discern how the divine-human partnership results in fruitful witness. The subsequent five chapters in this section explore the entire process. Here we should just single out some representative processes in three areas—language, learning, and leadership.

LANGUAGE: GOD TELLS HIS STORY

Scene: The urban guesthouse. You lean forward, pen and paper at the ready, as your friend tells his story.

"Like you, we poured ourselves into learning Russian; since it is the trade language, we needed to communicate well to government officials and businessmen. So initially, this made sense to us. But we discovered that while our friends were happy to discuss politics and money in Russian, they changed the subject whenever we brought up spiritual matters—or worse, talked specifically about Jesus.

"At first, we thought that people were not interested in spiritual issues. But no; new mosques were popping up all over the city, and we noticed a resurgence of fundamentalist Islam. We thought, 'Maybe people are hungry for God, after all.' So we spent a week praying and fasting, asking the Lord for discernment.

"Later that week, I met a new disciple of Jesus for tea. He said that he heard about Jesus, but because the message was in Russian, he thought Jesus was a foreign god and he didn't want anything to do with it. But then a cousin shared with him about the stories of the *Injil* in his own language, and suddenly Jesus made sense to him. He said, 'I would never accept a Russian Jesus. But when I heard about Jesus' love for me in the language of my heart, I knew that Isa al-Masih must be for me.'

"But when I heard about Jesus' love for me in the language of my heart, I knew that Isa al-Masih must be for me."

"As a result of that insight, we shifted our focus, committing ourselves fully to learn the heart language. We knew that once Jesus came alive for them in their language, they would know him as their Lord."

FRUITFUL PRACTICES:
1. *Seeking to communicate a culturally-relevant biblical message in the heart language of the people.*
2. *Sharing the Gospel in story form for oral societies.*
3. *Developing leaders with methods that fit the local context.*

The God who sent Jesus to take the form of a servant and live among us (John 1; Philippians 2) also speaks the language of our hearts. Because of this reality, some teams choose to focus on the heart language first, so they can tell the Good News much sooner. Still others, recognizing the need to communicate effectively in the trade language, the language of trade and education, assign certain members of their team to focus on the trade language while the rest of the team focuses on the heart language.

> FP 1: *Seeking to communicate a culturally-relevant biblical message in the heart language of the people.*

With respect to a culturally relevant biblical message (i.e., using Scripture that addresses the assumptions of the people's worldview and creates spiritual hunger), 99 percent of the practitioners said it was important or very important, and 94 percent said they practiced it. With respect to communicating the Gospel in the heart language of the people, 99 percent considered it important, and 86 percent practiced it.[65]

LEARNING: GOD REVEALS HIMSELF THROUGH THE WAY PEOPLE LEARN

> FP 2: *Sharing the Gospel in story form for oral societies (98% considered important, 73.5% practiced).*

Is it wise to teach literacy to oral societies so they can read the Bible? In previous generations, the answer was an obvious yes. Recently, however, some teams discovered that the answer is found by discovering how beliefs are embedded in the local worldview and how people learn about life. Teams generally conclude that the written Scriptures are best for peoples who are used to reading and writing; and the word in story form is best for oral cultures.

Consider this South Asian team, who discarded the use of written Bible studies and bound Bibles when they discovered the power of the Good News in story form. Observing how the local community passes on its values about God, community, and social 'rules', they learned to ask community leaders their 'rules' for telling stories, even asking them for help to craft biblical stories that relate to everyday issues such as truthfulness and forgiveness. Because community leaders were involved, these stories have become so popular that the imam uses

---

[65] Such a notation indicates that 99 percent of the participants felt that the practice was important or very important and 86 percent practiced it.

them in the local mosque! ("Stories and the Qur'an in South Asia," Interview #3 by Interviewer 02 at Southeast Asian Consultation in Spring of 2007).

This also reminds us that learning often occurs informally, within the existing web of relationships in the community. In the dusty remote villages of Africa, the rural society shares everything in community—including discussions about eternal issues. A team leader's wife discovered that celebrations and funerals were the best time to share such truths. The husband relates:

> *So when my wife shared a Gospel story to the group, the women engaged in animated and positive discussion, giving 'permission' for my wife to talk publicly about the Gospel. I discovered that this happens among the men as well. Now, our team attends all the public events and we are always ready with a Gospel story ("Sharing With Relational Groups in Africa," Interview #103 by Interviewer 129, Spring 2007).*

LEADERSHIP: GOD WORKS THROUGH FAITHFUL INFLUENCERS TO ESTABLISH COMMUNITIES OF FAITH

FP 3:   Developing leaders with methods that fit the local context.

The mentoring of leaders is planned and normally non-formal such as apprenticeship (98 percent considered important, 80 percent practiced).

Some teams, acknowledging that leaders can either be bottlenecks or avenues for their community, are slow to pass the baton of leadership until those potential leaders receive extensive training. Others, however, look for existing influencers of integrity and release them quickly. In the former, the team builds leadership principles in the emerging community. In the latter, the team employs existing leaders, empowering them quickly. Both approaches depend on the local context.

And both approaches have risks and rewards. Among the villages of this African people exist numerous mosques that are led by the village sheikh, or leader. "Daood," the team leader, entered such a village mosque one day; as an unexpected guest, he was invited to present a greeting. Instead of a standard greeting, Daood decided to tell the story of God's call to Abraham from Genesis 12:1–3. After briefly describing the idolatrous culture in which Abraham received his call and telling the story, Daood turned it over to the sheikh for his 'interpretation.'

The sheikh explained that while many people are seeking after God, the good news is that God is seeking us; he initiated his call to Abraham and is calling out a community of righteous faithful from Abraham; and that today God is calling their community to be righteous and follow God's will. He did not identify his own mosque as the company of righteous believers, but rather was calling a new community of transformed followers of God! ("Empowering Existing Leaders," Interview #19 by Interviewer 250, Spring 2007).

While there may be significant risk to such an approach, this team has discovered that the sheikh has validated the new community, defending its existence because he acknowledges that God is doing a new thing among his people. In such a case, faith is not a battle between "Christianity" and "Islam," but a total submission to God and to holy lives. As a result, the cross-cultural worker does not have to fight the stigma of "foreign intrusion."

CONCLUSION: THE FRUITFUL PRACTICES APPROACH

Your relationship with Mustapha or Miriam does not consist of formulas. For example, hospitality seems universally practiced, but is applied differently between cultures (in many cities, hospitality requires that one serve dessert late at night, while in others, that one must prepare an entire meal).

DISCOVERING FRUITFUL PATTERNS: THE FP APPROACH

1. Discover the most common effective practices for establishing fellowships.
2. Explore ways to apply these fruitful practices to your situation.
3. Evaluate your efforts after a season.
4. Share your results with others.
5. Begin the process afresh.

The existing list of Fruitful Practices is a snapshot of current wisdom among many teams across the Muslim world, not an exhaustive catalog of formulas. We are just beginning to discover the common practices of effectiveness between us. It serves as a helpful but limited benchmark of what God is doing among us.

As a benchmark, the Fruitful Practices are a description of effective works among Muslims, but are not a prescription of detailed instructions to follow. Neither should you expect any guarantees. While Fruitful Practices report what we see happening among us, there is no substitute for prayer and reflection. Even then, we should expect surprises, as Jesus reminds us: "The wind blows where it chooses, and you hear the sound of it, but you do not know where it comes from or where it goes" (John 3:8).

FRUITFUL PRACTICES ARE A BENCHMARK OF APPLIED WISDOM, NOT AN EXHAUSTIVE CATALOG OF FORMULAS. THEY ARE DESCRIPTIVE, NOT PRESCRIPTIVE. THEY ARE CORRELATIVE, NOT CAUSATIVE. THEY DO NOT REPLACE THE "GOD FACTOR," AND ARE NOT NECESSARILY UNIVERSAL IN SCOPE.

Even so, our search continues to "see and hear" what the Father is doing among Muslim peoples, as we discover more questions: "Are some Fruitful Practices limited to specific regions? How do Fruitful Practices compare between teams who are engaged in humanitarian efforts, and those who are engaged in business? As you commit to a Fruitful Practice approach to your work, how should you track your progress?" You may already have discovered some answers. Let us learn from you!

Scene: You have returned to the rustic and smoky guesthouse in your Central Asian city. This time, it is two years later, and you have been invited to meet a young worker who recently arrived in your area, hoping to share the Good News of Jesus. "Tell me the secret," he begs, trying to keep the despair from his voice. "What is happening here?"

You smile at the familiar conversation. "What do you mean?"

"How is it possible that so many of your Muslim friends are becoming followers of *Isa*?" he implores.

You place your tea on its saucer. "Let me tell you my story ..."

"My Father is glorified by this, that you bear much fruit and become my disciples" (John 15:8).

READING AND APPLYING GOD'S STORY OF HIS WORKS: THE BIBLE SHEDS LIGHT ON FRUITFUL PRACTICES

As we read the Bible with "Fruitful Practices eyes," we gain new insight into God's heart for fruitful work. Consider these examples:

Fruitful Practices help us to see how God is working through others so that we can join him in his work.

> *Very truly, I tell you, the Son can do nothing on his own,*
> *but only what he sees the Father doing; for what the Father does,*
> *so the Son does likewise (John 5:19).*

Fruitful Practices help us to bear much fruit and therefore glorify the Father.

> *My Father is glorified by this, that you bear much fruit and become my*
> *disciples (John 15:8).*

Fruitful Practices are a way to reflect on God's works in order to delight in what he is doing.

> *Great are the works of the LORD; they are pondered by all who delight*
> *in them (Psalm 111:2, NASB).*

Fruitful Practices empower us to determine what is best for our situation.

> *And this is my prayer ...to help you determine what is best, so that in the*
> *day of Christ you may be pure and blameless (Philippians 1:9–10).*

By studying Fruitful Practices, we hope to be good stewards of the manifold grace of God.

Like good stewards of the manifold grace of God, serve one another with whatever gift each of you has received (1 Peter 4:10).

Fruitful Practices reminds us to begin with the end in mind and consider how gatherings might generate movements of peoples who join the worshiping throng at the end of history.

After this I looked, and there was a great multitude that no one could count, from every nation, from all tribes and peoples and languages, standing before the throne and before the Lamb (Revelation 7:9).

Chapter 8

The Sowing of Witnessing

DAVID GREENLEE AND PAM WILSON

"A sower went out to sow."
Matthew 13:16

What does it mean to be *fruitful* in witness or evangelism? Fruitfulness is an elusive word, too often defined merely in terms of quantity. Long trainloads of wheat harvested from the far-stretching fields of India's Punjab speak of fruitful plenty. By comparison, the yield of a field of saffron is tiny but precious, the most expensive spice in the world.

And so it is when we evaluate fruitfulness in witness. We rejoice when we hear of large numbers placing their faith in Jesus Christ among Algeria's Kabyle. But we must view this against the backdrop of the apparent lack of response to Lilias Trotter's and Charles Marsh's long years of service.[66] Observers at the time may have rated them high on *faithfulness*, but with little grounds to commend them for *fruitfulness*. Seeking God's glory and compelled by the love of Jesus Christ, their observable fruit came much later.

In our analysis, from the start we recognize a diversity of settings. Clifford Geertz points to the vast difference between Muslims of Indonesia and Morocco—one of the few things they share in common is praying toward the same city, yet in doing so they face opposite directions.[67] Joshua Massey helps us see

---

66   See Patricia St. John, *Until the Day Breaks* (Carlisle: Authentic Media, 1994); Charles Marsh, *Too Hard for God?* (Carlisle: Paternoster Press, 2000).
67   *Islam Observed: Religious Development in Morocco and Indonesia* (Chicago: University of Chicago Press, 1971), 4.

"God's amazing diversity in drawing Muslims to Christ."[68] Seekers respond to various relational, intellectual, and supernatural motivations. Some go through a great struggle as they come to faith; others walk into a church and sincerely say, "Teach me to follow Jesus."[69] What appears to be fruitful in Algeria may be a failure in Southeast Asia, but we should at least listen, ask questions, and learn from one another.

As workers, we add a "human factor." Training, experience, and theological views affect fruitfulness while, as Richard Peace notes, "How we conceive of conversion determines how we do evangelism."[70] While we should all be people of love and integrity, the God-enabled means of witness of one person may be useless when tried by another. Our intention is to describe principles learned and lived out by those in witness among Muslims; it is not an assembly manual with guaranteed results.

WHAT FIRST ATTRACTED ME TO JESUS WAS THE WORD "FREE."
NOT GRACE, JUST SOMETHING WAS FREE, IT WAS FROM EUROPE,
AND I WANTED IT. ONLY LATER DID I FIND OUT THAT IT WAS A
BIBLE CORRESPONDENCE COURSE.
– A MOROCCAN MAN

Then there is the "God factor." We cannot predict *kairos* moments of his sovereign intervention. He sends dreams to some, but not to all; some are healed, others are not. While working out his purposes among the nations his hand is often hidden, as if in a glove.[71] God works through us, but grace is his from start to finish.

---

[68] "God's Amazing Diversity in Drawing Muslims to Christ," *International Bulletin of Missionary Research* 17, no. 1 (2000): 3–12.

[69] See Andreas Maurer, "In Search of a New Life: Conversion Motives of Christians and Muslims," in *From the Straight Path to the Narrow Way*, ed. David Greenlee (Waynesboro, GA: Authentic, 2006); also see David Greenlee, "How Is the Gospel Good News for Muslims?" in *Rethinking Our Assumptions: Toward a New Christian Understanding of Muslims in the 21st Century*, ed. Evelyne Reisacher et al. (Pasadena, CA: William Carey Library, forthcoming).

[70] *Conversion in the New Testament: Paul and the Twelve* (Grand Rapids, MI: Eerdmans, 1999), 286.

[71] Avery Willis, *Indonesian Revival: Why Two Million Came to Christ* (Pasadena, CA: William Carey Library, 1977); Dudley Woodberry, "A Global Perspective on Muslims Coming to Faith in Christ," in *From the Straight Path to the Narrow Way*, ed. David Greenlee (Waynesboro, GA: Authentic, 2006).

How We Carried out Our Analysis

Having stated these concerns, we affirm that fruitfulness can be enhanced by appropriate research and evaluation of the ways we show God's love. We do not approach this analysis as a marketing exercise, nor do we forget that statistics represent precious individuals. Our desire is to understand how we can better communicate to Muslims the love of God and the Gospel's good news. As fruitful practices (not a recipe book), these findings can be useful as a stimulus to reflection and serve as a basis for ongoing research and application.

Twenty statements of fruitful practices in evangelism were identified by a cluster of agencies in the four-year study leading up to the Consultation in the spring of 2007.[72] Of these, nine statements of fruitful practice emerged as the most important, and to these we give emphasis.

A Priority on the Local Context

FRUITFUL PRACTICES:

1. *Aiming to witness through social and relational networks (families, neighbors, community groups, etc.) as natural bridges to the formation of fellowships or churches.*
2. *Seeking to communicate a culturally relevant message. Use Scripture that addresses worldview issues and creates spiritual hunger.*
3. *Communicating the Gospel in the heart language of the people.*
4. *Seeking to be culturally appropriate (in dress, language, customs, hospitality, etc.).*

What kind of people do we serve? What are their concerns? What are the significant symbols and values of their culture? Do we know their story—both the ancient chapters as well as those written in today's newspaper? Experienced workers stress questions like these; four of the nine most fruitful practices are related to the context of ministry.

---

72   Two additional statements dealt with the role of children's ministry and the use of the Qur'an as a bridge in evangelism. Since affirmation of these and the literacy statements was quite low, we have not covered them in our analysis.

> FP 1: Aiming to witness or evangelize through social and relational networks (families, neighbors, community groups, etc.) as natural bridges to formation of fellowships or churches.

My wife asked a believer in our Sahel village, "When is the best time for me to share with women?" She thought she was going to say to make sure the husband is gone, at a time when not many people will be there. And yet the woman said the best time is at parties, wedding celebrations, circumcision parties, and even funerals where there are lots of women gathered.

My wife had tried one-on-one witnessing where women were polite and very uncomfortable, but all of a sudden in larger groups, everyone was very interested and giving approval of what was being said! One person might ask a question and another would feed off that question; they were very engaged.

The women feel a lot more confidence in the approval of a group rather than their own ability to make a decision on something that is strange or foreign. My wife has had countless opportunities in groups to share. A lot of times those individuals who are seeking would come to decisions or continue to show interest, but within that group there is an ability to actually be able to hear. It's like when they are one-on-one it falls on deaf ears, when they're in a group, there's much more interest ("Sharing with Relational Groups in [the Sahel]," Interview #104, Spring 2007).[73]

Jesus calls us to be willing to forsake even our families in following him (Matthew 8:22). But to the man delivered from Legion, Jesus said, "Go home to your family and tell them how much the Lord has done for you" (Mark 5:19, NIV). While Acts tells us of individuals who professed faith (the Ethiopian eunuch), we also see frequent reference to witness among entire families and households (Cornelius and the Philippian jailer).

---

[73] Stories have been edited for length and readability.

Reports of individuals coming to faith are increasingly common. Many North African believers started their journey of faith by secretly taking part in a Bible correspondence course. However, where there are reports of larger numbers coming to faith, witness along lines of social and relational networks seems to frequently be a factor.

Survey respondents ministering among communities practicing a more highly contextualized expression of faith to local culture give greater importance to this fruitful practice than those that are not (78 percent of those in C4–6 communities and 62.5 percent of those in C1–3 communities).[74]

> FP 2:   *Seeking to communicate a culturally relevant message, Scripture is used that addresses worldview issues[75] and creates spiritual hunger.*

We asked some Southeast Asian Muslim believers in Jesus to translate one of the books of the Bible on their own, putting it in ways appropriate for them. We asked them to think why they chose to use [some terms], and to check it in the community, but ultimately it was their book, they chose what to say. Arabic is a very honored language among Muslim people and especially in that area of the world, so they used a lot of Arabic terms.

They took people within their community, usually relatives, to go through what they translated. As they work through this with their families, relatives, and friends, they discuss the Scripture and the story and ask them questions. "What do you see? What do you hear?" And they are seeing Isa in a whole new way, and for the first time who he is ("Evangelism and Discipleship through Translation," Interview #53, Spring 2007).

---

74   See Figure 13.1 in chapter 13 for the C1–C6 continuum.
75   Assumptions and beliefs about what is real and how things fit together and happen.

One aspect of communicating culturally relevant messages is the use of local knowledge, just as Paul did in his sermon in Athens (Acts 17:16–34). Popular stories told by Muslims, such as the Nasreddin Hoca stories,[76] may provide us with helpful bridges to understanding.

We should consider the form of our message, whether spoken, sung, written, or acted out, since "a cognitive approach alone does not bring change in [Muslim] women's lives. They need to connect through experience on a relational level— with humans and the Divine."[77] Further, since "the content of every conscience is close enough to God's norms in order to be an initial reference point" in our witness, we should "speak of sin with reference to the indigenous conscience, particularly [the aspect]...in agreement with Scripture."[78]

A STORY OF NASREDDIN HOCA

Hoca was asked, "How would you prove someone was a saint?" He answered, "If I point at any stone or tree to come forward, it will come." At the same time, a plane tree was in front of him, so they asked, "Can you point at that tree so that it comes forward?" Nasreddin called out in a special voice for the tree to come forward, but not one leaf from the tree fell in front of him. So, he walked forward towards the tree.

His friends said, "You called the tree, and it didn't come. Why are you going to it?" He answered, "Saints are not self-centered people. If the tree didn't come to me, then I will go to it."

FP 3:   Communicating the Gospel in the heart language of the people.

A Central Asian MBB often speaks in Russian when he shares his faith with his friends in the city. But one day he spoke with his cousin Murat in their mother tongue. Murat later said, "Had you shared this with

---

[76]   See Idries Shah, *The Pleasantries of the Incredible Mullah Nasrudin* (New York: Penguin Arkana, 1993); *The Subtleties of the Inimitable Mullah Nasrudin* (London: Octagon, 1983); *The Exploits of the Incomparable Mullah Nasrudin* (New York: E.P. Dutton, 1972). He is known by various names (such as Juha in Arabic) throughout the Middle East and Central Asia.

[77]   Mary McVicker, "Experiencing Jesus: Reflections of South Asian Women," in *From the Straight Path to the Narrow Way*, ed. David Greenlee (Waynesboro, GA: Authentic, 2006), 129.

[78]   Hannes Wiher, *Shame and Guilt: A Key to Cross-Cultural Ministry* (Bonn: Verlag für Kultur und Wissenschaft, 2003), 367.

me in Russian, I would have never put my faith in Isa al-Masih. But because you shared it in …our heart language. I said this message must be for me" ("The Network," Interview #7, Spring 2007).

Females considered use of the heart language even more important than men did (94 percent of females, 82 percent of males). This may be true because the women they seek to reach are less likely than men to speak a trade language.

An MBB (Muslim background believer) from the Sahel provides a balancing perspective. "Globalization has made it such that a lot of youth are more proficient in the trade language than in their own mother tongue, even though it is their heart language, in which they cry and laugh. The race to catch up with globalization has made it such that we need not wait until we master the heart language before we pass on the Gospel" ("Value of Trade Language," Interview #14, Spring 2007).

FP 4:   *Seeking to be culturally appropriate (in dress, language, customs, hospitality, etc.).*

Worked out in practice, this principle takes on different forms. Some aspects, such as modest clothing and abstaining from alcohol, are common sense. More complex is to know how "modest" is defined in Istanbul as compared to Isfahan, in public places, or at a party for women. We might disagree on whether we should *always* respect the dietary customs of our host people, or for example, if we can properly enjoy such proscribed foods in private.

Discovering some aspects of cultural appropriateness—such as the subtleties of hospitality—takes time and helpful teachers. Other issues are more complex and harder to know how or what to change, such as insider terms used to describe God and religious experience. Further, we must learn what adaptation is not appropriate. A West African MBB was advised to use traditional Muslim dress in his ministry. Muslim friends, however, told him he was at best a clown, at worst deceptive. He found he had more response to his witness when dressed like "normal" Christians.

It is no surprise that women emphasized more than men the importance of being culturally appropriate (94 percent of females, 82 percent of males). Women, of course, are affected more than men on issues such as dress; women have most to lose if they do not comply with local norms.

Workers in rural areas are more likely to see this fruitful practice as very important than urban dwellers (90 percent of rural, 78 percent of urban). Cities generally afford more freedom, have more non-traditional influences, and more access to consumer goods. They foster complex networks of relationships that can span ethnic groups. This could result in workers making a broad adaptation but not in depth to a specific group's culture. Workers in cities may thus find it less essential to dress and behave in traditional ways. It is also possible that workers in the city gravitate to areas and neighbors most like themselves.

Other Fruitful Practices Related to the Context
In addition to the highlighted practices, some workers identified others.

» *Sharing the Gospel along gender lines.*

Women considered this more important than men (females 83 percent, males 69 percent). Those who have planted one or more churches find that sharing the Gospel along gender lines is less important than do those who have not yet planted a church (87 percent of non-planters, 67 percent of planters)—although there is no significant difference in reported practice. Perhaps once a church is planted, there are mixed gender relationships that provide for a greater sense of freedom, even if not always practiced.

» *Sharing the Gospel in story form.*

This is a method that not all have been trained to use, but one that some find significant in connecting to the learning styles of many of those we serve.

» *Addressing needs in their community as a tangible expression of the Good News (e.g., build a well, feed the hungry, minister to AIDS victims).*

This is more important among the oppressed (68 percent with oppressed, 53 percent with non-oppressed) and more practiced in rural areas (79 percent in rural, 66 percent in urban). Those serving C3 and C4 communities do not think this is as important as do those serving C5 and C6 believers

(47 percent in C3–4, 77 percent in C5–6), although the practice is similar. We wonder if this pattern reflects a need for some people to engage in such work—to obtain a visa, for example—even if they do not perceive it to be fruitful or important compared to their overall purpose of ministry.

FRUITFUL WORKERS RECOGNIZE AND ENGAGE THE CHALLENGES AT VARIOUS LEVELS

FRUITFUL PRACTICES:
5. *Being bold in witness and willing to risk.*
6. *Seeking opportunities to pray for the personal needs of their friends in their presence.*

Following Jesus and ministering to others is not always easy! Challenges come in various forms (2 Corinthians 9), but fruitful workers have found Spirit-enabled ways to face these challenges.

FP 5:   Being bold in witness and willing to risk.

I was visiting women in a prison, and realized one of the prisoners was near death. So I went into her room and sat on her cot and I was very bold. I mean, if we got caught doing this kind of thing...But I just asked [the prison staff for] a moment alone with her. So they stood back a little bit but watched us the whole time.

I said to her, "Do you realize that you might die from this?" And she said, "Yes." "But do you realize what may happen after you face God?" And I shared salvation with her and she accepted Christ.

She was totally in touch with her sin and the fear and she did die... It really gripped us but I realized how crucial some moments are. And had I said, "Oh, I shouldn't be so bold in the prison...I mean what if she tells on me or whatever." But when it is eternity staring you in the face—you act ("Chronological Bible Teaching," Interview #54, Spring 2007).

Boldness and risk are considered most important by those working among the oppressed (87 percent among oppressed, 76 percent among non-oppressed). In some settings, boldness is required to hand out Scriptures; in others it may take boldness to approach a government official for permission to carry out a community development project. It is taking a risk just to live in some situations; in other cases, risks may be like that of the woman in our story who dared to openly witness to a dying woman.

Boldness and risk characterize the life of a young man from East Africa. Born into a Muslim family, he came to faith as a teenager. Despite much suffering for his witness, his hope is strong: "I've gone through trials and rejection and persecution, but one thing I want to tell you ...So far we have come here due to the grace of God. God is faithful" ("MBB Approach to Evangelism," Interview #93, Spring 2007).

> FP 6: *Seeking opportunities to pray for the personal needs of their friends in their presence.*

We seek every opportunity we can to pray with people, whether they have rebellious teenagers, economic problems, or problems with their neighbors, but most often we pray with people when they are sick. [In some settings], we introduce ourselves and say, "We are not doctors; we are just normal people, but we believe in a supernatural God who is able to heal." And then, if the context allows, we read Luke 5:18–30 [where Jesus heals a paralytic and forgives his sins]. We're trying to plant the idea that Jesus has the authority to forgive sins.

But if we are in a context where that's not advisable, then we'll just tell a story. And we'll say, "I'm going to pray according to my own convictions and I'm going to pray in the name of Isa al-Masih." And then we go ahead and pray.

In several cases, [the MBBs] are involved in prayer and sometimes it is effective. In one case a young village woman ...prayed [for a sick woman] in the name of Isa al-Masih. There was certainly some reaction. But her father, who is not a believer, stepped in and said, "Don't bother her, she is praying in the name of Isa al-Masih" ("Prayer as Evangelism, and the Engel Scale," Interview #29, Spring 2007).

Other Fruitful Practices Related to Facing the Challenges

In addition to the highlighted practices, many listed:

> » *Praying for supernatural intervention (e.g., healing, demonic deliverance, dreams, etc.) and doing their part when God answers. The power of the Gospel is expressed in these ways.*

Significantly more than others, those working among the oppressed rather than the unoppressed rank it as very important (77.5 percent to 55 percent) and practice it more (88 percent to 75 percent).

FRUITFUL WORKERS KNOW THAT ONE PERSON OR ONE METHOD IS INSUFFICIENT

FRUITFUL PRACTICES:

7. *Encouraging MBBs to share their testimony.*
8. *Using evangelistic tools and practices that are reproducible.*
9. *Using various methods to share the Gospel. Fruitful workers do not rely on a single approach or tool.*

No person or method—not even any set of fruitful practices—is sufficient in ministry. Respondents to the survey, however, noted several approaches that were significantly fruitful, although they should not be taken as a "to do" list.

FP 7:   *Encouraging MBBs to share their testimony.*

A Central Asian woman heard the Gospel over a period of time, made a decision for Jesus, and started [witnessing] straightaway. Afterward she said it would never have entered her head to go and tell someone else about Jesus. But a friend had said to her , "Well, now, you go and tell someone else!"

She didn't need to be told how, who, where, or why, she just needed that little prod! Within a week, she met a friend she hadn't seen in a long time and said, "I am going somewhere tonight; why don't you come along? It will help you improve your life." So the friend came and within a few weeks came to faith!

She then spoke with a woman she knew at the bazaar and said something like, "You need to believe in Jesus." The woman replied, "That's the Russian God, isn't it?" She replied, "I don't know, read this." Within another couple of weeks, this woman also came to faith! These two plus the original woman are all in the church today, several years later ("Bold Believer in Central Asia," Interview #67, Spring 2007).

Despite encouraging exceptions, women are less likely to encourage MBBs to share their faith than men (63 percent of women, 83 percent of men). Evelyne Reisacher observes that North African MBB women "express both the desire to be close to their family and the pain of feeling rejected. They understand that it is not easy for their family to cope with their decision."[79] Perhaps such issues, and general social constraints, are weaker among men.

FP 8:   *Using evangelistic tools and practices that are reproducible.*

As a surgeon in a Christian hospital in Asia, everybody knows who I am. They come to us because we care for them.

When I start reading with someone, I say, "Let's spend some time reading." If they show interest, we tell them, "Before you come back next time you have to do the same with someone else." They always ask, "Who do I do it with?" I tell them, "Start with your wife, just sit down and tell your wife what you learned from me."

So right from the beginning they have that concept built in: what I learn, I share with someone else ("Discipleship as Evangelism," Interview #13, Spring 2007).

FP 9:   *Using various methods to share the Gospel. Fruitful workers do not rely on a single approach or tool.*

---

[79]   Evelyne Reisacher, "North African Women and Conversion: Specifics of Female Faith and Experience," in *From the Straight Path to the Narrow Way*, ed. David Greenlee (Waynesboro, GA: Authentic, 2006), 123.

Respondents pointed to numerous helpful methods used in sharing the Gospel, from music concerts and sports to Bible study with an individual. While a team or individual may focus on a specific aspect of witness, our experience is that Muslims who have professed faith in Jesus Christ speak of multiple influences and means of communication that God used to touch them with his love, power, and truth.

Other Fruitful Practices Related to Multiple Workers and Methods

Other practices that many practitioners considered important were as follows:

» *Continually evaluating the effectiveness of their methods and adapting as needed.*
» *Gathering seekers or believers as soon as possible to study and practice the Scriptures together.* Workers serving in rural settings are more likely to consider this very important than those in cities (82 percent rural, 71 percent urban). This practice is significantly weaker among those who have not planted a church (53 percent to 74 percent), possibly an indication of where the respondents are on a church-planting time line.
» *Expecting every team member to be involved in evangelism, while recognizing that different team members may have different roles.*
» *Making effective use of both local and expatriate workers.* Those who have planted churches practice this more than those who have not (88 percent to 71 percent), perhaps in part because those who have not yet planted a church may have few, if any, potential local co-workers.
» *Using Bible studies as an evangelistic tool,* as noted earlier.
» *Sowing broadly, using available media and technology* (e.g., Jesus film, Scripture portions, radio, cassettes).

QUESTIONS ARISING FROM VARIATIONS BY REGIONAL ORIGIN AND BY MINISTRY FOCUS

We noted several differences based on the region of origin of the respondents. For example, although a majority of workers from all regions consider it important to *seek to communicate a culturally relevant message (FP 2)*, a higher proportion of Western[80] workers (92 percent) than non-Westerners (80 percent) consider this as very important. Could it be that some non-Westerners have a smaller cultural gap to cross and thus place less conscious emphasis on this issue?

Sowing broadly (meaning a diversity of methods) is considered most important by those from the United States, less so by non-Westerners, while less than half of the other Western respondents rate this as very important.

Non-Westerners and those from the United States are significantly more likely to *encourage MBBs to share their testimony* than are other Westerners (84 percent to 67 percent), and place a higher importance on the *use of reproducible evangelistic tools and practices* (87 percent to 55 percent).

Further research and reflection might reveal roots of these differences in areas such as organizational strategy, missiological training, and cultural values typical of the respondents' home countries.

Beyond these points, there were differences on some issues between those working among Sunnis and the handful reported as serving among Shi'ahs. We recommend further research to compare perceived differences in fruitful practices among these groups.

CONCLUSION

God is drawing Muslims to faith in Jesus Christ. We, his witnesses, are weak (1 Corinthians 9:22), but we are also ambassadors (2 Corinthians 5:20). We are fragile jars of clay, but we bear a treasure, showing that "this all-surpassing power is from God" (2 Corinthians 5:7). Some of us may plant, others water. May we do so faithfully, enabled by God's Spirit, knowing that it is God alone who brings the fruitful growth (1 Corinthians 3:7).

---

80   In this section, by "non-Western" we mean countries of Latin America, Africa, and Asia.

Chapter 9

The Watering of Discipling

JOHN BECKER AND ERIK SIMUYU

"I planted, Apollos watered, but God gave the growth."
1 Corinthians 3:6

As we fly over Libya, the perfectly shaped circles that dot the North African landscape captivate us. Their verdant green contrasts richly against the dun-colored sand stretching across the vast Sahara. Massive high-pressure sprinklers, which pivot around a central point, create these amazing round oases. How incredible that life can spring out of barrenness with the skillful use of water!

This is only one of the countless irrigation systems engineered since the earliest method some 6,000 years ago. Yet no matter how diverse these methods are, they all rely on one thing: a source of water. They all have one goal: to supply the entire field, so that each plant has the exact amount of water it needs, neither too much nor too little.

Paul's beautiful analogy in 1 Corinthians 3 reminds us that this is also true in the spiritual world. We "farmers," messengers of the Good News of Jesus, must rely on only one source—the Master of the field. He is that central point around which we pivot, our source of life-giving water to nurture the Muslim fields to whose care we are committed. This is an intrinsic partnership, which involves skill on the part of us farmers as we co-labor with God, the giver of life. Without him, there is no harvest.

> Perhaps the most archaic and labor-intensive
> method of irrigation is the humble watering can.
> It is also the most intimate!
> The laborer has to get up close and personal
> with the plants receiving the water.

What is the best method to nurture the field with which we have been entrusted? Where, how often, and in what context does discipleship take place? To answer these questions, we must know our field and what resources are available to connect it to the water source.

As we examine fruitful discipleship practices in this chapter, we will need to keep in mind the variety of contexts from which these practices have been drawn and the consequent care with which they should be applied to any specific context.

MODELING AND BUILDING RELATIONSHIPS

Modeling the Christian life, building relationships, and demonstrating authenticity are key for effective discipling.

FRUITFUL PRACTICES:
1. *Working closely with new believers and modeling the Christian life.*
2. *Modeling and teaching a life of discipleship through their actions and relationships in the home, in service, and in persecution.*

The practitioners highlighted the following:

FP 1: *Working closely with new believers and modeling the Christian life (71% considered important, 88% practiced).*[81]

---

[81] Here and subsequently, such a notation will indicate that 71 percent of the participants felt that the practice was important or very important and 88 percent practiced it.

This was elaborated as follows:

FP 2: *Modeling and teaching a life of discipleship through their actions and relationships in the home, in service, and in persecution (91% considered important, 93% practiced).*

There was much discussion in groups at the Consultation on facets of this theme. At the heart of discipleship is relationship. An MBB (Muslim background believer) at the Consultation expressed what might be a common cause of anguish among Muslims: "Lots of people want to disciple and train me, but no one wants to be my friend."

To develop a strong relationship with an MBB, the messenger must demonstrate authenticity. This takes *humility* (a willingness to learn and admit fault)[82] and *availability* (enough contact points to model a Jesus-centered lifestyle.)

> The availability of the messenger
> to walk with the MBB,
> sharing in his or her struggles as much as possible,
> is one of the most fruitful activities
> in the discipleship process.
> Discipleship is not just giving content.
> It is relational.

MBBs must "see lives and learn stories" (Group 20, Spring 2007). It takes a servant heart for the team member to be available whenever needed; and it takes a servant's heart to open up to receiving from the MBB. This atmosphere of mutuality cultivates the freedom to share one's failures, confess sin, and give and receive forgiveness (Group 15 Discussion, Spring 2007). Effective modeling takes place when there is a sharing of life together.

It is not easy for team members when the imams are preaching against them, the local children are throwing stones at them, and adults are spitting at them! But messengers in this situation have a great opportunity to model how to bear up under persecution. Those who demonstrate a willingness to suffer

---

[82] In Eastern Europe, local believers complained that they felt unaccepted into the messengers' lives until the messengers were willing to show vulnerability and share their own struggles and failures.

alongside their Muslim brothers and sisters give a powerful encouragement to local believers (Group 6 Discussion, Spring 2007).

Modeling how a follower of Jesus feeds himself or herself from the Scriptures will teach MBBs how to find the answers far better than if the MBBs handed the answers. This prepares the new believers for the inevitable questions they will face when they begin sharing their faith, and it builds confidence that they do have answers.

CULTURALLY APPROPRIATE PRACTICES

Messengers must be aware of and sensitive to the culture.

> **FRUITFUL PRACTICES:**
> 3. *Learning culturally appropriate ways of confronting sin and restoring a repentant sinner.*
> 4. *Maintaining a respect for gender: normally, men disciple men, women disciple women.*

A team of messengers in West Africa had difficulty in discipling until they found a key to growing their disciples: using local proverbs to confront and correct. This team faced the challenge of confronting believers about their sin because of the perceived different set of values within the culture. For example, certain kinds of lying were used to protect their family or to survive, and so were not regarded as sin. The team came to realize that to confront or correct directly was not effective, but local proverbs were highly valued. This team decided to memorize popular proverbs and use them to address character issues. For example, when confronting pride, the team used, "Soap doesn't wash itself," meaning, "Don't praise yourself." And when confronting laziness, they said, "If you construct, God will meet you here," which meant, "You have to build first in order to have blessing." When they became fluent in the language of proverbs, their teaching began to reach people's hearts ("Using Proverbs," Interview #16, Spring 2007).

FP 3: *Learning culturally appropriate ways of confronting sin and restoring a repentant sinner (90% considered important, 91% practiced).*

Consultation participants cited many examples of using proverbs, stories, and indirect approaches that speak to 'honor and shame'[83] cultures.

Here is another example:

One woman, [the] first believer, taught me how to confront sin. She told me to confront the sin indirectly. For example, there is a group of three people, one of whom committed the sin. Even if you know which woman sinned, start talking about it [in the group]. [Talk] about how God can see everything and [that] we hope that God will touch the person's heart and cause her to repent...and so on. And we found this an effective way, because the people would come and repent, and they could be restored without shame. Saving face is very important in this society ("Discipleship and Leadership of Women," Interview # 23, Spring 2007).

FP 4: *Maintaining a respect for gender: normally, men disciple men, women disciple women (77% considered important, 93% practiced).*

Although this appears to be an obvious rule of practice, there are many stories of exceptions. In one-on-one situations, it is still best to keep it to one gender only. But many countries do not have such rules when it comes to group meetings. Older women have a place in the culture to teach men and can be considered spiritual leaders. In South Asia, Southeast Asia, Central Asia, Eastern Europe, and Africa, there is plenty of good fruit as a result of older women discipling men.

Significantly, no one at the Consultation shared any illustrations of men discipling women.

---

[83] Two all-important values in many cultures that are predominantly Muslim: honor and shame. "Gaining and maintaining honor is more to be valued than life. Avoiding shame, and as a result, shifting the blame to others is the only response when one's honor is threatened." In Bob Blincoe, "Honor and Shame: An Open Letter to Evangelical Leaders" *Mission Frontiers* 4 (2001).

"BELONGING BEFORE BELIEVING"

> **FRUITFUL PRACTICES:**
> 5. *Beginning discipleship before conversion (belonging before believing in some contexts).*
> 6. *Practicing locally appropriate and reproducible discipleship methods.*

Participants at the Consultation confirmed the experience of discipling before conversion, but how they do this and what they call it differ according to the context.

> FP 5:   *Beginning discipleship before conversion (belonging before believing in some contexts) (55% considered important, 76% practiced).*[84]

When a sown field is watered, the early stages of germination take place in the soil beneath the surface. This is also true of the process of emerging faith in the lives of our Muslim neighbors.

Scripture itself is not without ambiguity about when the apostles of Jesus actually *turned*,[85] though they were known to be his disciples from the outset of the three years he walked among them.

It is fruitful to start discipleship as soon as a significant relationship begins between the messenger and the Muslim friend. If the messenger is intentional about this relationship, whether through daily or monthly contact, this provides the environment for faith to take root. There may never be one moment of time when allegiance to Jesus is crystallized, because in many cultures, believers do not label a "point of acceptance" as do many North American and European Protestants. When a gradual process of turning to Jesus is accepted as natural, MBBs are more likely to be stronger in their faith (Groups 16 and 24 Discussion, Spring 2007).

---

[84]   Because community is so important to Muslims, it is helpful for seekers to experience loving fellowship, while exploring what it means to follow Jesus. Some people are persuaded relationally and emotionally before they are convinced rationally. This is what is meant by "belonging before believing."

[85]   The meaning of *straphete* in Matthew 18:3.

The typical journey of MBBs is gradually to align themselves to a different set of values and beliefs. It is common for a person to be a Muslim cognitively, but a follower of Jesus affectively and behaviorally, that is, the person's affections relate to Jesus, and his or her study is of the Bible (Group 2 Discussion, Spring 2007).[86] The extent to which the emerging believer feels free to make inquiries about the Bible is relative to the amount of freedom there is in meeting openly with the messenger. It is fruitful to give Muslim friends the freedom to determine how open to be.

Rolland Müller[87] describes how this freedom plays out in what he considers to be the five major concerns of the messenger in a discipleship relationship with an MBB:

» Keeping the follower of Jesus physically alive;
» Uniting the two faces (the two identities of Muslim and follower of Jesus);
» Encouraging spiritual growth;
» Coming out as a follower of Jesus; and
» Integrating the MBB into a fellowship.

In different contexts, the journey toward belonging occurs differently.

There is not unanimity about how much to include a pre-believing friend in the local gathering of believers. Many at the Consultation felt uncomfortable with the term "belonging before believing." This is especially true in fields such as North Africa and the Arabian Peninsula, where messengers must use extreme caution not to expose MBB communities to those who are not explicitly known to follow Jesus. In these contexts, the Muslim friend who shows interest in becoming a follower of Jesus is slowly introduced to members of the local MBB community.

As a result of this caution, the Muslim friend may take a longer journey toward belonging to a new community, and his or her only models of how to

---

[86] Cognitive, affective, behavioral: the idea that how we think (cognition), how we feel (emotion and affect), and how we act (behavior) all interact and go together. Specifically, that our *thoughts* influence our *feelings* and *behavior*, our *feelings* influence our *behavior* and *thoughts*, and our *behavior* influences our *emotions* and *thoughts*. These modalities are therefore interrelated, and change in one modality will in all probability influence at least one of the others.

[87] *The Messenger, the Message, The Community: Three Critical Issues for the Cross-Cultural Church Planter* (Turkey: Can Book, 2006), 110.

follow Jesus are the messenger or team of messengers. Obviously, in this case, the person cannot belong to the community until he or she professes to be a follower of Jesus.

In those contexts that can afford to be more open, inviting Muslim friends to gatherings of MBBs proves fruitful. From the beginning, they can witness faith expressed in relationships among their peers. And since their Muslim friends and family may reject them if they choose to follow Isa, it is important for them to experience a sense of belonging within the community of Jesus-followers. Examples from Central Asia and Southeast Asia demonstrate that whole communities are being formed around the concept of *belongers*. Usually what lies at the heart of this practice is an MBB who initiates the gatherings, often in the home of one of the Muslim pre-believers who is receptive. As discipleship takes place, a community of faith emerges spontaneously (Discussion of Groups 16 & 17, Spring 2007).[88]

ONE ORGANIZATION IN ASIA IS HAVING REAL FRUIT USING WHAT IS CALLED "TRAINING FOR TRAINERS." A MESSENGER GATHERS FOUR OR FIVE MUSLIM FRIENDS TO TEACH THEM STORIES FROM THE BIBLE. AS THEIR FAITH IN JESUS EMERGES, THEY IDENTIFY FRIENDS OR FAMILY MEMBERS WITH WHOM THEY WANT TO SHARE. GROUP MEMBERS ARE THEN ENCOURAGED OVER THE COURSE OF A WEEK OR TWO TO SHARE THE STORIES THEY HAVE LEARNED WITH THOSE THEY IDENTIFIED. TOGETHER THEY PRAY FOR ONE ANOTHER AND THEIR FRIENDS AND FAMILY. THE NEXT GATHERING IS THEN A TIME OF REPORTING, LEARNING NEW STORIES, AND CONTINUING TO PRAY.

EFFECTIVE AND REPRODUCIBLE PRACTICES

Communication must be effective.

Even the most skillfully engineered irrigation system is only as useful as its ability to deliver water to the plant. In terms of discipleship, this means that communication must be effective.

---

[88] Groups 16 and 17. In Central Asia, out of forty-five people who came to Christ, forty of them joined the fellowship before finding faith.

FP 6:   Practicing locally appropriate and reproducible discipleship methods (89% considered important, 93% practiced).

They choose resources and tools according to the local situation. These might include the following:

» Bible storying;[89]
» Chronological Bible storying;
» Alpha Course;[90] and
» Scripture memorization (83 percent considered important, 91 percent practiced).

In one South Asian country, security was tight, available literature was almost nonexistent, illiteracy among women was extensive, and large gatherings were forbidden. The team of messengers was forced to think 'outside the box' and use whatever was available as creatively as possible. They developed a teaching method that was based on simple objects and pictures to communicate the Bible and the lifestyle of a follower of Jesus. The hand became a symbol for praying for five friends. It also was a way to outline the epistle to the Romans. The Book of Acts was described as the body—Jesus, the head; the Holy Spirit, the heart; and the individual believers, the legs and arms. The team also adopted a Sufi teaching technique (*dhikr*[91]), using bullet points and sub-points as an outline, which they adapted to the entire Bible. *All these culturally and environmentally relevant discipleship tools proved to be easily reproducible.* Women were discipling each other, and fathers were teaching their children to memorize stories of the Bible with the help of simple pictures. The team members were greatly encouraged when they saw local believers teaching each other through these methods ("Appropriate Discipleship Materials," Interview #33, Spring 2007).

---

89   See chapter 16.

90   A course on Christian faith started at Holy Trinity Church, Brompton, a Church of England parish in London. By 2007, more then 10 million persons worldwide had taken the course.

91   *Dhikr* (*Zikr* in Urdu and *Zekr* in Persian, Arabic "pronouncement," "invocation," or "remembrance") is an Islamic practice that focuses on the remembrance of God. *Dhikr* as a devotional act that often includes the repetition of the names of Allah, supplications, and aphorisms from hadith literature.

> The most fundamental ingredient of this practice
> is that discipleship takes place in
> the heart language of the people;
> tools such as literature, audio recordings,
> films, and storying material
> are specifically geared for the local context.

The effectiveness of these materials increases when messengers take into account how members of the culture learn and pass along information. These considerations have proved especially fruitful in oral societies.

This practice also helps remove the false assumption that to become a follower of Jesus, one must leave one's cultural identity. When methodology and resources are produced locally, the MBB community feels a greater sense of belonging and ownership. This has proved true among communities where an established national church exists. In one situation in Central Asia, MBBs were initially encouraged to assimilate into the Russian Orthodox Church. There, they struggled to fit in and grow in their faith. They did not feel free to bring their friends and family members. This all changed when a few teams of messengers cooperated *in partnership with the MBBs* to create culturally relevant discipleship methods and tools. This was especially valuable because the MBBs had confidence in using these methods with their Muslim friends ("Discipleship Development," Interview #84, Spring 2007).

At the roundtable discussions and interviews during our Consultation, the Bible was universally acknowledged as the central tool in discipleship. Messengers were fruitful when they learned the local concerns so that they could teach the Word appropriately. When using chronological storying, they took time to adapt the stories to local situations.

LOCATION AND ARRANGEMENT

FRUITFUL PRACTICES:

7. *Selecting the places for discipleship that fit the situation and maturity of the emerging disciple.*

8. *Using a variety of effective discipleship methods (such as one-on-one, groups, etc.).*

The location and arrangements for discipling are strongly influenced by the context and the new disciples.

FP 7:   *Selecting the places for discipleship that fit the situation and maturity of the emerging disciple. (For example, secret or open meetings, in the community or in temporary exile—76% considered important, 91% practiced).*

FP 8:   *Using a variety of effective discipleship methods (such as one-on-one, groups, etc.—79% considered important, 92% practiced).*

Muhammad and Ahmed decided to take up the challenge of Manfred[92] to meet together, and so they borrowed a moped and met in an olive grove several kilometers out of town. What a delight it was to meet under a tree in the countryside away from the threat of curious onlookers. These Muslims who were discovering Jesus found it a free environment to share God's Word, express their worship, and meet other Muslims with the same love for Jesus. They still kept meeting regularly with the messenger, but they decided that they would also meet together without him on a regular basis. They wanted to depend on Christ and plant their roots in their own soil, and not in the "greenhouse" of a foreigner ("Meeting under the Olive Tree," Interview #37, Spring 2007).

The initial discipleship of an MBB is a crucial time for solidifying faith and obedience as followers of Jesus. In many contexts, it is not possible for this to take place in the open, so secret meetings (greenhouse environments) are essential. But as soon as possible, MBBs should be discipled together with other MBBs.

---

92   These are not the actual names of the people in the story.

In Southeast Asia, this is a standard discipleship practice. New believers are discipled more or less secretly for two weeks to three months, after which they are discipled more openly. The most important part of the discipleship is working through character and persecution issues as they arise. After this greenhouse care, most of the discipleship happens in the home gatherings of followers of Jesus, so there is positive peer pressure to deal with issues.

Several groups have found it fruitful to gather MBBs in groups for concentrated discipleship and teaching away from their immediate home environment. Neutral meeting places allow MBBs to have peace physically and emotionally without having to 'look over their shoulders' to see who is watching (Group 20 Discussion, Spring 2007). The weakness of this practice is that it is not as reproducible for the local MBBs because of the financial implications of traveling to another location.

In Eastern Europe, a team of messengers found it effective to take MBBs out twice a year to a family camp for up to two weeks. This was held in a different region of the country for security reasons. They provided corporate discipleship, as well as crisis and grief counseling ("Liminal Experiences for Leadership Training," Interview #28, Spring 2007).

Choosing locations other than the house of the expatriate messenger lessens suspicion in a high-persecution environment, which otherwise might lead to premature persecution. Also, alternative locations such as cafés and parks offer natural places for MBBs to bring their Muslim friends who are beginning a journey of faith (Group 20 Discussion, Spring 2007).

Though greenhouse discipleship is fruitful, MBBs still need to live out their faith in their local setting. One messenger working in North Africa said, "You can obviously modify the conditions in a greenhouse...if you plant a plant in a greenhouse and you water it the right way, and you get the light and the temperature right, it shoots up and looks great, but as soon as you come to transfer that plant from the greenhouse into the open soil, very often it doesn't handle that transition" ("Meeting under the Olive Tree," Interview #37, Spring 2007).

In any context, the decision about location and frequency should be worked out together with the MBBs who ultimately have to live with the consequences.

RELATIONSHIPS AND IDENTITY

FRUITFUL PRACTICES:

9. *Encouraging MBBs to develop relationships with other believers.*
10. *Encouraging MBBs to follow the Holy Spirit's lead and to apply biblical principles in establishing their identity in the community.*

Relationships with other believers and identity pose major challenges.

FP 9:   *Encouraging MBBs to develop relationships with other believers (80% considered important, 94% practiced).*

Center-pivot irrigation consists of several segments of pipe joined together and supported by trusses, allowing it to cover vast areas of soil. When MBBs are meeting and joining other MBBs, trust and timing are essential. In some contexts, imposters pose as followers of Jesus to watch and expose true MBBs. This creates a real threat to the emerging MBB faith community. The messenger must take great care in moving forward with this, even though it is absolutely essential to do this in order to create a viable MBB faith community.

Often, when MBBs actually meet one another, their suspicions about whether the others are true followers of Jesus dissipate. And by encouraging a professed MBB to meet together with other MBBs, one messenger in Africa reports he is able to ascertain the sincerity of that person's faith.

Often, a resistance to meeting for this purpose exposes the true motivation of the person for being in the relationship with the messenger. If it is not to follow Jesus, it is often based on an expectation of material good ("Following Biblical Principles on Discipline," Interview #115, Spring 2007).

FP 10:   *Encouraging MBBs to follow the Holy Spirit's lead and to apply biblical principles in establishing their identity in the community (83% considered important, 94% practiced).*

"Before I was a *musli* (by birth) Muslim, now I am an *usli* (true) Muslim." Some South Asian believers expressed their faith to others with this play-on-words, which allowed them to stay in their community. Eventually, they need to explain themselves, but this new identity allowed them to stay in the community long enough to get a fair hearing (Group 17 Discussion, Spring 2007).

When Muslims decide to follow Jesus, the identity they choose within their local community is an extremely important decision. The messenger should encourage them to do this in whatever way they feel led by the Spirit and their understanding of Scripture. This becomes an opportunity for the MBB to discover God's presence and guidance. A fruitful messenger will encourage the new believers to *expect God to provide* and to challenge them toward obedience to God's Word *without imposing the messenger's own biases* (Group 2 Discussion, Spring 2007). The mentor gives the MBB this freedom.

This choice of identity should:

» Be motivated by wisdom rather than fear;
» Preserve the MBB's witness; and
» Maintain links to family and community as much as possible.

The chosen identity should act as a bridge for the MBB to share his or her faith. When the MBBs have been given instruction and have carefully thought through their choice of identity, they will be prepared to respond to inquisitions appropriately, neither denying their faith nor raising unnecessary alarm with a poor choice of words.

Some MBBs desire a new identity to reflect the internal change that has taken place within them. Others want to retain their old identity in order to continue the benefits of cultural identification (Group 21 Discussion, Spring 2007).

WHAT ABOUT BAPTISM?

Three principles came out of discussions on the role of baptism in discipleship:

» It is administered to believers after some quality discipling.
» It is conducted by MBBs for MBBs as early as possible.
» It takes place in the presence of other believers, though the location and means may vary.

BACK TO THE SOURCE

We would not be exaggerating if we said that there were probably more questions than answers expressed by all those taking part in the Consultation and in the case studies that were the source of these Fruitful Practices. These questions reinforce our most basic need as messengers of the Good News—the need for the life-giving water of Jesus. The Lord says, "To the thirsty I will give water as a gift from the spring of the water of life" (Revelation 21:6). Therefore, as we labor over the fields we are tending, we remember that it is God who causes the growth (1 Corinthians 3:6). Let us constantly draw from this living water so that out of our "innermost being will flow rivers of living water" (John 7:38, NASB). *Let us pray that many Muslims will ask, "Give me this water, so that I may never be thirsty or have to keep coming here to draw water"* (John 4:15).

Chapter 10

The Gathering of Reproducing Fellowships

ERIC AND LAURA ADAMS

"I am the vine, you are the branches.
Those who abide in me and I in them bear much fruit."
John 15:5

Our goal is not just to proclaim the Gospel or to see a few individuals enter the Kingdom of God. Our purpose is nothing short of *establishing naturally multiplying communities of believers who follow Jesus within their cultural norms to the extent they can with integrity.*

The local church is the expression of God's transforming truth, power, character, and purposes. The most fruitful church plants have an identity that is firmly rooted in their own culture and includes a viable, attractive witness to the wider Muslim society. This might seem like common sense, but it is not always intuitive or common practice. *Cross-cultural workers often do not realize the subtle ways they can influence the emerging community to develop in very foreign and non-reproducible ways.*

The Church, grounded in its allegiance to God as King, is a dramatic witness that a community of ordinary people can be transformed. This community of faith is living proof to the surrounding Muslim society that the Kingdom of God has come, breaking into their culture to actively transform individuals and society. This is electrifying news to Muslims who spend their lives longing to please God, but often feeling that they fall short of his holiness.

This community of faith is the longed-for fruit of our ministry efforts. If established well, this community will remain long after any cross-cultural workers have left. It will continue to multiply spontaneously, leavening the society with the blessings promised to Abraham, impacting other cultures as God calls out apostles and church-planters to go from its midst to those yet unreached.

The church of Acts is not a historical oddity that merely existed for a brief while after Jesus' death. It is living and growing across the Muslim world today! Hearts are being brought to life; lives are being transformed by the Word-become-Flesh. Divine power is breaking in to heal, satisfy needs, and restore relationships. Believers are taking courageous stands in hostile communities—and winning the hearts of their neighbors by their acts of faith! They are even taking this Great Story to neighboring peoples. Muslims see God walking with friends and neighbors, people they know intimately. Their hearts are kindled with hope that he can walk alongside them, too.

What are the most important values influencing the vitality and expansive power of these faith communities? Here are some of the practices those working to establish Muslim-background-believer (MBB) communities have found to be most fruitful.

WORD AND WORSHIP

FRUITFUL PRACTICES:
1. *Using the Bible as the central source for life, growth, and mission.*
2. *Creating indigenous worship forms in their heart language (e.g., writing their own songs).*
3. *Sharing meals and the Lord's Supper, and practicing hospitality in appropriate ways.*
4. *Redeeming festivals and ceremonies (i.e., births, marriages, etc.).*

FP 1:   *Using the Bible as the central source for life, growth, and mission (99% considered important, 89% practiced).*[93]

---

[93]   Here and subsequently, such a notation will indicate that 99 percent of the participants felt that the practice was important or very important and 89 percent practiced it.

Scripture is the window into the heart of God, showing us his character and purposes. It reveals the way God views the unfolding of history and creation. The Bible's truths, discerned with hermeneutic integrity by local believers, must be at the heart of the emerging church, establishing the DNA of the local body as people who accurately handle the Word of truth (2 Timothy 2:15), and as people who listen and obey.

» Use a Relevant Translation

While the central importance of the Bible was not disputed, the issues that emerged in the small group discussions concerned access to and understanding of the Bible's truths. Among many Muslim peoples, there is still no full translation of the Bible. In some groups, translations that exist are less than ideal because they use outdated language or the language of 'near culture' (non-Muslim) peoples that communicates irrelevance or even unnecessary offense to Muslim hearts. Experienced field workers observe that translations prepared explicitly for a Muslim audience (using culturally meaningful terms and forms) significantly influence responsiveness to the Gospel.[94]

» Allow MBBs to Discern Interpretation

Even when Muslims have access to a culturally relevant translation, interpretation may still pose a problem. Each culture has its own worldview, the filter through which reality is mapped. Even when applying universal principles of Bible interpretation (hermeneutics), these different cultural worldviews mean that people will hone in on Scripture from different perspectives—and have a unique but only partial view of biblical truth.

Foreigners bring their own worldviews with them as they work cross-culturally. Unless they are conscious of how they are shaped by their worldview, they may assume their opinions represent the full teaching of Scripture. When they hear Muslim believers interpret biblical passages through a different worldview, the foreign workers may feel the need to 'correct' them, even force them to share their foreign viewpoint. This can cause dissonance in the new church, taint the faith of new believers with foreignness, and unnecessarily marginal-

---

[94]   John and Anna Travis, personal communication with author.

ize their witness to the Muslim society around them. We must all grapple with discerning the role of culture(s) and that of the Holy Spirit in interpretation of Scripture.

For example, many Westerners do not 'map' the supernatural as a significant part of daily life. However, many Muslim societies experience the supernatural as a daily reality, dealt with via charms, curses, interaction with *jinn* (spirits, angels, demons), and so on. While Westerners may skim over or not even recognize portions of Scripture that address supernatural realities, these passages might stand out to Muslims and inform a new understanding of how Jesus' people can relate to the supernatural.

Several practitioner case studies noted that inductive study of Scriptures can be quite fruitful with Muslim background believers: they observe what is written (whether through verbal retelling or through study of the written Word), understand what it meant to the original audience, interpret how God is speaking to them through it, and identify obedient steps he is asking of them. In this way, they develop an understanding of the Bible which is culturally relevant, that allows the Holy Spirit to speak deeply to their hearts, and which they can naturally discuss with their neighbors.

> FP 2:   *Creating indigenous worship forms in their heart language (e.g., writing their own songs) (78% considered important, 67% practiced).*

Worship refers to all aspects of our lives through which we acknowledge who God is and give him our devotion. In some societies, the term *worship* is used primarily for music and singing used during times of fellowship. This is only one small aspect of worship. Culturally relevant forms of worship can be expressed in celebration of the Lord's Supper, dance, poetry, drama, art, ritual, service, festivals, meditation, and more.

The focus of discussions at the Consultation was primarily on music and song. Not all felt that developing indigenous forms of music were important. Some communities find near-culture worship materials meaningful enough for use. In other areas, singing is not done for fear of exposure and persecution. In yet other cultures, music and song are perceived as immoral, and thus not relevant for expressing truths about God.

Many participants agreed that creating indigenous worship forms allows freer expression of devotion, and can be naturally attractive to non-believers. Culturally relevant worship can be deeply moving and strengthen community identity and bonds, while also eliminating the taint of 'foreignness' that can marginalize faith communities from their surrounding society.

Muslim background believers in community can best discern which forms of worship are most appropriate for the occasion, even if they seem strange to foreigners. Some participants encourage poets, artists, and composers within the believing communities to express their faith in art. Believers have even hosted regional gatherings of such artists to facilitate the production of worship resources.

FP 3:   *Sharing meals and the Lord's Supper, and practicing hospitality in appropriate ways (90% considered important, 91% practiced).*

In many Muslim cultures, hospitality and sharing a meal are a sacred trust, a bond that cannot be betrayed. This tradition resonates powerfully with the Lord's Supper as a context of bonding, blessing, peace, and reconciliation within the community, and with a universal church across cultures and history.

> *In many cultures,*
> *hospitality and sharing a meal are a sacred trust,*
> *a bond that cannot be betrayed.*
> *This tradition resonates powerfully*
> *with the Lord's Supper*
> *as a place of bonding, blessing,*
> *peace, and reconciliation*
> *within the community,*
> *and even with a universal church.*

FP 4:   *Redeeming festivals and ceremonies (i.e., births, marriages, etc.).*

While somewhat controversial (60 percent of participants saw it as important and 72 percent practiced it), many faith communities develop redemptive adaptations of traditional rites of passage. These include births, entering adulthood, marriages, death anniversaries, as well as celebrations and religious festivals—both Muslim and Christian. Many communities recognize that these events meet deep needs in their community. As one participant said, these rites embody "some of the highest expressions of life's deepest emotions." These events can reinforce fundamental touchstones of common humanity before God, and they can forge deep bonds in community identity.

MBB communities have adapted these traditional events to release God's blessing, replacing the role of the occult with the power of the Holy Spirit[95] and expressing the shift of their heart allegiances to Jesus' truth and power.[96] These adaptations are often public as well, communicating their convictions in culturally sensitive ways and giving another opportunity for their neighbors to experience God dwelling among them.

RELATIONSHIPS WITHIN AND WITHOUT

Believers' contexts have a profound influence on how they can express their oneness in Christ with all other believers while remaining in relationship with their community of birth.

> FRUITFUL PRACTICES:
> 5. *Fellowshipping as appropriate with the wider Body of Christ.*
> 6. *Having an identity in its own community without being absorbed by the wider non-MBB Christian community.*
> 7. *Working within relational networks with pre-existing trust bonds—family networks, work networks, friendship networks, student networks.*
> 8. *Involving women in ministry in contextually appropriate ways.*
> 9. *Seeking to bless and transform their wider community.*

---

[95] Paul G. Hiebert, *Anthropological Reflections on Missiological Issues* (Grand Rapids, MI: Baker Book House, 1994), 203–53.

[96] Charles Kraft, "Contextualization in Three Crucial Dimensions," in *Appropriate Christianity*, ed. Charles Kraft (Pasadena, CA: William Carey Library, 2005), 99–116.

Decide How Closely to Relate to Nearby Non-MBB Churches
Two fruitful practices emerged:

FP 5:   *Fellowshipping as appropriate with the wider body of Christ.*

FP 6:   *Having an identity in its own community without being absorbed by the wider non-MBB Christian community.*

The importance of relationships between the MBB fellowship and the wider Body of Christ provoked a complex discussion in the small groups. Only 34 percent felt the importance of cultivating these relationships, even while 62 percent practiced it. Experience from the fields tended to validate the *homogenous unit principle*.[97] That is, people feel most comfortable fellowshipping, and more able to forge a strong identity as a community, with others of their own culture and background.

There were several exceptions to this:

» In cities, where the anonymity and diversity of the urban environment suppresses ethnic distinctiveness, multi-cultural fellowships are more acceptable and viable.
» In areas where one ethnic group has very strong influence over another (usually due to historical political power, such as Russian influence in the Central Asian Republics), then those ethnic groups who have been subjected to the same power can more easily fellowship together.

For the most part, however, there was an innate tension between the principle of unity in Christ and the need for each emerging ethnic redeemed community to establish its own unique cultural identity. It is important to recognize that unity does not mean uniformity, and the Bible expresses ethnic diversity within the universal Body of Christ.[98]

---

[97]   "People like to become Christians without crossing racial, linguistic, or class barriers." Donald A. McGavran, *Understanding Church Growth* (Grand Rapids, MI: Eerdmans, 1970), 163.

[98]   See, e.g., Revelation 5:9.

In many fields, a near-culture church with a wealth of traditions has histori-cally existed, often for hundreds of years. In many instances, these churches have endured generations of hostility and treatment as *dhimmi*[99] (second-class though ideally protected) status from the Muslim majority society. As a result, these communities of faith have often developed prejudice, fear, or even hatred toward their Muslim neighbors.

A common, *unfruitful* case study observes Muslim believers trying to fel-lowship within one of these near-neighbor churches. Initially, they are accepted joyfully into the local church and allowed to share their testimony widely; some may even consider them to be "proof of the triumph" of Christianity over Is-lam. But their Muslim friends and family reject them for this behavior because they have demonstrated their new allegiance to a different (and hated) cultural group. Their friends and family now regard them as traitors and apostates. In this way, there is a forced break between the new believers and their social sup-port system; they must commit "cultural suicide," and their witness is lost to the Muslim society they have come from. Sadly, they also rarely become integrated into the near-neighbor church fellowship. Many return to Islam, not for lack of desire to follow Jesus, but because they have not found a new sense of belonging within the community of faith.

When Muslim-background-believing communities form in an area contain-ing one of these near-culture churches, they often feel pressured to conform to its traditions. The near-culture church has been Christian for centuries, so it presumably "knows the right way" for believers to live. Succumbing to these pressures can result in the new faith community taking on cultural forms that are not natural. Because those in the Muslim social majority perceive these MBB communities as aligning themselves with the "infidel" Christian culture, they marginalize the MBB community and neutralize its potential witness to Muslim society.

---

[99] Bat Ye'or, *The Dhimmi: Jews and Christians Under Islam* (Rutherford, NJ: Fairleigh Dickinson University Press, 1985).

Commit to One Another in Community

Many field workers labor diligently to disciple individual Muslim believers. When they bring these individuals together, expecting them to fellowship, they are dismayed that Muslims who are strangers to each other find it hard to trust each other. To share a secret with another can endanger you in many Muslim societies, putting you in that person's power. Becoming an infidel Christian is apostasy and can be punishable by death. No wonder strangers must work hard to earn each other's trust! "Bringing strangers together and calling them 'community' is not comprehensible in most contexts," said one practitioner at the Consultation. There is always the prior question of trust.

FP 7: *Working within relational networks with pre-existing trust bonds—family networks, work networks, friendship networks, student networks (97% considered important, 93% practiced).*

When these pre-existing networks begin to embrace faith in Jesus, they retain their trust and continue to relate even as they journey forward in faith.

> Bringing strangers together
> and calling them 'community'
> is not comprehensible
> in most contexts.
> There is always the prior
> question of trust.

While practitioners might need to communicate deeply with one individual at first, it is most fruitful when this seeker/believer chooses to be a gateway for the Gospel to spread within his/her natural relational networks. Many consultation participants encourage seekers to share what they are discovering about Jesus with family and friends in order to process their journey to faith together. In several case studies within a hostile environment, field workers encouraged seekers to demonstrate their changed heart, to be 'salt and light' to family and friends (to show love in action, rather than aggressively verbalizing their new beliefs), and even use qur'anic 'bridge' approaches[100] to earn a hearing for their new faith. This led to acceptance and further growth of faith within the family. It is a natural step to organize a relational network that believes together into a house church.

In many societies where participants worked, the idea of a community centered on Jesus was a new concept, without precedent. How ought new believers to relate to each other, bond together, and commit to one another as a community? Case studies revealed the importance of these communities studying the commands of Jesus[101] and how to live out his primary command to those who trust in him: love one another (and other biblical passages that tell Christians how they should treat "one another"). As the new believers discerned how to live out these commands and principles in a culturally relevant way, some workers encouraged them to commit to one another through a meaningful covenant or ritual, as a step in forging an identity as a community of believers following the Messiah.

Foreigners must understand their role in this process. They can be a powerful influence catalyzing the development of a healthy, culturally relevant community. But if the communities are to be fruitful and spread naturally, foreigners must resist allowing their cultural background, traditions, and biases to influence the emerging fellowship. As in Acts 15, new believers must have the freedom to develop their own traditions as followers of Jesus in their own culture.

Families, Women, and Children

Families are at the heart of a thriving MBB community. Until it attracts and integrates a core of stable families, the local believing community is weak and vulnerable. Emerging fellowships must address family issues, especially those of women and children.

In most Muslim communities, men and women often inhabit distinct subcultures, a result of the Muslim principle of *purdah*. Women are kept separate from men who are not blood relatives, and most often build their closest

---

[100] For more resources on this topic, see Patrick O. Cate, "Gospel Communication From Within," *International Journal of Frontier Missions* 11, no. 2 (April 1994); and Kevin Greeson, *The Camel: How Muslims Are Coming to Faith in Christ!* (Arkadelphia, AR: WIGTake Resources, 2007).

[101] George Patterson and Richard Scoggins, *Church Multiplication Guide: The Miracle of Church Reproduction* (Pasadena, CA: William Carey Library, 2002).

friendships with other women. Because of this reality, women practitioners must often minister to Muslim women apart from men, sharing their faith, teaching new believers how to mature, baptizing them, and even establishing a sense of community.

Many countries enforce laws explicitly forbidding anyone from teaching minors a faith different from that allowed by government or religious leaders. Some countries expel foreigners and imprison locals for proselytizing children who are not part of families within the believing community. Children are considered an integral part of the family in Muslim societies, and parental authority is respected. Many field workers stress the ethical importance of explicitly gaining parental consent to work with children. Parents commonly give permission to those who have developed goodwill and who ask for it. Seeking parental consent helps many workers develop excellent local community programs for all children, including education, health, vaccination, and sports programs.

> Emerging fellowships
> must address family issues,
> especially those of
> women and children.

In Muslim societies, it is most often the mothers who transmit religious values from one generation to the next. Because of this, many women who come to faith quickly begin to develop means to help their children understand Jesus, in turn leading them to faith. Muslim background believers at the Consultation described the plight of believing families in Muslim societies, even though this was not specifically addressed in our discussion of fruitful practices. Many desired more resources to help parents transmit their faith to their children and build their faith together as a family.

Often, some level of gender separation continues indefinitely, such as when women and men sit on different sides of the room or even meet at different times. Some communities, however, challenge cultural practices and emphasize the meeting together of whole families.

FP 8:   Involving women in ministry in contextually appropriate ways.

The Gospel gives Muslim women a new value and status, along with expanded roles in society.[102] Eighty-two percent of practitioners believe it is important to intentionally integrate women into the ministries of the local believing community, and eighty-three percent practice this. Our small group discussions revealed that Muslim women often feel empowered to do the following when they are thus valued and released to serve:

» Share their faith;
» Mentor younger female believers;
» Train children in the faith;
» Organize community services;
» Provide culturally appropriate leadership; and
» Retain the integrity of the family and community.

Bless and Transform the Wider Society

The local church not only transforms the individuals who enter it, but it can also be a powerful transforming and leavening force in the society around it. Many practitioners saw this as one part of bringing the blessing promised to Abraham to the Muslim peoples of the earth (see Genesis 12:1–3).

They identified attitudes that brought blessing: loving those who persecute you; turning the other cheek; walking the second mile; and refusing to perpetuate the adversarial cycle of rejection, prejudice, hatred, and revenge.

Where these attitudes are practiced within Muslim societies—even without an explicit verbal communication of the Gospel—goodwill is generated, and believers gain a hearing for the Good News. Merely presenting truth, without modeling transformation of lives, attitudes, and actions, provides a weak Gospel message. Conversely, living out the Kingdom without explanation is just as incomplete. The Kingdom must be lived, as well as preached, if we are to bear fruit.

---

[102]   Rodney Stark, "The Role of Women in Christian Growth," in *The Rise of Christianity: A Sociologist Reconsiders Christianity*, ed. Rodney Stark (Princeton, NJ: Princeton University Press, 1996), 95–128.

FP 9:   Seeking to bless and transform their wider community.

Eighty-five percent of participants practiced and 84 percent believed in the principle of blessing without discrimination. Any benefit went to all members of the surrounding community, not just believers. The ways and means described of blessing local societies covered a wide range of activities, most tailored to the felt needs in the community. Case studies included using money from collection jars at women's weekly Bible studies to feed local Muslim widows, voluntarily sweeping public streets, praying with non-believers, picking up trash, praying public prayers of blessing on the whole community, writing newspaper articles, helping the homeless, feeding mothers and children, providing marriage and family counseling, assisting with agriculture, building shelter, or providing primary health care, educational services, disaster relief, micro-enterprise loans, vocational training, community development, or business enterprises that created jobs.

In one area, when a neighboring village burned down, MBBs went in and rebuilt it. On another field, when Islamists destroyed a community center built by believers, the village rebuilt it brick by brick. In another case, an MBB so endeared himself to the Muslim community by his sacrificial service to them that they courageously protected him when threatened by Islamists.

Determine Whether to Verbalize Testimony

Many practitioners shared how they integrated their testimony into their activities. Others served without explicitly verbalizing the Gospel message, waiting until they had gained goodwill and a hearing, and then shared from their hearts. In many cases, the actions of Jesus' people spread his good reputation, gleaning a wider harvest of seekers (Acts 19).

> Merely presenting truth,
> without modeling transformation of
> lives, attitudes, and actions,
> provides a weak Gospel message.
> Living out the Kingdom
> without explanation is just as incomplete.

ACCOUNTABILITY AND DISCIPLINE

FRUITFUL PRACTICES:
10. Promoting accountability to one another.
11. Confronting sin and yet exhibiting grace for restoration after appropriate discipline.
12. Commonly meeting in homes or other such places, rather than 'church' buildings.

Accountability is inherent in the concept of the Kingdom. Its citizens respond in the obedience of faith to the Rule of the King. Jesus reasserted this when he said, "If you love me, you will obey what I command" (John 14:15, NIV). Jesus is *Lord*, as well as Savior. Accountability among believers is an act of love, preparation for the day when we will stand before the throne of judgment and mercy. We have access to the power of the Spirit to be transformed from the heart, conformed to the character of our King. This is what we were designed for.

> *FP 10:* *Promoting accountability to one another (88% considered important, 86% practiced).*

One participant said, "Accountability is the essence of discipleship." Many said that accountability must be integrated from the very beginning to become the DNA of the emerging community of believers. Cross-cultural workers must model this as an integral part of their faith. True accountability, many said, must be established from the outset as part of the cost of following the Messiah.

Genuine accountability requires trust within the bonds of personal relationships among believers. This is more easily established in small groups where people are more intimately acquainted with each other, especially if they are peers, close in age and stage of life. Transparency and honesty are contagious, and true friends will follow up with each other regularly on areas of vulnerability and temptation. Real accountability is like the guardrail at the edge of a precipice, protecting travelers from actions that are destructive to themselves and others.

FP 11: *Confronting sin and yet exhibiting grace for restoration after appropriate discipline.*

Effective accountability must also provide mechanisms for both reconciliation and biblical discipline. Eighty-four percent of participants considered this to be important, and 90 percent practiced it among themselves.

Willful human nature will often choose what is wrong—attitudes and behaviors incompatible with the values of the Kingdom of God—and remain unrepentant. There were many stories of self-identified "believers" who held character weaknesses such as gossip, abuse of power, addictive behaviors, or moral failings (such as theft or adultery), but were allowed to remain in community, even in leadership roles. When fellow leaders look the other way instead of holding people accountable for moral failings, the leaders open the door to deeply corrosive forces that can destroy the community of believers.

We all have natures that fall short of the holiness of God. The problem, as one participant commented, is not in having these failings but in not repenting when they are revealed to us. Workers cited several biblical narratives that can be helpful in teaching moral responsibility. For example, David and Peter both suffered the consequences of their lack of accountability, and Eli failed to address dishonor within his family.

Several participants note that in 'honor and shame' cultures, it is extremely difficult to address accountability, peacemaking, and discipline, because of the shame associated with admitting personal failings.[103] Believers need to be immersed in the knowledge that Jesus meets us in our shame, that he bore shame and humiliation for our sake.

Some workers find it helpful to use a third party, a trusted mediator, to address areas of correction in individual lives. Others have recognized the use of respected local proverbs or 'parables' as means of correction and encouragement.[104]

When the community of believers practices mutual correction, accountability, conflict resolution, and discipleship, they grow in godly character, responsible maturity, relational health, and spiritual power.

---

[103] Roland Müller, *Honor and Shame* (Philadelphia: Xlibris Corp., 2000).

[104] See chapter 9.

SELF-REPRODUCING COMMUNITIES

Church is a word with many meanings and associations. It is used to refer to a community of believers, a weekly gathering time, a building, a denomination, an institution, or the universal Body of Christ. Our understanding of the word is influenced by the particular Christian traditions of our own subculture and from our personal experiences. If we do not pause to acknowledge this, we might miscommunicate as we use the term.

At the Consultation, the 'church' we were discussing was defined as a community of believers or followers of Jesus who have come to faith from a Muslim background and gather to meet regularly. They express 'the church' through their biblically inspired involvement in each others' lives.

In societies in which there is hostility towards the concept of being Christian, it is vitally important to strip the Gospel message of foreign cultural traditions as much as possible and allow a culturally relevant expression of *following Jesus in community* to develop.

> The more a local church is
> defined by community,
> the more resistant the church is to persecution.

The more a local church is defined by buildings, assets, and institution, the more vulnerable the church is to persecution. Persecutors can use threats of taking away these rights and assets as leverage to control the church and silence the "voice of witness." The more a local fellowship is defined primarily by community (a network of relationships), the more resistant the fellowship is to persecution. This form of fellowship not only can survive environments of persecution but also often thrive and spread despite hostile scrutiny.[105]

> FP 12:   *Commonly meeting in homes or other such places, rather than 'church' buildings.*

---

[105]   See chapter 24.

Small house fellowships were the predominant form of MBB community represented at the Consultation. Such groups, which often network with one another, do not own buildings or significant assets. While only 75 percent of the participants felt that meeting in homes, rather than church buildings, was important, 86 percent practiced this on their fields. A rule of thumb brought out by practitioner case studies indicates that the greater the hostility of the society toward the Gospel—especially when persecution is a distinct threat—the smaller the size of the house groups.

After relational networks begin coming to faith and new believers are mentored, the next step is the forming of a house fellowship. One relational network is enough to start a small house group. House fellowships:

» Require little or no funds;
» Are less intimidating to seekers and new believers (when they are introduced by trusted friends);
» Can meet within a village or community immediately;
» Adapt easily to the cultural context;
» Are naturally relational and supportive;
» Are self-limiting in size, since only so many can fit comfortably in a house;
» Can easily and naturally reproduce; and
» Can be relatively 'invisible' to persecutors.

Case studies demonstrated that house fellowships thrive most when they are intentionally networked with one another (the earlier the better), so that despite their smallness they can enjoy a sense of wider community identity, mutual support, and encouragement. They can also work together on projects.

Determine When Higher-Profile Gatherings Are Appropriate

While house churches are the norm, many communities of MBBs pursue a publicly acknowledged identity and profile as well. This generally occurs in two situations:

» Where local hostility and persecution are low (for example where there is a secular government, or where Islam is only a thin veneer over a deeper non-Islamic cultural identity); and

» Where the community of believers has grown large enough and has relatively widespread recognition so that persecution no longer intimidates them.

Under these conditions, many MBB communities seek and receive a higher profile in society. They may even seek official recognition for their existence. They often meet more publicly in storefront churches or buildings dedicated for the purpose of worship. They also openly network together to develop resources and create institutions to serve their interests and needs.

Conclusion

Redeemed communities act as powerful redemptive forces within Muslim societies. When do these redeemed communities bear the most fruit? When they spring from the seed of the Gospel intentionally separated from the husks and chaff of foreign traditions. When they are allowed to take flower while drawing from local cultural soil and resources. When they are nourished by the "Word becoming flesh"—God's truth expressed through culturally relevant traditions and practices. When tended appropriately, the community of believers can be like the mustard seed that becomes a great plant to bless and nurture many. This is happening today within many Muslim societies, transforming those societies as well as the lives of believers and their families.

Chapter 11

The Equipping of Leaders

DEBORA VIVEZA AND DWIGHT SAMUEL

"The owner of the vineyard said to his steward,
'Call the laborers...'"
Matthew 20:8, NEB

"The things that you have learned from me...
entrust them to faithful people who will be able to teach others as well."
2 Timothy 2:2

INTRODUCTION

"THERE ARE NEVER TWO TIGERS ON ONE MOUNTAIN."
– A PROVERB ON LEADERSHIP FROM SOUTHEAST ASIA

As was noted in chapter seven, one of the ways God is drawing Muslims to himself is through faithful leaders. Yet the ideas we have about leadership formation and leadership in general vary widely. The proverb above illustrates this as it immediately raises questions in our minds. Is this true in my cultural context? Does this apply to all leadership situations—business, political, social, as well as to communities of faith? What traits of a leader does 'tiger' bring up in our minds—controlling and territorial, or energetic and proactive? These types of questions are evidence of the particular lens through which each of us views leadership. How, then, do cross-cultural workers and Jesus-centered communities deal with this multi-faceted issue?

In this chapter, we will highlight observations of some key things God is doing in communities of Jesus-followers with regard to leadership. From the wealth of data gathered at the Consultation, certain criteria for leadership selection and formation came up again and again, specifically the high value placed on character, contextual appropriateness, modeling in relationship, and empowerment.

CENTERED ON CHARACTER

FRUITFUL PRACTICES:

1. *Selecting leaders by character above credentials (for example, a person's level of literacy is not a primary qualification for leadership).*
2. *Training leaders within their immediate context, and as locally as possible.*
3. *Using Scripture as the textbook for leadership qualifications and training.*

Character alone does not necessarily prove ministry effectiveness. Neither is character understood as existing apart from gifting, calling, or culturally appropriate characteristics (e.g., age or experience). But no amount of competency can make one an effective leader in Jesus-centered communities if he or she does not have character.

FP 1: *Selecting leaders by character above credentials (for example, a person's level of literacy is not a primary qualification for leadership) (98% considered important, 75% practiced).*[106]

A cross-cultural worker in Southeast Asia told of one young leader who had a way about him that was attractive to people. He could draw people to himself and they would listen. However, it was discovered that he was sleeping with his girlfriend. When the workers brought it to his attention to see if he would

---

[106]   Here and subsequently, such a notation will indicate that 98 percent of the participants felt that the practice was important or very important and 75 percent practiced it.

repent, he refused. They had been considering working with him as a leader, but decided against it because of his refusal to change. In contrast, another man of about twenty-two years of age came to faith in Christ. Though he was a bit young and was not influential (and therefore probably not an obvious leadership candidate), his character was good. He loved his wife, he was faithful to do everything asked of him, and he "had a good way about him." The young man then introduced his father, a Muslim religious teacher in the village, to Christ. And the father became a follower of Christ too, quit his job, and has been going to other villages to begin sharing his faith. The worker concluded, "So credentials ...even charisma, were not what we would choose." When asked just what kinds of qualities were desired when referring to character, he elaborated: "Faithful to his wife, good to his children, surrounding community doesn't have anything they can accuse him of ...He's not power hungry, money hungry. So, he is above reproach" ("Character Proves Itself in Leaders," Interview #78, Spring 2007).

Many participants added that in addition to character, some kind of formal study or training can be helpful and contextually appropriate. This was often the case as leaders matured or the work of God developed in a certain area. But all agreed that character was more important, especially in the selection of leaders. Some quotes from the participants are:

We have people who have been through training but they have no character.

A leader who has character issues will reproduce that in followers. Our character is the number one thing (Small Group Discussion, Spring 2007).

In a moving story from Central Asia, one cross-cultural worker spoke about how the normal assumed progression from Gospel introduction to discipleship to leadership did not automatically result in healthy communities. It seemed that the leaders almost always floundered or fell away. After reflection and prayer, it was recognized that most had deeper issues in their lives. For example, many young people in this society grow up being told that they are worthless. Others have experimented with deviant sex. Because of this kind of brokenness, the cross-cultural workers realized the need for significant healing and found a form of healing prayer that helped them tremendously. The worker and others in the region now feel that this is a priority in their work ("Necessity for Healing Prayer in Discipleship," Interview #47, Spring 2007).[107]

Healing prayer is one approach to address this need. For others, it may require training in godliness, intentional one-on-one mentoring, some kind of counseling, or a combination of the above. The point here is that a deeper work in the character of a leader cannot be ignored.

Character and Movement

Additional data came from the general survey of all participants. There, in looking at Jesus-centered communities that showed signs of a movement, it was discovered that one of seven key characteristics is that community leaders meet the 1 Timothy 3 and Titus 1 leadership criteria that focus on character.[108]

Contextually Appropriate

Two practices related to cultural appropriateness.

FP 2: *Training leaders within their immediate context, and as locally as possible.*

Nine out of ten people at the Consultation were in agreement with this practice. One problem with sending leaders out of their context is that the further away they go, the less likely they are to return. In a case from North Africa, it was reported that out of more than twenty nationals sent out of the country for training during a several-year span, only two returned (Small Group Discussion, Spring 2007).

Some who have proved themselves to be leaders in the local context do, however, profit considerably from studying in another context that has resources not available locally and that can enhance the local ministry when the leader returns.

---

[107] For more on healing prayer, see chapter 18.
[108] Preliminary Summary of FP track by Knowledge Stewardship Team, September 26, 2007.

It is not always possible for leadership formation to take place in the immediate context. In one case in Central Asia where a wartime environment made leadership formation both difficult and dangerous, the workers have found it more effective to actually bring some members out once or twice a year to a retreat in a neighboring region. They brought them out as families, providing childcare, crisis and grief counseling, and leadership formation. The retreats lasted from one to two weeks. In addition, some key leaders came out separately to do specific training for a week or two. If they were out for too long, it became harder to get back in, and they wanted to get back in to their families anyway because of the danger ("Experiences for Leadership Training," Interview #28, Spring 2007).

FP 3: *Using Scripture as the textbook for leadership qualifications and training.*

Here is an account from the Middle East where the first community of faith has started more than ten others, most with their own leadership:

The situation of the people we were trying to reach was similar to the situation of the New Testament, the New Testament context. One thing that we tried to do was to provide tools and ways of presenting things that would be transferable, easily transmitted to others. And that involved trying not to rely too much on materials coming from elsewhere but to try to use the Word of God. One tool that we used in leadership training was to have a retreat every few months and to do an in-depth Bible study. I chose the book of Acts which showed how the Gospel spreads. We saw how the workers bring the Gospel in the beginning, how leaders are chosen, what is the basic preparation that one needs to give to the new believers, and what believers do in terms of fellowship and reproduction, the Lord's Supper, and the use of money. It was very interesting because I've been surprised by their obedience to Scripture ("Using Scripture in Training of Leaders," Interview #83, Spring 2007).

It is not hard to imagine why this was the highest in importance (93 percent) and practice (97 percent) among practices related to leadership. What we found to be most helpful, though, was how the Bible was actually used in various contexts. It requires a careful understanding of the local culture to impart the Word of God with the greatest impact. This practice is also relevant to the previous section on the centrality of character because the qualifications for leaders described in 1 and 2 Timothy and Titus center on character qualifications.

Modeled in Relationship

FRUITFUL PRACTICES:

4. *Modeling leadership through relationships more than through institutions.*
5. *Mentoring and forming leaders intentionally and usually informally, through practical experience.*
6. *Disciplers finding 'Timothys' to mentor and so produce reproducers (2 Timothy 2:2). Some use the term 'shadow pastoring.'*

As one of the participants said so clearly, "Modeling is important, and the best leaders are those who have had good models to follow. Christ showed the way for his disciples and set the pattern for one-on-one (i.e., life-on-life) leadership development" (Interview #33, Spring 2007).

> *FP 4: Modeling leadership through relationships more than through institutions.*

A young woman has been discipled by a cross-cultural worker in the Middle East. They used to live in the same city, but the cross-cultural worker was forced to leave the city. Now they are living an hour away from each other. "And so I have her come to my house so she sees us in our house," the cross-cultural worker explained. "She stays the night before. She's seeing how we work as a family, how we reach out through the prison ministry and reach out with lost friends. She asks me about my friends and prays for them, and I ask her about her friends and I pray for them. We talk about her personal discipleship of more purity and the basic disciplines. Then we talk about how she's discipling smaller groups." Through this relationship, the cross-cultural worker is helping the young national woman to develop her skills of leadership. It has been in this setting that she learned how to multiply her efforts through others, by training leaders who will train others (Interview #33, Spring 2007).

One participant told of a leader who had not been discipled in a daily context but was sent straight to Bible School. Later on in ministry, he did not display godly character and was eventually asked to leave. He added, "[Those in relationship] can observe you in whatever ministry you do as a leader. This is a great place to learn" (Small Group Discussion, Spring 2007).

Another participant summed it up like this: "Jesus sets the example in the New Testament with his disciples. He didn't do training in a formal way, but by doing ministry with them and spending time with them. He was teaching them through stories, experience, and living life together" (Small Group Discussion, Spring 2007).

This principle was the second highest in importance (83 percent) and practice (93 percent) of those pertaining to leadership development. 'Relational' does not necessarily mean being the person's best friend. The discussions and stories focused on the personal and 'walking side-by-side' aspects of relationship.

FP 5:   *Mentoring and forming leaders intentionally and usually informally, through practical experience.*

Even though leadership development is best accomplished with purposeful intent, the format is often non-formal. In one case, a female cross-cultural worker took two local women under her care and told us of the simple, non-formal model she used:

I met with one woman every day. Even when she was just married, she came to our house every day. Later when her husband began to take more responsibility in the community, she began to be involved in hospitality. I modeled the Christian life, and modeled leadership. She was very excited when the Lord asked her to do something like to be hospitable, or to pray. Another woman was focused on teaching. So I taught her how to teach and explain the Bible, and I told her to pray and ask the Holy Spirit to help her teach. And the Holy Spirit touched her and she is a very good teacher. Then I told her to find two other women who wanted to teach like her, and train them to teach as well. So it was like a mentoring-teaching situation ("Discipleship and Leadership of Women," Interview #23, Spring 2007).

From the comments of many participants, 'non-formal' was characterized by one-on-one time, in the home or other natural setting, and not in a classroom. It seemed especially important for imparting certain life lessons:

Non-formal relational time is key in getting to the heart of discipleship issues (Middle East).

Non-formal relational time is key in developing character (South Asia) (Small Group Discussion, Spring 2007).

Several participants indicated that some formal training may be good at the right time, but that it is still important to focus on godly character and leadership skills.

It takes too much time to give formal training when the groups are forming quickly. Informal leadership training is needed that can be done quickly. Formal training is for later.

I teach at a seminary; our students have appreciated the emphasis on practical learning. We're emphasizing a seminary that needs graduates to start a [community of fifteen members] during training or they don't graduate. [There is usually] too much emphasis on theory and not enough on practicality and application of learning (Small Group Discussion, Spring 2007).

FP 6:   *Disciplers finding 'Timothys' to mentor and so produce reproducers (2 Timothy 2:2). Some use the term 'shadow pastoring.'*

In studying the data gathered from participants, it appears that there is a direct link between mentoring new leaders and the likelihood of starting multiple communities.[109]

---

[109]   Preliminary Summary of FP track by Knowledge Stewardship Team, September 26, 2007.

When a local community both sends out its own cross-cultural workers and *mentors new leaders* in the community, the probability that a participant had started multiple communities is 78 percent. When neither of these things is happening, it is only 19 percent.

In Central Asia, a couple of enthusiastic local men shared the Gospel with those around them, resulting in a growing number of new believers. But they did not know how to develop these new believers, and because of security issues, the cross-cultural workers needed to stay in the background. One of the cross-cultural workers shared: "We were never going to be the ones heading things up, we were always going to be in the background working with the key leaders and helping them to lead the home groups and the house-based communities. So that's really how we functioned." The cross-cultural workers and the nationals discussed together what was going to cause a movement and how to reach the area. As the emerging leaders started doing more and going to villages, it became clear that this was the best approach. "They started to see fruit ...and right now, the places where it's really healthy and growing and multiplying is where they've done that."

WHO SHOULD LEAD— FOREIGNERS OR NATIONALS?

Fellowships led by a partnership between cross-cultural workers and national believers, a common model, were fruitful in establishing faith communities. However, faith communities led only by nationals seemed much more successful.

There were eighty-one participants who indicated they were involved with partnership-led communities and sixty-eight with nationals only–led communities. In the nationals only–led data, there were three reports of very high numbers of communities planted. Even taking those out leaves the nationals only–led group twice as fruitful. Only seven were connected to foreigner–led communities (not enough to give a fair count in the graph) that reported 1.4 as the average number of communities established.

At the same time, different cross-cultural teams in the area realized there was a need to help the key leaders develop resources in order to mentor, develop, and grow new leaders. They helped to create discipleship materials, as well as a curriculum for a small training center where they could develop local leaders. From the beginning a pattern was set—leaders following the trainer with a view to becoming trainers themselves. It all started in the capital city, but there are now three satellite locations that are working well and coordinated by local community members ("Discipleship Development," Interview #84, Spring 2007).

A very clear example of a discipler who finds a 'Timothy' to mentor and encourage was reported among women in the Middle East. A female cross-cultural worker began training a young woman who turned out to be very fruitful in her outreach. Within three to four months, there were twenty-four new followers of Jesus, and she was overwhelmed by trying to disciple all of them. She was mentored in the process of gathering the women who lived near each other into small groups and how to recognize new leadership. She now trains only the leaders of those groups (Interview #33, Spring 2007).

Reproductive mentoring is the passing on to someone of skills, character, and wisdom with the intention of that person doing the same with another. It is beneficial for those receiving the mentoring, and it is also an important factor in multiplying our efforts in establishing communities.

EMPOWERMENT–FOCUSED

FRUITFUL PRACTICES:

7. *Validating, affirming, and reinforcing the role of appointed leaders in the local church.*
8. *Helping the newly-gathered MBB community to choose their leaders wisely.*

It is clear that communities of faith are more likely to multiply when led by nationals only (see "Who Should Lead—Foreigners or Nationals?"). In the process of either passing on leadership or of affirming pre-existing leadership in the local community, it is important that cross-cultural workers do not exhibit control but instead be willing to let go, build up emerging leaders, and encourage learning even when that comes through mistakes.

FP 7:   *Validating, affirming, and reinforcing the role of appointed leaders in the local church.*

In a situation in Africa, one cross-cultural worker desired to see transformation come to the entire group. He realized the need for the community to be completely comfortable with the leadership even during the process of beginning to influence them toward a pursuit of God in Christ. He says,

> *Typically what we do is we ask the local people to choose leaders for their jamaa (group). This is before they ever hear about Christ. We initially start working with a community of people that has selected its own leaders so that they have a sense of ownership and being in control. It is naturally indigenous in a number of different ways. This has been both an exciting and a scary group because it's become large very fast. In just about three months the last meeting had about seventy-five adults and about as many children, which raises our profile enormously. It's not something we've actually wanted, but I think that because it is in the hands of the sheikh, his followers naturally show up and feel comfortable. Basically, they run the meeting. One of us will go and read some Scripture, after giving some background information, and then hand the discussion back to the sheikh to lead. This is a person who's never heard about Jesus from us. But he has said some very amazing things* ("Empowering Existing Leaders," Interview #19, Spring 2007).

Another similar group is now truly following Jesus and has begun to follow the same model to influence others.

The subject of control by cross-cultural workers came up often at the Consultation. A completely hands-off approach was found to be counterproductive by one participant. But many talked about the need for letting go of authority and a willingness to let new local leadership take ownership and initiative. Comments included the following:

We are still developing the leaders. I think it is fine to let local leaders make mistakes. Are we prepared to let local leaders make mistakes?

It is impossible at times to control how they are leading, and we need to back off even if we don't agree (North Africa) (Small Group Discussion, Spring 2007).

FP 8:   Helping the newly-gathered MBB community to choose their leaders wisely.

The selection of leaders is very important. One of the more significant questions that came up was concerning who chooses leaders for young communities of faith. In fact, a great deal of the discussion in the small groups focused on this and questioned the original wording of this practice since it could sound like outsiders have too much influence on this. Often, cross-cultural workers would choose leaders based on ideals of leadership from their home cultures, which could have disastrous results. Therefore, one participant suggested an alternate wording for this practice: "Purposefully studying the local structure of leadership and the local approach to leadership in order to be culturally appropriate in the selection of leaders" (Small Group Discussion, Spring 2007).

In a case from North Africa, cross-cultural workers were involved in choosing leaders for the fellowship. Since the older members were less literate and less willing, the expatriates looked to younger members for leadership, feeling that this was better than the outsiders leading. One younger man appeared suitable since he could read, was engaged in Bible study, and took initiative. However, after mishandling some money loaned to him, he failed to repent and to respond to discipline at which point both his leadership and his own faith unraveled ("Lessons Learned from Discipline in a Shame/Honor Culture," Interview #38, Spring 2007).

Could this have been avoided if the local believers had been wisely coached in choosing their own leader (e.g., showing them what God's Word says about the kind of leaders they need)? Would character issues and previous history have been more quickly discerned?

CONCLUSION

God seems to be bringing certain emphases into focus in the leadership of faith communities. Several key practices are proving fruitful, especially in the beginning of community formation. The character of a person is very crucial in the selection of those who will serve to build up the community. Careful consideration of a particular context is necessary for wisely choosing leaders, and for deciding how and where they will be trained. Jesus gave us an excellent example of forming leaders by modeling and handing off his authority, resulting in their personal growth and multiplication. As mentioned in the beginning of this chapter, we understand all things through a particular lens. To apply these fruitful practices, we need to be willing to lay aside our own lens and try to observe leadership with a new perspective.

Chapter 12

The Gathering of Teams of Laborers

ANDREW AND RACHEL CHARD

"'The harvest is plentiful, but the laborers are few;
therefore ask the Lord of the harvest to send out laborers into his harvest.'
Then Jesus summoned twelve disciples ..."
Matthew 9:37–10:1

Jesus began a certain story, "For the kingdom of heaven is like a landowner who went out early in the morning to hire men to work in his vineyard" (Matthew 20:1–16)[110] and that story is as poignant today as it was when he told it all those years ago. God has called us from different backgrounds and at different times to join those who would work for him, offering us all the same promises irrespective of when we join the work. As we reach into the lives of Muslims with the Gospel, we are part of that very story: the story of redemption in which God enlists people to work "in his vineyard," working to bring in his harvest. Witness, discipleship, and church planting are all part of that work, demanding cooperation; we believe that the natural medium for that is teamwork.

Team ministry was widely represented at the Consultation in Southeast Asia with participants representing 2,231 team members, offering us different models for consideration. Teamwork in ministry is hardly new! For centuries

---

[110] The importance of gathering a team of workers is noted in the parable even as the account goes on to focus on another aspect of the story.

such movements all over the world have begun with teams of pioneers striking off into new territory, whether as 'tent-makers' or as people more openly associated with traditional Christian ministries of word and deed.

Teams of church planters are better equipped than 'lone rangers' to reach remote people in difficult places, no matter how committed people on their own might be. The overwhelming witness of the Consultation's research is that in the bringing together of people with different gifts for the appointed task, there are numerous benefits that both bear fruit and lighten the load on individuals.

In this chapter we will look at significant factors in the formation and the life of fellowship or church-planting teams amongst Muslims, keeping the goal of church-planting movements in mind, and drawing on the accounts of the participants in the Consultation.

THE FORMATION OF TEAMS

FRUITFUL PRACTICES:
1. *Identifying the right leadership for the team.*
2. *Aiming for a large enough team.*
3. *Having members with a variety of gifts for the task.*

Teams do not just happen. The reality is still that the laborers are too few and they need to be intentionally brought together to create effective teams. Evidence shows that there are many factors involved in this information, so we shall look at some of the fruitful practices.

FP 1:   *Identifying the right leadership for the team (99% considered important, 86% practiced).*[111]

Across the regions represented at the Consultation, it was agreed that team leaders need to be wisely chosen, not left to fall into positions by default. When chosen by sending agencies or associated organizations, the team members can be added to the team with understanding of how that team needs to function in

---

[111]   Here and subsequently, such a notation will indicate that 99 percent of the participants felt that the practice was important or very important and 86 percent practiced it.

its target setting. One example is TIMO,[112] an organization that chooses people who have had significant experience in the mission field to lead a team of relative/complete newcomers through the learning process of entering an under-evangelized field with church planting in mind. A chosen leader may or may not have experience in the actual proposed setting, but their experience of the wider field can be hugely beneficial, as expressed at the Consultation by field workers in some of the most difficult places.

A second model is that the choice of leaders is made by the team, but this can only really work once the team members know one another well and are able to make an informed choice. One team reported that in their case a potential team leader worked with them for six months to see if the match was right, recognizing that experience was not the only issue, but that the potential for fruitfulness would become more obvious with time spent together in their setting.

THE QUALITIES PRACTITIONERS SAID THEY WANTED IN A LEADER:

- *An evangelistic heart*
- *Vision*
- *Faith*
- *Prayerfulness*
- *Ability to recognize gifts in others*
- *Praiseworthy character*
- *Experience*
- *Passion*
- *Ability to delegate*
- *Servanthood*
- *Love of people*
- *Availability*

Situations varying as they do, it might be that teams arise out of expatriate settings, or out of groups of committed nationals who share a burden for a place or a people. It is widely recognized that longevity on the field is not necessarily a positive factor and that there are various characteristics to be desired in team leaders.

---

[112] Training In Ministry Outreach (TIMO), a church-planting training program under Africa Inland Mission that seeks to combine training of inexperienced missionaries with gaining access to unreached or under-reached areas. In October 2007, there were thirty-two teams in a wide variety of settings. In 2005, after twenty years of TIMO teams, between 75 percent and 80 percent of alumni were still in service on the field. See www.timo-aim.com.

Recruitment of team members is no less an important factor as these will be the bulk of laborers for the given task, involving men and women of various ages. While acknowledging that every team will have its specific task in its specific setting, we need to ask what team member characteristics are commonly needed for a fruitful team ministry amongst Muslims? From the consultation research, we see that the following factors are most important.

FP 2:   Aiming for a large enough team.

This implies that team size matters, and it does. The average team size of consultation participants was nine adults (the number being raised by a few very large teams) although the majority of teams were less than nine in size. Team size in itself is not the key to fruitfulness, but a survey of the teams represented at the Consultation indicated the following:

» Teams with fewer than four adults showed a greater probability of *not* planting even one fellowship or church.
» Teams with eight or more adults had a greater probability of planting at least one fellowship.
» Teams with twelve adults showed a greater probability of planting multiple fellowships.

It would seem, therefore, that if our desire is to see church-planting movements, we need to be aiming for larger numbers of laborers in each team, supporting the strategy of sowing widely. Research suggests that five or six team members should be the lower limit of a team size.[113]

FP 3:   Having members with a variety of gifts for the task (99% considered important, 88% practiced).

It is common sense to form a team consisting of members with different, yet needed, gifts.

---

[113]   Preliminary Summary of FP track by Knowledge Stewardship Team, September 26, 2007.

AS SOMEONE WORKING WITH A DIFFICULT PEOPLE GROUP IN
KENYA WROTE, "GOD MAY USE ONE PERSON TO DRAW MUSLIMS
CLOSE, ANOTHER TO LEAD THEM TO FAITH, ANOTHER TO
DISCIPLE THEM. WE DON'T HAVE TO DO EVERYTHING!"

Once again there are different models. Some organizations do not actually go to the field until a team has been put together. Leaders are selected and then the team is recruited, all before entering the field of ministry. Another model is that new personnel go to the field and join either an existing team, or join a group of others who in their own time form a team. However it is done, though, teams should be constructed wisely with the task in mind.

IN EACH PLACE, ONE PARTICULAR BALANCE OF GIFTEDNESS MAY
BE BETTER THAN ANOTHER. A WORKER FROM THE MIDDLE EAST
WRITES THAT BRINGING IN TOO MANY WORKERS WITH TEACHING
OR PASTORAL GIFTS CAUSES STRUGGLES; IT IS BETTER THAT THEY
COME AS EVANGELISTS. FROM THE ARAB WORLD, A WORKER
REPORTS THAT A COMBINATION OF SPIRITUAL AND PRACTICAL
GIFTS WAS CRITICAL TO TEAM UNITY AND FUNCTIONING IN
THEIR MINISTRY SETTING. THIS IS ECHOED BY MANY PRESENTLY
SERVING IN MUSLIM FIELDS.

Team leaders and members of church-planting teams should be prepared to embrace a wide variety of ministry within one team, freeing team members up to work where their gifts and passions lie, but keeping all that the team does connected to the vision. There needs to be recognition that working within one's skill set will energize workers, while working outside one's skill set often leads to early attrition.

> **FRUITFUL PRACTICES:**
> 4. *Recognizing that women are essential members of the team and serve effectively.*
> 5. *Valuing language learning proficiency (especially in the local or heart language over the trade language) and culture adaptation.*
> 6. *Valuing prayer and a growing walk with God.*
> 7. *Having a vision and focused intention.*
> 8. *Being flexible in strategy and willing to adapt and modify.*

FP 4:   *Recognizing that women are essential members of the team and serve effectively (97% considered important, 92% practiced).*

Not only do women have significant roles in the team structure, but in the Muslim world, they have access to women and children even while men are restricted in this area. Also, women team members are usually able to talk at a deeper level with Muslim women much sooner than male team members are able to with Muslim men.[114]

FP 5:   *Valuing language learning proficiency (especially in the local heart language over the trade language) and culture adaptation (99% considered important, 95% practiced).*

Across the world where people are seeking to reach Muslims with the Gospel, field workers are committing themselves to learning the language of the hearers, and of consultation participants a majority use the heart language of the target people as opposed to a trade language. Many people find language-learning an uphill struggle, but most of us would also say that every ounce of effort is worthwhile. Language-learning takes us into the culture, not just as we draw close to the people to use the language but also as the language itself reveals cultural truths and even cultural secrets. One worker said, "Language is a must. Without language you are not reaching the heart of the people." Yet another said, "I have been a language coach for many years and have found that lack of language really affects the effectiveness of the member." Tom and Betty

---

[114] See chapter 5.

Brewster, who pioneered the LAMP method of language learning, coined the phrase, "Language learning is ministry": one that has echoed in our own ears for all the years we have been on the field.[115]

The message from the cross-cultural worker reaching out to Muslims is that language is an essential practice because it is fruitful. The reality is that the attrition rate in workers who do not learn the language well is faster than for those who do. One vulnerable group are mothers with young children, who frequently struggle to get out and learn language well. Having said that, those who are not good with languages should not lose heart, for within fellowship-planting teams there needs to be an acceptance that different people have different aptitudes. The mutual accountability must still be there, but tempered by this understanding and driven by a strong desire for each team member to succeed by reaching their potential. We need to look carefully at how we go about learning language, embracing methods that are truly practical for the majority of people.[116] It is important for a team to include at least one member of High Language Skill (HLS). Based on a survey of the 280 practitioners from around the world and the 738 MBB communities and the 5,800 field workers then represented, there was a 43 percent probability that a team with at least one HLS member, having incorporated learning preferences (oral or written) into team strategy and working in the local language, would have planted multiple churches and an 83 percent probability of having planted at least one church. Without those three ingredients, there was shown to be a 93 percent probability that not even one church will be planted.[117] Obviously, many other factors influence any given situation.

The issue has been raised that in some ministry settings the local people do not want others to learn their language. It may be that they are suspicious of motives, or that they closely guard their language, not wanting it to be understood by others. This will demand great sensitivity and patience as God softens their hearts to feel good about their language being learned. In some cases, other reasons overrule the normal language-learning practice.

---

[115] Language Acquisition Made Practical (LAMP). This method keeps people right in the ministry setting and frequently enables even the very timid language learner to succeed. See www.instantweb.com/linguahouse.

[116] In addition to the LAMP method above, PILAT and SIL also have good pre-field language acquisition courses.

[117] Preliminary Summary of FP track by Knowledge Stewardship Team, September 26, 2007.

SOME PEOPLE WORKING IN SOUTHEAST ASIA WERE FACED WITH
THE REALITY THAT THEIR TARGET PEOPLE DID NOT WANT THEM
TO LEARN THEIR LANGUAGE BUT WANTED BADLY TO LEARN
ENGLISH. THE TEAM DECIDED TO CHANGE THEIR STRATEGY OF
LANGUAGE LEARNING AND BEGAN TO MINISTER IN AND TEACH
ENGLISH INSTEAD, RESULTING IN FRUITFULNESS. THIS WAS A
KIND OF 'REVERSE ADAPTATION' OF THEMSELVES AND THEIR
APPROACH TO ADAPT TO THE FELT NEEDS OF THE PEOPLE.
(DISCUSSION GROUP, SPRING 2007)

If the whole point is communication of the Gospel to Muslim peoples, then we need to do whatever is best to communicate.

Cultural adaptation is certainly attached to language learning, but how teams adapt is going to vary from ministry setting to ministry setting. Scripture urges us to move cross-culturally in order to win other for Christ (1 Corinthians 9:20–23), but not surprisingly, there is considerable breadth to how this is applied. Some Gospel workers assume the local dress and the daily habits of the local people to a high level, while others do so just a little to demonstrate unity with them and yet choose to retain individual freedom. Of course, identification with local people means more than outward appearances and may well demand an alteration in the way we think—for example, about time, possessions, and personal space—but each place is unique. No culture stands still and fruitful church planters will be sensitive to changing values in their communities, needing wisdom from God as to how to deal with those changes. One field worker writes that she has needed, over time, to find a balance between living the way of the local people and yet having some personal space to maintain sanity and to be able to be fruitful over the long haul.

FP 6:   *Valuing prayer and a growing walk with God.*

This was expressed in various ways:

» Practicing an intimate walk with God (99 percent considered important, 95 percent practiced);

» Involvement in sustained prayer, fasting, and spiritual warfare (99 percent considered important, 75 percent practiced); and

» Mobilizing extensive international, focused prayer (99 percent considered important, 74.5 percent practiced).

GODLINESS IS MORE IMPORTANT THAN STRIVING TO REACH MINISTRY GOALS.

At the Consultation, there was strong agreement that teams need to be made up of people of spiritual maturity who practice an intimate walk with God and who are committed to growing godly character as individuals and as teams, not just seeing goals reached. One team leader writes, "We bring two coaches in twice a year to provide accountability for our spiritual walk," and another worker writes, "We need to build accountability structures in all we do and model."

FP 7: *Having a vision and focused intention (98% considered important, 92% practiced).*

A Memorandum of Understanding or similar document lessens the myriad of potential distractions. A worker from East Africa said, "As an ongoing team, we have a Memorandum of Understanding, which states our vision and our goals. We have written down our core values and our commitment to one another as team members. All these things help us to hang together when there are struggles within the team or when there are discouragements in ministry that might otherwise entice us to give up."

As teams understand their context better or as the context changes, this leads to a complementary practice:

FP 8: *Being flexible in strategy and willing to adapt and modify (99% considered important, 93% practiced).*

FOSTERING FRUITFULNESS IN TEAMS

> **FRUITFUL PRACTICES:**
> 9. *Surveying and assessing the needs of the people, profiling their identity and the status of the Gospel.*
> 10. *Building a team mentality.*
> 11. *Demonstrating love for the people.*
> 12. *Partnering with others for fruitfulness.*

There are a number of practices that have fostered fruitfulness in teams.

FP 9:   *Surveying and assessing the needs of the people, profiling their identity and the status of the Gospel (96% considered important, 65% practiced).*

There is significant benefit in getting such an overview of the host people before beginning any king of ministry among them. Of course, living with them will provide the most information on a local level, but church-planting teams would do well to understand also the overall status of the people group. There are organizations that do just this, with prepared questionnaires for carrying out the survey.[118]

FP 10:   *Building a team mentality.*

Getting to know one another well and learning to care deeply for one other needs to be worked on consistently. Of course, team building takes many forms, some made possible pre-field and others not until in the field.[119] Time needs to be invested in orientation and in learning how team members think and feel, how they express themselves (or do not), and how they react to different personalities. This will be largely the job of the team leaders who will often find their team members to be ready and willing but also sensitive to being hurt while perhaps being insensitive to hurting others, the common combination of people in culture shock. Of course, location contributes a lot to how

---

[118]   See, e.g., TIMO (www.timo-aim.com) and CAPRO, a global movement of African origin (www.capromissions.org).
[119]   See Richard Scoggins, *Building Effective Church Planting Teams: A Handbook for Team Leaders and Mentors,* http://www.dickscoggins.com/books/teams.php.

team building can happen, but for many team members, knowing that within the team there is to be mutual support, love, respect, and accountability from the start can provide solidarity and comfort at a time when much of life is changing dramatically. Moreover, establishing mutuality within the team means that as time goes by, there will be more naturally a sharing of one another's triumphs and the carrying of one another's burdens.

Someone working as part of a team in a closed country wrote, "Whenever anybody won a victory or had an opportunity to share the Gospel with somebody ...it refreshed all of us no matter how much difficulty we were personally experiencing."

As in 1 Corinthians 13, the chief quality in building a team mentality is love, which leads to the next fruitful practice.

> FP 11:   *Demonstrating love for the people (99% considered important, 96% practiced). The team needs to be put together for love; leadership must be servant-like; all of the team's ministry must arise out of love. Our love must show the uniqueness of God's love through Christ.*

Showing the love of God through acts of kindness, community development projects, or in the day-to-day shared living with Muslim people does not go unnoticed. Acting and living in love show followers of Jesus to be different from other people. When we actively seek ways to demonstrate love—especially for the unloved—they ask what it is that drives us to do such things. Over and over again, fellowship-planting teams testify about how Muslims have first been drawn to learn about Christ because his followers demonstrate that their belief in him makes them more loving.

Fruitful practices 5, 6, and 7 above also contribute to the quality of fruitfulness in teams, as do various forms of partnering.

> FP 12:   *Partnering with others for fruitfulness:*

> » *Partnering with Muslim leaders, such as a "man or woman of peace"* (87 percent considered important, 51 percent practiced).

One strategy that some see as very effective for church-planting teams involves finding a 'man or a woman of peace' (based on the principle in Matthew 10:11) or someone in the locality who might be called a 'fire-starter', that is, one who is well respected and has the ear of the people or one who has the ability to get things going in their communities (96 percent considered important, 60 percent practiced). There was a strong objection by many at the Consultation to the idea of actual 'partnering' with non-believers, but many see value in building relationships with influential people, whether their influence be social, religious, or political. Undoubtedly, a good relationship with authorities based on openness and mutual respect is of great value in many contexts. Being good friends with Muslim leaders can be a huge blessing, fostering greater respect for one another, which builds bridges for communication of the Gospel.

ONE PARTICIPANT WROTE,
"WE HAD A MUSLIM MAN WHO WAS INTENSELY
INTERESTED IN JESUS. HE LOVED JESUS AND HAD THE RESPECT
OF MANY PEOPLE IN THE COMMUNITY. HE STARTED TELLING
PEOPLE ABOUT THE *INJIL* (GOSPEL). WE DID NOT SEEK HIM;
GOD GAVE HIM TO US."

» *Partnering with same-culture or near-culture evangelists who share the vision* (94% considered important, 74% practiced).

They bring with them a much deeper level of understanding than expatriates often have, while generally avoiding the pitfalls that seem to accompany the presence of expatriates. We do need to recognize that this practice is not always without significant pitfalls, and in practice statistics indicate that in regions of the world where there is a mature national church, for example in parts of Africa or in the Philippines, partnering with national evangelists occurs a great deal more than elsewhere. In some places, however, barriers have arisen between the national church and Muslims that are hard to overcome from either direction.

Consider this story from the Consultation of a fruitful church-planting team in Southeast Asia, made up of one expatriate worker and various national workers. It demonstrates the fruitfulness in their setting of working with near-culture witnesses (including MBBs), gives a different model for team formation, and demonstrates team building:

> *Three and a half years ago, a missionary who has been involved in Asia for forty years began to work with a team of three Southeast Asian women, one of whom was an MBB. He was involved in their recruitment but then took on the role of a facilitator/coach, while remaining completely absent from the church-planting setting. A national mission organization oversaw the women's administration, fund-raising, accountability, and communication with their home churches. Initially he worked with them on vision and strategy, also involving the national mission organization. It was very much a team approach and yet he met with the women only three or four times a year for team-building, vision-casting, interpersonal mentoring, and to hear news of what was going on and what fruit they were seeing.*

> *The team has used what the expatriate calls a Transformational Development Model, which involves community health, literacy, and community mobilization, bringing in national groups to help with those areas where the team lacked the needed expertise. This model created a platform through community development for entering the area and then for planting fellowships, the goal being to raise the level of health and education and to mobilize the community to be involved in its own development, while planting fellowships. Without this, their religious activities would have been strongly rejected.*

> *With time, the national mission organization increased their responsibility for the women, and the expatriate took even more of a back seat. The beauty of this model is that in keeping expatriates out of the picture, it has allowed for indigenization to occur more naturally. As the development took place, so too did the church planting, resulting in two small house fellowships being established in the two primary communities, where previously there had been no Christian witness. People from two other communities have asked for the team to come to them, too.*
>
> *Having provided know-how in the early days without which they could not have done the job, the expatriate is now mostly superfluous.*

This is a model that deserves serious consideration by those who have been field workers for a long time, know the language and culture, and have much to offer in terms of advice and support.

Of course, in many Muslim ministry settings there can be few same-culture evangelists (at least for some time) and near-culture evangelists may actually have prejudices and conditioning (or be perceived as having such behavior by local people) that is counter-productive to the work rather than helpful for it. The Consultation brought to light evidence that sometimes, if the near-culture evangelists are in fact Christian Background Believers (CBBs), the cross-cultural jump can be too big even for willing workers who have not been well trained in cross-cultural ministry. But of course this is not always the case, and 'near-culture' is a broad term. Others point out that it can be more fruitful to work only with the believers in the emerging Christian community rather than bringing in people who are still relative outsiders.

» *Partnering with other agencies* (92 percent considered important, 85 percent practiced).

How much a team will partner with others will depend partly on how much freedom is allowed by the government. It does seem rather obvious to us that it is fruitful to make use of other people's expertise, for example, in translation work, community development, or education. It does need to be said, though, that even if formal partnership is not happening, communication between agencies is imperative. There is little worse than discovering that another agency is doing either the same work targeting the same people or the same area—sometimes with disastrous consequences—or that the work of one agency is undermining the work of another. These problems are exacerbated if the agencies are working in close proximity, possibly even working from a common base.

A FIELD WORKER WRITES THAT SOMEONE FROM EACH AGENCY IN HIS OR HER LOCALITY WOULD GET TOGETHER AND SWAP INFORMATION AND MATERIALS, BRING NEWS OF PROJECTS, AND GIVE TESTIMONIES OF WHAT WAS HAPPENING IN HIS OR HER MINISTRY. IT WAS A VERY POSITIVE RELATIONSHIP WITH ENCOURAGEMENT FOR EVERYBODY INVOLVED.

In Central Asia, four agencies came to the realization that it could be very fruitful to work together, sharing resources and personnel, acknowledging that they shared much the same vision for their work. They asked the question, why would they start four networks of house-churches when they could work together on planting one network? They drew up basic guidelines for the network, drawing their work together in unity and yet making allowance for some of the theological differences represented by the agencies, recognizing that it did not matter if there were some variations in some of the churches' theological positions and in so doing crossed both agency and denominational barriers. As one agency has moved location, the others have stepped in and picked up the agency's responsibilities. If personnel have gone on furlough, others within the network have done their best to fill the gaps, allowing for an almost seamless flow among the four agencies. The result has been significant fruitfulness in church planting.

» *Partnering with local churches* (87 percent considered important, 62.5 percent practiced).

There is evidence of benefit in, where possible, bringing the local ministry to Muslims under or in association with a local church while being free to keep the vision and required identity of the church-planting work. There is agreement that 'local' national pastors like to be involved alongside expatriate efforts, able to advise and assist where possible, but this issue is also fraught with problems and questions. Where there are big cultural differences between the believers of existing churches and the Muslims to whom a witness is occurring, a point of healthy contact can be hard to find. Unless those very churches themselves become charged with passion for Muslims, there often seems little chance of being able to integrate MBBs into the existing congregations/cell groups. It does happen—one person tells of a local church that "has been mobilized to become a community of belonging for MBBs," but the reality is that other CBB groups just do not seem to be able to get the point about the need to make some changes to welcome MBBs. One suggestion made by various people is that instead of partnership with whole churches, church-planting teams should find individuals within them who will join the work among Muslims. An MBB points out that even if there are risks in getting local churches too involved, it is possible to get them involved in praying for the outreach to Muslims, but from his experience, he warns that care is needed, and it depends very much on the context of the work. This also applies to partnering with a national church, for example, a denomination that exists within the country of ministry that may or may not have a 'local' church in the specific ministry area.

CONCLUSION

With all that we see in the media, it is not surprising that reaching out to Muslims with the Gospel is seen by many as the work of a few brave men and women, but this is so unfortunate! While the task does present its particular challenges and even dangers, it also offers us a chance to move among people who by and large are people of principle and honor, sincerely committed to their religious teaching. Although we have some significant differences in understandings, there is much that many of us can learn from Muslims, and many who have spent time living with them testify to much that is good and godly in the Muslim worldview.

Having said that, leaving one's home or comfort zone is rarely without struggle, and in fact Jesus gave a special promise of blessing to those who are separated for the sake of the Gospel (Matthew 19:29). Accepting this struggle to be normal for people from all cultures and backgrounds, it does not surprise us that God has given us ways to deal with it. We believe that after the significance of having the Word of God to teach us and being indwelt by the Spirit of God as our counselor and guide, the next greatest provision for us as 'workers in God's vineyard' is the concept of teamwork. Have we not seen in this chapter how working as a team brings strength and ability for the task? Can we not see how much good sense it makes to work in teams whenever possible? No, it will not be problem-free, and team members will not always feel that their team is the best they could have. However, what better way is there to combine strength and skills, passion and wisdom, to blend differentness with grace, in order to bring fruitfulness—in order to bring in the harvest?

Part 3

Emerging Issues in
Fruitful Practices:
Birds, Rocks, Sun, and Soil

Chapter 13

Factors Affecting the Identity That Jesus-followers Choose

JOHN AND ANNA TRAVIS,
WITH CONTRIBUTIONS BY PHIL PARSHALL

*"Day by day, as they spent much time together in the temple,
they broke bread at home and ate their food with glad and generous
hearts, praising God and having the goodwill of all the people."*
Acts 2:46–47

Historically, very few from the world's mega-religions of Islam, Hinduism, and Buddhism have ever become followers of Jesus.[120] Today, however, compared with other eras, larger numbers of Muslims have turned in faith to Jesus. This phenomenon has resulted in the formation of many hundreds of Muslim background Christ-centered fellowships (*ekklesia*) worldwide. In the 1990s a simple tool was developed, the C1–C6 continuum, to describe six types of these fellowships presently seen in the Muslim world.[121] The purpose of this chapter is to identify some of the factors that appear to be influencing the type of fellow-

---

120 For the first 2,000 years of church history, virtually all who have come to Christ, whether from Europe, Asia, or Africa, have been animists or worshippers of localized national or ethnic deities. Few have ever come to faith from the huge, ancient mega-faiths. In the words of David Bosch, "by and large, Christianity has not been very successful among those people who are adherents to what often ...is termed the great religions—Islam, Hinduism, Buddhism, etc." David Bosch, *Transforming Mission* (Maryknoll, NY: Orbis Books, 1991), 477.

121 See Phil Parshall, "Danger! New Directions in Contextualization," *Evangelical Missions Quarterly* 43, no. 4 (1998): 404–406, 409–410; John Travis, "The C1–C6 Spectrum?" *Evangelical Missions Quarterly* 34, no. 4 (1998): 411–15; John Travis, "Must all Muslims Leave Islam to Follow Jesus?" *Evangelical Missions Quarterly* 34, no. 4 (1998): 411–15.

ship, in terms of the C1–C6 continuum (henceforth referred to as the C-scale), that Muslims either join or form once they know and begin to follow Jesus.[122] We present these factors with several caveats.

The C1–C6 Continuum: Six Types of Christ-Centered Communities Found in the Muslim World					
C1	**C2**	**C3**	**C4**	**C5**	**C6**
Traditional church using a language different from the mother tongue of the local Muslim community	Traditional church using the mother tongue of the local Muslim community	Contextualized Christ-centered community using the mother tongue and some non-Muslim local cultural forms	Contextualized Isa-centered community using the mother tongue and biblically acceptable socio-religious Islamic forms	Community of Muslims who follow Isa yet remain culturally and officially Muslim	Secret or underground Muslim followers of Isa with little or no community

Fig. 13.1

First, though greater numbers of Muslims have decided to follow Jesus than ever before, the number of these new believers is still very small in comparison to the Muslim population worldwide (at least 1.3 billion). With so many millions of Muslims yet outside the knowledge of Jesus, all should be circumspect when drawing conclusions at this point in history. Second, in this chapter we are writing about Muslims who have chosen to follow Jesus *primarily* as a call of God on their lives (even though some political, ethnic, or socio-religious realities may have secondarily contributed to the decision). As many have noted, this call of God often comes about in part through dreams, visions, miraculous answers to

---

122 Numerous articles have appeared on the topic of the cultural factors that impact forms of witness and worship in Muslims contexts. By the late 1970s, all positions along what may now be described as the C-scale had been articulated in seminal articles. See John D.C. Anderson, "The Missionary Approach to Islam: Christian or 'Cultic'?" *Missiology: An International Review* 4, no. 3 (1976): 258–99; John W. Wilder, "Possibilities for People Movements Among Muslims," *Missiology: An International Review* 5, no. 3 (1977); Harvey M. Conn, "The Muslim Convert and his Culture," in *The Gospel and Islam: A Compendium*, ed. Don McCurry, abr. ed., 79–113 (Monrovia, CA: MARC, 1979); Charles H. Kraft, "Dynamic Equivalence Churches in Muslim Society," in *The Gospel and Islam: A Compendium*, ed. Don McCurry, abr. ed., 114–28 (Monrovia, CA: MARC, 1979). Two later key works to appear were Phil Parshall, *New Paths in Muslim Evangelism* (Grand Rapids, MI: Baker Book House, 1980); and J. Dudley Woodberry, "Contextualization among Muslims: Reusing Common Pillars," in *The Word among Us*, ed. Dean Gilliland, 282–312 (Dallas, TX: Word Publishing, 1989).

prayer, and personal study of the *Injil* (the New Testament).[123] Third, although we are looking at a macro-view involving factors, trends, and statistics, it is with a profound sense of awe and reverence that we do so. We realize that what God does in the Muslim world comes down to what God does in each Muslim heart. Our hearts resonate with these words of Jean-Marie Gaudeul:[124]

> *My first thought is a sense of wonder at God's ways of leading people toward a real, live encounter with himself. We are treading on holy ground as we examine the extraordinary variety of personal experiences through which God revealed his tenderness and love to so many millions of human beings. Each human conscience is a holy temple where the Lord meets his children and draws them to himself.[125]*

Fourth, we will endeavor not to mention countries, ethnic groups, or numbers in ways that could cause anyone harm. With statistics, we mention only very general numbers such as hundreds or thousands. With these four caveats in mind, we now turn our attention to some findings of the 2007 Global Trends and Fruitful Practices Consultation (GTFP Consultation).

Some Findings from the 2007 GTFP Consultation

Participants at the recent 2007 GTFP Consultation, who have worked among Muslims and seen fellowships planted, met for several days to share their experiences. Each participant was asked to state the number and types of fellowship(s), in terms of the C-scale, that they have seen planted or were involved in planting in the countries where they worked. The results confirmed what many had suspected. Hundreds of fellowships are being formed; all positions along the C-scale are represented. C1 was the primary type of fellowship for 1 percent of participants, C2 for 5 percent, C3 for 28 percent, C4 for 37 percent, C5

---

123   J. Dudley Woodberry, Russell G. Shubin and G. Marks, "Why Muslims Follow Jesus," *Christianity Today* 51, no. 10 (2007): 80–85. Woodberry et al. have collected approximately 750 questionnaires from Muslim background believers (MBBs) from thirty countries and fifty ethnic groups focusing on their reasons for following Christ. The findings indicated that dreams and visions were an important factor in their decision to follow Jesus with 27 percent having a dream or vision before they accepted Jesus, 40 percent at the time of accepting Jesus and 45 percent after they had accepted Jesus.

124   Jean-Marie Gaudeul has collected and analyzed histories of approximately 100 MBB men and women of all ages from twenty different countries. See *Called from Islam to Christ* (East Sussex, UK: Monarch Books, 1999).

125   "Learning From God's Ways," in *From the Straight Path to the Narrow Way*, ed. David Greenlee (Waynesboro, GA: Authentic, 2006), 81.

for 21 percent, and C6 for 8 percent (percentages are rounded to the nearest whole number). This shows that for the majority of cross-cultural workers in attendance (86 percent), the nature of the work on which they reported falls into the C3–C5 range. The data indicate no significant difference in terms of fruitfulness (number of fellowships reported per participant) among those in the C3–C5 range. Characteristics associated with emerging movements were most strongly seen in C4 and C5 work. We now turn to factors that appear to influence the type of fellowship in terms of the C-scale that Muslims either join or form once they begin to follow Christ.

Factors That Impact the Context of MBBs

Ideally within Muslim societies, religion, culture, and politics form a united, integrated whole. As Martin Goldsmith states:

Islam is within the whole warp and woof of society—in the family, in politics, in social relationships. To leave the Muslim faith is to break with one's society. Many a modern, educated Muslim is not all that religiously minded; but he must, nevertheless, remain a Muslim for social reasons, and also because it is the basis for his political belief. This makes it almost unthinkable for most Muslims even to consider the possibility of becoming a follower of some other religion.[126]

Yet in spite of this idealized unity within Islam, numerous political, social, cultural, religious, and historical factors impact individual Muslim contexts at the ground level, determining in part the ways in which Muslim background believers (MBBs) in Jesus[127] follow Christ.[128]

---

[126] "Community and Controversy: Key Causes of Muslim Resistance," *Missiology: An International Review* 4, no. 3 (1976): 318.

[127] In this chapter, we use the term MBB for believers from a Muslim background who have decided to leave Islam as they follow Christ as well as for Muslim believers (sometimes referred to as MBs) who have decided to follow Jesus from inside Islam.

[128] Some of the factors mentioned in this chapter, based on the authors' observations, overlap with the five circumstances described by J. Dudley Woodberry that tend to create openness for the Gospel. These five circumstances are political factors (especially resurgent Islam), natural catastrophes coupled with the loving response given by Christians, migrations of Muslim populations to new areas, the desire for blessing or power that has been met when healing prayer is offered in Jesus' name, and finally, ethnic and cultural resurgence on the part of some Muslim minorities. "A Global Perspective on Muslims Coming to Faith in Christ," in *From the Straight Path to the Narrow Way*, ed. David Greenlee (Waynesboro, GA: Authentic, 2006), 11–13.

IN SPITE OF THIS IDEALIZED UNITY WITHIN ISLAM, NUMEROUS
POLITICAL, SOCIAL, CULTURAL, RELIGIOUS, AND HISTORICAL
FACTORS IMPACT INDIVIDUAL MUSLIM CONTEXTS AT THE
GROUND LEVEL.

Political factors are multifaceted. Some Muslim societies have secular, demo-cratic governments with relative religious freedom. Some are kingdoms under autocratic rule. Some Islamic countries are under *shari'ah* law where, although seldom enforced, the penalty for conversion to another religion is death. Those who follow God's call to al-Masih (the Messiah) instinctively consider C-scale-type options in light of the political realities of their context. Some become C6 (secret or underground) believers, or to use Gaudeul's term, "catacomb Christians."[129]

Social factors come into play at the grassroots or communal level. How much leeway is there *socially* in a given context to follow al-Masih? In some locations, regardless of the government's stance, the impact on marriage, family, and the immediate circle of relationships is the determining factor in the decision of how to follow Jesus. In some parts of Africa, and in certain areas of Indonesia as well, Muslims and Christians live side by side, at times one family having both Christian and Muslim members.[130] In other settings, leaving Islam is tantamount to social suicide resulting in divorce, loss of one's children (if a mother makes this choice), loss of income and status, physical violence, or even honor killing within families. Whereas a hard-line political or social stance in some Muslim countries influences MBBs toward options to the right of C4, it has also been an impetus for some moderate Muslims to turn from Islam and look for other spiritual options, such as are available in C1, C2, or C3.

Closely related to the political and social factors are demographical, histori-cal, and cultural ones. We may be able to imagine how these realities might in-spire MBBs to move toward various places on the C-scale. In any given Islamic milieu, does a significant Christian minority exist? If so, are those Christians open to receiving Muslim background believers as equal members in their

---

129   *Called from Islam to Christ* (East Sussex, UK: Monarch Books, 1999), 264–65, 288.

130   While most of North Africa is Muslim, some parts of West Africa at the village level have this type of diversity and pluralism. While Indonesian ethnic groups tend to embrace one religion as a whole, among two of the Batak groups of Sumatra and among some segments of the Javanese, there appears to be room for an individual to be Muslim or Chris-tian and still be accepted by the community.

fellowships? Are these Christians largely nominal, or do they have a vibrant faith in Christ? Are current Christian–Muslim interactions friendly, distant, or hostile? How long ago did the society embrace Islam, and how intertwined is Islam with the local culture now? Is ethnicity dearest to the people, or has religious identity become the stronger tie that binds? Is there room in a given context for one to be, for example, an authentic Turk, Kazak, Tunisian, or Saudi and not be a Muslim? In some Islamic milieus, this type of pluralism exists to a certain extent; in other places, it is rare or entirely missing.

Closely linked to this are the aspirations and future directions in which Muslims of a particular ethnic group are headed. Are they in a time of innovation, or even trying to break free of a past that, in part, involved Islam?[131] How much has globalization, Westernization, or post-modern thought influenced the society? On the one hand, globalization causes some Muslims to search for spiritual life options outside what they have known. On the other hand, globalization causes many Muslims to deepen their commitment to Islam, longing for a return to the stability of the past.

Ethnic realities also play a part. Some Muslim nations are multi-ethnic; others are relatively mono-cultural. Where several distinct Muslim ethnic groups live side by side, does one group tend to politically, economically, or socially oppress other Muslim groups? This trend is seen today, for example, with some Berbers, many African Muslims, and some Kurds in the Middle East all feeling oppression at the hands of fellow Muslims.

Socio-religious variance is also a contributing factor. Are there mystical Islamic orders led by charismatic leaders, or syncretistic Muslim groups incorporating folk practices into their local expression of Islam? Many Muslims of a Sufi orientation have regarded Isa (Jesus) as the model for life. Not only may the presence of folk or Sufi expressions of Islam open the way for the Gospel, but they may also increase the possibility for new local expressions of Islam, including those centered on Jesus and the Bible (the "previous scriptures" of Islam, the *Taurat*, *Zabur*, and *Injil*).

Another crucial factor is the interaction that the people have with those called 'Christians' in the past. Are the only 'Christians' they have ever known colonial European soldiers and administrators? Has there ever been an authentic,

---

131   This seems to have been the case with numbers of Muslims who were formerly under communist rule in some areas of Eastern Europe and Central Asia.

loving, relevant messenger of the Gospel living in their midst?[132] Is there a Bible in the local language, and does it use the terminology and literary forms of the Muslims? Have Gospel messengers, past or present, communicated a primarily spiritual message focusing on the Good News of the life, death, and resurrection of Jesus for all peoples, or have Muslims essentially heard messages on the superiority of the Christian religion and their need to change religions to be saved?[133] This question is highly relevant because Gospel communicators, whether nationals or expatriates, regardless of the context of a given people, can influence the type of faith that emerges in terms of the C-scale, due to their own personal preferences.[134]

Finally, on an individual level, what has the experience of Islam meant to a particular Muslim? Does he observe noble spiritual pursuit or hypocrisy on the part of his co-religionists? Does she sense safety and spiritual nurture, or overbearing control on the part of Muslims closest to her? Does the Islam he know teach him to live morally in the fear of God? Does the Islam she know insist that she practice occult rituals, even involving overt appeasement of spirits? Did he or she come to faith along with many others, or alone? In addition, God's calling on particular MBBs may influence whether they decide to pioneer Jesus communities inside or outside the religion of their birth, or opt for a new home in an existing community where effective discipleship is well-developed. The following four case studies help illustrate factors described in this section.

A RECENT CASE STUDY

This first case study involves a nation of tens of millions of Muslims who have historically been quite resistant to the Gospel. Christianity, the nominal affiliation of their former Western colonizers, has been perceived as a depraved

---

[132]   A recent survey indicated that the lifestyle and witness of Christian(s) whom MBBs had known personally ranked number one in their decision to follow Jesus. See J. Dudley Woodberry, Russell G. Shubin, and G. Marks, "Why Muslims Follow Jesus," *Christianity Today* 51, no. 10 (2007): 80–85.

[133]   While the issue of religious identification will eventually come up, messengers of the Gospel must emphasize the biblical truth that we are saved by grace through faith in Christ, not by joining a religion per se.

[134]   A case in point of the possible effect of the messenger's C-scale preference is Achmad (pseudonym). Some non-Muslim background believers tirelessly shared the Gospel with him and prayed for him over an extended period. After a supernatural encounter with God, he accepted Christ and became a C1 believer in their church. Years later he learned from others of options to the right of C1 and joined a C4 group. After more time passed, Achmad sensed God's call to join a C5 group, as he deemed it most favorable for reaching family and friends yet outside the full knowledge of Jesus. Other members of his family, however, came to faith and opted for C1. This illustrates that personal preference may vary from individual to individual within the same country, area, neighborhood, or even family, and that the personal preference of messengers can impact C-scale choices of MBBs.

religion, characterized by eating forbidden food, drinking alcohol, and living an immoral life. On the other hand, the *ummah* (community) provides an integrated worldview with Islam at its core, and a solid foundation of self-identity. Being, belonging, and conforming are high societal values in this nation, forming a barrier against any extreme action such as converting to Christianity. Such a change of allegiance would be seen as a denial not only of Islam but also of family, friends, and society in general.

The common local expression of Islam in this particular nation can be characterized as Folk Islam. Muslims readily give allegiance to a holy man, who oversees a grouping of devout disciples, and is regarded as a vice-regent of Allah on earth. He exhibits supernatural powers of healing and exorcism. Finally, a shrine is built over his coffin where an annual pilgrimage takes place on the anniversary of his death. There is an ongoing tension between the minority of fundamentalist Muslims and the majority of folk Muslims. Only in recent days have the orthodox begun to have an impact on the population in their call to move toward a *shari'ah*-based interpretation of Islam.

A few decades ago in this nation, a devastating internal disturbance aligned Muslim against Muslim. Thousands of co-religionists were murdered and raped, and their houses burned. This brutality caused many to seriously question the validity of their personal religious allegiance to Islam.

Around this time, a team of cross-cultural expatriates began a new work to invite Muslims to follow al-Masih. Perhaps the most important help to this effort was the production of a Muslim-friendly translation of the New Testament. Prior to this, the only Bible translation available used non-Muslim vocabulary, making it largely distasteful and irrelevant to Muslim readers. Distribution teams of national Christians worked throughout the country, selling the Muslim-friendly Scriptures at a reasonable price. The stage was being set for a movement to Christ.

It was stated that on average, only two Muslims had turned to Christ per year over the past fifty years in this country. Obviously, radical rethinking was imperative. The urgent question before the team was how to contextualize the Gospel message while maintaining biblical fidelity. A Muslim entering one of the country's Western-style, non-Muslim background, minority national fellowships would find many rituals either unfamiliar or repugnant, or both: no provision for washing before prayer; people worshipping with their shoes on, sitting on pews; no prostration before almighty God; no one praying toward Mecca; singing instead of chanting; a sense that church members were uncomfortable in the presence of non-Christian-background people.

ON AVERAGE, ONLY TWO MUSLIMS HAD TURNED TO CHRIST PER YEAR OVER THE PAST FIFTY YEARS IN THIS COUNTRY.

In Islam, form and meaning are closely aligned. The team in this case study made a decision to retain old forms as much as possible, but inject them with biblical meanings. With the exception of directional praying, all of the above were quite easily adopted into the worship schema of the emerging MBB fellowships.

Because of the Muslim perception of the word "Christian," a suitable alternative was sought. "Followers of Isa" became a designation that was appreciated. This moved the focus from an unappreciated label ("Christian") to Isa himself, whom Muslims revere as a prophet. Currently, many MBBs simply refer to themselves as "believers."

Solving the issue of baptism was a huge task, not yet entirely resolved. Since Muslims regard Christian baptism as a moment of forsaking one's religion, family, and friends, the team pondered an alternative. Could a rite of initiation serve as a functional substitute for baptism? Would the exclusion of water and a simple profession of allegiance to Christ lessen the misunderstanding? After a great deal of prayer and discussion, it was decided that the rite of water baptism should be retained. However, every effort is made to explain to Muslims that believer's baptism is about allegiance to Christ, *not* a forsaking of familial and social relationships.

This particular case study falls in the C4 range of the C-scale. Numerous other groups have carried out similar approaches throughout this country. Some proceed further in their contextualization process than others, yet these groups are fellow evangelical believers, desirous that Muslims come to saving faith in Christ. It is safe to say that there are many thousands of MBBs in the country today. There is some persecution, but considering how the new communities have grown in the past few years, this is less of a problem than one would have anticipated.

THREE SHORTER CASE STUDIES

In a study from another country, a large number of Muslims have recently decided to follow Isa. Some of the dynamics described in the case study above, such as Muslim-friendly translations of Scripture, also occurred. The main difference between these two movements is one of religious identity. While the first case study describes a non-Muslim C4 movement, this second study describes a C5 expression of faith in Christ (i.e., new followers of Isa remain culturally and officially a part of the Muslim community). In this movement, the MBBs have what might be called a parallel worship experience. On the one hand, they simply carry out their normal life as Muslims in terms of such disciplines as daily prayers, fasting at Ramadan, and Muslim holidays. At the same time, they meet weekly in simple Jesus-centered home fellowships where they study the *Injil* (the New Testament) inductively, pray for each other and, as a community, serve each other and the poor in their neighborhoods.

This small movement has grown very quickly, particularly through family networks, as one Muslim shares with another the good things that God through Isa has done for them. Similar to the first case study, this nation had been under the domination of a Western "Christian" country. However, in spite of the negative impression Muslims have concerning Christians in general, there is a strong, substantial Christian minority made up primarily of non-Muslim background ethnic groups. In fact, in this multi-ethnic country, there are hundreds of Muslim background fellowships reflecting all positions along the C-scale.

The third study comes from a country that is 99 percent Muslim, yet has a secular national government. Several thousand Muslims have become Christians in the past few decades. Many of these new followers of Jesus were nominal Muslims, including university students and political socialists. The fellowships that have been formed are C2 and C3 in nature. They use the language of the local Muslim population, yet the worship style is not Islamic as it is in the first two case studies. The C2 groups borrow music forms from the West, whereas C3 groups have an ethnic flavor to their worship music. The believers in this movement want to be called Christians with full government recognition of their identity and their fellowships.

The fourth study involves a movement with thousands of MBBs from one ethnic group that was largely Christian before the advent of Islam. This group, which eventually converted to Islam, has always felt suppressed socially and politically by the dominant ruling Islamic ethnic group that effectively controls the country. In part, they are coming to faith in reaction against Islam. This movement has seen many signs and wonders. The new believers, as in the third case study, want to be known and recognized as Christians. Within this movement are C1, C2, and C3 fellowships, some using Bible translations in European languages, and others in their own ethnic languages.

FACTORS INFLUENCING C-SCALE CHOICES

We begin with C6 because many, perhaps even most, Muslims begin their journey with Jesus as secret or underground believers. The social climate that would most influence an MBB toward the C6 position would be an Islamic government that has declared the changing of religion illegal, even punishable by imprisonment, violence, or death.[135] C6 believers might also be found where social pressure against conversion is extremely high.

C5 communities may emerge in contexts similar to where C6 is found, except that the social or political environment allows for Muslims to meet and be known as ones who receive the Bible as the Word of God, while remaining legally or culturally Muslim. This calls for the new believers to maintain exceedingly close relationships with family and community leaders. The existence of such C5 expressions of faith depends largely on the ability of the MBBs to show that they are truly a part of the local community and then find ways to express biblical truth in forms and categories Muslim friends and neighbors can accept. Our Consultation data indicate that this is occurring in a number of places.[136]

---

[135]   It is interesting to note from the GTFP data that two areas of the world, the Arab world and Iran, show a significant number of participants associated with C6 ministry.

[136]   Of the various points on the C-scale, C5 has been the most controversial. Many articles have been written both for and against this approach. The earliest articles alluding to the need for a C5 orientation came from Anderson (1976), Wilder (1977), Kraft (1979), and Conn (1979). Parshall (1998), an authority on contextualization among Muslims, stated that he believes C5 is dangerous and should only be a temporary or transitional position for MBBs. This concept is also brought out in Phil Parshall's *Beyond the Mosque* (Grand Rapids, MI: Baker Book House, 1985). Articles written in favor of this approach by field workers came from John Travis, "The C1–C6 Spectrum?"; John Travis, "Must all Muslims Leave Islam to Follow Jesus?"; and from H.M. Weerstra and J. Massey, eds., *International Journal of Frontier Missions: Muslim Contextualization* I 17, no. 1 (2000), which featured articles by Bernard Dutch, Joshua Massey, J. Travis, and Andrew Workman, Stuart Caldwell, and Richard Jameson and Nick Scalevich. For more recent articles supporting the C5 approach, which is often referred to as *insider movements*, see John and Anna Travis, "Appropriate Approaches in Muslim Contexts," in *Appropriate Christianity*, ed. Charles Kraft (Pasadena, CA: William Carey Library, 2005); J. Dudley Woodberry, "To the Muslim I Became a Muslim?" in *Contextualization and Syncretism: Navigating Cultural Currents*, ed. Gailyn Van Rheenen (Pasadena, CA: William Carey Library, 2006), 143–157; Rick Brown, "Brother Jacob and Master Isaac: How One Insider Movement Began," *International Journal of Frontier Missions* 23, no. 3 (2007): 41–42; and Kevin Higgins, "Acts 15 and Insider Movements among Muslims: Questions, Process and Conclusions," *International Journal of*

WHEREAS C3–C6 GROUPS TEND TO BE FORMED BY MBBs,
MBB GROUPS ASSOCIATED WITH C2 AND C1 FELLOWSHIPS
TEND TO BE EMBRACED BY OR AFFILIATED WITH A NATIONAL OR
INTERNATIONAL ORGANIZATION OR DENOMINATION.

C4 fellowships are found in contexts where MBBs no longer feel comfortable being Muslims, but resonate strongly with Islamic forms (see the first case study above) and long to remain in close relationship with Muslim family and friends. Often, they are not comfortable with a Christian affiliation either, due to the many negative associations. Many refer to themselves as simply "believers" or "followers of Isa." Our Consultation data indicate many of these fellowships exist worldwide as well.

C3 fellowships exist where MBBs have a high regard for their ethnic forms but have rejected Islam. They wish to be known as Christians, although without Western or foreign forms. Numbers of these types of fellowships are found worldwide as well.

Whereas C3–C6 groups tend to be formed by MBBs, MBB groups associated with C2 and C1 fellowships tend to be embraced by or affiliated with a national or international organization or denomination.[137] In the group-oriented societies of much of the Muslim world, there may be a desire to join whatever is the largest and strongest expression of faith, with strength and size being more important than familiar religious forms. Some C6 believers at times fellowship secretly with C1 fellowships, even using C1 or C2 forms in their secret life of faith.

MISSIONAL IMPLICATIONS

What are the missional implications of what has just been described for those who long to share the love of al-Masih with Muslims?

First, while we rejoice that many Muslims in many contexts are finding the Savior, we recognize these are only some of the first fruits among

---

Frontier Missiology 24, no. 1 (2007): 29–40.

For two recent articles that urge caution in the C5 approach, see Timothy Tennent, "Followers of Jesus (Isa) in Islamic Mosques: A Closer Examination of C-5 'High Spectrum' Contextualization," *International Journal of Frontier Missions* 23, no. 3 (2006): 101–15; and Gary Corwin, "A Humble Appeal to C5/Insider Movement Muslim Ministry Advocates to Consider Ten Questions," *International Journal of Frontier Missiology* 24, no. 1 (2007): 5–20. Both Tennent and Corwin, like Parshall, strongly advocate contextualization, but believe the C4 approach is preferable to C5.

137   In the fourth case study, MBBs founded indigenous C1- and C2-style fellowships.

millions still to come to a knowledge of Jesus. Different contexts require different approaches.

Second, we must realize that sharing the Gospel with Muslims is "not about us" but rather about God and the Muslims whom we are called to serve. Scripture indicates that messengers of the Gospel must be willing to adjust their ways for the sake of those without Christ (1 Corinthians 9:19–23). The determination of a point on the C-scale should not be on the basis of what cross-cultural workers are "comfortable with" but rather should be a matter of God's leading and the needs of the people in a particular context.[138]

Third, in those places where a Christward movement occurs, it tends to initially impact only one niche or segment of society. Depending upon the factors mentioned above, not the least of which are the messenger and the nature of the message communicated, fellowships formed at first may tend to fall in a similar place on the C-scale. However, as with any new movement or social innovation, there are generally early adopters who accept the change most quickly, who may not be representative of the society or group as a whole. Therefore, additional approaches at various places on the C-scale may be needed in time for the full harvest to come in. Let us, as MBBs and cross-cultural workers, live out faith in Christ according to our own conscience and calling, blessing others whose calling may differ from ours. May we rejoice in all the ways God is calling Muslims to himself through Jesus the Savior.

---

[138] On philosophical, strategic, or theological grounds, some MBBs and cross-cultural workers are opposed to certain positions on the C-scale. We are not suggesting that one violate his or her conscience or calling. Within those parameters, however, a worker should be as flexible in approach as possible for the sake of those not yet in Christ, even as churches and para-church organizations in many parts of the world today offer a wide range of spiritual options depending upon the context of the community.

Chapter 14

Factors That Facilitate Fellowships Becoming Movements

DAVID GARRISON AND SENECA GARRISON

"Some fell into good soil, and when it grew,
it produced a hundredfold."
Luke 8:8

"All over the world this Gospel is bearing fruit and growing,
just as it has been doing among you since the day you heard it and
understood God's grace in all its truth."
Colossians 1:6, NIV

If you have come this far, you are special. Less than 1 percent of the world's Christians ever share their faith with a Muslim. But if you are reading this book, then you are likely in that 1 percent. If you are a Christian in an Islamic country, then you know what it costs to live and serve as a minority. Within the ranks of Christians sharing their faith with Muslims, perhaps you are one of those who has actually seen Muslims come to faith in Jesus, and you have begun discipling and even gathering these new followers of Christ into fellowships. If this describes you, then you are indeed a choice and blessed servant of God!

Could it be that God has even more in store for you? Could God be preparing you to go beyond a witness, a discipling relationship, or even a church-planting work among Muslims? Perhaps God has chosen to fill you with a more outrageous vision, a vision born out of the question, "What would it take to see *all* of these Muslims come to saving faith in Jesus Christ?"

We call this the WIGTake or "What's it going to take?" vision. Once God plants it in your heart, it changes everything, because this vision will not release you until new fellowships are multiplying rapidly throughout the people to whom God has called you. This rapid multiplication has come to be known as a church-planting movement. It is an indigenous, rapid reproducing of new believers and new fellowships that sweeps through a people group. Akin to Donald McGavran's notion of people movements,[139] church-planting movements emphasize the distinctive of reproducing, multiplying, indigenous fellowships.

What does it take to go from a fellowship plant to a multiplying movement? If the answer were simple, then perhaps every fellowship planter would be participating in a movement today. The truth is, church-planting movements, like redemption and salvation, remain cloaked in a mystery of divine and human interaction. Though mysterious, they remain prevalent enough to convince us of their reality and their possibility.

We can be encouraged that we understand much more about the dynamics and inner workings of church-planting movements than we did even a decade ago. This increased understanding can help serious students of these movements to avoid many needless dead ends and nonstarters in the quest to see true fellowship multiplication among a people.

What are some of the lessons we have learned? In this chapter, we will consider seven lessons learned and five dead ends to avoid. Let us begin by identifying the dead ends. That way, if you are just beginning your ministry, you can avoid them; or if you are already headed down a wrong path, you can reverse course and proceed down a more promising route.

---

[139]   See Donald A. McGavran, *The Bridges of God* (New York: Friendship Press, 1956).

DEAD ENDS

1. *Church-planting movements are immaculate conceptions.* Immaculate means unstained or untainted by human involvement. There is enough of the miraculous in every conversion experience to fill us with awe and wonder, but a good reading of the Bible teaches us that God has intentionally reserved significant roles for human agents in his great drama of redemption. You must believe this is true, or you would not have troubled yourself to witness to a Muslim in the first place. Jesus promised to send his followers "out to fish for people" (Matthew 4:19). Every person who knows how to fish realizes that fishing is a learned skill, not a miraculous discovery. We do God no service when we ignore the roles that he has assigned to us and decline his invitation to learn how to become effective fishers for people. Application: *Do not blame God for the absence of a church-planting movement among your people. Instead, learn all that you can about how God is at work in such movements. Seek to align yourself and your ministry with the ways God has chosen to work.*

2. *More is better.* There remains a widely held opinion among mission advocates that a responsive people should be flooded with foreign workers. The view draws its momentum from a misguided harvest missiology and a misunderstanding of Jesus' instructions to, "Therefore ask the Lord of the harvest to send out laborers into his harvest" (Luke 10:2). More workers are needed for the harvest, but the best place to find these new workers is in the harvest field itself. One of the surest ways to kill an indigenous movement is through 'foreignization,' the process of identifying an emerging Gospel movement with a foreign culture. Christ "became flesh and dwelt among us" (John 1:14, KJV). Christ was an outsider who came into our world and took on the peculiar flesh, language, and culture of a single people. As the New Testament Gospel spread, it did not remain dominated by its original Jewish flesh, language, and culture. Instead, the Gospel assumed

the unique flesh, language, and culture of *each* nation, tribe, and language in which the Gospel was shared. Application: *Build your team out of nationals, particularly new followers of Christ from the people you are seeking to reach. They will gain skills and confidence as they labor alongside you, ultimately eclipsing you as the movement unfolds. The resources for the harvest are* in *the harvest!*

3.   *The show-me syndrome.* Too many movements have been aborted by the desire for a tangible, institutional facility to validate the first fruits of success. How often have pastors and churches from the West pushed Christian workers to produce a church building that can be photographed and displayed like a war trophy, when what is needed most is a grassroots movement of transformed lives? New believers can and will find their own facilities, whether they are in homes, parks, storefronts, or catacombs. When *they* find the right time, *they* will choose to become more visible to the broader public. Our efforts to shortcut that process are unnatural and, ultimately, counterproductive. Application: *Resist the temptation to erect a monument to your ministry. Instead, encourage new believers to meet in their own homes. This will quickly and naturally contextualize the movement and greatly enhance its reproducibility.*

DEAD ENDS

1.   *Church-planting movements are immaculate conceptions.*
2.   *More is better.*
3.   *The show-me syndrome.*
4.   *Ministering to the dead.*
5.   *It is really about you.*

4. *Ministering to the dead.* As followers of Christ, we naturally want to do the work of our Lord, and that will always involve ministering to the needs of the less fortunate. The ministry impulse for every follower of Christ is undeniable, because it emanates from the Spirit of Christ that dwells within us. But we must never forget that beyond the temporal need there is an eternal need. Application: *Integrate witness into every kind of ministry. Our ministry should be such that it attracts others to ask concerning the hope that is within us (1 Peter 3:15) and be attracted to follow Christ.*

5. *It is really about you.* The profound message, "It's not about you!" applies to the Great Commission as well. God wants us to be faithful in his service, but he also expects us to be fruitful (Luke 13:6–7; John 15:8). We must get beyond thinking that our role is simply an opportunity for us to exercise our talents or some test of our spiritual endurance. *It is not about us!* The Great Commission is about God's glory being revealed to and embraced by the world. Your role is that of an emissary, an ambassador, a vessel, an instrument. Dying to self is the beginning of "becom[ing] all things to all people, so that I might by any means save some" (1 Corinthians 9:22). Following Paul's example, we must constantly place our ministries on the altar, evaluating them in light of God's Word and his mission. If you have not seen fruit in your ministry in a long time, then try a different approach. Application: *If you have spent years laboring without seeing any results, it is not time to quit; it may be time to try a different approach. The stakes are eternal, so refocus your faithfulness on the pursuit of fruitfulness.*

Now that we have identified a few dead ends, let us shift our attention to some lessons that we have learned that can lead us toward church-planting movements.

LESSONS LEARNED

1. *There are five elements in every church-planting movement.* One of the most insightful lessons of the past few years has been the realization that every church-planting movement has five inter-dependent, reproducing elements. These are as follows: a) effective ways of initiating a Gospel witness; b) an effective Gospel witness; c) immediate, basic discipleship; d) effective fellowship formation; and e) ongoing leadership development. One could write volumes on each of these five elements, but in this chapter we will have to settle for only a few brief comments.

First, in church-planting movements, followers of Jesus have found a *way or ways to easily begin a conversation* that leads to a clear Gospel witness. This point is so very basic and simple that most Jesus-followers miss it altogether, yet doing so means a movement or even a harvest will never take place. It is well worth your time to learn how to effectively initiate a conversation about Jesus in each type of setting. In some Muslim countries, the most effective catalyst has come through Islam itself. We see this when followers of Christ begin with the words, "I have been reading something in the Qur'an that has given me great hope and encouragement. Can I tell (or ask) you about it?" This leads to a qur'anic walk through passages about Isa al-Masih (Jesus) that culminates in a clear Gospel witness. Others direct their witness to family members or close friends who know them best with a brief testimony of how their lives were before Jesus and how it has been since he came into their lives. If the family member or friend shows interest, these opening lines are followed by a simple explanation of how the person can also come to faith in Jesus Christ.

The second element, *an effective Gospel witness*, means a witness that is heard, understood, and accepted by those hearing it. This is not to say that the message will be received by everyone who hears it, but if no one is accepting it, then there may be something wrong with the message or the way it is being communicated. For outsiders, contextualization can help. Insiders will contextualize more naturally, particularly if they have recently turned in faith to Jesus. It is equally important that the Gospel witness be widespread in order to optimize the likelihood of finding someone whom the Holy Spirit has been preparing to receive the message. The Bible calls such a person a "son of peace," and the New Testament is filled with examples of both men and women who fit this description (Luke 10:6; 19:2; John 4:7; Acts 3:2; 10:1). As the movement gains momentum, it will become evident that the most effective witnesses are the new followers of Christ themselves. They are the ones who can best relate to their friends and family and have the ability to naturally contextualize the Gospel for them.

The third element is *immediate discipleship,* which follows as soon as possible after a new commitment to follow Christ. Immediate discipleship grounds a new follower of Christ in the fundamentals of the faith and helps them learn how to feed themselves from the Bible. It also launches the new follower of Christ on the path of daily communion with God through prayer and Bible study. When done properly, immediate discipleship will equip and commission the new Jesus follower to share their faith with friends and family. For this reason, the discipler must also prepare the new follower of Christ to expect persecution as a part of the price of following a crucified Lord.

The fourth element, *effective fellowship formation*, requires intentionality and a plan to plant multiplying fellowships. When fellowship formation is done well, it knits new Jesus-followers into a community of fellow disciples who will nurture and encourage one another as they follow Christ. A viable, healthy fellowship reproduces the life and work of Jesus Christ within the community and exponentially multiplies the work of the Christian worker as it transforms an outsider movement into a movement within the community.

Finally, church-planting movements cultivate and *multiply new leaders.* The methods employed may include formal doctrinal training, but always involve steeping the emerging leaders in the daily, practical work of a fellowship leader. Multiplying home fellowships are natural spawning grounds for this kind of leadership development because they offer so many opportunities for emerging leaders to assume partial leadership roles as they hone their gifts for greater future service. There are many ways to enhance leadership development, and spiritually hungry new followers of Jesus will inhale every kind of training made available. For this reason, they must learn early the importance of evaluating every breeze that blows by the standard of God's Word.

Every movement of multiplying fellowships finds some way to accomplish each of these five elements. In fact, it has become relatively easy to see in many fellowship-planting efforts that die out the absence or deficiency of one of these crucial elements. The most effective fellowship-planting movement strategies not only exhibit these elements, but they also have managed to integrate them into a seamless rhythm of multiplication. Application: *Examine your own fellowship- or church-planting efforts to see if you have deficiencies in one or more of these five elements. Make corrections as needed.*

In addition to these five elements, there are other valuable insights that have been captured over the past few years.

2. *Oak trees begin as acorns.* At the same time that more and more Western and Korean workers are coming out of mega-churches, God is also choosing to unfold church-planting movements through small, reproducing home fellowships. Workers without a background in home fellowships have important lessons to learn if they are to navigate a church-planting movement. While there is nothing wrong with fellowships beginning small, they must still be fellowships nonetheless. Just as an acorn possesses the entire genetic DNA of a fully mature oak tree so, too, must a small house fellowship embody each of the essential elements of a church as described in God's Word. Essential marks of a fellowship include worship, sharing, ministry, discipleship, and outreach. If these core markers are to characterize a healthy fellowship-planting movement, then they must first be evident in the life of each follower of Jesus and in every new house fellowship that is planted. Application: *Begin a house fellowship in your own home. It will teach you invaluable lessons as you practice the very vision you are seeking to replicate among your people.*

LESSONS LEARNED

1. *Practice the five essential elements of a church-planting movement.*
2. *Remember that oak trees begin as acorns.*
3. *Build a foundation of training and modeling.*
4. *Utilize accountability loops.*
5. *Ask yourself, "How many of my people will hear the Gospel today?"*
6. *Make use of a reproducible fellowship paradigm.*
7. *Demonstrate boldness in the face of persecution.*

3. *Training and modeling.* In fellowship-planting movements, training is a foundation on which the movement stands or falls. What kind of training? Training that produces multiplying opportunities to share the Gospel, broad and effective Gospel witness, multiplying new disciples, the planting of vibrant reproducing fellowships, and ongoing leadership development. In fellowship-planting movements, those shepherding the movement invest enormous amounts of time and effort training their national partners to pursue each crucial element of a church-planting movement. However, training without a personal investment remains shallow and detached. The best way to add depth to your training is to practice what you are teaching. Application: *Put into practice what you are training your national partners to do. Walk with them as they share their faith, disciple new believers, form new fellowships and raise up new leaders.*

4. *Accountability loops.* Jesus recognized the importance of accountability; that is why he sent out his disciples two by two. Not only did they have vertical accountability with his insistence that they report back to him on what they had accomplished (Luke 10:17), but they also experienced peer accountability as they spurred one

another on to faithful witness and obedience to his commission. This pattern of peer accountability continued throughout the history of the early Church (Peter and John; Priscilla and Aquila; Paul and Barnabas; Paul and Silas) and is still found in explosive church-planting movements today. The difference between teaching (which too often goes in one ear and out the other) and training is *accountability*. Training reinforced by accountability produces results. Application: *Complete each training session with concrete action steps. Agree to meet with your trainees weekly to "see how we've done." Remember that you can only demand accountability if you are willing to submit to it yourself.*

5. *How many of my people will hear the Gospel today?* This is the question that haunts those who have embraced the WIGTake ("What's it going to take?") question. In church-planting movements, we see the question go beyond "How many people will I share my faith with today?" to the bigger, more strategic question of "How many will see and hear?" This question, like the WIG-Take question, propels one beyond oneself to multiple streams of Gospel witness cascading out through hundreds and even thousands of national partners. Application: *Make a list of ways that your people can experience and hear the Gospel. Now, implement the list. Teach your national partners to do the same. Then keep adding to the list on a regular basis.*

6. *Have a reproducible fellowship paradigm.* If a fellowship is to be reproduced, then it must be both reproducible and reproducing. This has led practitioners to move away from churches with paid leadership, at least in the early stages. Paid leaders, even those whose support is drawn from their own members, have a disincentive to start new groups as this would tend to erode the financial basis for their own ministry. Professional (paid) leaders have a natural inclination and financial incentive to grow their churches larger rather than start multiplying new churches. Application: *Gather some friends to begin your own "laboratory"*

house fellowship. You will learn more about helping others start a fellowship and reproduce a new fellowship by trying it yourself.

7. *Boldness in the face of persecution.* Of course, this is easier said than done, but that fact makes it no less true. In places where we have seen church-planting movements, persecution has not been absent, but it has been accompanied by a bold Gospel witness. In similar settings of persecution where the response has been extreme secrecy or anonymity, we do not see a movement of new fellowships result. It is not inordinate to ask, "Does a bold witness ever result in martyrdom?" The answer is yes. Veterans of Gospel witness in the Muslim world will tell you, though, that the reports of martyrdom far exceed the incidence of martyrdom. In many parts of the Muslim world, the fear of persecution is quite possibly the single greatest barrier to the people being reached and must be overcome. Application: *There needs to be a more open expression of the fact that we are followers of Christ.*

FINAL LESSONS

Some final lessons learned will serve as a conclusion to this chapter. These are the deepest lessons. We have learned that God's heart for Muslims far exceeds our ability to comprehend. We can only begin to imagine the depth of his love for the Muslim world when we gaze into the face of the One who carried their sins and ours to the cross. This is why we leave home and family to take the Gospel to a people who may not want to hear it. *His* love constrains us (2 Corinthians 5:14).

And, for this reason, we should not be hasty in shaking the dust from our feet. Those instructions from Jesus in Luke 10:11 are too often cited by those who would question why time and resources should be spent on the resistant world of Islam. Why, they ask, should we expend limited resources for a people so seemingly hostile to the Gospel?

GOD'S HEART FOR MUSLIMS FAR EXCEEDS OUR ABILITY
TO COMPREHEND.

God appears to be answering that question by unfolding fellowship-planting movements in some of the most resistant places on earth. Whether in Cuba, China, northern India, or Bangladesh, God continually shows us that he is "not wanting any to perish, but all to come" to faith (2 Peter 3:9).

In church-planting movements, when the going gets tough, successful practitioners have chosen to *innovate* rather than abandon the lost. What they often discover is that it is not the Gospel that has been rejected, for who could honestly reject the God of all creation taking on the form of a Servant to bear upon himself the penalty for our sins? Instead, it is the way the message is proclaimed or the culture in which the message is wrapped that prompts resistance. And so these effective practitioners keep looking for new ways to present the timeless Gospel, so that by all means they might save some.

A Triple Blessing

Jesus-followers are blessed with a Gospel that translates, one that begins with the Incarnation—God's translation of himself into our fallen world. This divine model invites us to follow his pattern as well. We have permission to innovate, to try new ways to break through the barriers of opposition before we shake off the dust from our feet.

Jesus-followers are also blessed with an ethnically diverse, worldwide community of Great Commission co-laborers. We would be foolish not to partner with and learn from our brothers and sisters around the world. There is still so much to learn about how God is at work fulfilling his Great Commission. If the Body of Christ only knew what the Body of Christ knows, then the Body of Christ would know all that it needs to know to complete the work of Christ in the world. Think about it.

Finally, Jesus-followers are blessed with the promise that God's Holy Spirit is already at work all around us, even among the most unreached peoples of the earth. Our task is to find where God is at work and to engage those we find, beginning with those whom his Holy Spirit has prepared, offering to them a clear reason for the hope that is within us (1 Peter 3:15).

With all of these lessons, resources, and blessings available to us, how can we help but feel very special indeed!

Chapter 15

Bible Storying and Oral Use of the Scriptures

JACK COLGATE

*"Then beginning with Moses and all the prophets,
he interpreted to them the things about himself in all the scriptures."*

Luke 24:27

Amir and his wife did their best to make me feel welcome. I sat cross-legged on the floor of their small living room. A few small end tables and a television set stood like lonely sentinels in the sparsely-decorated room. I had dropped by to greet Amir's family on their return from the village after the month of fasting. They were back to run a fairly thriving small roadside business selling breakfast rice porridge. But today's conversation was laced with concern and worry over the troubling economic climate. Amir explained, "This is not like the monetary crisis of eight years ago. We weren't worried back then. Now we are. We pay over twice what we used to pay for kerosene. And I don't know if our customers will want to buy our rice porridge if we increase our prices."

What could I say to Amir and his wife? I told them a story, the story of Jesus healing a blind man. Before healing him, Jesus asked, "What do you want me to do for you?"

After I told the story, I said to Amir and his wife, "God can still heal blind people. But you're not blind physically. However, you are like that blind person. What lies ahead is dark, and you are groping about to know where to go." Amir and his wife nodded in agreement. I continued, "Well, then, what do you want God to do for you?"

Amir and his wife paused for a moment, then answered, "We want God to bless our business."

"Then let's ask God to do that right now! May I pray for you?" They willingly agreed.

The telling of Bible stories—one type of which is illustrated by this account of my interaction with Amir and his wife—is undoubtedly one of the fruitful practices that God is using today to reach unreached peoples, including Muslim people groups. In the last two to three decades, the use of various Bible narrative or storytelling formats for witness and discipling has increased dramatically. In recent years, this heightened attention to narrative has been included as part of a broader focus: a recognition by mission strategists and practitioners that the majority of the population of the world's unreached people groups is oral (illiterate, functionally illiterate, or semi-literate) in communication and learning styles.[140] This realization is now shaping strategies for evangelism, discipling, and the training of leaders among oral learners.[141] Results of the Global Trends and Fruitful Practices (GTFP) Consultation survey confirm the prevalence of oral styles of communication and learning and the importance of strategic attention to orality: 71 percent of Muslim people groups among whom GTFP participants work have an oral learning preference. Ninety-one percent

---

[140]   Published literacy figures for many countries are mostly unreliable as a measure of functional literacy. For example, the government literacy figure for the province of the Asian country where my wife and I live and work is more than 92 percent. However, my research pointed to a number of factors indicating a stronger presence of orality than the government figures would lead us to believe. Among these factors are low figures for mean years of schooling and for school participation rate, poor ability to read among youth, low figures for new publications per year and for newspaper circulation rates, the nature of the local language as primarily a spoken and not a written language, and the predominant use of the Arabic Qur'an as an orally recited word.

[141]   Grant Lovejoy et al., eds., *Making Disciples of Oral Learners*, Lausanne Occasional Paper, No. 54 (Pattaya, Thailand: Lausanne Committee for World Evangelization, 2005). This is a helpful booklet that explains orality, introduces chronological Bible storying, and describes recent strategies and collaborative efforts to reach the world's oral learners. See also www.oralBible.com and www.onestory.org for more information on this growing movement within mission circles.

of survey participants noted that strategies of their respective teams reflect an understanding of this learning preference. Furthermore, teams who understand the learning preferences (whether oral or literate) of their people group and incorporate this into team strategy were more fruitful (in terms of numbers of fellowships planted) by 340 percent!

THE TELLING OF BIBLE STORIES IS UNDOUBTEDLY ONE OF THE FRUITFUL PRACTICES THAT GOD IS USING TODAY TO REACH UNREACHED PEOPLES.

One of the strategies that individuals and teams are using to plant Gospel seed among Muslims is Bible storying. Thus, I open this chapter by describing briefly two ways of Bible storying. I then present three reasons why the use of Bible stories is particularly appropriate and fruitful for use among oral seekers and disciples of Jesus in the Muslim context. The telling of Bible stories, however, is not the only way that the Scriptures are being used fruitfully in Muslim settings. Thus, I describe a number of other ways that the Bible is being used among oral seekers and disciples of Jesus: as lectionary/book of corporate readings, song book, prayer book, and source of creeds. A case study highlighting the combining of these simple, reproducible ways of engaging Scripture is then presented, followed by some concluding comments.

CHRONOLOGICAL BIBLE STORYING

Of the various types of narrative or chronologically-developed Bible teaching or storying formats, chronological Bible storying has probably received the greatest attention among cross-cultural workers in the last decade. Chronological Bible storying is a method of presenting scriptural truth through telling a series of Bibles stories that maintain the chronological flow of Scripture. The stories are told without interruption or added commentary. Each telling is followed by simple questions to prompt review (or retelling) of the story and elicit discussion and application. Various storying tracks can be developed, corresponding to the various stages of evangelism, discipling, fellowship planting, and leadership training. Many materials about and resources for chronological Bible storying are now available.[142]

---

[142]   See, for example, the resources and links at www.chronologicalBiblestorying.com and www.oralBible.com.

POINT-OF-NEED BIBLE STORYING

Aside from chronological Bible storying, another type of fruitful use of scriptural narrative is point-of-need Bible storying.[143] In this type of storying, a single Bible story is told to address a particular need. The account of my interaction with Amir and his wife provides an example of this type of storying. The various Bible storying materials and resources that I have reviewed seem to give less emphasis to the telling of single stories. Yet this kind of Bible storying has the potential to bear fruit among Muslims, particularly among women who in most cultures tend to share their heartaches, griefs, and concerns more openly than men do.[144]

The telling of single Bible stories does not need to be only female gender-directed, though. Both Muslim women and men face many troubling concerns and needs. Thus, when I conduct Bible storying workshops, I now include a module suggesting various Bible stories that address the concerns of the people group among whom we live.[145] These include stories and parables that portray the following concepts:

» God seeing and caring for the needy and the poor;
» God caring for those who are wounded in heart and suffering in spirit;
» God's judgment (for those grappling to understand natural disasters);
» The danger of living in fear, panic, and jealousy;

---

[143] The descriptive phrase "single stories related to ministry needs" also appears in the glossary entry "Bible storying" in Lovejoy et al., *Making Disciples of Oral Learners*. Two other types of Bible storying mentioned are the telling of thematic story clusters and the telling of Jesus stories first rather than beginning with the usual Old Testament stories that lead up to Jesus.

[144] J.O. Terry compiled these stories in response to the custom among Muslim women in North Africa, the Middle East, and South Asia of gathering to share their stories of hardship. Terry's hope is that women will begin to hunger for an experience of forgiveness and blessing from God as they hear stories from the Old Testament and from the life of Jesus. The stories can bridge into a prayer ministry for the women or into a series of evangelistically-oriented Bible stories. See J. O. Terry, "Good News for Those with Stories of Grief: A Message for Women Who Share Stories of Personal Misfortune and Grief" (unpublished manuscript, Media Consultant for Asia and the Pacific, International Mission Board, Southern Baptist Convention, 2000).
However, Mary McVicker cautions that for women in her South Asian context, storying must connect at the level of their experience. "For story as a method, the temptation is to emphasize the content—concentrating on the message and its cognitive processes (the facts, logic, and arguments enclosed in the story)—rather than the experience of the story itself, which is the core of the women's processing that enables her to understand truth." See Mary McVicker, "Experiencing Jesus: Reflections of South Asian Women," in *From the Straight Path to the Narrow Way*, ed. David Greenlee (Waynesboro, GA: Authentic, 2006), 323.

[145] These concerns have been discerned as we have gone deeper in relationship with Muslims. Thus, in workshops, I present an overall storying approach that includes two other important aspects of narrative: storying from our own lives and learning to ask good questions and listen well in order to draw out the stories from the lives of our listeners.

» Good news for those who hide shame and feel remorse for their sin;
» Divine healing and deliverance from demons through Jesus the Messiah;
» The danger of turning to occult practices or practitioners
» The importance of forgiving others; and
» God's help for those who lack confidence and feel inferior.

WHY USE BIBLE STORIES?

"TELLING STORIES—THAT IS OUR WAY": A CASE STUDY

BY ANNIE WARD

For the last ten years, my husband and I have been working in a Central Asian country where we have witnessed a great hunger for God's Word. We responded to this interest by reading the Scriptures (especially the Gospel of John) with Muslim seekers and saw some come to faith. After six years, I was introduced to chronological Bible storying. My husband and I, together with a colleague, decided to experiment with telling Bible narratives rather than simply reading them aloud. It was already our habit to read and sing Scripture whenever we hosted guests or were guests ourselves. When we switched to telling the stories, however, interest increased, and we experienced more spiritual openness as well as a desire to own and read the Scriptures.

We also tried this with a family of believers whom we had been discipling. Although this family is very literate, they are members of a local culture that prefers oral communication—speeches are not written down, and stories and poetry are widely used. All of us began to take turns to learn (in advance of the meeting) and then retell a Bible narrative (beginning in Genesis). We used colloquial language so that every family member, including the children, became a "teacher."

At each gathering after the narrative had been told, someone would retell the story, and others would make corrections if necessary. We would then discuss what the story meant for our lives. We found that maintaining eye contact engaged the listeners as did asking simple observation questions in chronological order. Essentially, this enabled the retelling of the story through question and answer (e.g., "Where did this happen? Who was there? What did he or she say or do? And then what happened?")

We were surprised to find that these simple changes made our studies in God's Word at once more accessible and reproducible. Reading a text and explaining it was not immediately reproducible, but telling the stories and communally discussing their application for our lives proved far more fruitful. Some of the children even started telling stories to their school classes!

My friend Zenab later explained how learning to tell Bible stories had better equipped her to spread the Word to friends, neighbors, and family:

> *When we read from the Bible I couldn't understand it, but you knew Jesus better than I, so I thought that was the way it had to be done. But when the stories were told it went into my heart, and I was able to tell others.*

> *When we read from Scripture, I got tired and wondered when we'd be done, but when we started narrating the Scriptures I didn't want to stop! It awakened my interest and my questions surfaced and could be dealt with.*

After Zenab learned a repertoire of stories, she was able to share accurately with people in a context where having a written copy of the narrative would be inappropriate or lead to persecution or both. Zenab also uses a children's picture Bible with nonliterates, reading the narrative aloud first and then retelling it. She has learned that it is difficult to remember a story if she tries to memorize verbatim from the Scriptures. Furthermore, the story is less accessible to her listeners. Instead, Zenab prefers to simplify stories in her own words, taking care to retain essential details. After Zenab has told a story, she will often look at the text later and tell the person(s) if she has been inaccurate or has missed something important.

In the past, typical women's meetings in our area of believers and seekers have been modelled on the methods used by expatriate workers. Some women prepare and read from notes; others share their thoughts, then together the group reads a text that illustrates them. Zenab comments:

> *They don't tell stories. We read from Scripture and talk about a theme, but it isn't so interesting that way. I don't want to hear something prepared a week in advance. I want to hear something that comes from the heart.*

Zenab is a "woman of peace," respected by men and women alike and a gifted storyteller. She is currently overseeing several groups composed of both believers and seekers where the Scriptures are a central focus. The Word is spreading through these existing social networks of family and neighbors. Some group members enjoy reading; others can read but do not. Still others cannot read at all. However, everyone likes to hear the stories! The Bible as story seems to awaken greater interest, and many will ask for a copy of the Scriptures to read for themselves or with neighbors or family or both.

I asked Zenab how many in the groups retell Bible stories to others rather than reading them aloud. She explained that few are able to do this well because the text of the Bible itself, especially with its unfamiliar names, creates a barrier to learning and retelling the stories. In contrast, local classics with even antiquated language can be retold because of their familiarity.

We concluded from this that it might be advantageous to delay introducing the written Scriptures even to very literate group members until listeners are familiar with many of its narratives in an oral way. By interacting with the Bible narratives orally first, they will be better equipped to share them with others in a more accessible and reproducible manner.

Asked about her use of storytelling, Zenab says, "Telling stories—that is our way, that's what we used to do at school, that is how we lay a foundation for our lives."

Storying from the Bible is appropriate and fruitful for at least three reasons. First, it is based upon an understanding of the Bible as God's story, which is perhaps the most fundamental interpretive category for the Scriptures. There is an overarching, historically grounded story in general chronological order to which the whole of Scripture testifies. God's story tells of God at work in human history from creation to the end of time for the salvation of all peoples and for his ultimate glory.[146]

In the language of our "adopted" country, my wife and I like to remind the believers in Jesus whom we disciple and train that the Bible is the "High (or Great) Story." The main actor in this great story is God himself. God is the "central character" who "is present explicitly or by implication" in almost every narrative.[147] Thus, the Bible is a holy book that "points us to the grace of God active on our behalf more than to our obligations to God."[148] In this sense, the whole of the Bible could be called a Gospel, and its stories highlight the riches of God's grace.[149] This focus on God's story and on God as the central character contrasts with the focus in popular Muslim piety on the prophets themselves as examples to emulate.

THE FRUITFULNESS OF BIBLE STORYING

1. *The Bible is the "High Story."*
2. *Much of the content of the Bible itself is in narrative form.*
3. *Most Muslims are oral rather than literate in their communication and learning styles.*

---

[146]   Its main parts would include the creation of the world and of humanity, humankind's fall into sin, God's redemptive work in and through the patriarchs and his people Israel, a climax or central scene in the birth, life, death, resurrection, and ascension of Jesus Christ, the stories of the early believers (i.e., the church), and the expected return of Christ and the new creation.

[147]   Walter C. Kaiser, Jr., *Preaching and Teaching from the Old Testament: A Guide for the Church* (Grand Rapids, MI: Baker Academic, 2003), 70.

[148]   John Goldingay, *Models for Interpretation of Scripture* (Grand Rapids, MI: Eerdmans, 1995), 56.

[149]   Even the stories of God's wrath against sin portray God's judgment as his "strange" and "alien" task that must be viewed in the framework of his great and everlasting compassion (Isaiah 28:21; Lamentations 3:33; Psalm 30:5; Isaiah 54:7–8).

Secondly, Bible storying is a biblically appropriate practice, because—quite obviously—much of the content of the Bible itself is in narrative form. "Narrative is the preferred genre of the biblical text."[150] The tendency to mine precept, principles, and three-point sermons from Scripture has sometimes blinded literate readers and students of the Bible to the actual story form of much of the Bible. Bible storying encourages a use of the Scriptures that accords with its actual narrative form.

Thirdly, Bible storying is a particularly fruitful practice for use among Muslims, because—as noted earlier—most Muslims are oral rather than literate in their communication and learning styles. As oral learners, they respond better to concrete stories than to the sharing of abstract principles or isolated Bible verses. Many times my wife and I have observed how stories lead Muslims to discover God and his grace in transforming ways.

OTHER WAYS TO USE THE BIBLE ORALLY

The Bible is not only God's story, however, as demonstrated by the content of the Bible itself. Although the bulk of the Scriptures take the form of story, the Bible contains more than just narrative. It also includes a setting forth of the law and instructions for worship, wisdom literature, prophetic writings, visions (apocalyptic literature), letters of the apostles, poetic expressions and songs of praise, prayers, thanksgivings, calls to worship, laments, confessions of sin, and benedictions. Thus, corresponding to these non-narrative parts of the Bible, there are at least two other broad interpretive categories for the Scriptures: God's Word and the response of God's people.[151]

In addition to using the Bible as storybook, then, these two other categories for Scripture suggest a number of other ways that we can use the Bible fruitfully in oral Muslim contexts. Most notably, we can use the Bible as a lectionary or book of corporate readings (when approaching the Bible as God's Word) and as song book, prayer book, and source of creeds (when approaching the Bible as the response of God's people; see Figure 15.1).

---

150   Kaiser, *Preaching and Teaching from the Old Testament*, 63.
151   The categories of God's story, God's Word, and the response of God's people presented here come from John Goldingay, *How to Read the Bible* (London: Triangle, 1997).

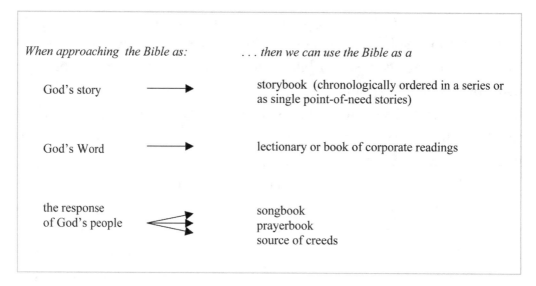

When approaching the Bible as:

...then we can use the Bible as a

God's story   ⟶   storybook (chronologically ordered in a series or as single point-of-need stories)

God's Word   ⟶   lectionary or book of corporate readings

the response of God's people   songbook
prayerbook
source of creeds

Fig.15.1

A Case Study of Simple, Reproducible Scripture Use for Oral Disciples

A number of years ago, my wife and I started to gather regularly with three individuals who work for us. Two were women with minimal knowledge of Islam who had already made professions of faith in Jesus the Messiah and were leading a gathering of a few women. The third was a younger Muslim man with a higher level of knowledge about and adherence to the pillars of Islam.

Our desire was to model a simple way of engaging the Scriptures and of gathering that was reproducible, that is, that they in turn could repeat for use with others in their family and broader social networks. During our gatherings, we combined the various oral uses of Scripture that are presented in this chapter.

Over the first number of gatherings, I told (in adapted chronological Bible storying style) a short series of Bible stories. This series started with the stories of creation and of Adam and Eve's fall into sin, continued with a few Messiah-anticipating Old Testament stories and ended with the story of Jesus' birth and an abbreviated story of his death, burial, resurrection, and ascension. Sometimes we read the Bible story (or parts of it) out loud together. The women also asked on a few occasions to take with them the actual written Bible story, since they did not feel confident in their ability to retell the story accurately to others.

Since we live in a large urban area with good comprehension of the national language, and since our three employees were from two separate people groups, we used the national language (rather than the language of the dominant local people group). After the telling of the story, simple questions were asked to facilitate recounting of and interaction with the story. We would always close by praying for one another.

After this initial storying phase, we continued to gather regularly, reading at first in lectionary style through the book of Mark. Then we read through Acts and most of Genesis. To date we have also read through most of Exodus as well as James, Titus, John, and other passages. We are currently rereading Mark, and the women have also read through thirty selected psalms that we gave them.

Because we have the Scriptures accessible in digital format, I print and hand out one chapter at a time. These Scriptures are printed on folio-size paper, in landscape format (i.e., like a normal book), with two columns and size 16-font letters big enough for those with poorer eyesight to read.[152] New Testament Scriptures are taken from a translation of the New Testament that uses names and terminology that are meaningful to Muslim readers.[153] Shorter portions are chosen, and these are read slowly, verse by verse, often twice (and occasionally even three times). Simple questions are asked that encourage the recounting of and interaction with the selected reading. Sometimes the story or parts of it are replayed or retold.

For our gatherings, I also prepared a small booklet of Bible prayers and scriptural or Scripture-based creedal-type statements (some in the language of the local people group as well). These are recited together, and on occasion I have sung certain Bible prayers.[154]

---

[152] Colleagues in other Muslim settings have told me that because of a high view of the importance of the Holy Book, using portions of Scripture printed on normal paper might not be appropriate. Furthermore, a maturing movement to Jesus will undoubtedly need bound volumes of printed Scripture.

[153] For more information on issues surrounding the meaningful translation of the Scriptures for Muslim readers/hearers, see Tim James, "Working with Colleagues from Other Faith Traditions," *International Journal of Frontier Missions* 23, no. 2 (2006): 61–66; John Travis, "Producing and Using Meaningful Translations of the Taurat, Zabur and Injil," *International Journal of Frontier Missions* 23, no. 2 (2006): 73–77; and Brad Williams, "The Emmaus–Medina Intertextual Connection: Contextualizing the Presentation of God's Word," *International Journal of Frontier Missions* 23, no. 2 (2006): 67–72.

[154] In security-sensitive contexts where corporate singing might be inappropriate, an individual singer or cantor can sing or chant softly. Lyrics may be a verbatim quoting or a poetic adaptation of biblical texts. Benefits of setting Scripture to music are at least twofold: music touches the affective and even physical aspects of our being, and meter, rhyme and melody serve as mnemonic aids in the memorization of Scripture.

The two women have become vibrant and bold leaders in their respective families and social networks. They take the Scripture portions and photocopy them, and these are read out loud together in gatherings that they lead. Printed and bound New Testaments or other Scripture portions have also started to be used. In some cases, designated readers (or lectors) read the passage (particularly if there are poor readers or illiterates in the gathering). To date, they lead or have helped to birth multiple gatherings of followers of Jesus and seekers that follow the simple, reproducible model of Scripture use and gathering described here. Men take part in some gatherings and some are starting to emerge as leaders. The young Muslim man who works for us has not yet made a clear verbal confession of faith in Jesus as Messiah and Lord, but he prays movingly during our gatherings. He also tells the Bible stories to his children and has taught his oldest daughter to pray spontaneously in the national language (rather than just by using recited, memorized qur'anic prayers in Arabic).

CONCLUDING COMMENTS

This case study presents one model for use by gatherings of faithful followers of Jesus that are multiplying in an oral Muslim context. There are other fruitful models as well, as the accompanying case study from Central Asia indicates. Undoubtedly, however, any model that is to be fruitful in an oral Muslim context will need to be based upon a simple and reproducible (i.e., able to be multiplied by oral disciples themselves) engagement with the Scriptures.

In our context (where there are available written Scriptures), this engagement with the Bible has gone beyond a pure chronological Bible storying approach. Why? First of all, not too many oral-culture followers of Jesus in our Asian context feel comfortable or confident in telling a Bible story orally. But they are more confident to read Bible stories and portions out loud—even if poorly—and to lead others to read out loud those same Scriptures, followed by lively interaction. Perhaps this is because for Muslims there is already a strong recognition of the importance of the holy written word. Thus, the focus on reciting or reading out loud together the Scriptures fits their understanding of what should happen in a gathering.[155] Secondly, these disciples of Jesus have

---

155   Interestingly, the main way that the Scriptures are being engaged in a significant turning to Jesus in an oral Muslim South Asian context appears to be patterned after the lectionary/book of corporate readings model. Cross-cultural workers associated with this movement use the phrase "manuscript Bible study" to describe this engagement with Scripture. However, we literates tend to associate "Bible study" with the tools, skills, and methods of literate Bible study that are

an appreciation from their Muslim upbringing of the importance of reciting creedal statements and simple prayers from the Scriptures.

Muslims are accepting God's special revelation in Jesus the Messiah. They are engaging the *Taurat, Zabur,* and *Injil* in languages that they understand— storying, reading, reciting, singing, praying, and confessing it in creedal style. Fruit is being borne for God's glory.

But God's heart is for even greater fruit. Thus, may we who are literate cross-cultural workers continue to model simple, reproducible ways of engaging Scripture. This will facilitate the continued growth of Spirit-led, Scripture-fed movements to Jesus among oral-culture Muslims.

---

not very reproducible among communities of oral disciples of Jesus. Thus I prefer to use the phrase "using the Bible as a lectionary/book of corporate readings" to describe this way of engaging Scripture.

Chapter 16

Expatriates Empowering Indigenous Leaders

ABRAHAM DURÁN, MICHAEL SCHULER,
AND MOSES SY

*"Two are better than one,
because they have a good reward for their toil.
For if they fall, one will lift up the other."
Ecclesiastes 4:9–10*

The aim of every church planter is to see multiplying churches that lead to people movements through self-propagating, self-supporting, and self-governing churches. As we are all aiming for this, we often see three phases that many of the movements today have been going through. In the first phase of a real pioneering, church-planting situation we often start with a 'parent-to-child' or 'older-to-younger sibling' relationship between the expatriate workers and the national leaders of the Muslim background believers (MBBs). In the second phase, we move into a 'sibling-to-sibling' relationship, and lastly, the expatriate worker should take the role of an 'uncle or aunt'. This means having the role of an outside adviser who knows the situation and has the confidence of the local leaders.

Wherever possible, it is favorable to move as quickly as possible into a 'uncle or aunt' role as this is the phase where the fastest growth is happening. In some cases, expatriate workers can start a sibling-to-sibling relationship with local leaders right from the beginning or even slide directly into the role of 'uncle/ aunt' to some local leaders. In any event, as we have the aim of seeing all Muslim unreached people groups (MUPGs) reached for Christ, we might find ourselves often in a parent-to-child or older-to-younger sibling relationship at the beginning as there are no local leaders at all in this people group.

> ### THREE TYPES OF RELATIONSHIPS
>
> 1) *Parent-to-Child (or Older-to-Younger Sibling)*
> 2) *Sibling-to-Sibling*
> 3) *Uncle or Aunt*

The following experiences of having parent-to-child, sibling-to-sibling, and uncle/aunt relationships come out of church-planting activities in North Africa, Central Asia, and the Middle East.

THE PARENT-TO-CHILD OR OLDER-TO-YOUNGER SIBLING RELATIONSHIP

In a pioneer situation where we go through the steps of sharing the Good News with the first people, discipling the first believers, and training the first leaders, we should have in mind two Bible verses that will lead us to the following principles in this article:

Principle 1: Train faithful leaders who are able to train others. Paul wrote, "What you have heard of me through many witnesses entrust to faithful people who will be able to teach others as well" (2 Timothy 2:2).

Principle 2: They must increase, I must decrease. John said, Jesus "must increase, but I must decrease" (John 3:30). In the same way John wanted to see Jesus increase and himself decrease, expatriate workers need to see themselves decrease and local leaders increase.

Choosing Local Leaders

Especially in a pioneering situation, we are often in danger of choosing the wrong people as leaders. This danger can arise for various reasons such as expectations from the society of choosing the oldest person even if he or she is not really qualified, or choosing a young intellectual who does not really have the acceptance of the society even if he or she fits the biblical qualifications. A good principle of choosing the first leaders is given by Paul: "And after they had appointed elders for them in each church, with prayer and fasting they entrusted them to the Lord in whom they had come to believe" (Acts 14:23). The word 'they' in the Greek context could mean the apostles as well as the believing community. Certainly when the Jerusalem Council chose people to go with Barnabas and Paul to speak to other churches, they said, "It has seemed good to us in assembly to choose men and send them to you" (Acts 15:25). In this way, the leaders are accepted by the local community and are usually the ones who have been leading the community already. As Greg Livingstone used to say: "Leaders are the ones who are leading!"

They Must Increase, But I Must Decrease

There are two models that have been used to follow this important principle —the local leaders must increase and the expatriate leaders must decrease.

1. In several cases, the expatriate leader is present at the church meetings and models servant leadership to the whole group. At the beginning, he or she is leading part of the gathering with the aim of handing responsibility over to the identified leaders as quickly as possible. This phase can take a few weeks or months (hopefully not years). The quicker the expatriate worker empowers the national leaders, the better.

2. Many people are choosing the 'shadow pastoring' model. The expatriate leader is not present at the gatherings, but is coaching the local leaders right from the beginning. This often seems to be a quicker and better way to see local leaders actually leading and having responsibility for the gathering. In order to see this model working well, there must be a real 'man or woman of peace' (an

influential member of the Muslim community who acts as a
bridge for fellowship development). Next to the man or woman
of peace might often be a bolder person who opens doors in
the neighborhood or country. This is often a passionate, radical
person who takes the Gospel and runs with it; he or she is willing
to be in the front and give everything to see it come to his or her
people. The fellowship is built around the people of peace, but
the bolder people bring people into the Kingdom of God.

In North Africa, where one of us has been working for ten years, we have
seen both. We started with the first option as there was no national believer
available, and it took us some time to identify the first local leaders. Later on,
we used the second option with faithful men and women as we were 'shadow
pastoring' them. This was much more fruitful, multiplied far more quickly, and
the local leader had the honor of leading right from the beginning. Out of experience, I would choose 'shadow pastoring' wherever possible.

Allowing Them to Make Mistakes—As a Parent or Older Sibling Still Carrying the Responsibility

Regardless of the model that is chosen, local leaders need to know that the
expatriate leaders are around as their 'parents' or 'older siblings'. They need to
have a place where they can come back, talk, and pray things through. This
might often require the expatriate leaders spending several hours per week with
the emerging leaders. Expatriate leaders need to 'back up' local leaders. If local
leaders are making mistakes, expatriate leaders may need to bear the responsibility for the consequences on their own shoulders if necessary—the same way
a parent often has to bear the responsibility for the actions of their child.

As in many honor and shame cultures, one of the worst things that can
happen for a person is to 'lose face'. For this reason, expatriate workers need to
develop deep and solid relationships with the local leaders so that shame will
not hinder local leaders' growth in their leadership after having made mistakes.
Expatriate leaders need to confirm them in their leadership, encourage them,
build them up, and help them to get God's vision for themselves as leaders. At
this point, it is often helpful to point to biblical leaders and how they dealt with
mistakes in their own lives.

Pointing to the Bible as the Major Resource for Questions

Especially at the beginning, there are many questions for which the new leaders need to have answers: What will the gathering of believers look like? What position in the society should it have? How should the new believers be called? Expatriate workers are often in danger of sharing their own points of view or convictions rather than helping new leaders to discover through the Bible what the Holy Spirit is saying to them. As earthly parents or older siblings in faith for the emerging local leaders, we need to train them not to expect answers from us but to seek the heavenly Father who is revealing himself to his children through his word.

Spending Time with Leaders

Spending time with local leaders is key to their development. Jesus himself spent three years training his disciples. A practical way of doing this is to organize weekends with key leaders, sometimes including their families. As was mentioned above, one of the key issues is to build up trust with local believers. Trust is built by spending time and sharing our lives with them. Important steps in the lives of local leaders often happen in such special times with their 'parents in faith'.

Preparing Them for the Next Phase—Sibling-to-Sibling Relationship

1. In some cases, this is the time where the pioneer worker(s) who started the whole work might have to move to a different location. Those who have served as parent or older sibling figures for the local leaders move on, and other people from the expatriate team might move into a sibling-to-sibling relationship with the local leaders. In our situation in North Africa, when the time came to appoint the third elder over several house fellowships, we wanted the two local elders to appoint the new elder. The answer of the elders was: "As long as you are here, you are our father in faith. We cannot appoint this third elder, as it would be a sign that we are not honoring you. Once you are gone, we will be able to appoint new elders ourselves."

2. In another instance, expatriate leaders stayed in the city for two years to prepare the MBBs for taking over more and more leadership. Expatriates have been in a sibling and uncle/aunt relationship for a long time and stayed in the region as local elders were leading and taking the responsibility. Therefore, it is not always necessary to move on, but certainly necessary to 'pass on the baton'. Expatriates were focusing on things other than being the primary motor of the local fellowship-planting work. They were mentoring leaders and helping with nationwide alliances, doing Scripture ministry, providing teaching and discipleship material, and so on. The local leaders knew that the expatriate role had changed and that the expatriates were not their parents anymore. This, in turn, encouraged the local leaders to take on more responsibility and to fulfill key leadership roles.

THE SIBLING-TO-SIBLING RELATIONSHIP

Moving from a parent-to-child relationship to a sibling-to-sibling relationship is a crucial step in forming healthy communities of believers. The believers should understand that they are not 'under' the expatriate workers but equal partners with them. This is a normal step in healthy relationships, but when it comes to working with local brothers and sisters, many expatriate workers struggle to find a good way to empower them. Moving away from a paternalistic relationship and toward a genuine partnership is the key.

MOVING FROM A PARENT-TO-CHILD RELATIONSHIP TO A SIBLING-TO-SIBLING RELATIONSHIP IS A CRUCIAL STEP IN FORMING HEALTHY COMMUNITIES OF BELIEVERS.

A sibling-to-sibling relationship helps local leaders to grow into their role as leaders of an emerging fellowship or church. Tom Steffen refers to that phase as 'passing the baton'.[156] Our local sisters and brothers have very much esteemed our assistance and advice, but with their growing maturity, they were also keen to make sure we do not take the baton (control) back into our own hands.

---

[156] See Tom A. Steffen, *Passing the Baton: Church Planting That Empowers* (La Habra, CA: Center for Organizational & Ministry Development, 1997).

Working with local leaders as equal partners will build them up. In this phase, decisions need to be made together. We should make sure that local leaders take on ownership, not just for the believing community, but also for any present and future action. It is their community after all. Being siblings means reducing our own role and influence by lifting them up as the leaders of the church.

In a church-planting effort in Central Asia, workers followed the concept described by the acronym 'MAWL.' This stands for 'Model, Assist, Watch, and Leave.' While a parent-to-child relationship refers more to modeling, a sibling-to-sibling relationship can be described as the phase of 'assisting and watching.'

Watch the Timing

Parents have to care for their children as long as they are small and needy, but there will be a time when children have to start making decisions and choices for themselves. Church planters want to see the local brothers and sisters growing steadily and becoming more responsible for the community. It is extremely valuable to plant the right ideas and concepts from the beginning. The emerging church should have the 'DNA' of local leadership, and local ownership should be ingrained as early as possible. It is important to communicate the vision and process clearly and early. The local believers should know that 'we are walking together for a limited time.' The goal is to see them become fully self-sustainable in the right time.

Share the Responsibilities and Burdens

As siblings, we are partners. Now it is the time for local leaders to take charge of meetings and give direction to the church while expatriates support their growth in leadership. This is done, essentially, by spending time with them, evaluating the last meeting, studying the Word, and helping them prepare for the next meetings. Our primary role in this phase is to assist and train local leaders. Over time, they will grow in their confidence and experience. Our focus should be on teaching, casting vision, growth in biblical knowledge, the basics of church planting, and character building.

Have Locals Become More Visible

As John the Baptist realized, followers of Jesus should become less important while Jesus becomes more important in our lives. Likewise, in this phase of church planting, local brothers and sisters should increase in their role, while expatriates decrease. Expatriate leaders need to lift local leaders up instead of trying to cling to the more prestigious role of being their spiritual parents. As siblings, expatriate leaders support local leaders as peers and allow them to step into the spotlight. This is a natural and healthy process, but very often it goes against the desire of expatriate workers to 'be in control' and to make sure the church develops in a healthy way.

Help Them to See Issues from a Different Angle

As expatriates support local leaders to step into increased responsibilities, local believers will see things differently. Expatriates and locals have different cultural lenses and come from different backgrounds. It is a natural process of maturing for leaders to wrestle with different views and find a common understanding. As local leaders grow in confidence, their voice will also increase in volume and force. However, they should still be able to accept the experience and knowledge of the expatriate workers to help in balancing viewpoints.

Have the Courage to Submit to Their Advice

When local leaders really lead, they must know that expatriates do not undermine the leaders' authority. Even if ideas are different and expatriate leaders might try to balance some of them, expatriates need to be careful to leave the responsibility in local leaders' hands. Sometimes, expatriates might feel that the local leaders are going in a direction that might not be the best one. But they need to be able to make mistakes and learn from them. At the same time, mistakes provide an opportunity for loving evaluation of the situation together with expatriates. This might show where more teaching is helpful. More and more, expatriates should ask the local leaders for advice and learn from them how they see the future of the emerging church.

Resist the Temptation to 'Jump in and Rescue'

Expatriates should not take the baton back if things go wrong. This is probably clear to everybody, but experience shows that expatriates often struggle not to step back in. Who does not feel the urge to take back the helm when the ship is about to crash on the shore? As expatriates partner with local sisters and brothers in order to see them growing in leadership, expatriates need a lot of wisdom in assisting without controlling.

A few years ago, several expatriate leaders felt that several local leaders were being influenced by a foreign organization that held questionable views about financing and church-planting strategies. As an expatriate team, we wrestled with our role and came to the conclusion that we would caution the local leaders about this liaison but let them move on if they felt that this was God's way for the future church. They went on with this group but, soon after, came back, having experienced some disappointment. This has provided a great opportunity for growth in maturity without the expatriates jumping in and overruling the local leadership's decisions.

Be Their Resource Person

A crucial role of the expatriate workers is to link local leaders with outside resources. By this, we do not primarily mean money. The local followers of Jesus need to understand that they are part of the universal church and have a part to play in the Kingdom of God outside their own tribe or country. The church-planting effort in Central Asia included preparing discipleship and elder-training material in the local language, helping with creating contextualized worship music and songs, setting up an inconspicuous Bible school, supporting the Old Testament translation project, and so on. Some expatriate workers try to avoid talking about support from the outside because it can destroy the church. However, experience has shown that with globalization and the Internet revolution, local leaders will, sooner or later, get in contact with potential donors from outside. It is better to discuss this issue with them openly and to make them aware of the potential damage that outside resources might cause to their beloved fellowship.[157]

Prepare to Move on to Becoming Their 'Uncle/Aunt'

As peers to the local leaders, assistance is usually limited to a certain time frame. The goal is to establish strong local leadership. The believing communities should form their own identity and vision under indigenous leadership. Eventually, foreign church planters will withdraw from the actual scene even more and will move into the phase described by the terms 'uncle/aunt'.

---

[157] See chapter 17.

The Uncle/Aunt Relationship

Paul was not only a pioneer-apostle and a remarkably effective church planter, taking the Good News about the Kingdom of God where the Gospel was not yet known. He was also exceptionally good at transferring to the local believers the responsibility to spread the Gospel among their own people. He remained an outside adviser who knew the situation and had the respect and confidence of the local leaders. We call this stage being an 'uncle/aunt' to the local leaders.

The main reason that we have Paul's inspired letters to the Galatians, Corinthians, Thessalonians, and more is that he remained committed to the fellowships he had planted and felt a responsibility to stay in touch with them. He tried to spend whatever spiritual capital the Lord had given him to stir the fellowships to continue in the right doctrines and practices that he considered essential for spiritual growth and effective communication of the Good News to others.

In the Middle East, we had the opportunity of planting the Gospel among a major non-Arab ethnic group and seeing a tangible demonstration of its power as our friends followed Jesus and influenced their families and friends with his teachings.

Through successes and mistakes, we consider the following three areas to be important in being an uncle or aunt to local leaders:

1. Uncles/aunts need to be known among local leaders as fathers/mothers;
2. Uncles/aunts need to be motivated by love; and
3. Uncles/aunts need to maintain effective communication.

Uncles/Aunts Need to be Known among Local Leaders as Fathers/Mothers

Paul wrote to the Thessalonians:

As apostles of Christ we could have been a burden to you, but we were gentle among you, like a mother caring for her little children. You are witnesses, and so is God, of how holy, righteous and blameless we were among you who believed. For you know that we dealt with each of you as a father deals with his own children, encouraging, comforting and urging you to live lives worthy of God, who calls you into his kingdom and glory (1 Thessalonians 2:6–12, NIV).

In other words, he was able to be an 'uncle' to them and to write them and advise them about their local situation, though he was no longer in their context, because he first had been a successful father. Usually, good parents of local leaders are those who have been living with them side by side. They were successful because they had been good parents and siblings. During this time, the local leaders had come to understand that, by the grace of God, the Lord had been using the expatriate workers (through their acts of wisdom, purity, courage, and generosity) to build the local church. On this basis of confidence, the expatriate worker has influence as an uncle or aunt to the local leadership, giving advice even if he or she is not living in the same place anymore.

THE MORE WE BECOME A 'GREEK TO THE GREEKS' AND A 'JEW TO THE JEWS,' THE BETTER PARENTS, SIBLINGS, AND, FINALLY, UNCLES OR AUNTS WE CAN BE FOR THE LOCAL LEADERS.

The more we become a 'Greek to the Greeks' and a 'Jew to the Jews' (1 Corinthians 9:19–23), the better parents, siblings, and, finally, uncles or aunts we can be for the local leaders. This is because we will understand the situation of the local leaders to the extent that we were able to identify with them. Likewise, the leaders may respect more and listen better to someone they feel is not alien to their environment. One of the keys we discovered in the work in the Middle East was the essential nature of becoming men and women worthy of honor in the sight of local leaders.

Uncles and Aunts Need to be Motivated by Love

If we do everything right, yet we do not have love, we are nothing (cf. 1 Corinthians 13). Paul says to the Thessalonians:

So deeply do we care for you that we are determined to share with you not only the Gospel of God but also our own selves, because you have become very dear to us (1 Thessalonians 2:8).

It is our experience that local leaders see the difference between workers who are just trying to achieve something and those who want to do something together with them, through the love of God, for their people and their nation.

Expatriates must be willing to share with them more than the Gospel message. They need to be available as a second family when local leaders need a place of rest, a prayer, or a listening ear. As parents and siblings, this is done very close to the people, and uncles and aunts will continue this role even if they are further away.

Uncles and Aunts Need to Maintain Effective Communication

Paul stayed in contact with the churches through occasional visits, through sending faithful team members with pastoral gifts, and through writing letters. In some cases, he was able to go back and have a more extended field visit after the leadership was firmly established and respected by the church.

Paul also used communication to show the believers that he was praying for them, was aware of their struggles, was committed to their success, and was willing to facilitate them. He used the letters and visits to give encouragement toward perseverance in the work, but when needed, he was able to correct them kindly, always doing what he could to support their leadership.

Today, expatriate leaders need to visit the growing churches in person. Certainly, we also have the great opportunities of using technological tools such as phones, e-mail, and other modern communication methods, which enable us to communicate with local leaders all over the world. This makes today's role of uncle or aunt much easier than in earlier times. Having said this, we should not underestimate the importance of visiting the local leaders on the field. There is a saying among Muslims: *"Where the eye or the words or the thoughts can go, the feet are not there."* In other words, we can think about people, talk with them, and even see them; but it is only when we are physically present that people feel the real power of our love for them.

CONCLUSION

Expatriate workers need to pray to find faithful people among the unreached peoples. Expatriates need to teach them how to love Jesus and help them to become transformed into his image in the same way that parents want to see their children grow up to become responsible adults.

In the sibling-to-sibling role, expatriate workers and local leaders work together in equal partnership. This is a time when confidence grows between local and expatriate leaders, when they are working together as iron sharpening iron. Expatriates can also gain deeper insight into the culture with the help of local people, and local people can benefit from the wisdom of their elder siblings in the Lord.

The uncle or aunt is usually living in a different place, but continues to have influence in the local church by being in close contact with the leaders through different communication methods and through visits to the field.

Chapter 17

Are We Nourishing or Choking Young Plants with Funds?

J. R. Meydan and Ramsay Harris

> *"As for what was sown among thorns,*
> *this is the one who hears the word, but the cares of the world*
> *and the lure of wealth choke the word, and it yields nothing."*
> *Matthew 13:22*

Are there ways that we utilize funds in the Muslim world that actually *choke* the plants instead of *nourishing* them? Jesus' explanation of the seed that fell among thorns is a universal warning to his people in all cultures, all nations, and all generations. The writers of this chapter willingly confess that, as individuals and as the Body of Christ in the Western world, we ourselves have at times succumbed to the "worries of this life and the deceitfulness of wealth." And as we seek to be Jesus' ambassadors among Muslims, we might at times inadvertently be encouraging the growth of the thorns instead of the plants. But before we make our case, let us give a few very important disclaimers.

While we advocate wisdom and discretion in the use of outside funds when planting churches in the Muslim world, we do not wish to suggest that humanitarian aid, community development, relief work, or generosity toward local believers in times of crisis and need has no place in living out the Gospel in Muslim countries. The Scriptures have much to say about generosity and the responsibility of followers of Jesus to give of their resources to others—to all people, not just to those who follow Jesus.

Nor do we wish to imply that there is absolutely no scope for financially supporting local leaders. The Fruitful Practices research revealed that in some of the successful church plants studied, local leaders do indeed receive some kind of foreign funding.[158] But beyond showing that in most of these cases there is some type of "accountability to respected local leaders for the use of these foreign funds,"[159] it was beyond the scope of the research to reveal the *how, where, when, who,* and *why* of this funding. And, of course, the research focused on *successful* church plants, not on all of the situations where funding was used *unsuccessfully.* All who labor long-term in developing countries realize these issues are complicated, and require much prayer, deep understanding of local cultural values regarding money, a great deal of time to get to know local believers so that we are not "hasty in the laying on of hands" (1 Timothy 5:22), and consistent discussion among missionaries and local believers so that our unity in Christ is not marred by how we handle funds.

ARE THERE WAYS THAT WE UTILIZE FUNDS IN THE MUSLIM WORLD THAT ACTUALLY CHOKE THE PLANTS INSTEAD OF NOURISHING THEM?

Unwise use of foreign funds can of course damage the work of God in any context. But certain specific realities in the Muslim world present particularly acute challenges—perhaps unique challenges—for the use of external funds.

First, God is using world events and the media to give many Christians a burden and passion to reach out to Muslims. This is a positive development, but one consequence is that an unprecedentedly large number of Christian organizations and donors are interested in "having a ministry" in some Muslim context, while security concerns mean that relatively few of these wish to place resident workers in Muslim countries where they might develop a deep understanding of local cultural values and deep relationships with local believers. At the same time, the number of MBBs (Muslim background believers) in

---

[158] Of the Consultation participants, 61 percent said they used foreign funds wisely for outreach and development (in a way that does not impair local responsibility) and 43 percent said the local fellowship takes the initiative in sponsoring projects and supporting workers, and avoids reliance on outside sources.

[159] Eighty-two percent of the fellowships practiced "accountability to one another."

most Muslim contexts is tiny, and most are new in the faith. So, relative to non-Muslim contexts, the Muslim world has a disproportionately large number of donors seeking partnership with a disproportionately tiny number of mature local believers. This imbalance between the number of eager donors and the number of recipients means that unwise use of money may have a more profound distorting effect on church-planting ministry, unintentionally "choking" the faith of young believers.

A second reality of the Muslim world is that Muslims have preconceived assumptions about how Christian missions operate. Muslims assume that the principal methods Christian missionaries intentionally use to lure Muslims away from Islam and into Western Christian culture is by buying them off with gifts and money (often under the guise of relief and development), by sending young attractive women to seduce their young men, or by brainwashing their children. We can scarcely overstate how angry the Muslim public feels over this perceived methodology of Christian missionaries. Muslim leaders and the Muslim press warn against it constantly, and ordinary Muslims are furious when they see any behavior by missionaries that seems to confirm these assumptions.

Granted, these assumptions are incorrect. The motivation of virtually every Christian around the world who desires to see Muslims encounter Jesus (and especially those who would take the time to read this book) would never operate with the intention to "lure" Muslims to Christ through bribery, seduction, or brainwashing. Furthermore, we have seen Islamic missionary organizations that use money in precisely the way they denounce in Christians. But that does not mean we should disregard Muslim fears on this issue. The fact of the matter is that some of our actions as missionaries can unintentionally reinforce this misconception. Sometimes by our handling of finances, we can inadvertently appear to be "buying Christians" in Muslim lands.

A third reality is that with few exceptions Muslim-majority countries tend to be in the developing world, with the related problems of widespread unemployment, lack of basic necessities, fierce competition for resources, poverty, and significant disparity in lifestyle between rich and poor. Sixty percent of the world's poor are Muslims, and many of the world's poorest countries are majority-Muslim countries. As a result, whether we like it or not, most missionaries in Muslim contexts are in a relative position of power, with the potential to provide money, jobs, prestige, and financial resources. In short, to those whom they seek to serve, missionaries can be seen more as bearers of financial resources leading to survival here on earth, than of Good News leading to eternal life.

Perhaps the best way to illustrate the above problems is to share a few case studies. The following are all true stories, from four different majority-Muslim countries, with names and a few small details changed to protect the identities of those concerned. In each case, we talked personally with the people involved.

THE CASE OF MAHMOUD

Mahmoud comes from a country that is more than 90 percent Muslim. As is typical in many such countries, the tiny evangelical movement in his country is overwhelmingly composed of people from the non-Muslim minority. For decades, the missionaries in this country prayed that God would raise up an MBB couple from the largest ethnic group in the country who would have the gifts, calling, and character to pastor a church in the capital city.

After many years of prayer, the Lord raised up Mahmoud and his wife. Both were MBBs from the largest ethnic group. Mahmoud was the son of an imam. He had suffered horrific persecution at the hands of his family, but had stood faithfully and heroically for Christ. He clearly had leadership gifts and a sense of calling to ministry. The missionaries who had led him to Christ and discipled him began training and grooming him for church leadership.

About this time, a large evangelical organization decided to open an office in the capital city. They were launching a US$100 million humanitarian program that would span several different countries in the region, and they decided to locate their regional headquarters in this city.

This organization had a worldwide policy of preferring to hire "national Christians," rather than foreigners or local non-believers, to do basic office jobs. So they came into this country looking for mature national Christians to hire. Because the national evangelical movement was tiny, they found very few candidates. They set the salary scale based on their worldwide policies, not based on knowledge of local salary scales. You can guess what happened: they offered Mahmoud an administrative office job that paid a salary fully five times what he could ever hope to earn as a pastor.

The missionaries felt profoundly ambivalent about this. On one hand, they were deeply disappointed to have their dreams for the church leadership dashed. On the other hand, they did not want to stand in Mahmoud's way or keep him and his wife in poverty when the missionaries themselves were reasonably well-off.

This evangelical organization was initially very happy with Mahmoud's work. They appointed him to a high-status job in the accounting department of a program handling millions of dollars. A year later, disaster struck: Mahmoud was caught embezzling money. He was fired by the evangelical organization, but they graciously agreed not to press legal charges against him. He was publicly discredited in the eyes of other local believers. He was deeply embittered by what he felt was mistreatment by his fellow-believers who had been his employers. He dropped out of church and ceased to live for Christ. Over the years since then, healing has slowly come in his relationship with the Lord, with the church, and with his former employers. But he is no longer seen as a potential church leader by himself or by other local believers.

ZAYDAN'S TRANSLATION JOB

Zaydan is an MBB elder in an MBB church. He has won two dozen Muslims to Christ and has planted a daughter church. However, one day rumors began circulating among both missionaries and local MBBs in his city that Zaydan was guilty of financial wrongdoing and was no longer qualified for church eldership. The missionary who was discipling Zaydan investigated these rumors.

In most cases, the rumors turned out to be based on miscommunication, not on actual wrongdoing. But one rumor was particularly noteworthy. Several people had noticed that during one particular month, Zaydan had suddenly become very generous financially toward other MBBs in his own church and in other churches. He gave very generous gifts to a number of other believers in need. The sums of money involved were clearly beyond what he could afford on his modest monthly salary as a government functionary. When people asked him where the money had come from, he either gave evasive answers or refused to answer at all. This convinced many people—both MBBs and missionaries—that he had come by the money through dishonest means.

It was another MBB elder who finally succeeded in finding out what had happened. Zaydan had received the money confidentially from Tom. Tom is a relatively new missionary from a large, respected evangelical mission. Tom has not yet learned the language or the culture very well, but he is zealous for the Lord and wants to make an impact on the country for Christ. Tom's mission is well-known for a particular discipleship program it uses, and it provides training to other groups in how to use this discipleship program in various contexts. Tom asked Zaydan to translate some of the training materials into Zaydan's mother tongue.

This translation project was very sensitive from a security standpoint, so Tom asked Zaydan to promise not to tell *anyone* at all about it, and Zaydan agreed. Tom paid Zaydan a sum of money that was fairly modest by the standards of Tom's budget and by the standards of what Tom's mission was accustomed to paying, but the sum of money was huge in comparison to Zaydan's monthly income. When Zaydan asked Tom whether he could at least tell the missionary who was discipling him about the project, Tom insisted that no one must know.

When people began to ask Zaydan about the financial source behind his sudden generosity, he found himself in an impossible situation. He had given Tom his word not to tell anyone about the translation project. So he gave evasive answers or refused to reply to questions. We might never have found out the truth if it were not for another MBB elder who made an inspired guess and went to Tom and forced Tom to tell him what had happened.

Zaydan's reputation was seriously damaged by this series of events. Though people have now been told that there was no dishonesty involved, there is still a residual feeling of tainted trust in him as an "above reproach" church elder.

Imam Ahmed and the Guest Speaker

Ahmed is a Muslim cleric (imam). The US$38 per month he earns by leading mosque prayers, signing marriage contracts, conducting funerals, and tutoring children in Qur'an recitation is enough to support his wife, three children, and widowed mother in their small village. They sometimes do not have extra money for medical bills or schoolbooks, but Imam Ahmed is thankful that they get enough to eat, and he tries his best to serve his community as a moral and religious leader. Now he looks at the letter in his hand, and knows he has a decision to make. He leans against the wall on his porch and thinks over the events of recent days.

Over a period of many months, an old classmate had been talking with him about Isa Nabi (the Prophet Jesus). Imam Ahmed has longed to be at peace with God, and was drawn to Jesus when he saw the change in his friend's life.

One day, Imam Ahmed was invited to come and hear someone talk about Jesus from the Bible and the Qur'an. At the gathering in his friend's home, he was surprised to see about ten or eleven other men, most of whom he knew personally from his village. The man who spoke was obviously knowledgeable about both the Qur'an and the Bible and a true scholar. Ahmed was intrigued to hear evidence that the law cannot save anyone, and asked if he could hear more.

So when he was invited again a few weeks later, Imam Ahmed went with expectation, greeted the various men from his village with enthusiasm, and introduced himself to the one or two men with whom he was not yet acquainted. One of these newcomers, Rahul, had traveled all the way from the capital city and was very friendly, exchanging phone numbers and addresses with everyone present. Imam Ahmed could not understand why this seemed to make the man who was teaching uncomfortable. But the meeting began, Imam Ahmed heard about how Jesus is the fulfillment of the law, and something stirred in his heart and mind—could this be the truth?

Only a few weeks later, he received a letter in the mail from the capital. Rahul, the man who had exchanged addresses with him and the others at the previous meeting, invited him to the capital city for two days of meetings about the Prophet Jesus. If he agreed to come to these meetings, his bus fees, room, and board would be provided, plus another US$20 in cash. What an invitation! He wanted to hear more about Jesus, he had never been able to afford to travel to the capital city, and he could actually earn some extra money. He eagerly wrote back and agreed.

When he traveled to the capital, he was surprised to see at least 150 others at the meeting, and even more surprised at the tall foreigner who was introduced as the speaker. This foreigner and the other men and women with him (who were seated in the front of the room in chairs) looked and sounded like television movie stars, adding to Imam Ahmed's bewilderment. Could this man, who comes from a people who are steeped in sin (as is evident from the television), possibly know anything about God? But as Rahul introduced the guest speaker, he reminded the group that the foreign guests were generously providing them all with US$20 and their room and board, and encouraged everyone to listen attentively and enthusiastically. And so this foreigner proceeded to speak with a loud, passionate voice, and Rahul translated. It was difficult to understand everything that was said, but overall it was an interesting time.

ONE MORE QUALIFICATION FOR SPIRITUAL LEADERSHIP?

A relatively wealthy local believer set down her cup of tea, put her hands on the table, leaned forward, and said, "Of course you should partner with local believers. But why do you foreigners seem to pick out the worst of our people to shower with resources, while ignoring those who are mature and able to lead in a godly way? This is not helping the church in our country at all!"

So how should we, as outsiders, choose our local partners? The Apostle Paul wrote that an important part of establishing an ekklesia (local Body of Christ or church) in a new area is to appoint local leadership. The books of Titus and 1 Timothy list many necessary qualifications for spiritual leadership, including the need for the leader to be the following:

- *above reproach*
- *not overbearing*
- *respectable*
- *able to teach*
- *mature*
- *exemplary in marriage and parenting*
- *self-controlled*
- *hospitable*
- *not a lover of money*
- *upright*

But too often, as mission organizations and churches around the world who want to reach Muslims for Christ, we unintentionally communicate to local believers that the most important qualification for spiritual leadership is the ability to speak an international language (such as English, Korean, Spanish, or French). We convey this by consistently providing financial support to the local believers who can communicate with us and translate for us.

From our perspective, we are hastening the day of Christ's return by using effective and efficient methods. After all, we think, it takes years and a lot of financial investment for one outsider to learn the language well enough to communicate effectively, and funding locals is much more expedient. But since we must have some level of communication even to transfer funds, we naturally gravitate to those believers with whom we can communicate. In doing this, do we accidentally suggest that language learning skills are more important than character? An important truth that should be obvious but is often overlooked is that there may be a good number of godly and tested MBB leaders who are excellent communicators in their own mother tongue but who cannot speak one word of a foreign language.

The most prominent theological seminary in one South Asian country has English on the curriculum for every semester, and students know that if they can master English as well as get a degree in theology, then they are almost guaranteed to find a sponsor who will fund their ministry efforts. Their sponsors live far away from the realities of the local believers' daily lives, and do not consistently have the opportunity to observe whether or not these potential national partners are hospitable, above reproach, respectable, or disciplined in relating to family and community. Instead, the sponsors must make the decision to fund the ministry based upon vision trips, occasional reports, and follow-up visits where the communication takes place in the sponsor's language, effectively eliminating any local accountability.

Certainly, learning another language is a necessary skill for cross-cultural ministry. But this is the responsibility of those called by God to cross cultures. Language learning should not be the qualification for someone whose job description is to shepherd a flock locally or witness locally. The Apostle Paul did not include it on the list, and neither should we.

During meals and breaks, Imam Ahmed chatted with the other participants and heard everyone talk about the various organizations that provide funding for meetings like this one. Imam Ahmed was surprised to learn that many of the participants received a salary or stipend from foreigners in order to attend meetings and host them in their village area. He realized he could earn significantly more money this way than through his village clerical duties.

Also during meals and breaks, the foreign guests chatted with Rahul, the only local person present who could speak their language. He had been such a gracious and helpful host to them since their arrival. The foreign guests had journeyed to the country on a "vision trip," praying about how God might use them to advance God's Kingdom in this Muslim land. They were delighted for the opportunity to share something from God's Word to brand-new, Muslim background believers, and prayed that God would use it to encourage and strengthen these believers.

When the foreign guests learned from Rahul that Imam Ahmed was a new believer who had come to this meeting for the first time, it generated much excitement, especially when they learned that Imam Ahmed was a Muslim cleric. The foreign guests saw Imam Ahmed's presence at the meeting as significant evidence that their host and translator, Rahul, was doing a very important work in the country, and was worthy of their further financial support and partnership. And since Imam Ahmed was already a religious teacher, they deduced that he might be an excellent pastor or evangelist, and that this could be the answer to their prayers for national partners. They returned home and reported to their church about Rahul's ministry, and about their opportunity to share God's Word with more than 150 eager, new believers. They also told the moving story about how Imam Ahmed, the Muslim cleric, had put his faith in Jesus and is now sharing his faith with his community. The church enthusiastically decided to support Imam Ahmed in this new ministry.

Back in his own home, leaning against the wall of his porch, Imam Ahmed looks at the letter he received from Rahul. He is confused by the offer to work for Rahul and receive regular funding from the foreign guests, and also amazed at the prospect of tripling his income as a cleric. But he will have to handle this carefully. If the village finds out that he is being paid by foreigners to teach something different from what they regularly hear in the mosque, his family will be driven out, and perhaps harmed. He decides that he will continue to go to his friend's house to hear the teaching about Jesus, and will encourage some of his close relatives to go with him.

A month later, Rahul visits to find out how things are going and to give Imam Ahmed his stipend. Imam Ahmed tells him about all the different people who go to the meetings to hear about Jesus and mentions that the group meets regularly. He receives the stipend gratefully as it will help pay some needed medical bills. Rahul is likewise delighted to write in his next newsletter to the Western donors about the budding ministry of Imam Ahmed in his home village.

WHO IS DISCIPLING KHADIJA?

One of us was visiting in Khadija's country and had the privilege of getting to know this lovely MBB sister. She had a beautiful testimony of how Jesus Christ had changed her life, and her joy in the Lord and sweet spirit were deeply evident. We asked her about her current growth in discipleship, and she shared the following with us, her eyes shining with joy:

"On Monday mornings I meet with Sally from YWAM for Bible study. Then on Monday afternoons I get together with Anke and Maria of OM for prayer. On Monday evening I attend the weekly fellowship dinners at the home of the Smiths of AWM. Then on Tuesday mornings I meet with Katie of another agency for a discipleship session. On Tuesday afternoons I get together with Marie of the Southern Baptists for fellowship ..." And so she continued, describing to us each day of her typical week.

Since we knew that she was unmarried and did not live with her family, we wondered how she could earn an income to live on if she was so busy with Bible studies and prayer meetings every weekday. We asked, in a polite, oblique way, what she did for a living, to get income. Continuing her joyful, angelic smile she told us:

"On Monday mornings I meet with Sally from YWAM for Bible study. Then on Monday afternoons I get together with Anke and Maria of OM for prayer. On Monday evening ..." At first we did not understand what she meant—why she was repeating the same story she had just told us about her discipleship program. As she explained further, we began to understand. Each of these wonderful missionary sisters in Christ with whom she met was also financially generous. Some were more generous than others. Whenever Khadija had a financial need, she would humbly, discreetly share a prayer request about it with these missionary women. Usually most of them would give something. It all added up to enough money for Khadija to live on. In effect, Khadija's full-time job, which was earning her a full-time income, was to be "discipled" by all of these different women.

When we talked with some of these missionaries, we discovered that most of them did not know how many other missionaries were also "discipling" Khadija. Each was writing prayer letters home about their discipling ministry with this one MBB woman. More importantly, they did not know how much money other missionaries were giving. They had no idea that it was all adding up to a full-time job with a full-time income.

THE CASE OF AISHA

Aisha was one of the first people in her 100 percent Muslim country to believe in Christ. She was passionately committed to the Lord and led more than a dozen relatives and friends to Christ. She experienced remarkable visions and was used in healing the sick in Jesus' name. She had a job with a modest salary, and was not financially dependent on anyone.

One day, representatives involved in planning and preparing an important international evangelical conference visited Aisha's country. They met with the on-site missionaries and said that they had funds to bring three national believers to represent Aisha's country at this important conference. The missionaries replied that the church was still not established and that the handful of national believers were not yet at the point of maturity to be ready to fly around the world to attend such a conference. However, the conference representatives insisted that the invitation was for nationals only, and they suggested that the missionaries were being arrogant if they were unwilling to allow adult MBBs to decide for themselves what they were ready to handle.

Finally, one missionary couple introduced Aisha to the conference planners. She attended the conference and came back more on fire for Jesus than ever before. She was deeply inspired by the vision she caught for being part of the worldwide Church. She also came back with a list of names and addresses of Christians around the world who wanted to stay in touch with her. Her presence at the conference had generated quite some excitement, since no believer from her country had ever before in history attended an international Christian conference.

Soon Aisha began receiving and accepting invitations to conferences all over the world. Her non-believing Muslim husband suspected (unfairly) that she was committing adultery on all of her international travels. He was an alcoholic and a violent man. He began to beat her regularly to the point of endangering her life. Finally he divorced her.

Sometime later, Aisha met a fine young MBB man, and the two were married. He had no job, but they both had enough conference invitations to keep them traveling full-time. They discovered that they could earn enough income to live on through their conference attendance. They took the *per diem* allowance often given at such conferences and used it to buy merchandise that they then brought back home in their luggage and sold at great profit—often to the missionaries in their country. They were able to beat the market prices for such merchandise because they brought it through customs without declaring the merchandise or paying customs duty on it.

As they got to know various churches and wealthy Christians in America, Europe, and Korea, they found that their generous brothers and sisters around the world wanted to help them financially to facilitate their ministry in this totally unreached country. They began receiving regular donations from a variety of sources. They in turn were generous with their new-found wealth and helped other MBBs. This generosity, combined with their evangelistic zeal and gifting, resulted in an MBB church numbering perhaps twenty-five members under their leadership.

Problems began to develop as some MBBs felt that they were not getting their fair share of the financial assistance. They accused Aisha and her husband of concealing how much money they were receiving and of hoarding most of it for themselves. Aisha and her husband insisted that this was not true, but they felt pressure to attend more conferences to generate more money. There was of course no accounting, no control-mechanism, and no transparency about what money was flowing in and out, so we do not know whether the accusations were fair or not.

> OVER A PERIOD OF YEARS, THE MBB CHURCH GREW IN
> NUMBERS, BUT THE FINANCIAL JEALOUSIES AND RUMORS GREW.

Because Aisha and her husband had children, they usually could not both travel at the same time. But they needed financially to travel to conferences as often as possible. Over time, they got to the point where on perhaps 95 percent of the days of the year one of them was away at a conference while the other was staying home with the children. This was not good for the children, and it was not good for the marriage, since they were spending very little time together as a family.

Over a period of years, the MBB church grew in numbers, but the financial jealousies and rumors grew, and the stress on the marriage grew. It all exploded when Aisha discovered that her husband had committed adultery on one occasion while they were apart. He repented and asked forgiveness, but the hurt was too deep. She began seeing other men (but not committing literal adultery) to attempt to restore her self-image as an attractive woman. The other MBBs were deeply disillusioned by this, and suddenly all of the jealousies and rumors about finances exploded into a major dispute. The church totally collapsed, and the fallout has caused serious hurt to all of the other MBB fellowships in the country.

SO WHAT SHOULD BE DONE? A CODE OF ETHICS?

Most effective, long-term church planters among Muslims—both missionaries and mature MBB leaders—agree that the problem described above is a huge problem, and most agree that there is no good solution to the problem. Most of the problems described above originated with well-meaning foreign Christians who had not learned the language and the culture and/or had not lived long-term among the Muslims whom the Christians want to touch for Christ. In many cases, if these brothers and sisters had known the damage they would cause, they would have acted differently. Do those who have deeper linguistic and cultural understanding and experience—whether cross-cultural workers or mature MBB leaders—have a responsibility to give clearer leadership to our well-meaning brothers and sisters?

MOST OF THE PROBLEMS DESCRIBED ABOVE ORIGINATED WITH WELL-MEANING FOREIGN CHRISTIANS WHO HAD NOT LEARNED THE LANGUAGE AND THE CULTURE AND/OR HAD NOT LIVED LONG-TERM AMONG THE MUSLIMS WHOM THE CHRISTIANS WANT TO TOUCH FOR CHRIST. IN MANY CASES, IF THESE BROTHERS AND SISTERS HAD KNOWN THE DAMAGE THEY WOULD CAUSE, THEY WOULD HAVE ACTED DIFFERENTLY.

One form which such leadership might take would be for a broad group of senior, respected field leaders, including both expatriate workers and mature MBB leaders, to craft a set of ethical guidelines that represent a consensus governing the use of money, conference invitations, scholarship offers, job offers, and so on by foreign Christians in Muslim contexts. Of course, some groups might be unwilling to abide by such guidelines. But we believe that the majority of our well-meaning brothers and sisters would attempt to abide by such guidelines if they were clearly written and came from a broadly-based group of field leaders whom they respect.

The following might be included in such guidelines:

1. The decision to follow Christ involves sacrifice and self-denial (Matthew 8:20; 16:24–26). Nothing should be done that gives the impression—either to new believers or to the surrounding Muslim community—that people are receiving or may receive financial or material rewards for believing in Christ. This is particularly important to consider in the context of relief and development work.

2. New believers must be sensitively taught the dignity of work and not be encouraged to be dependent on handouts (1 Thessalonians 4:11–12; 2 Thessalonians 3:10).

3. Those in Christian ministry who receive any financial support—whether they are expatriates or locals, and whether the source of support is foreign or local—should be making a financial sacrifice to be in ministry. That is, it should be clear to all that the

minister could have made more money in another line of work
(1 Corinthians 9:14–18; 2 Corinthians 2:17; 1 Peter 5:2).

4. Just as most donors would not fund expatriate workers who are
   not accountable to some responsible organizational structure for
   their personal finances, use of ministry funds, and general Christian character, so any support of MBB leaders should be contingent on the establishment of at least an informal local oversight
   committee that knows the leader's overall financial picture and
   personal Christian character, and that is able to keep the leader
   accountable. That committee should be composed primarily of
   people who know the local situation intimately and who have no
   personal financial interest in the matter (2 Corinthians 8:19–21;
   Acts 20:4).

5. No funding should be kept secret from the oversight committee
   (2 Corinthians 4:2).

6. We should not "be hasty in laying on hands" (1 Timothy 5:22; 1
   Timothy 3:6). Church leaders need time to develop and demonstrate maturity in Christ.

7. Conference invitations and scholarship opportunities should
   be contingent on their reinforcing a believer's commitment and
   relationship to their local church and its leadership, not undermining it (1 Corinthians 14:12).

8. The local church should be taught the principles of tithing and
   offerings (Malachi 3:8ff.). Any external funding should fulfill the
   criterion of not undermining the motivation of local MBBs to
   tithe and to give to others.

The foregoing is not intended as a definitive set of guidelines. Rather, it is intended as an initial list to stimulate discussion that might lead to a consensus on guidelines that might then be proposed to the worldwide Christian community.

CONCLUSION

The most effective, long-term church planters we know among Muslims generally agree that "there are no really good solutions to these problems." But they also agree that they have a fairly clear idea of what some *bad* solutions are. If we can move toward a set of agreed-upon ethical guidelines, then perhaps we can prevent future tragedies in the lives of precious MBB brothers and sisters like Mahmoud, Zaydan, Imam Ahmed, Khadija, and Aisha. Perhaps we can learn to nourish God's plants in a way that does not choke them with thorns, but instead helps them to flourish.

Chapter 18

Relevant Responses to Folk Muslims

CALEB CHUL-SOO KIM AND JOHN
& ANNA TRAVIS

*"A number of those who practiced magic arts
brought their books and burned them."*
Acts 19:19

Folk Muslims live in a world where evil forces and invisible beings, both real and imagined, wreak havoc in their daily lives. To combat attacks from this dangerous, unseen world, folk Muslims have devised numerous traditions and practices. This chapter describes the world of the folk Muslim and the felt needs it expresses and which the Gospel must address if these Muslims are to see its relevance—a different set of needs than those which Christian witnesses traditionally address. Further, when these Muslims decide to follow Christ, there are commonly deep issues from occult practices, hurts, and lack of forgiveness that require a ministry of inner healing and prayer for them to experience true health and freedom in Christ. The chapter will conclude with a description of this ministry in concrete situations.

The Muslim Spiritual World

Most non-Western people do not see as sharp a distinction between the "natural world" and "supernatural world" as Westerners usually do.[160] In most folk Muslim societies, such a distinction becomes quite absurd. Muslim communities are intrinsically spiritual since life revolves around Islamic cosmology and religious tenets. The universe is understood in terms of the qur'anic concept of God's creation, consisting of both the human world and the unseen world.[161] The unseen is directly connected with the human world. This may well be what is expressed by the two worlds in Surah 55:31. Most Islamic traditions understand this as the duality of the living world, including both human beings and *jinn* (spirits).[162] Therefore, what appears to be "natural" is actually touched by, and connected to, what we call the supernatural or the unseen world. A large portion of ordinary Muslims daily experience a world in which they encounter innumerable spiritual beings and forces that are hostile and menacing to their earthly well-being. In the following, the beliefs of many Muslims about their struggle with the unseen will be described.

Formal Islam and Folk Islam

The faith and practice of common Muslims can be described in terms of two different, yet interconnected, religio-cultural expressions. The first, what some call "formal" or "official Islam," is used to refer to the ideological aspect of Islam proper. It focuses on "high" religious issues—human existence, ultimate realities, and religious duties. The six articles of *iman* (belief), the five pillars, *jihad* (the Muslim struggle "in the way of God"), the efforts to emulate the lifestyle of Muhammad, and other beliefs, characterize the nature of formal Islam. These official aspects of the faith have been commonly understood by outsiders as truly representative of Islam. A significant proportion of ordinary Muslims, however, live in a world that contains spiritual elements and practices often found outside formal Islamic ideology or are tangential to it.

These spiritual elements and practices constitute the other face of Islam, often referred to as "popular" or "folk Islam." Many of these popular beliefs and practices

---

160 See Charles Kraft, *Anthropology for Christian Witness* (Maryknoll, NY: Orbis Books, 1996), 197–198; Paul Hiebert, Daniel Shaw, and Tite Tiénou, *Understanding Folk Religion* (Grand Rapids, MI: Baker Books, 1999), 35.

161 See Ibn Kathir, *Tafsir Ibn Kathir*, abr. ed., trans. Safi al-Rahman Mubarakfuri, vol. 1 (Riyadh, Saudi Arabia: Darussalam, 2000), 73.

162 See Cyril Glassé, *The Concise Encyclopedia of Islam* (New York: Harper Collins Publishers, 1989), 211.

originate from pre-Islamic local traditions. Nonetheless, the majority of Muslims, including a number of leaders, do not condemn these practices, in part because they often appear Islamic, having some basis in certain Islamic traditions (*Hadīth* or *Sunna*). Islamists like the Wahhabis condemn these beliefs and practices, but many common Muslims consider such practices part of Muslim religion and culture.

Thus, folk Islam is composed of beliefs and practices that have been tacitly endorsed by certain *Hadīth* traditions, or that have been passed down from certain pre-Islamic local traditions, and have been absorbed and integrated into the Muslim culture. The effect of this is that any given Muslim culture contains at least three religio-cultural components: normative Islamic features, Hadīth-based Muslim traditions, and pre-Islamic local traditions.

At a practical level, folk Islam deals mainly with everyday problems that are seldom touched upon, much less resolved, by formal Islam. The broad acceptance and practice of folk Islam indicate that the needs of many Muslim hearts are not satisfied by formal religion. It also shows that many Muslims are anxious and afraid about the affairs of the invisible supernatural world around them. Folk Islam addresses the 'here-and-now' problems. Thus, folk Islam resides in the real lives of Muslims who have worries, questions, and dissatisfactions.

To many, official Islam is primarily intellectual, leading to institutionalized laws and theologies along with formal rituals. However, it should be noted that both the terms "folk Islam" (popular or low Islam) and "formal Islam" (normative, orthodox, or high Islam) are terms that describe dynamic religious aspects of Islam observed in any Muslim society. Unlike the concept of syncretism, a large proportion of Muslim individual holds both formal and folk Islamic world-views, although the proportion of each worldview may differ from individual to individual (or from society to society), depending upon each individual's cultural upbringing.

FOLK ISLAMIC WORLDVIEW

Having briefly described both formal Islam and folk Islam, we now turn to a more focused discussion of folk Islamic worldview. In doing so, it is helpful to use the framework for analysis of religious systems provided by Paul Hiebert.[163] By adopting this framework, the folk Islamic worldview can be depicted as

---

[163]   See the original model in Paul Hiebert's article, "The Flaw of the Excluded Middle," in *Anthropological Reflections on Missiological Issues* (Grand Rapids, MI: Baker Book House, 1994), 194.

shown below in Figure 18.1 (note that it, like other folk religions, is composed of personal beings and impersonal powers or forces).

	Personal Beings		Impersonal Forces[1]		
Unseen or Supernatural Realm	Cosmic Beings based on High Islam	*Allah, angels (archangels and many others)*	Cosmic Forces based on High Islam	*God's absolute power and preordination (qadr), the Book (the Qur'an)*	Other World
Empirical Realm (Folk Islam)	Other Beings in Low Islam	*the prophets (in Paradise), dead saints, ancestors, Iblis (the chief jinni or the Devil), all other jinn (many with names), etc.*	Local Forces in Low Islam	*magic, sorcery, astrological forces (power of astrologic time and space), divination, Baraka, merit of dhikr, evil eye, evil tongue, curses, talisman, amulet, reading of the Qur'an, drinking of the qur'anic writings, etc.*	This World Empirical Realm (Folk Islam)
Seen or Natural Realm	Social Relations in Low Islam	*Muslims (holy men and ordinary Muslims), other religious people (Christians, Jews), nonbelievers (Mushirukun), animals, etc.*	Natural Science in Low Islam	*natural medicines (plants and herbs both from Islamic traditions as in Hadith[2] and from pre-Islamic local traditions), and other local sciences*	

[1] Hiebert uses the term "organic analogy (or metaphor)" in place of "personal beings" and "mechanical analogy (metaphor)" in place of "impersonal forces." See also Bill Musk, *The Unseen Face of Islam* (Kent, UK: MARC, 1989), 192.

[2] See Imam Ibn Qayyim Al-Jawziyya (1290-1350), *Natural Healing with the Medicine of the Prophet* (translated and emended by Muhammad Al-Akili, Philadelphia, PA: Pearl Publishing House, 1993), a good example to demonstrate Islamic traditional medical science.

Fig.18.1

As shown in Figure 18.1, the boundary between the high and low aspects in the folk Muslim worldview corresponds more to the distinction between the categories of "Other World" and "This World" than to the division between the "Unseen (or Supernatural)" and "Seen (or Natural)" realms. "This World" is also parallel to the "Empirical Realm," which is the arena of folk Islamic beliefs and practices. This means that low Islam, consisting of folk Islamic features, is concerned mostly with this-worldly experiences. Most personal beings that belong to the category of the unseen world, except Allah and his angels who are far beyond human approach, are perceived to be part of "This World." They are the objects of human experience, interaction, and manipulation like those in the Seen world, and most of them are unfriendly to humans. Also a part of "This World" are countless spiritual forces, most of which are hazardous to the human world.[164]

Folk Muslim Beliefs about Spiritual Beings

Many folk Muslims see God as distant, unconcerned with the earthly problems that affect everyday life. God's primary business is to determine the final destiny or fate of each person. This means that Muslims often feel they must deal with the various spirit beings of their reality—dead saints, ancestors, jinn, and other types of traditional spirits—on their own.

Among the spiritual beings, jinn[165] seem to be most feared. They are perceived as social members and thus classified as part of the earthly domain in spite of their supernatural, invisible nature. They have intellect, emotion, and will.[166] This Muslim view of jinn is actually derived from Islamic traditional teachings, based on the Qur'an and the Hadith.[167] According to the canonical traditions, jinn are treated as another species of creation, spiritually parallel to the human race (Surah 55:33). Jinn were created by God from fire (Surah 15:27; 55:15),

---

[164]   Hiebert has already pointed out the fault of the exclusion of this psycho-spiritual world by Westerners, calling this supernatural yet experiential realm the "excluded middle." See his article "The Flaw of the Excluded Middle."

[165]   In Standard English, "jinni" is singular and "jinn" plural.

[166]   In popular belief, jinn may have bodies, too. If they do, they must have weight and density similar to that of the air. See Ahmad H. Sakr, *Al-Jinn* (Lombard, IL: Foundation for Islamic Knowledge, 1994), 115. Thus, it is believed that jinn also eat, drink, marry, produce offspring, and die, just as human beings do. If *jinn* do not have bodies, they use human bodies to manifest themselves. This is a Muslim folk theory of what anthropologists call spirit possession.

[167]   Caleb Kim has extensively discussed the canonical accounts of jinn as well as folk experiences of jinn in the fifth chapter of his book *Islam among the Swahili in East Africa* (Nairobi, Kenya: Acton Publishers, 2004). See also Abu Ameenah Bilal Philips, *The Exorcist Tradition in Islaam* (sic.) (Sharjah, UAE: Dar al Fatah, 1997) and Umar Sulaiman al-Ashqar, *The World of the Jinn and Devils*, trans. Jamaal al-Din M. Zarabozo (Boulder, CO: Al-Basheer Company, 1998).

whereas human beings were created from dust (Surah 22:5). However, jinn are notorious for their evil and malevolent nature toward human beings. For this reason, they are called "devils" (*shayatin*).[168] They are also rebellious toward God, although some of them converted to Islam when they became fascinated with Muhammad's recitation of the Qur'an (Surah 72:1–15). Even religious (Muslim) jinn are apt to afflict people with all kinds of diseases and personal problems for no apparent reason. Certainly jinn are "to man an avowed enemy" (Surah 17:53). In folk understanding, therefore, jinn ought to be avoided if possible, and appeased through appropriate rituals if people get in trouble with them.

Beliefs about Supernatural Forces

It is not only spiritual beings that threaten human well-being, but spiritual forces as well. Unless these are controlled and manipulated, social or individual security will be at stake. Some people are believed to possess these powers and can use them to harm others. The evil eye, for example, is a type of spiritual force that Muslims in many parts of the world believe has a devastating effect. Curses, spells, and charms are also feared. Some Muslims fear that even compliment-ing someone about a pretty baby girl might provoke an evil jinni's curse upon her because of envy of her beauty. One's failure in business might be caused by someone's spell or curse put upon the business. One's boyfriend may leave her because her rival uses more powerful charms than hers.

There are so many unidentified enemies in life that it is difficult to know who is a friend and who is not. Because of this kind of fear of evil forces, Mus-lims always yearn for more *baraka* (blessing) or power to protect themselves against them, either through the purchase of magic charms, amulets, talismans, and the like, through the services of "power people" (local shamans, healers, exorcists, etc.), or through the performance of precisely designed rituals. For this reason, both 'helpful' and 'harmful' magic (i.e., both witchcraft and sorcery) are popularly practiced among folk Muslims. Failure to control and manipulate spiritual forces for their own benefit can spell disaster.

---

[168] Kim, *Islam among the Swahili*, 82. The Muslim use of words referring to jinn is often confusing. To clarify the usage, it needs to be noted that the mischievous or harmful jinn are generally called *shayatin* (the plural form of *shaitan*) meaning "devils." Thus "jinn" and "shayatin" are not different types of spirits. The *shayatin* (devils) can be understood as evil jinn.

FOLK ISLAMIC PRACTICES

The harmful spiritual beings and forces are perceived to be of great peril to Muslim individuals and societies. Because of this dread of the spirit world, Muslims feel the need for assistance from power people or practitioners who are able to deal with the hostile surroundings. It is often observed that such practitioners even come from 'orthodox' Islamic leadership in some places. The practitioners offer their services for a fee in a way similar to the way medical doctors provide their expertise for the health of their community.

THE HARMFUL SPIRITUAL BEINGS AND FORCES ARE PERCEIVED TO BE OF GREAT PERIL TO MUSLIM INDIVIDUALS AND SOCIETIES. BECAUSE OF THIS DREAD OF THE SPIRIT WORLD, MUSLIMS FEEL THE NEED FOR ASSISTANCE FROM POWER PEOPLE OR PRACTITIONERS WHO ARE ABLE TO DEAL WITH THE HOSTILE SURROUNDINGS.

If someone is believed to be afflicted or inhabited by jinn, he or she will go to a practitioner. If the practitioner tends toward a more orthodox form of Islam, he will use the Qur'an to deal with the evil spirits. Generally, the practitioner will recite some qur'anic chapters (often the thirty-sixth Surah, *surah Yasin*) to chase away the jinn who have harmed the patient. The practitioner commonly reprimands the afflicting or inhabiting spirits with an authoritative voice to take away the cause of the sickness and leave the patient alone.

If, however, the practitioner's religious predisposition is more toward folk Islam, the healer is likely to employ a variety of pre-Islamic elements from local traditions, such as drumming, dancing, burning incense, or performing a séance. However, these folk-oriented practitioners are also likely to incorporate into their dealing with spirits some official Islamic rituals and forms of prayer and chanting. These practitioners do not generally try to exorcize the spirits, but rather attempt to pacify them.[169] Whether attempting to drive the demon out with qur'anic verses or pacifying it through folk rituals, the cure or deliverance is often only temporary.

---

[169]   This type of approach to evil spirits to heal the sick or possessed is called "adorcism" by some anthropologists. See Luc de Heusch, *Why Marry Her? Society and Symbolic Structures*, trans. Janet Lloyd (Cambridge, UK: Cambridge University Press, 1981), 156.

Apart from seeking help from practitioners, ordinary Muslims also use a myriad of practices to protect their families and communities against evil spirits and forces. They often visit shrines or tombs of dead saints, believing that dead saints can pass on their blessings (*baraka*) to the living through various veneration rituals. They may also perform official Islamic rituals such as the practices of the five pillars (originally designed to enhance the Muslim focus upon the oneness of Allah), in order to magically obtain more *baraka* (blessing).

Some Muslims also focus on particular days, dates, times, months, and seasons that they believe have particular spiritual meaning. Failure to observe the right time for certain activities may cause a calamity. Various locations and directions also have spiritual significance to some Muslims such that they are vigilant to face the right direction and to find the right place for certain actions, determined by folk traditions. Many Muslims are, therefore, extremely careful to observe all kinds of rules in order to secure their welfare against the hostile spiritual environment. From all this we can see that the minds of folk Muslims are filled with many kinds of fears: fear of fate, fear of an unknown future, fear of unknown enemies, fear of the unseen world, fear of wicked jinn, fear of angry ancestors, fear of sicknesses, and so forth.

POWER ENCOUNTER:
A CHRIST-CENTERED RESPONSE TO FOLK ISLAM

In light of the belief systems described above, what is the relevance of the one the Qur'an calls Isa al-Masih (Jesus the Messiah) to the needs of the world's folk Muslims? Do Jesus and his followers have a response to the Muslim fear of jinn and evil forces, their quests for physical healing, and their hopes to be blessed in this life and the life to come?[170]

During Jesus' earthly ministry, he and his followers proclaimed a message of eternal life while freeing myriads of people from demons, diseases, and disorders. These miraculous acts of God's power, such as healing and deliverance, are often referred to as *power encounters*. Muslims who have accepted Jesus often mention that some form of God's miraculous power intervening in human

---

[170] The Qur'an portrays Jesus as a great healer who even raised the dead (*Surah Ali Imran* [3]:43–49 and *Surah al-Maidi* [5]:109–10).

affairs was instrumental in their decision to follow Christ.[171] Their accounts reveal two types of power encounters. The first involves sovereign acts of God such as visions, spiritual dreams, angelic visitations, and miraculous answers to prayer that occur without human involvement. The second type involves miracles that occur as followers of Jesus use their authority in Christ (Luke 9:1–2; 10:17–19) to heal the sick, cast out demons, and pray for troubled hearts and minds.[172] The remainder of this chapter will focus on this second type of power encounter,[173] with emphasis on a holistic approach to healing prayer.

A Holistic Approach to Healing Prayer

As the description of folk Islam above indicates (see Figure 18.1), folk Muslims see life holistically, without the sharp division Westerners generally perceive between the visible material world and unseen spiritual world.[174] The people Jesus healed in first-century Palestine possessed a worldview not unlike that of many modern-day folk Muslims. As Scripture indicates, Jesus healed holistically touching bodies, souls, and spirits. A holistic approach to healing prayer among folk Muslims today needs to include at least three types of prayer that heuristically we refer to as *breaking* prayer, *healing* prayer, and *deliverance* prayer.[175] These types of prayers are described below.

Breaking Prayers

Breaking prayer deals with breaking spiritual bondages (somewhat similar to negative spiritual forces in Islamic worldview), and is characterized by specific renunciation and repentance. It covers areas such as occult folk Muslim practices that invoke spirits (Deuteronomy 18:9–14), generational bondages

---

171   For descriptions of power encounter and power ministries among Muslims, see J. Dudley Woodberry, "The Relevance of Power Ministries for Folk Muslims," in *Wrestling with Dark Angels*, ed. C. Peter Wagner and Douglas Pennoyer (Ventura, CA: Regal Books, 1990), 313–31. See also Vivienne Stacey, "Practice of Exorcism and Healing," in *Muslims and Christians on the Emmaus Road*, ed. J. Dudley Woodberry (Monrovia, CA: MARC Publications, 1989), 291–303.

172   Praying for troubled hearts and minds may also be referred to as inner healing, in contrast to outer or physical healing.

173   This is not to imply that this second type is more important. We emphasize the second type only because this is where we as Christ's servants are called to work. We should pray, however, always asking God to perform more and more of his sovereign miraculous signs and wonders.

174   For an excellent treatise on this subject, see Bill Musk, *The Unseen Face of Islam* (Kent: MARC, 1989).

175   For an excellent description of these three types of prayers (although he uses different terminology), see Charles Kraft, *Defeating Dark Angels: Breaking Demonic Oppression in a Believer's Life* (Ann Arbor, MI: Servant Publications, 1992).

(Lamentations 5:7; Psalm 79:8, 9), ungodly "soul ties,"[176] judgments of self or others (Matthew 7:1, 2; James 4:11, 12; Romans 14:4), vows made outside God's will (Proverbs 20:25; Matthew 5:33–37; Leviticus 5:4–6), and curses (Psalm 62:4; 109:28; James 3:9–10; Proverbs 26:2; Galatians 3:13; Romans 12:14). It also covers any other sin or activity that may have given Satan an open door into one's life. It is not uncommon in the life of folk Muslims to find many of these destructive practices. Renouncing and repenting are referred to and illustrated often in Scripture (e.g. Ezekiel 14:6; Daniel 4:27; Proverbs 28:13; 2 Corinthians 4:2; Acts 19:18–19).

Healing Prayer

Healing prayer consists of both physical healing and inner healing. Physical healing happens as diseases, injuries, and physical handicaps are brought before the Lord in prayer. Scripture is replete with examples of physical healing.

Inner healing, on the other hand, deals with wounds of the heart, painful memories, and destructive thought patterns. This generally takes place as the one seeking healing (the *prayee*) and the one leading the prayer time (the *pray-er*) go together before the Lord in prayer, asking God to remind the prayee of any incident(s) where the prayee's heart was wounded. As the prayee remembers (see Psalm 42:4; Lamentations 3:19–20),[177] she or he verbally describes ("pours out," see Psalm 38:9; 64:1; 62:8; Matthew 26:36–44) to God the emotions connected with the incident, being honest about even the worst reactions. The prayee then asks God to show something of himself at the point of pain (Psalm 34:18; 69:17), trusting that even at the darkest moment, God was actually present (Psalm 139:7–16). The pray-er and prayee wait before God until he does what only he can do; heal the wound and lift the pain (Psalm 94:19; 147:3). It may be necessary at this stage to move back and forth between breaking prayers and healing prayer. Often, healing comes more readily when breaking prayers are spoken to address any issues that surface during the recollection of memories.

---

[176] Ungodly soul ties refer to unhealthy bonds with others caused by such actions as sexual relationships outside marriage, or relationships with power people (shamans, certain curers, some martial arts teachers). Both healthy human ties as well as unhealthy soul ties are alluded to in Scripture (e.g., Genesis 2:24; Leviticus 26:13; Colossians 2:2; Ephesians 5:21–25; 6:1–4; Galatians 1:10; Proverbs 29:25; Jude 14 and 16 [Samson's soul ties with women]; 1 Corinthians 6:15–17).

[177] The emphasis in this model is not on the details of the memory (endeavoring to avoid the possible problem of "false memories"); the emphasis is on the negative emotions that surface, and waiting on God to bring healing and freedom.

A HOLISTIC APPROACH TO HEALING PRAYER
INCLUDES

1. *Breaking prayer*
2. *Healing prayer*
3. *Deliverance prayer*

In these healing moments, God tenderly communicates with the prayee via a still small voice (1 Kings 19:12), a mental picture or vision (e.g., Acts 10:9–16), a Scripture verse brought to mind, a physical sensation, miraculous peace (Daniel 10:18, 19), or simply a sense of his presence (Exodus 33:14).

During the days of Jesus' earthly ministry, we find numerous cases of inner healing as he touched and restored people's troubled hearts, emotions, and souls through his powerful, loving words and deeds. Jesus brought about inner healing in the restoration of the guilt-ridden Peter (John 21:15–19), the socially ostracized woman at the well (John 4:4–42), the despised Zacchaeus (Luke 19:1–10), the grateful prostitute honored by Christ (Luke 7:36–50), the rescued adulteress (John 8:2–11), the blind man emboldened by Christ (John 9:1–41), the ceremonially unclean hemorrhaging woman (Mark 5:25–34), and the tormented, feared wild man freed of myriads of demons (Luke 8:26–39). In each of these touching encounters with Christ, we see Jesus healing more than physical bodies: he heals broken hearts and shattered lives; he takes away rejection, shame, and sorrow.

Essentially, healing prayer entails helping people to be still and listen to God, spiritually experiencing his love and healing power, similar to the way people experienced it when Jesus walked on earth. How can this occur when Jesus, though alive, is not present in body with us? The answer is that wherever we are gathered in his name, until the end of the age, he is with us, and spiritually we can hear our Shepherd's voice (Matthew 18:20; 28:20; John 10:4–16, 27). Humans by nature are meant to experience the Lord's presence, but not all take advantage of this (Psalm 16:11; 91:1; 139:7).

Of course, experiencing the presence and healing of Christ is highly subjective, yet Muslims with whom we have prayed seem to know when Isa has touched them in a special way. Tears often follow as they then effortlessly forgive the one who offended them (Matthew 6:12–15; 18:21–35), renounce the desire to blame God (Job 40:8), and repent of sin (Proverbs 28:13; 1 John 1:9–10), often committed as a wrong reaction to pain (Ephesians 4:26, 27). A new sense of joy (Psalm 28:6, 7), either then or shortly thereafter, can be expected. Some may need this type of prayer repeatedly over a short period of time or on different occasions throughout their lives.

Deliverance Prayer

Deliverance prayer or simply deliverance is the ordering out of demons from the life of the prayee with the authority given us in Christ (Ephesians 6:12; Matthew 10:8; 28:18). If sufficient breaking prayer and healing prayer have occurred,[178] this process of ordering demons to leave can be quite simple and straightforward. At other times, the demons resist expulsion, and a struggle takes place. We have observed both types of reactions during prayer sessions with Muslims.

An important aspect of deliverance prayer is that it should not be seen as restricted only to evangelism or witnessing; we have seen numerous examples where new Muslim followers of Jesus have needed deliverance prayer for months or even years after their salvation. Contrary to what is sometimes assumed, demons do not always leave automatically at the moment one enters the Kingdom of God.[179] Healing and deliverance are often a process.

Holistic Healing Prayer and the Three Encounters

It is helpful to look at healing prayer as a form of power encounter in light of Kraft's three encounters ministry model.[180] In this model, power encounter is seen as a means of opening hearts to experience God's truth (truth encounter), which hopefully will lead to allegiance to God through Christ (allegiance encounter). Furthermore, in terms of planting Isa-centered home fellowships

---

[178] Breaking and healing prayers take away footholds the Devil may have gained in a prayee's life; thus, the expulsion of demons is easier.

[179] John Travis, as a part of doctoral research, recorded many case studies of Muslims who became followers of Jesus, yet years later needed deliverance from demons. Many well-known evangelical scholars and professors who have had experience with deliverance ministry believe that a true follower of Christ can be "demonized" (*daimonizomai* or "under the influence or inhabited by a demon"). Examples of such scholars include Merrill Unger, Chuck Swindoll, Ed Murphy, Neil Anderson, Clinton Arnold, Fred Dickason, and Charles Kraft, to name a few. For an excellent treatment of this topic, see the second chapter of Clinton Arnold, *3 Crucial Questions Regarding Spiritual Warfare* (Grand, Rapids, MI: Baker Books, 1997).

[180] See Charles Kraft, "What Encounters Do We Need in Christian Witness," *Evangelical Missions Quarterly* 27 (1991): 258–65.

among folk Muslims, Kraft sees the three encounters occurring over time, impacting witnessing, discipleship, and leadership development.[181] This three encounters pattern is clearly seen in Scripture, especially in the life and ministry of Jesus and the first believers (e.g. Mark 5:1–20; John 4:1–26, 39–42; John 9; Acts 2:1–41; 3:6–26; 5:12–16; 8:4–8). In short, holistic healing prayer is not an end in itself, but rather is part of a larger divine plan of seeing all people turn in allegiance to God through Jesus Christ.

Two Examples of Healing Prayer with Folk Muslims

The following examples of healing prayer involve Muslims that we (Anna and John) have known personally. The first example is that of a powerful Muslim shaman who had come to know Isa al-Masih through the amazing love shown him by Tazim,[182] an MBB (Muslim background believer in Jesus) from the same ethnic group. Shortly after coming to faith, the shaman went into a violent rage, tearing up his house and acting out of his mind. Tazim had never directly encountered demons. However, due to his familiarity with Gospel accounts, he assumed the behavior was demonic and said, "In the name of Isa al-Masih, come out!" The shaman instantly fell to the floor, and for the next two hours, one demonic presence after another was expelled. I (John) arrived after the deliverance was over and found the former shaman sitting peacefully on the floor of his bamboo house, seemingly in his right mind. He then willingly surrendered to us all of his occult paraphernalia (many charms and amulets) and together we prayed over the objects, smashed them with a hammer, then burned and buried them. Over the ensuing months, the former shaman continued to be discipled by Tazim, and through his witness, several other families believed.

The second example is the story of Mariha. Mariha's husband was discretely a follower of al-Masih, yet Mariha was still outside the Kingdom. This lovely couple invited us to their home, and Mariha and I (Anna) had the chance to start praying right away. Mariha had much pain related to her relationship with her mother, who had died a number of years before. The Lord showed Mariha

---

181   Kraft's three encounters model (1991) includes "three stages" of spiritual development where, over time, a follower of Jesus matures and increasingly experiences more power, truth, and deeper allegiance to God.

182   A pseudonym. Throughout the remainder of this chapter, all names used in case studies are pseudonyms as well.

vivid scenes from her childhood, all revolving around the theme of her mother. When the intense pain surfaced (she could feel it physically in her body), she poured out her heart to God, not holding anything back. Over and over, Isa made himself known in each memory, taking away the pain from when she was a little girl and showing his victory over the demons also present in many of the scenes in her mind.

At last she sighed, "O God, did my mother ever love me at all, even just a little bit?" We waited. There was nothing, no memory of love or nurture, just bellowing tears of emptiness. But then the tears seemed to change. Mariha could barely get the words out, "I see his face! Love beams are shining from his face into my heart, filling the emptiness ...I am stepping back a bit ...I see the full picture now ...He is hanging on the cross and I am at the foot of his cross."

When we ended the time of prayer, Mariha asked me, "So what does the cross mean?" God was revealing one of the truths so difficult for most Muslims to accept: the cross of Christ. Mariha was so blessed over what God did for her, she arranged for another family member, who had experienced emotional difficulties for several years, to also receive prayer. His first question to me (John) when we met for prayer was, "What does the cross mean?" Both Mariha and her relative later came to Christ through the witness of faithful friends.

Closing Words

Jesus loves Muslims. He came for them; he died for them. He longs for them to enter the Kingdom and experience all that God has for them. Many folk Muslims seek healing, blessing, deliverance from evil, and the hope of a better life both now and in the hereafter—just what the people of Palestine sought in Christ's time. God has equipped his people with spiritual authority in Christ and power to heal and cast out demons in his name. With love, humility, and Spirit-breathed boldness, let us take this healing power to Muslim brothers and sisters whom our Master has called us to serve.

Chapter 19

Pre-Field Preparation to Sow

DON ALLEN AND ABRAHAM DURÁN

*"For this reason, since the day we heard it,
we have not ceased praying for you and asking that you
may be filled with the knowledge of God's will in all spiritual wisdom
and understanding, so that you may lead lives worthy of the Lord,
fully pleasing to him, as you bear fruit in every good work and
as you grow in the knowledge of God."*
Colossians 1:9–10

THRIVING IN THE MIDST OF CHAOS

Famine in Darfur. Insurgency in Iraq. Political upheaval in Pakistan. The headlines make it clear: in the Muslim world, uncertainty is common. In any Muslim country, you very well may experience disaster, political upheaval, or war. In some places, the local people respond by welcoming you into their communities to bring humanitarian aid. In other places, they respond by revoking your visa. Life certainly feels more predictable back home!

BEFORE YOU LEAVE FOR THE FIELD, LEARN TO THRIVE AMID
HARDSHIPS, TELL STORIES WITH CULTURAL SENSITIVITY, AND
RESPECT MUSLIMS' STRONG COMMUNITY BONDS WHILE YOU LIVE
IN *COMMUNITAS* WITH YOUR OWN TEAM.

A Latin American team worked in northern Iraq between 1993 and 2007 during some of the most unstable years of that region. They lived through many civil wars, the second Gulf War, terrorism, epidemics, constant unpredictable changes in the cost of living, an invasion of their city by Saddam Hussein's forces, loss of visas, closed doors from Iraq, Turkey, Syria, and Iran, personal and governmental threats, and numerous other hardships.

Did all this trouble force them out of their adopted country? No! By God's grace, they facilitated a church movement that thrived through persecution and hardship.

We might thrive when things are going smoothly, but can we do it in the midst of upheaval? This is an important question, because you will very possibly establish your ministry within a context of uncertainty, at best. Among the 300 workers in the Muslim world who were surveyed, 40 percent of them live in an area where there is some kind of social or political upheaval.

New workers frequently experience a gulf between what they have learned in the classroom and what they *really* need to know when they arrive on the field. They must be trained to adapt and learn from the moment their feet hit the ground, because in the 'known' Muslim world, conditions may change rapidly, and in 'pioneer' locations, life is even more challenging.

Prospective messengers need *preparation for field realities,* as well as *equipment for effectiveness.* Stirred by the vision of "a great multitude ...from every nation ...standing before the throne" (Revelation 7:9), a new generation of workers yearns for fruitful veterans to teach them how they did it! They do not just want to know, "Was it effective then?" They want to know, "Is it effective *now?*" They aspire to be like the people of Issachar "who had understanding of the times, to know what ...[they] ought to do" (1 Chronicles 12:32).

A growing number of pioneers choose to go where life is most uncertain— where the church is *not*—because that is where God's power is so often revealed most gloriously! As you can see in Figure 19.1, the majority of new fellowships emerge from the most unsettled locations.[183]

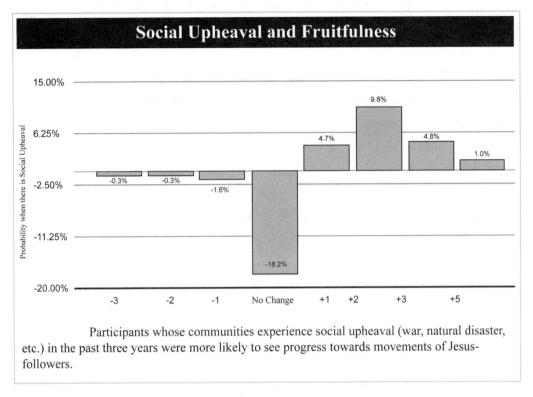

Participants whose communities experience social upheaval (war, natural disaster, etc.) in the past three years were more likely to see progress towards movements of Jesus-followers.

Fig.19.1

RITES OF PASSAGE

Should it surprise us that workers in God's vineyard can thrive amid strife and upheaval? Not if we read the New Testament. As the Apostle to the Gentiles, Paul was no stranger to danger, even going so far as to *commend his hardship as a mark of his apostolic calling*: "Three times I was beaten with rods. Once I received a stoning. Three times I was shipwrecked; on frequent journeys, in danger from rivers, danger from bandits, danger from my own people, danger from Gentiles" (2 Corinthians 11:25–26; cf. 12:12). It is not only the MBB fellowships but the messengers themselves who suffer in serving. Yet those willing to suffer are most likely to succeed.

---

183   See chapter 20 on "Islamism and Receptivity to Jesus" and chapter 24 on "Recapturing a Missiology of Suffering."

There is a way to prepare to 'suffer well', if we are willing. Many of us, lacking experience with danger, can learn from the Maasai people of Kenya. Anthropologist Victor Turner, in his research of coming-of-age rituals among the Maasai, discovered that boys 'become men' when they are thrust out of the village and are allowed to return only after they have proved their bravery in the midst of danger.[184]

Future Gospel ambassadors may benefit from a similar rite of passage in order to demonstrate their capacity to persevere, innovate, and thrive in pioneering areas. Real-life examples abound:

> » Urban dwellers challenge their stamina and courage in 'Outward Bound' courses or 'wilderness boot camps'.
> » Families leave their comfortable suburban homes to carve out redemptive communities in the inner city, ministering to the poor or to refugees.
> » College graduates conduct disaster relief in the remote regions of Central Asia, rather than establish lucrative practices in their own countries.

HOW DO THEY SHARE THE GOOD NEWS IN WAYS THAT RESONATE?

The Holy Spirit uses such testing to conduct his refining work, as trainees face hardship and difficulties they never experienced before, making difficult choices, adapting to new challenges, overcoming obstacles. After they have allowed themselves to be humbled by these circumstances, they are far better equipped to fulfill their apostolic calling to tell the Gospel simply and humbly in ways that will resonate in Muslim hearts.

How do they share the Good News in ways that resonate?

---

[184] *The Ritual Process* (Ithaca, NY: Cornell University Press, 1969).

"Storying" the Gospel

Most Westerners are trained to think and communicate in terms of objective statements. Many Latin Americans and some Asians receive Western-shaped education and learn to state truth as propositions. But among most people we serve, life's important truths are passed on through stories.

Stories have the power to change people. Jesus used parables to communicate the good news of God's powerful work. We must become powerful storytellers like Jesus, with a clear understanding of the following if we are to communicate the Gospel to our beloved Muslim friends:

» The cultural context of Bible stories, such as "The Good Samaritan" and "The Prodigal Son." These stories provide powerful images and lessons when seen from their original cultures;[185]
» How our own culture has impacted our understanding of the story, possibly in ways we have not previously recognized; and
» How local culture impacts our listeners' understanding of the story.

When we fail to consider these issues carefully, we communicate the Gospel from our own frame of reference, rather than from that of our focus people. As Tom Steffen points out, "Christian workers often overlook the fact that different worldviews and expectations should call for different ministry approaches. Rather than taking time to create new evangelism models, they often rely on models that won *them* to Christ or those used by esteemed mentors."[186]

One Middle Eastern team avoided this pitfall by adapting the tale of the Pharisee and the Publican as a contemporary story to highlight the futility of all religion in reaching God without a personal relationship with him. Another team in Central Asia used a well-known local folk story as a backdrop for telling the Gospel. Let your imagination soar as you prayerfully consider how to use stories to illustrate forgiveness, peace-making, hospitality, or improving relationships in your neighborhood.[187]

---

185 For an example, see Kenneth E. Bailey, *Poet and Peasant and Through Peasant Eyes: A Literary-Cultural Approach to the Parables in Luke* (Grand Rapids: William B. Eerdmans Publishing Company, 1983); *Jesus through Middle Eastern Eyes: Cultural Studies in the Gospels* (Downers Grove, IL: IVP Academic/InterVarsity Press, 2008).

186 *Connecting God's Story to Ministry* (La Mirada, CA: Center for Organizational and Ministry Development, 1996), 63.

187 For more on communicating through stories, see chapter 15 on "Bible Storying and the Oral Use of Scriptures."

Top Five Skills for Godly and Effective Pioneering Messengers

Here is a model for informal prefield preparation. This "Five C's" approach aims to help fellowships prepare future cross-cultural workers 'in their own backyard' to develop skills and practices that they must have on the field. I include some suggestions for each area. These are lifelong habits which the person needs on the field.

Communion with Christ

Skills to develop: you increasingly grow in your relationship with God; thrive in hardship and uncertainty; and discern how God is working in order to join him in that work.

Preparing for the field: experience failure and explore what God may be teaching you. Find a mentor or spiritual director. Practice 'hearing' from God. Deepen your practice of personal worship and dependence upon God. Make notes on the ways in which God is working around you. Be diligent in spiritual growth.

Character

Skills to develop: you demonstrate increasing measures of the fruit of the Spirit in your life as you cooperate with God's transforming work; you practice godly communication; and you persevere in hardship.

Preparing for the field: Overcome life-dominating patterns of sin. Practice the 'put off/put on' dynamics of godliness (Ephesians 4:17; Colossians 3:1–7). Monitor your ability to handle stress and bad times. Finish the projects that you start. Be a champion of the Holy Spirit's work in others. Invite counsel from others. Become a skilled listener and encourager.

Community

Skills to develop: you actively pursue peacemaking; positively contribute to the team; and demonstrate joyful godliness in marriage or singleness.

Preparing for the field: join a mission team and work toward its success with no expectation of what you will get out of it. Observe the unique contributions of each member to the success of the team. Promote peacemaking; reconcile with someone (Hebrews 13:17; Matthew 18:15–17). Model purity in singleness and marriage.

Content

Skills to develop: while serving, you effectively apply the Bible, missiological principles, and effective professional skills.

Preparing for the field: Explain the basic message and key themes of the Bible. Help others to respond to important life questions with Bible passages. Study the Bible on your own as the chief resource for faith, practice, and sharing the Good News. Explore the cross-cultural dimensions of biblical teaching, especially in the book of Acts. Attend a *Perspectives* course or *Encountering the World of Islam* or more extensive courses offered by many seminaries, colleges, and universities. Understand the basic beliefs and practices of Muslims, both the formal (qur'anic) and informal (hospitality, gender relationships, authority, power, etc.).

Competence

Skills to develop: you become more effective in sharing the Gospel; relate well with others cross-culturally; and reproduce yourself in leadership.

Preparing for the field: Get involved with refugees, immigrants, or international students; spend a lot of time with them. Share stories from the Bible, and work hard at being more effective in this. Look for God-seekers and help them to discover Jesus and become a disciple. Find where Muslims gather and befriend them. Mentor someone else. Start a seekers group in your neighborhood; train someone in the group to become the leader.

WHOSE VIEWS?

In America, it is more common to talk about Jesus with one person at a Starbucks than with an entire family around the dinner table (especially when fewer and fewer Americans eat dinner together). In Latin America, however, one typically shares the Gospel with an individual in front of his or her whole family. The Book of Acts records examples of people such as Cornelius and the Philippian jailer, who both came to follow Jesus within the context of family, as is typical among Muslims.[188] Sometimes when the cohesion of the group is too strong and negative you may need to start with an individual because to consider a new idea in the midst of everyone whose opinion you value is overwhelming, but then use two safeguards: give a group vision from the beginning (you and your family) and delay pressuring for a decision until there has been a rumor in the family for some time and several are ready to take that step together or are sympathetic to the step.

The transforming power of the Gospel is dimmed by cultural insensitivity. An experienced worker in Central Asia warns: "To suggest we want to 'Christianize' Muslims in Central Asia is to say that we want them to become Russians and adopt the culture of 'Christian Stalin.' We do not want to convert anyone to a different culture. Instead, we want [them] to see how the Gospel speaks to [their] *own* culture" ("Interview with a Cross-cultural Worker," Southeast Asian Consultation, Spring 2007).

THE TRUTH MUST BE TOLD
WITH CULTURAL SENSITIVITY AND
IN THE PREFERRED LEARNING STYLE OF THE PEOPLE
IN ORDER FOR THEM TO GRASP IT.

That is why we must discern the effects of both cultures—our own, as well as the one we adopt. Only then can we craft a story that avoids offense and connects to life as it is lived among our adopted people group. That is why we must explore how people prefer to learn. Literate learners think in terms of information, propositional truth, and order. Oral learners think in terms of story and

---

[188]   Bill Musk, *Touching the Soul of Islam* (Crowborough, UK: Monarch Publications, 1995), 44–66.

lessons. This is an important consideration, because often, *how* we tell the truth is just as important as the truth itself.

Fruitful messengers understand and apply this concept. For example, in a rural mountain village adjoining a major city in South Asia, a team discovered patterns of bitterness between leading families. Knowing that their people pass on important truths through stories, the team crafted tales of forgiveness and reconciliation and told them to the key families whenever they gathered together. These stories were so well received, the families now re-tell them at the mosque! ("Stories and the Qur'an in Southeast Asia," Interview #3, Spring 2007).

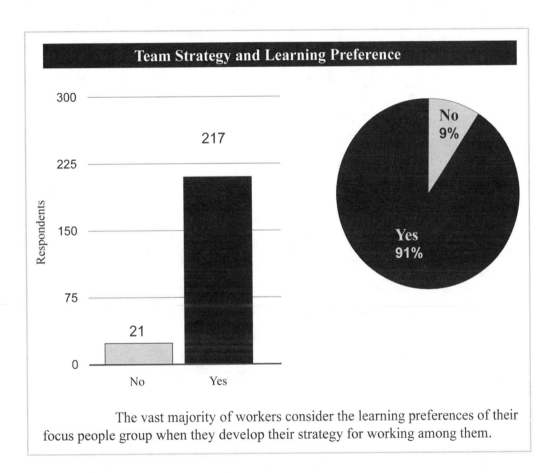

The vast majority of workers consider the learning preferences of their focus people group when they develop their strategy for working among them.

Fig.19.2

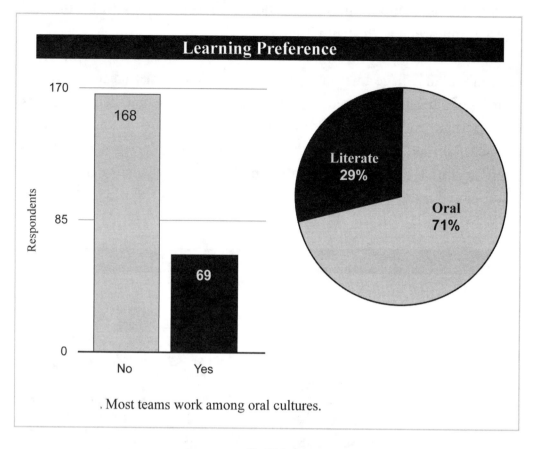

Fig.19.3

CONNECTING STORIES OF GOD'S KINGDOM
TO "THEIR" STORIES

The key to pre-field preparation is readiness to study culture. You can practice this by studying culture in your own city. Here are some suggestions from anthropologist and linguist J. Daniel Hess:[189]

1. Know your story. Explain to someone you know how the Gospel impacts your life.
2. Choose a family or a neighborhood from a different culture and study how its members communicate truth. Take notes on the

---

[189] *The Whole World Guide to Language Learning* (Yarmouth, ME: Intercultural Press, 1994). See also Dan Sheffield, "Assessing Intercultural Sensitivity in Mission Candidates and Personnel," *Evangelical Missions Quarterly* (January 2007): 22–28.

patterns of communication. Do they tell their family history? What lessons are taught? How do they pass along key knowledge of life or faith? What biblical stories connect to the themes in this group?

3. You can discover the *cultural story of your people group* by exploring how they practice hospitality, how they teach their children, and other common activities of their daily lives.

4. Practice telling the Good News in the relational network of your adopted people. Be ready to tell a story at any moment! Perhaps you can tell the parable of the Two Sons (Luke 15) and invite your hearers to explain its meaning.

5. Serve on a disaster relief trip. As you visit with local families, take note of the stories they tell about disaster, survival, and so on.

SERVING WITHIN THE COMMUNITY

Throughout the Muslim world, the community plays a significant role in establishing fellowships. For some tribal groups in Africa, important matters are discussed only when the villagers all meet together; they do not discuss important topics privately. Since the Gospel is an important topic, workers share the Good News at the community meetings. Together and openly, the villagers discuss the implications of following Jesus until there is a consensus ("Telling the Story in Relational Groups in North Africa," Interview #129, Southeast Asian Consultation, Spring 2007).

THE COMMUNITY IS A LIVING ORGANISM, A SPIDER WEB
THAT LINKS EACH PERSON IN A COMPLEX NETWORK OF
RELATIONSHIPS.

Since the community is the conduit for passing along good news as well as bad, existing social networks can transform into whole communities of Jesus-followers![190]

---

[190] One gains significant insights by viewing the biblical narrative through the eyes of social networks. A cursory study of the Greek word *oikos* in the Gospels and Acts demonstrates how the Gospel flowed through these natural relationships.

Increasing numbers of workers in the Muslim world are tapping into the potential of this dynamic for catalyzing disciples within existing communities. Until recently, teams frequently encountered two impasses in their efforts to establish fellowships: an inability to create a cohesive fellowship among estranged believers and an inability to establish MBB leadership. It is hard to underestimate the difficulty of forming a community with Muslim strangers who each came to Christ through radically different channels and from different communities. It is equally difficult to appoint leaders from within a group in which no one has any leadership experience. But gatherings and leaders are likely to emerge naturally when webs of relationships are used to transform the community.

Since Muslims may adopt the Gospel through their social networks, more Gospel messengers now seek to plant the Good News within existing social structures such as neighborhood committees, sewing circles, or apartment complexes. Discerning workers encourage leaders to emerge from within those circles, and they provide leadership training early in the process.

Preparing for Field Realities

Here are two good methods for new recruits to gain practical experience in establishing a community of faith before heading to the field:

Conduct a Mini–Ethnography of a New Community
The 'community' could be as simple as a football tailgate party for a local team or a similar event or program that attracts a gathering of people. Candidates study this mini-culture by interacting with those who attend, asking questions, and simply observing their behavior.[191]

Intern with a Veteran of the Muslim world
Under the mentorship of the veteran field worker, new recruits choose to live in an area of the city where Muslims live and gather, in order to befriend and serve them. In that context, they learn how Muslims live by asking many questions. With their mentor's guidance, candidates explore the implications MBBs face when they choose to follow Jesus. Mentors structure practical

---

[191]   To learn more about the value of careful observation and study, read Samuel H. Scudder, "The Student, The Fish, and Agassiz." Teachers refer to this article to learn the principles of inductive Bible Study, but it is also a valuable tool for exploring culture (see http://www.bethel.edu/~dhoward/resources/Agassizfish/Agassizfish.htm).

assignments such as sharing a Jesus story in a gathering of Muslims or appointing a seeker to find other seekers who will join them in a study of the Kingdom of God.[192]

PROMOTING TEAM RELATIONSHIPS TO FULFILL THE VISION[193]

Are you a team player? Do you work and play well with others? Most workers in the Muslim world belong to a team, which can have as few as three members or as many as thirty. In a recent survey, 300 veteran workers across the Muslim world indicated that their team health is either "excellent" or "good." If you plan to go to the Muslim world, you will most likely be part of a team that will need to work together! As conduits of the life-changing Gospel, we must demonstrate Christ-likeness in the following areas of team life:

» Sharing a common vision;
» Exercising grace in the midst of disagreements;
» Practicing biblical peacemaking; and
» Praying for one another, as well as our Muslim friends.

Even though all team members are followers of Jesus who share a common calling to take the Gospel to the same people group, they cannot assume that all their values will be automatically lived out in their team. Many veteran cross-cultural workers have shared horror stories of teams that fell apart for various reasons.[194]

Teams often become dysfunctional when their members expect the team to function as a church, meeting all their needs for worship, prayer, friendship, and encouragement. If the team leader (or the team's Memo of Understanding) is unclear that its purpose is task-focused, it is likely that someone will be unhappy.

So, then: is the team a community, or is it a mission?

---

[192] A recent survey of 300 workers reveals that a cluster of factors, when practiced together, foster the multiplication of fellowships. The most influential factor, according to the survey participants, is that leaders and fellowships make their own decisions (Preliminary Summary of FP track by Knowledge Stewardship Team, September 26, 2007).

[193] See chapter 12.

[194] Some reasons for team failure: clash of culture or personality, disagreement over vision, poor leadership, wrong assignment of roles and tasks, and unclear goals.

Communitas Before Community

Ralph Winter suggests that a cross-cultural team engaged in spreading the Good News is primarily a mission, not a community. In his defining article on the "two structures" of God's redemptive purpose, he proposes that the church is a modality: it focuses on the nurture of its members. The missionary band, on the other hand, is a sodality: it exists as a mission. In this explanation, Winter helps us understand that team members should not expect from their team the same extent of nurture that is intended for a church. The team bands together because it is on a God-ordained task: to establish Jesus-centered communities where there are none.[195]

If Winter is right, the team is a *communitas*, a community that exists because of a common task. It is a group that comes together in order to achieve something; in other words, the goal is primary. Like the Celtic communities of the Middle Ages, people of faith come together because they are on assignment. Such a task-oriented community looks and feels different from the nurturing community of the church back home.[196]

So how do Gospel messengers prepare for this kind of team life? It helps to practice before you leave for the field. As you work with others to accomplish a goal, you discover the value of their contributions. Start practicing *communitas* now. Gather a team. Start a ministry from scratch. Observe the interpersonal dynamics. 'Map' your relationships. Note how you can improve your share of the work. Celebrate your progress. Congratulations! You are preparing for the field.

Training-in-Life for the Rest of Your Life

If you adopt the kind of training suggested here, some of your colleagues may be concerned that you want to eliminate older training methods. Will this new approach replace formal training programs provided by seminaries and institutes? Are books no longer necessary? Obviously, there is no perfect training.

---

[195] "The Two Structures of God's Redemptive Mission," in *Perspectives on the World Christian Movement* (Notebook Edition), ed. Steven Hawthorne and Ralph Winter (Pasadena, CA: William Carey Library, 1999), 131–33.

[196] This is not to suggest that a person's needs should not be met. What it does mean, however, is that the apostolic band is called to sacrifice, to suffer, and to expect that their own needs will not be met. Paul says it well in 2 Corinthians 6:3–10. For an excellent summary of *communitas*, and its implications for cross-cultural work, see Alan Hirsch, *The Forgotten Ways: Reactivating the Missional Church* (Grand Rapids: Brazos Press, 2006), 217–29.

The best is that which takes advantage of many types of preparation, including courses in seminary and university. If necessary, assure your colleagues that God wants you to be prepared for changing times, and *that* requires a variety of approaches.

To summarize: Keep the end in mind. Practice risk-taking. Tell God's Story and your story. Learn how people learn. Practice *communitas*. These things make for an effective witness anywhere—in your hometown as well as in Muslim homelands.

Part 4

Emerging Issues in Global Trends: More Birds, Rocks, Sun, and Soil

Chapter 20

Islamism and Receptivity to Jesus

MOUSSA BONGOYOK

"Those who go out weeping, bearing the seed for sowing,
shall come home with shouts of joy, carrying their sheaves."
Psalm 126:6

Today, Islamism has become a major theme of study. Experts from various backgrounds analyze it, and in the process they raise many questions. One question that sowers of the Good News may consider seriously is related to the relationship between Islamism and receptivity to Jesus. Is Islamism a hindrance to receptivity to Jesus or a catalyst?

Our main goal in this chapter is to answer that question. In order to do this properly, however, there is a need to define "Islamism" and to explore "receptivity to Jesus." The first part of the chapter will clarify terms and concepts. Then the following aspects will be considered in the order presented: Islamism as an obstacle to receptivity to Jesus, Islamism as a catalyst for receptivity to Jesus, and practical suggestions for maximizing the potential of openness to the Lord Jesus Christ in contexts impacted by Islamism.

PRELIMINARY CLARIFICATIONS

The abundant literature on Islamism does not necessarily make the task easier for those who are studying it. In fact, some authors leave the readers with more confusion than ever before. For this reason, let us define Islamism before moving further.

What is Islamism?[197]

Islamism, as used here, is the ideology held by fundamentalist and conservative Muslims that all of life, including the political and social realms, should be regulated by the way of God. For Sunni fundamentalists (i.e., those who return to the fundamental documents), this means a return to the Qur'an and the example (*sunnah*) of Muhammad and the early community (*salaf*) recording the reports of their words and deeds (*hadith*). For Sunni conservatives, the guiding texts also include law (*shari'ah*) as developed in four recognized schools of law through the third Islamic century.

Shi'i Islamists of the major Ithna 'Ashariyya branch are conservatives guided by some slightly different hadith and another school of law that authorized the first twelve imams after Muhammad to speak '*ex cathedra*', and in Iran since the Islamic Revolution of 1979, a leading jurist has been chosen to provide political "guardianship" over the people. The Islamists contrast with liberal Muslims who may want to be guided by Islamic values from the Qur'an, hadith, and shari'ah but may support democracy, and such 'human rights' as religious liberty, equality of women, and so forth.[198] Islamists may be peaceful[199] or militant, for there are resources for either in Islam's authoritative texts.

When Do We Know that People are Receptive to Jesus?

At first glance, this question seems to be of no value in an Islamic context since almost all Muslims have a deep respect for Jesus because they consider him to be one of the greatest prophets. Most of my Muslim friends tell me that they do not have any problem with Jesus but that their real problem is with Christianity. Nevertheless, two critical questions need to be asked: What do they

---

[197] From J. Dudley Woodberry, "Current Trends in Islam" (course syllabus, Fuller Theological Seminary, Pasadena, CA, 2004).

[198] See Charles Kurzman, *Liberal Islam: a Sourcebook* (New York: Oxford University Press, 1998).

[199] See Raymond William Baker, *Islam Without Fear: Egypt and the New Islamists* (Cambridge, MA: Harvard University Press, 2003).

mean by Jesus? Is the fact that they accept him as one prophet among others enough for their salvation? Answers to these questions will help us to clarify the concept of receptivity to Jesus.

Jesus Christ is a historical figure described both in the Bible and the Qur'an. The descriptions are not the same. The Bible recognizes his divinity and affirms his death and resurrection, all denied as most Muslims understand the Qur'an. Are these Muslim teachings insurmountable obstacles? Fouad Accad writes, "I have studied the Qur'an for thirty years; I've found it overwhelmingly pro-Christ, pro-Christian and pro-Bible."[200] I agree with him at this point. Though the differences between the qur'anic Jesus and the biblical Jesus seem to be great, the similarities are so numerous that Christians and Muslims can find common ground and build on it for constructive and friendly discussion.

The Qur'an and the Bible agree on his virgin birth, his faultless nature, his miracles, and many of his titles. Instead of elevating walls between the two religions and destroying the chances of fruitful communication, it is better to build bridges on these similarities. There is enough evidence in the Qur'an to help a genuine Muslim seeker of the Truth to understand that Jesus is not only a simple human prophet among others. Thus there is much about Jesus to which a Muslim is naturally receptive. However, with the rise and expansion of Islamism, is it easy for a Muslim to be receptive to Jesus as Lord and Savior?

ISLAMISM AS AN OBSTACLE TO RECEPTIVITY TO JESUS[201]

Many Muslims who were willing to know more about Jesus because of the Christian literature they read or the contacts that they had with their Christian neighbors seem to have been discouraged by Islamists for various reasons. In my context of ministry in Africa, I have identified six major hindrances.

Fear of Islamist Attack

Not all Islamists are necessarily violent. Nevertheless, many Islamists have perpetrated terrorist attacks in various parts of the world, and there are more threats ahead if we refer to their own declarations on the Internet and through other media. This situation has created fear on both sides. Some Christians fear

---

[200] Fouad Elias Accad, *Building Bridges* (Colorado Springs, CO: Navpress, 1997), 10.

[201] For a fuller discussion of much that follows in this chapter, see my "The Rise of Islamism among the Sedentary Fulbe of Northern Cameroon: Implications for Theological Response," Ph.D. diss. Fuller Theological Seminary, School of Intercultural Studies, 2006.

for their lives and prefer not to be involved in witness among Muslims. There are also many Muslims who may have been more receptive to Jesus if there were no clear Islamist menace. Unfortunately, militant Islamists have killed many Muslims who have become followers of Christ. However, violence is not the only method that they use.

Islamist Economic Power

In many nations of the majority world where poverty is a big challenge, rich Arab nations are investing large sums of money. In Africa, for example, Islamist movements are spending millions of dollars on scholarships, social projects, and military or political movements that support their agenda. Many people go to these movements in order to receive financial or material help. People do not necessarily embrace Islamist movements because they are convinced that their ideology is the best, but simply because they are poor and unable to meet their family's basic needs for food, health care, clothing, and so on. In the process, they move further from the Gospel, sometimes even with the blessing of their governments.

SIX FACTORS THAT HINDER RECEPTIVITY TO CHRIST

1. *Fear of Islamist Attack*
2. *Islamist Economic Power*
3. *Government Policies*
4. *Open Fight against Christians*
5. *Christian Silence*
6. *Anti-Christian Propaganda*

Government Policies

Paul Marshall has documented the spread of extreme shari'ah law throughout the Muslim world in, for example, Iran, two of the four provinces of Pakistan, the northern provinces of Nigeria, and northern Sudan. In all these cases, there have been restrictions against Christians and conversion from Islam.[202]

---

[202] Paul Marshall, ed., *Radical Islam's Rules: The Worldwide Spread of Extreme Shari'a Law* (Lanham, MD: Rowman & Littlefield Publishers, 2005), 1–17.

Open Fight against Christians

In some cases, there has been open fighting against Christians, as in Sudan, Nigeria, and parts of Indonesia. In other cases, Muslim followers of Christ in, for example, Afghanistan, have apparently been killed by their own families.

Christian Silence

To me, the saddest situation is when Christians flee their responsibility because of the Islamist threat and become silent even when they have opportunities to preach the Good News in both favorable and unfavorable circumstances (cf. 2 Timothy 4:1–2). I was very sad once, when I learned from a former Muslim who is now a follower of Christ that some Christians he went to in order to enquire how to become a follower of Christ advised him to remain a Muslim because they were afraid of the consequences of his conversion for them. I understand that there are circumstances where Christians need extra wisdom in order to survive and stay in the context, but we must avoid hiding behind silence and disobeying the Lord's command to preach the Good News to all peoples. This includes Islamists, even when they criticize or oppose the Church openly.

Anti-Christian Propaganda

We live in a world where Christianity in some contexts is less and less influential. Multiple scandals in Christian circles do not make it easier for people to perceive the positive sides of Christianity and the benefit of its teachings for our societies. Rather, people seem to be more and more hostile to Christian values, and Islamists are among those who are very aggressive in inundating the media with anti-Christian propaganda.[203] Many people who do not know otherwise trust the words of the media. Even some of those who were favorable to Christianity begin to doubt or even oppose it.

Obviously, these hindrances do not help Muslims or even non-Muslims to become more receptive to Jesus. Fortunately, however, this is just one side of the issue. Let us look at the other side.

---

[203] One of the best African perspectives on this topic is M. Tadjé Eonè's book, *Et si le terrorism manipulait les media?* [*What if terrorism was manipulating the media?*] (Chennevières-sur-Marne, France: Editions Dianoïa, 2005).

ISLAMISM AS CATALYST TO RECEPTIVITY TO JESUS

In regard to what was said above, one may be tempted to conclude that Islamism is an obstacle to receptivity to Jesus. This is true sometimes, but, in Sub-Saharan Africa (where I live) and in other parts of the world, we have observed more receptivity to the Gospel since the rise of Islamism. Warren Larson in a doctoral dissertation, since published, has shown how the sale of Bibles and the numbers of inquiries and Jesus-followers increased in Iran after the Khomeini Revolution of 1979 and after Zia ul-Haq tried to institute shari'ah law in Pakistan (1984–1986).[204] Similar growth in the number of Jesus-followers followed the imposition of shari'ah laws by President Numeiri in Sudan in 1983 and following strife between Islamists and the Algerian government after the latter had canceled elections in 1992 that the Islamists were winning. There were, of course, other factors influencing receptivity.

Actions by Moderate Muslim Scholars and Leaders

Many Muslim scholars are denouncing the Islamist threat and are openly supporting Christians. As Quinn and Quinn wrote, "The modernists-progressives represent a new development in Islam. They look analytically at Islamic tenets and believe one must not apply Islamic law too literally or try to transpose seventh-century systems into a twenty-first-century setting. The South African imam and author Moulana Farid Esack is a voice for such a tendency."[205] John Azumah made almost the same comment about Farid Esack in his books,[206] but he is just one among many others. Some of the Muslim scholars have even discovered the real face of Jesus when they were doing research about Christianity, and today they are followers of Christ. Other Muslims have come to Christ for completely different reasons.

---

[204] See Warren Fredrick Larson, *Islamic Ideology and Fundamentalism in Pakistan: Climate for Conversion to Christianity?* (Lanham, MD: University Press of America, 1998), also on CD "The World of Islam: Resources for Understanding," version 2, J. Dudley Woodberry, General Editor (Colorado Springs: Global Mapping International, 2006), and "Islamic Fundamentalism in Pakistan: Its Implications for Conversion to Christianity" (Ph.D. diss. Fuller Theological Seminary, School of Intercultural Studies, 1996).

[205] Charlotte A. Quinn and Frederick Quinn, *Pride, Faith and Fear: Islam in Sub-Saharan Africa* (Oxford: Oxford University Press, 2003), 25.

[206] John Azumah, *The Legacy of Arab-Islam in Africa* (Oxford: Oneworld, 2001), 199.

Muslim Anger against Terrorist Acts Perpetrated by Islamists

The September 11, 2001, attacks against the United States seem to have divided Muslims into three main groups: those who completely agree with the militant Islamist ideology, those who are not quite sure what to think about it, and those who are openly against Islamism. Among the third group of Muslims are many people who are deeply disappointed by radical Islamists and have come closer to Christians. Many Muslim voices rise against the terrorism that is perpetrated in the name of Allah not only against non-Muslims but also against their fellow Muslims. A growing number of Muslim scholars think that such actions are not in tune with true Islamic doctrine.

In Sub-Saharan Africa (where it is common to find Christians, Muslims, and followers of African religions in the same family), people are deeply shocked by Islamist attacks against other members of the family or an ethnic group no matter what religious conviction they have. Once, Islamists attacked a Christian village in southern Sudan by surprise and wiped it out. When folk Muslims from a neighboring village learned what happened, they were angry at their fellow Muslims who killed innocent Christians, and consequently, most of them decided to abandon Islam and to become followers of Jesus. This is a recent event that illustrates what Tertullian said: "The blood of the martyrs is a seed for the Church." It is sad to notice that, all over the world, radical Islamists are shedding the blood of innocent followers of Christ; but the Lord is great and there are more people following Christ than those who are murdered.

SEVEN FACTORS THAT ENCOURAGE RECEPTIVITY TO CHRIST

1. *Actions by Moderate Muslim Scholars and Leaders*
2. *Muslim Anger against Terrorist Acts Perpetrated by Islamists*
3. *More Opportunities to Talk About Jesus*
4. *Islamists Who Have Met Christ on Contemporary Damascus Roads*
5. *Christian Maturity in Times of Trial and Persecution*
6. *Intense Prayers Result in Wonderful Answers*
7. *More Training and Planning*

More Opportunities to Talk About Jesus

Amazingly, with the rise of Islamism, there are also increasing numbers of opportunities for Christians to share their faith with their Muslim neighbors. On the one hand, Muslim scholars have taken the initiative to meet Christian leaders or scholars. For example, Mustapha Cherif, an Algerian Muslim philosopher, took the initiative to write to Pope Benedict XVI and succeeded in talking to him in private about Islam on November 11, 2006.[207] Recent dialogues between Muslims and Christians in response to the Muslim overture of "A Common Word Between Us" are another example.[208]

On the other hand, when folk Muslims and less-educated Muslims hear Islamist teachings about Christianity, most of them (at least in our context) are surprised because the Islamist teachings are different from their personal experiences with Christians. Because of this, Muslims sometimes go to their Christian neighbors and ask questions about the Bible or about the Christian faith. In the process, believers have opportunities to share their faith. This way, Muslims get to know the beauty of Christian faith, the depth of Christian doctrine, and biblical teaching about Jesus. The outcome is remarkable: there are more Muslims who become followers of Jesus in the process.

Islamists Who Have Met Christ on Contemporary Damascus Roads

Just like Paul who met Jesus on the road to Damascus (Acts 9:1–18), some Islamists have met Christ while studying the Bible and Christian theology with the clear intention of using that knowledge against Christianity. In various parts of the world, more Muslims are reading the Bible, and some of them have already found Jesus and committed their lives to him. Testimonies are available on the Internet and in various publications.[209]

When events like this occur, Christians are encouraged, and they gain strength and confidence as they follow their Lord Jesus Christ even in difficult times.

---

[207] There is a detailed report on Mustapha Cherif's encounter with the Pope. See Mustapha Cherif, "Ce que j'ai di au pape ..." *Le Nouvel Observateur*, no. 2195, November 30, 2006, 6ff.

[208] See www.acommonword.com; www.yale.edu/faith/abou-commonword.htm; J. Dudley Woodberrry, "A Call to Evangelicals to Respond to a Significant Muslim Overture," http://www.christianitytoday.com/ct/2007/octoberweb-only/143-42.0.html, also on www.acommonword.com/mediaresources.

[209] Jean-Marie Gaudeul, *Called from Islam to Christ: Why Muslims become Christians* (Crowborough, E. Sussex, 1999); J. Dudley Woodberry et al., "Why Muslims Follow Jesus," *Christianity Today* (Oct. 2007), 80–85.

Christian Maturity in Times of Trial and Persecution

One striking observation I made in more than fifteen African nations that I visited is that, before the rise of Islamism, a good percentage of Christians who were living in Muslim contexts were spiritually weak. With the advent of Islamism, many have become more serious about their Christian faith, have started to attend church or Christian meetings more regularly, and have decided to hold more prayer meetings (including prayer nights, prayer with fasting, and chains of prayer twenty-four hours a day). They are spiritually stronger. The fruits of their commitment are tangible. They listen to the Lord and obey his commands. Because of this, they have become true salt and light in their environments. Many Muslims who observe these Christians are attracted to Jesus by the quality of life of the Christian community. The Muslims see the difference between Christians and non-Christians.

Who could imagine that Islamism could push the Christian community into deeper spirituality? The ways of the Lord are definitely mysterious and wonderful. But this is just one aspect of the multiple blessings of trials and hardship.

Intense Prayers Result in Wonderful Answers

Somebody compared prayer to the railroads and the train to God's blessings. The more that Christians pray, the longer the railroad is, and the further God's blessings go. There is wisdom in this image. God answers prayer, and each believer can share a testimony of God's special answer to prayer in his or her life. But, when things go well, Christians pray little. In times of difficulties, there is more prayer. Prayer should not be seasonal. The world needs believers who, like Daniel, are committed to praying faithfully several times a day in all circumstances.

With the rise of Islamism, more believers pray fervently, and God is at work. Muslims experience dreams, visions, healings, and multiple miracles. In one city, Christians decided to adopt all the mosques in their neighborhoods and to pray five times a day for all those who attended them. Shortly after the Christians began praying, many Muslims witnessed that they saw Jesus in dreams and visions. A rich Muslim businessman said that the Lord Jesus showed him heaven and told him: "If you want to come here, believe in me." He went by himself to the church and committed his life to Jesus. Nobody had witnessed to that Muslim before, but God listened to Christians' prayers and led him to Jesus by the power of his Holy Spirit. As the community of believers takes prayer seriously, the Church will hear more and more testimonies like this in various parts of the world as well. The Lord will not only lead more Muslims to salvation, but he will also give more wisdom to church leaders as they train believers and seek God's direction.

More Training and Planning

This is a paradox, but many blessings come out of the Islamists' threats. Because of Islamism, many church leaders realize that their knowledge of Islam is not sufficient. In Francophone Africa, for example, many denominations have just started to send students for Islamic studies or to organize seminars on Islam and witness among Muslims. So far, Bangui Evangelical Graduate School of Theology is the only evangelical seminary in Francophone Africa that trains at the graduate level in missiology and Islamic studies, as does Nairobi Evangelical Graduate School of Theology in Anglophone Africa. Both schools are exploring the possibility of developing doctoral programs. Many other schools are preparing to launch similar programs at a variety of educational levels. At the same time, church leaders are strategizing. The outcome of their effort is already visible with the increasing receptivity of many Muslims to Jesus.

There are even more exciting times ahead. The results will even be greater if Christians (and especially church leaders), wisely and intentionally maximize current opportunities.

HOW TO MAXIMIZE THE POTENTIAL OF RECEPTIVITY TO JESUS

Christian thinkers and mission practitioners need to deepen reflection on this issue. I salute the effort of the 2004 Lausanne forum in Thailand and particularly the production of Lausanne Occasional Paper No. 50.[210] Similar works need to be produced, for there is hope to further God's Kingdom. Here are a few suggestions for all Christians.

---

[210] David Claydon, ed., *The Impact on Global Mission of Religious Nationalism and 9/11 Realities*, Lausanne Occasional Paper, No. 50 (Pattaya, Thailand: Lausanne Committee for World Evangelization, 2004).

Pray More

In the Bible, God gives wonderful promises to those who pray (Psalm 50:15; Matthew 7:7–11; Philippians 4:6–7; 1 Peter 5:7). The Lord is ready to do greater things on behalf of the Muslim community, but it seems like the baskets of prayer are not ready to receive God's multiple blessings. In reality, the best way to maximize non-Christians' receptivity to Jesus is to pray for them more regularly and more deeply, and to do it with pure hearts (cf. Isaiah 59:1–2). An African proverb says: "If the cooking pot is boiling, it is because there is fire underneath." The same wisdom applies to prayer. The fervent prayer of Christians is like a fire, and it will produce dynamic spirituality and greater impact on non-Christians in general and Muslims in particular because the Lord is ready to do greater things if those who love him ask him to intervene.

It is very important to pray, but it is also important to be patient and faithful in difficult times.

MAXIMIZE RECEPTIVITY BY:

- *Praying more;*
- *Being faithful to the Lord;*
- *Responding wisely to Islamist attacks;*
- *Being involved in joint activities;*
- *Training church leaders and lay people; and*
- *Training and involving more MBBs and Islamists.*

Be Faithful to the Lord

It is not easy for human intelligence to agree with Tertullian that martyrdom is a seed. However, a simple glance at Church history is sufficient to realize that it grew more in times of trials and persecution. On the other hand, it was weaker in times when the Church was dominant and was not facing a major threat. For this reason, followers of Christ need God's assistance in such a way that they remain faithful to God even if there is a menace to throw them in the furnace like the three companions of Daniel (Daniel 3) or in the lion's den like Daniel himself (Daniel 6). The Lord has promised to be with his disciples every day until the end of time (Matthew 28:20). He will be with us. His presence will be a great source of comfort. His Spirit will be a great source of joy for those who trust in God. His divine hand will hold his children no matter what happens to them. Nothing will happen to believers if the Lord does not allow it, and he will not allow it if it is not the right time to suffer hardship, imprisonment, or physical death. In all cases, the result will be more souls coming to Christ, more receptivity to Jesus. No price is high enough for that.

Faithfulness to the Lord is essential, and knowing how to react properly in the event of an Islamist attack is also important.

Respond Wisely to Islamist Attacks

Violence leads to violence, and it is rarely the best response to an Islamist attack. Non-violent methods need to be explored and applied. Jesus encouraged his disciples not to respond violently to their enemies (Matthew 5:33–37). Acting differently is not the wisest thing to do. I am aware that it is easier to expand on this theoretically than to handle violent attacks in real-life situations. But Stephen illustrates to us how to do the right thing at the right time (Acts 7:54–60), and later Paul, who approved his murder, was led to Christ and became one of the most devoted and influential Christian leaders of all time. There are many Pauls among the Islamists. As Christians, let us bless them instead of cursing them.

One pastor in northern Nigeria gave good advice to his church members when Islamists completely destroyed their church building on a Sunday morning just before the service in the late 1990s. Christians were tempted to retaliate and destroy the neighboring mosque. But their pastor, who was formerly a Muslim, told them to forgive and pray for their enemies instead. They did so, and the Lord glorified himself because the Muslim community was deeply moved by the Christians' attitude. Consequently, many Muslims in the neighborhood decided to become followers of Jesus.

Be Involved in Joint Activities

Currently, there is lot of literature about Christian–Muslim dialogue. Personally, I think that most scholarly discourses on that subject do not start in the right place. The right approach seems to be pragmatic and relational. Two questions need to be asked: What are the felt or real needs of the community? What can Christians do together with their Muslim neighbors in order to meet these needs? This is the first step.

The second step is to identify key people and key venues that will help Muslims and Christians to move from good intentions to concrete actions. It is when Christians and Muslims work together that they will get to really know one another, to appreciate the value of human relationships, and to be more inclined to peaceful cohabitation. It will also create a climate where it will be easier for Muslims to become followers of Christ or at least to listen peacefully to their Christian neighbors. This is happening almost every day in Sub-Saharan Africa, where Christians and Muslims work together in various projects like building and running a school or a clinic, digging a well, educating the community about the danger of religious extremism,[211] and similar activities.

Train Church Leaders and Lay People

If the church is to play a key role in educating the whole community, it must train its leaders and the church members at all levels, including those who prefer oral methods. Of course, this requires contextual approaches, proper training methodology, and transferable tools. The need is obvious. The goal is to train all believers so that they become mature disciples of Christ capable of training others (2 Timothy 2:2) and putting into practice their spiritual gifts. When this occurs, the church will never be the same, and there will be revolution in witnessing and social work. If the training is done faithfully, both theoretically and practically, more people will be attracted to Jesus. But, for greater outcomes, there is a special category of Christians that needs more attention.

Train and Involve More MBBs and Islamists

There are more Muslim background believers (MBBs) today than ever in Church history. However, most of them are not educated or trained properly. A few MBBs are in spiritual leadership positions. Although church leaders need wisdom and discernment in selecting and training Muslim followers of Jesus at the right time of their spiritual pilgrimage and in the right schools or loca-

---

[211] Authors like Carolyn Fourest and Fiammeta Venner draw the attention of the public to the fact that 9/11 does not only show the danger of Islamism but also shows the danger of the return of all extremisms. Carolyn Fourest and Fiammeta Venner, *Tirs croisés* (Paris: Calmann-Levy, 2003), 9–16. This observation deserves proper attention. Extremism is dangerous whether it is Muslim, Jewish, Hindu, Christian, or from any other source.

tions, they should be more proactive about it. The best witnesses among Muslims are former Muslims. The best pastors in any given context are those who come from that milieu. Insiders will bring new perspectives in our methodology. Sometimes, they will completely change the way we engage in witnessing and worship Jesus—this is the right time in history to listen to them carefully, to examine everything in the light of the Bible, and to be humble enough to change traditions or methods that need to be changed. The shift of the center of gravity of Christianity is God's sign that things must be done differently. Do we hear the voice of the Holy Spirit through it?

CONCLUSION

As I conclude this chapter, the image of Samson's riddle comes to my mind. He said: "Out of the eater came something to eat. Out of the strong came something sweet" (Judges 14:14). This riddle was given in a particular context with a particular meaning, but it can be applied to Islamism and put this way: "Out of the Islamist threats can come unique opportunities to lead more people to Jesus."

The rise of Islamism is challenging. Sometimes, it hinders Christian activities. Overall, however, if the Church sees the rise and expansion of Islamism with spiritual eyes, the Church will discover unique opportunities to do God's mission and to harvest souls who are ripe enough for salvation. Followers of Jesus will be strengthened and encouraged to carry out the task of bearing witness to Jesus with more zeal and wisdom. In reality, Islamism makes the Muslim community far more receptive to Jesus, and this approachability would increase if Christians did the right thing at the right time with the Lord's heart and power.

Chapter 21

Toward Respectful Witness

Transcribed from a talk by
Joseph Cumming

*"Always be prepared to give an answer to everyone
who asks you to give the reason for the hope that you have.
But do this with gentleness and respect."*
1 Peter 3:15 NIV

I am speaking about "Respectful Witness" in the context of contemporary interfaith encounters with Muslims, and coming from a North American perspective. Obviously, when you speak of "contemporary encounters," immediately you think about the aftermath of 9/11, and the way that has profoundly impacted Muslim–Christian relations.

One of the things that I think is remarkable is God's ability to bring good things out of evil. What happened on 9/11 was very evil. Many of the things that have been done in reaction to that since then have been very evil. But God has brought great good out of it. One of the things that God has done to bring good out of it is to open doors as Paul says in 1 Corinthians 16: "A wide door for effective work has opened to me ...and there are many adversaries" (1 Corinthians 16:9).

MUSLIM–CHRISTIAN RELATIONS

Since 9/11, Muslim leaders of the world have been more interested than ever before in history in talking with Christian leaders, and trying to sort out the problems between our two faith communities, which, between us, constitute the majority of the human race. And if we do not learn to get along, we are going to "have a worldwide confrontation." They are conscious of that, and they are anxious to talk with us.

MUSLIM LEADERS OF THE WORLD ARE MORE INTERESTED
THAN EVER BEFORE IN HISTORY IN TALKING WITH CHRISTIAN
LEADERS, AND TRYING TO SORT OUT THE PROBLEMS BETWEEN
OUR TWO FAITH COMMUNITIES, WHICH, BETWEEN US,
CONSTITUTE THE MAJORITY OF THE HUMAN RACE.

I have had the privilege of receiving some amazing invitations since 9/11. Several months after 9/11, I was invited to speak at al-Azhar University. For those who are not familiar with al-Azhar, it is the dominant institution of religious scholarship for the 85 percent of the Muslim world who are Sunnis. No matter where you go in the Sunni Muslim world, in the little village mosque, the imam there was trained by somebody who was trained by somebody who was trained by somebody who trained at al-Azhar.

This institution, which has about 400,000 students worldwide, trains the elite scholars and leaders of the Muslim world. I was invited to speak, several months after 9/11, on a topic, which, if you know anything about Islam, you will know is very controversial, and that is, "Did Jesus Christ die on the cross?"

Now, 99.9 percent of Muslims will tell you very emphatically that Jesus did not die on the cross. They believe that God replaced Jesus with a substitute and took him up to heaven alive. And this is a very emotional point for most Muslims, so it is quite stunning, actually, that they would invite me to this bastion of Islamic orthodoxy to speak on this topic. The department chair who introduced me said, "You have heard it said in the news media that Islam is an intolerant and bigoted religion. We're here today to prove otherwise. We've brought in this scholar today, and he's not a Muslim, and he's not an Arab. He's a Christian, and he's an American. And we've invited him to speak on a very controversial topic: 'Did Jesus Christ die on the cross?' And I just want to say, 'Take your liberty, brother.'"

Now, I am Pentecostal, so I like it when they say, "Take your liberty, brother." And in response to such a magnanimous invitation, what I did, and what I have done in such institutions, is simply look sympathetically at the Islamic texts themselves, because if you have looked at the texts of the Qur'an, you know that there is one verse in the Qur'an that seems at first glance to deny that Jesus died on the cross, and there are three other verses in the Qur'an that seem at first glance to affirm that Jesus did die on the cross. And you say, "Well, which is it?" And how do you reconcile these? And so I went through all the major Muslim commentaries on the Qur'an through the centuries, the ones that Muslims see as most authoritative, the ones that at al-Azhar they study every day. I simply looked up those four verses to see what they had to say.

It was very interesting to see that they all agreed that this is actually an open question, that there has actually always been a minority opinion in the Muslim world that Jesus might have died and risen. Now, I did not push a Christian point of view. I simply went objectively through these texts that the greatest Muslim scholars in history had written, and it is more or less indisputable that they all say, "This is an open question, and it is permissible to hold the view that Jesus did die and rise."[212] And after I shared this at al-Azhar with a standing-room-only audience, we opened up for questions and answers, and this went on for hours. Eventually, I had to go because I had a flight to catch, but there was a beautiful moment when one woman student said to me, "Sir, we've learned a lot from you about what the Qur'an teaches and about what Muslims believe about the crucifixion of Christ. But I'd like to know, what does the crucifixion of Christ mean to you?"

Then I shared with all of these professors and scholars and students at al-Azhar how Jesus changed my life, how when I was a young man, I was lost in sin, headed toward alcoholism, experimenting with drugs and sexual immorality, and contemplating suicide, and how Jesus broke into my life, and was willing to forgive my sins by his death on the cross, and how that changed my life.

---

212 For an overview of these leading qur'anic commentators who allow for a real crucifixion and resurrection, see Joseph Cumming, "Did Jesus Die on the Cross? Reflections in Muslim Commentaries" in J. Dudley Woodberry, Osman Zumrut, and Mustafa Koylu, eds., *Muslim and Christian Reflections on Peace: Divine and Human Dimensions* (Lanham, MD: University Press of America, 2005), 32–50.

As I shared, tears began to pour down people's faces, and they began to applaud, and they stood up, and began to cheer. Now, that is not the image that we get of Islam, in the American news media at any rate.

"DIALOGUE"

When I was starting out in the ministry and in earlier years when I would hear the word "dialogue," I would immediately react negatively and say, "I don't want to be involved in that." I do not know if any of us have had that kind of feeling, and the reason that I have declined to take part is that because I thought that the first ground rule for inter-faith dialogue was, "You are not allowed to believe that your faith could be valid for the whole human race."

Since I cannot accept that premise, then, I assumed that excluded me. But the rules for inter-faith dialogue are changing. For example, a few years ago, I was at a remarkable inter-faith dialogue, which was a quiet, off-the-radar-screen meeting that brought some very top-tier Muslim, Christian, and Jewish leaders together.

On the first morning, one of the Christian seminary presidents said, "I want to set some ground rules. The first ground rule for inter-faith dialogue is that if you believe that your faith is the only true way for the whole human race, you should not be participating in this dialogue."

Now, it so happened that I was in the position of translating for him into Arabic at that time. It is always a challenge to translate something you do not agree with, and the Muslim delegates were furious. They said to me, "What is this guy thinking? He invites us to his country, and the first thing he does is tell us, 'You're not welcome.' Because of course we believe Islam is the true religion for the whole human race. If we didn't, we wouldn't be Muslims!"

And then they said something very interesting. "We want to work with you Evangelicals, because we feel like we have something in common with you Evangelicals." Another Muslim leader said, "We want to be talking with Christians who take scripture seriously." I think the very shape of what dialogue is all about is changing in the world today.

BRIDGES

Once, I had the opportunity to meet with the Lebanese Ayatollah, Sheikh Fadlallah. Together with Ayatollah Sistani, Sheikh Fadlallah is one of *the* single most influential Shi'ite leaders in the Arab world. Ayatollah Sistani is more frequently in the American news media. Sheikh Fadlallah is probably more influential throughout the Arab world, but they are both very influential. Sheikh Fadlallah is mainly known in the American news media as the founder of Hezbollah. Although he no longer leads Hezbollah, the people in Hezbollah certainly still look to him for spiritual guidance.

Sheikh Fadlallah's anti-American credentials are well-established. I was hoping to meet with him, but it turned out that the only day I was free in Lebanon was the day before Ashura, the holiest day of the year for Shi'ite Muslims. That is the day they commemorate the martyrdom of Hussein, the grandson of the prophet Muhammad.

Even though it was like asking for an audience with the Pope on Christmas Eve, we called ahead to ask for an audience with Sheikh Fadlallah. His secretary replied, "There is no way he has time." But then the secretary got back to us and told us, "Actually, Sheikh will give you five minutes. But I want you to understand, after four minutes and fifty-five seconds, I want you standing up, and saying, 'It's time to go.'" We agreed.

I went and I prayed over the few days before I met with him, and I said, "Lord, tell me what to say, because we will spend a minute shaking hands for the television cameras, and then I will have two minutes to say something; he will have two minutes to say something; and then the time will be up. What can I say in two minutes that will both show respect for him and his religious convictions, and bear faithful witness to Jesus Christ?"

I prayed and agonized, but could not get a real sense of clarity for what I should say. I had a few ideas, but it was not until we were on the way to the meeting that I figured out what I wanted to say. We were driving through a very poor area of south Beirut that had recently been demolished in the war, and I saw a banner for Ashura over the road that said in Arabic, "The victory of blood over the sword." What this meant was that Hussein, in Shi'ite belief, when they came to kill him, could have called on God, and God would have enabled him to kill all of his enemies. Instead, he voluntarily laid down his sword and allowed them to massacre him, and in so doing, in Shiʻite belief, he gained a position of intercession for the forgiveness of the sins of others.

JESUS, WHEN THEY CAME TO KILL HIM, COULD HAVE KILLED HIS ENEMIES, BUT INSTEAD, HE LAID DOWN HIS LIFE FOR THEM IN LOVE, AND WHILE HE WAS DYING, PRAYED FOR THEIR FORGIVENESS. I BELIEVE THAT THIS ACT IS THE KEY TO FORGIVENESS FOR THE WHOLE HUMAN RACE, AND THAT THIS IS THE KEY TO BREAKING THE CYCLE OF VIOLENCE AND RETRIBUTION AND REVENGE IN THE WORLD TODAY.

Now, does that sound familiar? At that point, I felt the Holy Spirit say, "That's what I want you to talk about." We went, and we shook hands, and then Sheikh Fadlallah said, "What do you have to say?" I shared what I had seen on the banner, and I said, "This is how I understand it: Hussein could have killed his enemies, but instead, by laying down his life, he won the greater victory." He replied, "Yes, that is what it signifies for us." I said, "That's what I believe about Jesus, that Jesus, when they came to kill him, could have killed his enemies, but instead, he laid down his life for them in love, and while he was dying, prayed for their forgiveness. I believe that this act is the key to forgiveness for the whole human race, and that this is the key to breaking the cycle of violence and retribution and revenge in the world today."

Now, I expected the Sheikh to say, "Right, but we do not believe that Jesus died on the cross." I did not know that someone had given him a copy of my paper the night before, the same one that I had presented at al-Azhar. He had apparently read it. He turned to his followers and said, "I totally agree with every word this Christian man of God has just said."

After five minutes—four minutes and fifty-five seconds—I stood up to go as I had been instructed, and he said, "Where are you going? I need to talk to you! There is a lot more I want to talk to you about!" He kept me for two hours, at the end of which I had to go, because I had another commitment. I can tell you, when we walked out, the people in the waiting room did not look friendly toward me.

In the course of the conversation, he asked me about many different things. He asked me about the Trinity, and I explained what we believe about the Trinity. He asked me about the integrity of the text of the Bible, and I explained what we believe about that. Of course, he asked me about political questions. The day before I visited him, the Israeli Defense Force had been trying to do one of their "targeted executions" of a Hamas leader in the West Bank. They fired a missile at the building he was supposedly in, and they missed. They hit two little boys who were playing soccer in the street. I think they were fourteen and eleven years old, and they were instantly killed. That night, on the television screens of the Arab world, you could see the mangled bodies of these two little boys, whose only crime was that they played soccer on the wrong street on the wrong day.

Sheikh Fadlallah asked me, "What do you have to say about this as a Christian?" I said, "Well, I look at the suffering of all innocent victims of violence and oppression and injustice, regardless of whether they are Israeli, or Palestinian, or Lebanese, or American, through the lens of the suffering and death of Jesus Christ. If it were not for the suffering and death of Jesus Christ, I might wonder at times whether God had abandoned the human race, whether God cared. But in the suffering of Jesus Christ, I see the sign of God's solidarity with all innocent victims of violence and suffering and oppression.[213] That's how I understand the suffering and death of these innocent Palestinian boys." He turned to his followers and said, "I agree with every word this Christian man of God has just said."

RELATING

It was several months later that the Abu Ghraib scandal broke, and the image of that poor man standing with electrodes on his hands was broadcast all over the world, and millions of Muslims asked their leaders, "How are we supposed to think as Muslims about this?" One answer would be the tribal answer: "We are the Muslims, they are the Christians. They are trying to kill us, so we need to kill the Christians before they kill us." That would not be the answer I would want them to give.

---

[213] For more on this concept, see Jürgen Moltmann, *The Crucified God: The Cross of Christ as the Foundation and Criticism of Christian Theology*, trans. R.A. Wilson and John Bowden (Minneapolis, MN: Fortress Press, 1993).

Interestingly, and perhaps not coincidentally, Hezbollah did not give the tribal answer. Instead, under the influence of Sheikh Fadlallah, they put out a video on their television channel, in which they took images and music from the movie "The Passion of the Christ" and morphed them together with images of innocent Iraqis suffering at the hands of American troops. Then, they issued a press release, explaining that they understood the suffering of the Iraqi people through the lens of the suffering and death of Jesus Christ: "The suffering of Jesus Christ is a universal theme. It is something in which everyone, including Muslims, believes."

Now, I cannot tell you for certain that it was because I put that idea in Sheikh Fadlallah's mind, but certainly, what they said was exactly what I had suggested to him.

If you viewed that video just "as an American," you might say, "Why do they have to go make our troops look so bad again?" If, instead of viewing that video as an American, you viewed that video as a Christian, you might say, "Wow, millions and millions of Muslims in the Middle East are being told by Hezbollah, 'When you think of the suffering of the Iraqi people, think of the suffering and death of Jesus Christ.'"

A Struggle

In the remaining part of this talk, I would like to share something very important: a challenge for Christians, especially American Christians. Part of what I will share may be hard for some to take. I want to preface it with a little personal note, because you might think, as I share, "Is this guy naïve about the menace of militant Muslims in the world today?" I want you to know that I have personally survived two attempts by Muslim extremist crowds to lynch me: once, because I was an American in 1986, and once because of my witness to Jesus Christ in 1989. I have received more death threats from Muslim extremists through the years than I can count. I have been arrested, I have had my home searched, and my Bibles have been confiscated. The police have interrogated me about my witness to faith in Jesus Christ, and I have close friends who have been tortured. I think I have earned the right to say I am not naïve about Islamic extremism. But I want to ask: What does our Christian faith say about the attitude we should have as Christians toward Islam and Muslims in the world today? I believe that since 9/11, there is a titanic struggle going on in the heavenly realms. It is a struggle that most Christians are completely unaware is taking place. It is not a struggle between Muslims and Christians or between Muslims and the West. Rather, I am talking about a struggle within Christianity itself, a struggle for the soul of the Christian faith.

What image springs to the minds of most Christians when they think about Muslims? The Twin Towers, Osama bin Laden? What image do you think first springs to Jesus' mind when he thinks about Muslims? The image that first springs to my mind is of a woman, who, when the police came to arrest me, risked her life to rescue me from prison. She came from an ethnic minority group that was being persecuted and "ethnically cleansed" at the time, and despite her terror of the police, she rounded up fifty people from the whole neighborhood to come and plead with the police not to imprison me. That is the kind of person who springs to my mind when I think of Muslims.

SINCE 9/11, THERE IS A TITANIC STRUGGLE GOING ON IN THE HEAVENLY REALMS. IT IS NOT A STRUGGLE BETWEEN MUSLIMS AND CHRISTIANS OR BETWEEN MUSLIMS AND THE WEST. RATHER, I AM TALKING ABOUT A STRUGGLE WITHIN CHRISTIANITY ITSELF, A STRUGGLE FOR THE SOUL OF THE CHRISTIAN FAITH.

I think that when Jesus thinks about Muslims, he thinks about the fact that 60 percent of the world's poor are Muslims. As the apostle Paul said, "They asked only one thing, that we remember the poor, which was actually what I was eager to do" (Galatians 2:10).

I could turn that around and ask: What sort of images spring to the minds of most Muslims when they think about Christianity? For many, the images that come to mind are of Christians oppressing Muslims. And many of those who are oppressing Muslims openly claim to be Christians. September 11 has set a question before the Christians of the world, a question that we were able to ignore before 9/11, and that now we are no longer at liberty to ignore. The question is: Is the Christian faith primarily a tribal identity? (We are the Christians, they are the Muslims.) Or, is the Christian faith primarily costly discipleship to Jesus Christ the Crucified?

For many people before 9/11, the lines between these two things could be blurred. They were able to think about following Christ and think about Christianity as a tribal identity. That is no longer possible, because the answer that we give to that question is going to take us in different directions in the world today.

TRIBES OR DISCIPLES?

If the Christian faith is primarily a tribal identity, where does that take us? It takes us to the belief that, "We must fight to defend the survival of Christian civilization. If necessary, we must kill the enemies of our civilization before they kill us. We must pray that our God gives us victory over their 'Allah-god.'" On the other hand, if the Christian faith is primarily costly discipleship to Jesus the Crucified, then we must gladly lay down our lives in love for Muslims and share with them the precious Good News of Jesus, so that they may come to know his Gospel of salvation.

The answers to the "tribal identity or costly discipleship" question take us in opposite directions. If, when thinking of Muslims, we think of the Christian faith as a tribal identity we might ask: How do we avoid being killed by them? How do we prevent terrorist attacks on our homeland? How do we stop their encroachment in our countries? But if we think of the Christian faith as costly discipleship, another set of questions governs how we think of Muslims: How can we love Muslims? How can we share Good News with them with gentleness and respect (1 Peter 3:15)?

We have to choose one way or the other. What does Jesus say about this? He says, "If any want to become my followers, let them deny themselves and take up their cross and follow me. For those who want to save their life will lose it, and those who lose their life for my sake and the sake of the Gospel will save it" (Mark 8:34–35).

So we have to choose—self-preservation or self-giving for the Gospel? You cannot have it both ways. A prominent televangelist said, "The message of peace and reconciliation under almost all circumstances is simply incompatible with Christian teachings as I interpret them. This 'turn the other cheek' business is all well and good, but it's not what Jesus fought and died for. What we need to do is take the battle to the Muslim heathens, and do unto them before they do unto us!"

What does Jesus say? "If anyone strikes you on the right cheek, turn the other also" (Matthew 5:39). "But I say to you, love your enemies, and pray for those who persecute you" (Matthew 5:44). "Put your sword back into its place, for all who take the sword will perish by the sword. Do you think that I cannot appeal to my Father and he will at once send me more than twelve legions of angels? But how then would the scriptures be fulfilled, which say it must happen in this way?" (Matthew 26:52–54).

A Decision

You have to decide: self-preservation or self-giving for the Gospel? People will make sacrifices for their country that they would not be willing to make for God. If you think, how many followers of Christ are working for God among Muslims worldwide? Back in 1982, it was about one per million. Today, it is a lot more, maybe about 10,000 followers of Christ working among 1.3 billion Muslims.

But now think, what is the number of Evangelicals serving with the military in Iraq today? Well, if there are 162,000 U.S. troops in Iraq right now, maybe 10 percent of them are evangelical Christians; so 16,200 Evangelicals will go to Iraq for their country. That is a lot more than are willing to go to the Muslim world for their Savior to serve Muslims in Jesus' name.

YOU HAVE TO DECIDE: SELF-PRESERVATION OR SELF-GIVING
FOR THE GOSPEL?

Those military personnel are risking their lives, and society says, "That's beautiful." They endure separation from family and difficult living conditions, and everyone says, "That's heroic." When Jesus' followers do the same, everybody says, "Oh, are you sure you should be putting your family through that?"

What does the Bible say? "Our citizenship is in heaven, and it is from there that we are expecting a Savior, the Lord Jesus Christ" (Philippians 3:20). What does the Bible say? "This is how we know what love is: Jesus Christ laid down his life for us, so we ought to lay down our lives for one another" (1 John 3:16 NIV).

HENOTHEISM

Throughout history, whenever any nation has been at war, and has become convinced that their very survival and way of life are at stake, they have been tempted by a heresy known as henotheism. The *Random House Unabridged Dictionary* defines henotheism as the worship of a particular god as by a family or a particular tribe without disbelieving in the existence of others.

Let me give you an example of henotheism from World War II: "*God mit uns—God with us.*" It is a verse from the Bible, and though it means that in Jesus we see that God is with the whole human race, it was interpreted as "God with our tribe, against our tribe's enemies." This henotheistic heresy has the potential to completely destroy the Christian church.

More recently, a U.S. Army general was speaking to a large evangelical Christian church, describing a battle with a warlord in northern Africa, and he said, "I knew that I need not fear, because my God was more powerful than his god! I knew that my God was the true God, and his God was a demon!" That is henotheism. Though the general later apologized, the church did not apologize. Why? Because in henotheism, this is what we people want their military leaders to say, that, "Our God is going to help us beat their 'Allah-god.'"

What does the Bible say? "Is God the God of Jews only? Is he not the God of Gentiles also? Yes, of Gentiles also, since God is one" (Romans 3:29–30). Of course, if God is the God of the pagan Greeks, then how much more so of Muslims? I think it's very clear in the Bible that there is not, "Our God who is going to help us beat their God," there is only one God who is the God of the whole human race.

CONCLUSION

It used to be commonly said that Islam was Satan's greatest masterpiece. I believe that is not true. I believe that Satan's greatest masterpiece was the Crusades. Why? Is it because the Crusades were the worst atrocity that ever happened in history? I think Hitler was worse. Stalin was worse. Pol Pot was worse. What is so horrible about the Crusades is that it was done under the symbol of the cross, that Satan succeeded in distorting the very heart of the Christian faith.

The cross is at the heart of the entire Christian faith, and for the Muslims and the Jews of the world, what does the symbol of the cross now signify? The cross now signifies, "Christians hate you enough to kill you." What is the cross supposed to signify? It is supposed to signify, "God loved you enough to lay down his life for you, and I love you enough that I would lay down my life for you." Satan succeeded in taking the very heart of the Christian faith, and turning it around to mean not just something different, but to mean the exact opposite of what it was supposed to mean.

What would be a greater victory in the post-9/11 world? Would it be to tempt Osama bin Laden to hijack a few more airplanes? That would be a minor victory for Satan. Or would it be to tempt the Christian community to abandon their historic faith in Jesus Christ, delivered once for all to the saints, and to turn it into a tribal, henotheistic religion predicated on enmity with our neighbors? I think that would be a much greater victory for Satan.

What does the Bible say? "If any want to become my followers, let them deny themselves and take up their cross and follow me. For those who want to save their life will lose it, and those who lose their life for my sake and the sake of the Gospel will save it" (Mark 8:34–35). As followers of Jesus, we must follow in his footsteps, deny ourselves, and serve Muslims, just as Jesus himself "did not come to be served, but to serve"(Matthew 20:28).

Chapter 22

Peacemaking and Church Formation

David Shenk and Ahmed Haile

"The fruit of the Spirit is ... peace."
Galatians 5:22

"Blessed are the peacemakers,
for they will be called children of God."
Matthew 5:9

Ahmed was born into a Muslim nomadic home in Somalia; David is the son of pioneer missionaries in Tanzania. We both responded to the call of the Holy Spirit to follow Jesus, Ahmed in his youth and David as a child. Our responses introduced us into joyous reconciliation with God and with others, and although our parental homes were vastly different, each of us knows that the church is the fellowship of the redeemed, and each of us has reconciled bearing witness to the *shalom* of God.

THE PEACE OF ISLAM AND THE PEACE OF THE GOSPEL

The Muslim community is also committed to peace. The term "Islam" (to submit) is formed from the same Arabic root as *salam* (peace). Yet the theological narrative that forms the Muslim peace mission is very different from that of a Christ-centered community. The Hijrah is at the heart of the Muslim narrative. For twelve years Muhammad had proclaimed the early portions of the Qur'an in seventh-century Mecca, but he was not successful in gathering a viable community of believers around him. The polytheistic Meccans strongly resisted his message.

Then an invitation came from Medina (175 miles to the north) for Muhammad to become an umpire between the tribes. He accepted that invitation; the secret migration of his followers to Medina is known as the Hijrah. That is the beginning of the Muslim era. He was welcomed as a leader who would bring peace to the ethnic tensions in Medina. In Medina, Muhammad successfully used political power to establish peace as well as establish the Muslim community. The Meccan enemies of the Muslim movement were defeated in the battles that ensued, and within eight years, the Meccans accepted peace. Muhammad entered Mecca with 10,000 troops as he extended the peace of Islam throughout the city.

On that day of triumph, Muhammad proclaimed, "Truth hath come, and falsehood hath vanished away" (Surah 17:81).

Six hundred years earlier, Jesus was at the height of his popularity in Galilee after his miraculous feeding of 5,000 people. The Galileans insisted that he become their king, but Jesus rejected the invitation, instead setting out for Jerusalem, where he would meet arrest and crucifixion. In his dying, he cried out in forgiveness for those who had crucified him. In his crucifixion and resurrection, Jesus triumphed over all principalities and powers.

In one of his resurrection appearances, he showed his wounded hands to the fearful disciples and proclaimed, "Peace be with you. As the Father has sent me, so I send you. Receive the Holy Spirit" (John 20:21–22).

THE CHURCH: A FELLOWSHIP OF RECONCILIATION

The Muslim Hijrah takes us in the opposite direction to the way chosen by Jesus. Messiah-centered peace is the way of the cross. The peace of the Messiah is in receiving and offering forgiveness. That is a gift of grace that political systems cannot create. In fact, political systems such as that created by Islam are inclined to become strongholds that resist the way of the cross. The Christian calling is to encounter those strongholds and bring them into captivity to the mind of Christ (2 Corinthians 10:3–5). The mind of Christ is foolishness to the world, but Christ crucified is the power of God (1 Corinthians 1:22–24)!

That is the story of our journey in ministry among Muslims; it is a journey engaging Islamic strongholds in the powerful peacemaking "weakness" of the cross. This is the reason we believe that vulnerable peacemaking and church formation flow together.

PEACEMAKING MINISTRIES AMONG SOMALI MUSLIMS

The Somali people live throughout Somalia and much of northeastern Kenya, eastern Ethiopia, and Djibouti. In essence, the Somalis are 100 percent Sunni Muslim. In the early 1960s, David and his family joined the Somalia Mennonite Mission team in Somalia. That is where we, Ahmed and David, met. It was in the emerging congregation in Mogadishu that we learned to know each other as brothers.

In the 1970s, political changes foisted Marxism upon Somalia. David and his family were required to leave by the Marxist regime; Ahmed left because of the stranglehold of atheistic ideology upon the educational system. Consequently, our ways converged in Eastleigh, the mostly Somali-Muslim area of Nairobi in Kenya, Somalia's southern neighbor. We believed that God had placed us in Eastleigh to be a visible witness to the peace of the Messiah. For that reason, we rented a five-apartment complex where Christians from different ethnic or national backgrounds lived as a fellowship of worship, reconciliation, service, and witness. We were a visible sign of the peaceable kingdom of Jesus the Messiah.

Our community was a few yards from a mosque of Sufis. (This is mystical Islam that influences most Somali Muslims in the form of the movement known as *Sufi Al Sunna wal Jamaha.*) We sometimes visited the imam and met with Muslim leaders and their disciples for tea or dinner with occasional conversations about faith. The Sufi communities across Somalia have always been committed to intercommunity peace within societies that were often in conflict. Our Christian community of peace was modeled contextually so that it made sense within the Sufi-Somali milieu. We served the Eastleigh community in a variety of ways, especially with a quiet reading room where students could study away from the congestion of their homes.

That ministry has developed into the Eastleigh Fellowship Center, where hundreds of Muslims come every week. They participate in diverse ministries from weight lifting to one-on-one literacy tutoring. For Somalis, who are exceedingly mobile, this center is known as an oasis of peace for many throughout northeastern Africa.

We worked with a center-based team in a four-year effort developing a contextual Bible study course for Muslims known as the *People of God*. As a community committed to peacemaking, we took the course to key Muslim leaders, and asked for their comments before publishing. We wanted the course to be a bridge, not a wall. One of the Muslim polemists, who often preached in the neighborhood of the center, was so appreciative that we sought his counsel that he actually counseled us on how to write one chapter in such a way that Muslims could hear the Christian message. The cleric commented after the changes were made, "I disagree with what you have written, but now I can hear your message! I will not object to Muslims taking this course."

The *People of God* in East Africa has introduced the Gospel to up to 1,000 Muslims annually with little or no objection from the Muslim community. Hundreds have come to faith in the Messiah. Its distribution center for East Africa is the Eastleigh Fellowship Center.

A fellowship of believers in the Messiah emerged, and we teamed together with others in leading that fellowship. In later years, as militant Wahabism began to take root in Eastleigh, it became prudent for the believers to meet in other areas of the city, but many of those who participate in the several Somali fellowships in Nairobi have been touched by the grace of God through the ministries of the Eastleigh Fellowship Center.

THE *PEOPLE OF GOD* IN EAST AFRICA HAS INTRODUCED THE GOSPEL TO UP TO 1,000 MUSLIMS ANNUALLY WITH LITTLE OR NO OBJECTION FROM THE MUSLIM COMMUNITY.

Other partnering agencies developed a sister community in the town of Garissa within the Somali nomadic heartland of northeastern Kenya. The leaders met with the leading Sufi cleric of northeastern Kenya to receive his blessing in their commitment to developing a Christian community of reconciliation. The physical layout of the center was modeled on that of the Sufi center: a worship round house, a meeting house, a common dining round house, and sleeping/living round houses. Just as in Nairobi, participants were believers in the

Messiah who came from diverse ethnic and national backgrounds. They became a sign of the peace of the Messiah throughout the region. On one occasion, when scores of houses were burned in inter-clan conflict, that center was a beacon of hope and recognized as an oasis of peace.

The ministry has gone through many transformations, including shifts in location. Today, there is significant focus on prayer for healing of those traumatized by the wars of Somalia. Many Muslims come for the prayer ministries of the Christian team. The Holy Spirit uses the ministry of prayer to extend the healing touch to Jesus the Messiah to Muslims, and occasionally, those who come for this ministry of healing prayer report that they have seen a vision of Jesus the Messiah who has met them and touched them with healing grace. At this writing (January 2008), Kenya is in political turmoil, and ethnic conflict is spreading. The peace team continues its presence in Garrisa in the midst of the conflict as a community of peace, prayer, and hope within the turmoil.

AN AMBASSADOR OF PEACE

In the late 1970s, Ahmed left Eastleigh for the United States, where he began academic peacemaking studies. He then returned to Somalia as an ambassador of the Prince of Peace. After his marriage to Martha, the Somali government unraveled in inter-clan wars, and the Hailes left Somalia.

However, Ahmed is from a clan in Somalia who are recognized as the peacemakers. His conviction is that within the pre-Islamic Somali traditional culture, there are peacemaking themes that have analogies with Old Testament themes, particularly a commitment to restorative justice and covenant known as *hher*. He therefore decided to return to Somalia alone to work within the clan structures as a peacemaker. Just before his departure, several Somalis from his clan met him in Washington, D.C. and threatened him for his commitment to the Messiah. Ahmed responded, "If you kill me, I want to assure you that my family and the church will forgive you, for that is the way of the Messiah." They were amazed, and probed him with questions about the nature of the peace that Jesus offers.

So he left for Mogadishu, Somalia, to broker peace between the warring factions. However, clans at war usually do not view peacemakers kindly. One of the factions fired a rocket into the building where Ahmed was staying, and his leg was destroyed. The whole city heard about what had happened, and the few disciples of Jesus living in Mogadishu did their best to find a way to airlift him to Nairobi. An ambulance plane flew him to Nairobi, and then he went on to the United States. The doctors' assessment was that he would not live, yet the Lord touched Ahmed and he survived as a one-legged peacemaker.

After his recovery, he and the family returned to Kenya, where he currently teaches peacemaking at Daystar University and is a participant in the pastoral leadership of the Somali believers in Nairobi. Some three decades after we joined hands and formed a team committed to being a sign of the peace of the Messiah in Eastleigh, Ahmed and his family continue to carry that vision forward. David was recently in Nairobi joining in the Sunday worship under the great tree in the yard of the Hailes with about eighty followers of Christ, including many joyous children along with the women and men. (In Somalia, children could not attend worship, and women were rarely or never present.) That day David was filled with joy by seeing how the Lord has prospered the vision that was planted in our hearts three decades earlier when we moved into Eastleigh.

MANY KEY CLAN LEADERS COME TO MEET WITH THIS CHRISTIAN PASTOR TO SEEK COUNSEL AMIDST THE PERPLEXING GYRATIONS OF THE PEACE-BUILDING PROCESS FOR THEIR WOUNDED MOTHERLAND.

During one congregational retreat in mid-2006, David served as a resource person. For one session, the participants read the passage about the woman who calls her neighbors to rejoice with her when her lost coin is found (Luke 15:8–10). Most of the Somali women are refugee widows. They enacted the account, and when the coin was found, the women began an exuberant traditional dance with cries of joy. These socially marginalized and poor refugee widows exclaimed, "Jesus is the woman in the story; we are the coin. Jesus is dancing for joy, for he has found us! That is why we also dance."

Ahmed continues his mission as a peacemaker, and in fact, the great tree in the Haile yard is known as Ahmed's tree. Because of the endemic violence in Somalia, many key clan leaders live in Nairobi and occasionally come to Ahmed's tree to meet with this Christian pastor to seek counsel amidst the perplexing gyrations of the peace-building process for their wounded motherland.

Their respect for Ahmed helps to provide space for the fellowship of Jesus-followers.

Like Ahmed, Somali believers in the Messiah who are committed to peacemaking are salt and light within these current turbulent times. The same is true of a cluster of Somalis who had been students in Somalia Mennonite Mission schools a generation ago, and who are now working for peacemaking, although they are committed to Islam. These peacemakers are sometimes nicknamed "Muslim Mennonites" by their Somali companions. They have been influenced by the salt of Christian schools, and bring peacemaking gifts to the table that are recognized with appreciation by those who long for a reconciled Somali society. Some of these peacemakers have worked with Christian teammates to develop literature of peacemaking that has been widely distributed within Somali situations of conflict.

DIALOGUE WITH MUSLIMS

A further development during those early years in Eastleigh was a dialogue that David wrote with a Muslim colleague, Badru D. Kateregga, who taught at the university where David was a lecturer in world religions. The book they authored, *A Muslim and A Christian in Dialogue*,[214] is confessional. In the first twelve chapters, Badru shares his faith, and David responds to each chapter as an evangelical Christian. In the second half, David shares his faith and Badru responds as a conservative Sunni Muslim. The purpose is limited—building understanding in a peacemaking way. David's hope is that this book would address key misunderstandings, and thereby contribute to the kind of peacemaking that provides room for the church to develop.

David never imagined how widely this peacemaking effort would reach, nor the ways that this book would help to provide space for the church within some quite restrictive Muslim societies. We will share two examples: Kosovo and Indonesia.

Kosovo

In the ethnic cleansing wars in Kosovo of the late 1990s, Serb militias sometimes killed Muslim families, burned their houses, and placed crosses in the em-

---

214   See Badru D. Kateregga and David W. Shenk, *A Muslim and a Christian in Dialogue* (Scottsdale, PA: Herald Press, 1997).

bers, causing thousands to flee into Albania or Macedonia. Especially in Albania, Christian agencies and churches ministered to the devastated Kosovo Muslim refugees. Through this witness, some Kosovar refugees became believers, and as they returned home after the wars, some formed churches. Most are Muslim background believers who are not well received by the wider Kosovar Muslim community. Eighty percent of Kosovo is Muslim, with 20 percent Catholic and Orthodox. As Kosovo struggles toward its future, having declared its independence on February 17, 2008, the constitution brokered by the United Nations recognizes these three religious communities: Muslim, Catholic, and Orthodox. Evangelicals have been concerned that there was no recognition of their presence.

It was therefore surprising when a key member of the Islamic faculty at the university agreed to a public dialogue on peacemaking with David. Such a dialogue would indicate tacit recognition of the legitimacy of the presence of Evangelicals in Kosovo. The professor agreed to the dialogue because he was impressed with the spirit of the Shenk–Kataregga dialogue. The event held in the spring of 2006 was advertised across the country; the Evangelical Alliance sponsors rented the largest hall that accommodated 600 people. When the time came for the dialogue to begin, the room was completely full, with most key Muslim and Christian leaders present. The thrust of the Muslim presenter was that one must strive for justice because without justice there can be no peace. David agreed but observed that justice alone can never bring healing to Kosovo, where every family has been touched by atrocities. Surely forgiveness is needed.

"Where can forgiveness be found?" the Muslim colleague asked. David spoke of Jesus, who in his crucifixion reached out in forgiveness to those who were crucifying him. The mostly Muslim audience was amazed.

The next day, a reporter from the leading weekly news magazine in Kosovo interviewed David. She began by asking, "Since I represent a Muslim-owned newsmagazine, I do not want to interview you about Jesus. Why are you committed to peacemaking between Muslims and Christians?" David responded, "Because of Jesus."

Ninety minutes later, she closed her pad, observing, "Our theme has been the peace of Jesus. I do not know if the owners will permit this to be published." They did! The editors ran a double-page center spread on the theme of the peace of Jesus. Soon, the chief *khadi* (Muslim jurist) of Kosovo requested to have lunch with the head of the evangelical association to explore the peace of Jesus in bringing healing to Kosovo. Soon thereafter, the Muslim leadership opened the door for a constitutional recognition of the evangelical churches in Kosovo.

Later, David returned to Kosovo and was invited to address the Islamics Department on the theme of 'Faith and Freedom' and was informed that this was the first time a non-Muslim had addressed that department. David's presentation grounded freedom within a God-centered commitment, a conviction that was quite different from the assumptions of the Islamics department. The Holy Spirit is not confined by political constraints; nevertheless, we are grateful when the political order respects the freedom of people to choose their faith. Within Islamic societies that kind of recognition cannot be assumed; it needs to be nurtured through peace-building initiatives of the church.

Indonesia

In a very different region of the world, Indonesia, peacemaking initiatives are exceedingly pertinent; sometimes there has been isolated violent conflict between Christian and Muslim communities, such as Solo in Central Java. In 1998, large sections of the center of the city were damaged in riots. The issues were complex: ethnicity, wealth and poverty, Christians and Muslims. A young pastor stepped forward to give leadership to Muslim–Christian peacemaking. As a contribution to building bridges, a joint Muslim–Christian peacemaking committee decided to publish *A Muslim and a Christian in Dialogue* in Indonesian.

The pastor also initiated peacemaking efforts with an Islamist group, which had been responsible for some church burnings and even some killings. When the pastor first went to the home of the militant commander, the officer said, "You are an infidel, and I can kill you."

The pastor persisted, returning occasionally to drink tea with the commander. Then the pastor invited the commander and his officers to fly with several pastors to Banda Aceh to work with a Christian team in post-tsunami reconstruction. Surprisingly, the commander accepted, and in the two weeks he and the pastor roomed together, they became friends. One evening, as the Muslim Islamists were sitting with the Christian team, the commander wept. He explained, "My heart has melted within me. I am overcome when I think of the ways we have treated you Christians, and when I see you respond with such great love among the Muslims of Banda Aceh."

Early in 2007, David was invited to Solo for the official launching of *A Muslim and A Christian in Dialogue.* One venue for the launch was a gathering of eighty key Muslim, Buddhist, and Christian leaders, and the second venue was the Islamists' command center. About thirty Christians participated, with at least that many of the Islamist militants, who were mostly armed and dressed in their militia uniforms. This center commands 10,000 members of a militia in Java. We sat in a circle, and then the Islamist spokesperson said, "We are Islamists. Our mission is to fight to defend Islam and kill our enemies."

David responded, "When one kills one's enemies, that actually creates more enemies. We are disciples of Jesus, and he taught us to love and forgive our enemies. In that case, one does not have an enemy." They were surprised. This Messiah-centered theology was radical! Then the pastor, who was sitting by the commander, gave him a copy of *Dialogue.* The man lost his composure, and after the pastor sitting by him placed an assuring hand on the commander's shoulder, the commander said, "I am overcome, for this book is revealing another way. It is the way to respect and love the person with whom you disagree, rather than using violence against him."

WHEN ONE KILLS ONE'S ENEMIES,
THAT ACTUALLY CREATES MORE ENEMIES. WE ARE DISCIPLES OF
JESUS, AND HE TAUGHT US TO LOVE AND FORGIVE OUR ENEMIES.
IN THAT CASE, ONE DOES NOT HAVE AN ENEMY.

The commander ordered fifty copies of *Dialogue* for all his officers. As the relationship has developed between the commander and the pastor, they have pledged to cooperate in building trusting relations between churches and the Muslim communities in Java. When the commander learns of a potential church burning by one of his militia groups, he contacts the pastor. With the encouragement of the commander, he works proactively to ameliorate the threat.

The church that the pastor leads in Solo has grown significantly during these years that the pastor has been engaged in peacemaking. People are attracted to the peace of Jesus the Messiah. Now, however, they have a new challenge: the church building is overcrowded, and so the congregation needs to plant a new church. That is often a major challenge in Indonesia, for it is difficult to get permission to build churches. However, in Solo, the commander of the Islamists is advocating with the authorities for permission for a new church facility. The commander says, "You have become my good infidel friend!"

David asked the pastor how he accounts for this transformation, from being addressed as "infidel whom I can kill" to "my good infidel friend." The pastor responded, "Lots of cups of tea!—And the Holy Spirit."

CONCLUSION

We, Ahmed and David, are grateful for the ways that simple and modest commitments to peacemaking have contributed to the development of fellowships of Somali Muslim background believers. We are also grateful for ways that these commitments have borne fruit in several peacemaking commitments in other regions, even into the command center of Islamists in Central Java. Our conviction is that peacemaking prepares the spiritual and cultural soil of Islamic societies for hearing and receiving the Gospel. It prepares the society for church formation.

Islam is a stronghold. Our conviction is that this stronghold can only be addressed in the spirit of the crucified and resurrected One who, with his wounded and uplifted hands blessed and commissioned his timid disciples, "Peace be with you. As the Father has sent me, so I send you. Receive the Holy Spirit" (John 20:21–22).

Chapter 23

An Integrated Identity in a Globalized World

Patrick Lai and Rick Love

"Now you have observed my teaching, my conduct,
my aim in life, my faith, my patience, my love,
my steadfastness, my persecutions and suffering ..."
2 Timothy 3:10–11

Since the 1980s, tentmaking has re-emerged as an important aspect of serving in the Muslim world. More recently the focus has been on doing business as mission. Yet too little attention has been given to the challenge of doing excellent tentmaking or business as mission while being a fruitful disciple maker. Most individuals tend to emphasize one role or the other. Few people have been able to combine effectively the roles of disciple maker and tentmaker/business-person (henceforth in this paper we will use the terms tentmaking and business as mission interchangeably unless clearly stated).[215]

Today, we face an even greater challenge. In the past, we thought we could live in two worlds with two identities. To the church, we were missionaries. To our Muslim friends, we were teachers, business owners, non-governmental organization (NGO) leaders, and so forth. In fact, we were trying to be both. But the tension between this dual-identity (the work-ministry schizophrenia

---

[215] We included both terms in the introduction of this paper since tentmaking can include activities outside business, e.g., relief and development, teaching.

that many cross-cultural workers feel) has been heightened in the twenty-first century.

One effect of the rise of Islamic terrorism is that Muslims and those serving in the Muslim world have a higher profile on the world stage. Suddenly, more people are interested in what we do, simply because we live in and serve as bridges to the Muslim world. In addition, we now live in an interconnected, globalized (Google-ized!) world. With a few clicks of the computer, anyone can easily discover that the person the church considers to be a missionary is the person the Muslim neighbor knows as a businessperson or teacher (and vice versa).

This dual identity results in anxiety for some. They feel as though they are hiding their true identity and face the nagging fear they may be found out. It also makes it hard for some cross-cultural disciple-makers to maintain a clear conscience before God and others (cf. Acts 24:16). The result is a lack of integrity and lack of boldness to share the Gospel.

While our intentions have been good, many of us have not walked in integrity before God and our Muslim neighbors. This lack of integrity is not pleasing to God. Because of this, we need to go beyond traditional views of tentmaking and disciple making to seek an integrated apostolic identity[216] for the twenty-first century, which helps us walk in greater integrity. To find the way forward, we need to go backward. We need to take a fresh look at what the New Testament teaches about doing business as mission or tentmaking and how it helps us bear fruit with credibility, integrity, and boldness.

EVIDENCE OF TENTMAKING ON ALL OF PAUL'S JOURNEYS

A cursory reading of the New Testament seems to indicate that Paul did very little tentmaking. Many people tend to see him as a full-time Christian worker who did tentmaking only when he needed money. However, there is clear biblical evidence that he spent time making tents during all three of his journeys. Moreover, Paul viewed his work and ministry as integrated. Tentmaking was no "cover" or mere "platform." Certainly, his apostolic calling was the driving force of his life.[217] But just as certainly, work played a central role in the fulfillment of his calling.

---

[216] We define apostle as a cross-cultural disciple maker serving in a pioneer context—a "sent one" who forms communities of Jesus-followers where Christ is not named (Romans 15:20).

[217] "I do all things for the sake of the Gospel" (1 Corinthians 9:23, NASB).

The New Testament does not provide enough evidence about Paul's tentmaking to draw indisputable conclusions about how much time he worked. Some who are pro-tentmaking tend to go beyond the evidence to make their point, while others who see tentmaking as insignificant minimize the evidence. Let us examine the evidence afresh.

First Journey

The book of Acts does not describe Paul's tentmaking activities during his first journey (Acts 13–14). However, Paul clearly alludes to it in his discussion about his rights as an apostle: "I and Barnabas ...*must work for a living*" (1 Corinthians 9:6, NIV). This implies that Paul worked to support himself on his first journey since he teamed up with Barnabas only on his first journey.[218]

Second Journey

Both Acts and the epistles mention Paul's tentmaking activities on this journey. Acts 17 describes Paul's ministry to the Thessalonians, and both letters to the Thessalonians describe his long hours and arduous work doing manual labor.

> *You remember our labour and toil, brothers and sisters; we worked night and day, so that we might not burden any of you while we proclaimed to you the Gospel of God (1 Thessalonians 2:9).*

> *For you yourselves know how you ought to imitate us ...we worked night and day, so that we might not burden any of you. This was not because we do not have that right, but in order to give you an example to imitate (2 Thessalonians 3:7–9).*

---

[218] Gordon D. Fee, *The First Epistle of Corinthians* (Grand Rapids: Eerdmans, 1987), 404. As Fee notes, "The mention of Barnabas is especially intriguing. Why not Silas, for example, or Timothy? The answer almost surely does not lie with the suggestion that Barnabas had also visited Corinth, but with the probability that traditions about the apostles were well known. And in this case Paul and Barnabas in particular were known to have worked at a trade when they evangelized." See also Ruth E. Siemens, "Tentmakers Needed for World Evangelization," in *Perspectives on the World Christian Movement*, ed. Ralph D. Winter and Steven C. Hawthorne (Pasadena, CA: William Carey Library, 1999), 737. Siemens writes, "The first journey: Paul and Barnabas took the Gospel through the island of Cyprus and the Galatian–Phrygian region. In 1 Cor 9:6 Paul suggests they already supported themselves at that time and continued that financial practice when they formed two separate teams."

We can draw a number of significant conclusions about doing business as missions/tentmaking and apostolic calling from these passages.

1. Paul worked hard and put in long hours in his secular occupation. "Aching arms, tired fingers, calloused hands were a daily experience for this tentmaker. He paid a high price for his integrity. But he felt it was worth the price to fulfill Christ's mission."[219]

2. Paul made tents to serve as an example to others. Perhaps he aimed to challenge the commonly held aversion for manual labor held by many Greeks.[220] But certainly, "Paul regarded idleness, which was endemic in Greco-Roman society, as inappropriate for the Christian believer. So he deliberately set the example of hard work to support himself and called upon his [followers] to imitate him."[221]

3. He did not see his work as a distraction from his calling as an apostle.[222] New Testament scholar Gordon Fee observes about Paul's tentmaking: "At least as early as the mission to Thessalonica, what was originally a necessity had developed into a studied expression of his mission."[223]

[219] David A. Hubbard, *Thessalonians: Life that's Radically Christian* (Dallas, TX: Word Books, 1977), 22–23.

[220] See Simon J. Kistemaker, *New Testament Commentary* (Grand Rapids: Baker Books, 1993), 141. Kistemaker helps us understand the differences between Jewish and Greek views of manual labor: "Every Jewish boy had to learn a trade, usually from his father, to support himself. Jesus became a carpenter, John and James fishermen, and Paul a tentmaker. Even though Paul's trade was considered menial, he was not at all ashamed of it. In both Acts and Paul's epistles, references to Paul's readiness to work with his own hands abound (see, e.g., Acts 18:3; 20:34; 1 Cor 9:6; 1 Thes 2:9; 2 Thes 3:8). Yet in the Hellenistic culture of that day, Greeks disdained manual labor. They were of the opinion that physical labor had to be performed by slaves. By working with his hands Paul lowered his status in the eyes of local citizens."

[221] P.W. Barnett, "Tentmaking," in *Dictionary of Paul and His Letters*, electronic ed., ed. Gerald F. Hawthorne, et al. (Downers Grove, IL: InterVarsity Press, 1993).

[222] See Siemens, "Tentmakers Needed for World Evangelization," 737. Siemens notes: "An inductive study and careful correlation of all the relevant passages show that self-support was Paul's deliberate policy, part of his well-designed strategy."

[223] *The First Epistle of Corinthians*, 179. See also 1 Thessalonians 2:9; 4:11; 2 Thessalonians 3:6–13.

Ronald Hock has probably published more research on Paul's tentmaking than any other New Testament scholar. He has shown that far from being peripheral to Paul's apostolic calling, tentmaking was an integral part of it. "More than any of us has supposed, Paul was *Paul the Tentmaker*. His trade occupied much of his time ...[H]is life was very much that of the workshop ...of being bent over a workbench like a slave and of working side by side with slaves."[224]

Paul's work at Corinth is the most explicit and detailed description of his work as a tentmaker.[225]

> *There he met a Jew named Aquila ...with his wife Priscilla ...and because he was a tentmaker as they were, he stayed and worked with them. Every Sabbath he reasoned in the synagogue, trying to persuade Jews and Greeks. When Silas and Timothy came from Macedonia, Paul devoted himself exclusively to preaching, testifying to the Jews that Jesus was the Messiah (Acts 18:2–5, NIV).*

Paul began his ministry at Corinth by working as a tentmaker during the week with Aquila and Priscilla. "Every Sabbath"—implying some sort of routine—Paul would minister in the synagogue. After an unspecified period of time, Silas and Timothy brought a financial gift from Macedonia[226] that enabled Paul to stop the work of making tents and reprioritize his time to minister in other ways. Though Paul's apostolic *modus operandi* was tentmaking, he also accepted financial support so that he could give more time to discipleship and leadership training. In addition, accepting support enabled the churches to participate with Paul in his ministry. Paul's concern was for the giver, as much as for the gift (Philippians 4:17).

---

224   *The Social Context of Paul's Mission* (Philadelphia: Fortress, 1980), 67.

225   Craig S. Keener, *The IVP Bible Background Commentary: New Testament* (Downers Grove, IL: InterVarsity Press, 1994), 375. "By this period, the term translated "tentmaker" was also applied to leatherworking in general. As a leatherworker, Paul would have been an artisan. Artisans were typically proud of their work, despite the long hours they had to invest to succeed, and were higher than peasants in status and income; but they were despised by higher classes, who thought labor with one's hands degrading (see the conflicts described in the introduction to 1 Corinthians). Their long hours in their shops afforded them much time to talk while doing their work, but Paul apparently is able to discontinue the labor (1 Cor 4:12) when his companions bring a gift from the Macedonian church (v. 5; 2 Cor 11:7–8; 12:13; Phil 4:15). Corinth's agora (central marketplace) had the longest line of colonnaded shops in the empire."

226   From the church at Philippi. See Philippians 4:14–15.

WORKERS NEED TO BE ACCOUNTABLE BOTH TO THEIR SENDING CHURCH AND TO THE LOCAL COMMUNITY.

This passage in Acts highlights the strategic need for workers to be accountable both to their sending church and to the local community. There is an old saying, "He who pays the piper calls the tunes." Tentmakers have a reputation of being most accountable to the people who pay their salary. As Phil Parshall puts it, "Most tentmakers I know are all business and no ministry." Clearly, one way of being held accountable to doing ministry is to be partially dependent on the church for our income. Working in paid local employment holds us accountable financially and in other ways to the community where we live. For Paul, clearly, there were two sources of support—both from his tentmaking work and from supporting churches.

THIRD JOURNEY

Paul's farewell address to the Ephesian elders in Acts 20:34–35 makes it clear that Paul worked as a tentmaker during his ministry at Ephesus:

> You know for yourselves that I worked with my own hands to support myself and my companions. In all this I have given you an example that by such work we must support the weak, remembering the words of the Lord Jesus, for he himself said, "It is more blessed to give than to receive."[227]

Paul's calloused hands made tents to support himself, meet the needs of his team, and modeled hard work for the sake of the emerging church.

At Ephesus, Paul's tentmaking and apostleship were a seamless whole:

> Paul had the use of the building of Tyrannus from 11 A.M. to 4 P.M. Tyrannus no doubt held his classes in the early morning. Public activity ceased in the cities of Ionia for several hours at 11 A.M., and ...more people would be asleep at 1 P.M. than at 1 A.M. But Paul, after spending the early hours of the day working making tents, devoted the midday hours of burden and heat working at his exhausting business

---

[227] See also 1 Corinthians 4:12; 2 Corinthians 11:23, 27; 1 Thessalonians 4:11.

of teaching and discipling. His zeal and energy were such that he must have infected his hearers, so that they were willing to sacrifice their siesta for the sake of listening to Paul.[228]

Hock argues that "The workshop was a recognized social setting in Paul's day for intellectual discourse."[229] Thus, Paul's demanding schedule allowed time for both tentmaking and teaching, and his work as a tentmaker enabled him to share the Gospel freely in the context of his work. In other words, his tentmaking job enhanced his church-planting effectiveness.

Paul's Background and Training: An Integrated View of Work and Ministry

As a rabbi (Acts 22:3), Paul would have been trained both in the Scriptures and in a secular trade to support his ministry.[230] The importance of this bi-vocational emphasis is reflected in rabbinic traditions. Rabbi Zadok said, "Make not of the Torah …a spade wherewith to dig …whosoever derives a profit for himself from the words of the Torah is helping his own destruction."[231] Rabbi Gamaliel declared, "An excellent thing is the study of the Torah combined with some worldly occupation, for the labor demanded by them both makes sin to be forgotten. All study of the Torah without work must in the end be futile and become the cause of sin."[232]

Though trained as a Jewish rabbi, Paul was an apostle to the Gentiles (Romans 11:13). Thus it is important to understand the social and intellectual milieu of the Greek world in which he served. Wandering itinerant Hellenistic philosophers were common in Paul's day. These philosophers supported themselves

---

[228] An analysis of the Western Greek text of Acts 19:8–9 has led F.F. Bruce to this conclusion in *Commentary on the Book of the Acts* (Grand Rapids: Eerdmans, 1975), 388–89. In *A Textual Commentary on the Greek New Testament*, 4th ed. (New York: United Bible Societies, 2001), Bruce M. Metzger notes regarding Acts 19:9, "The interesting addition in the Western text ('[Paul] argued daily in the hall of Tyrannus *from the fifth hour to the tenth*' [i.e., from 11:00 a.m. to 4:00 p.m.]) may represent an accurate piece of information, preserved in oral tradition before being incorporated into the text of certain manuscripts. Were it present in the original text, there is no good reason why it should have been deleted."

[229] Ronald F. Hock, "The Workshop as a Social Setting for Paul's Missionary Preaching," *The Catholic Biblical Quarterly* 41 (1979): 450.

[230] In *The Social Context of Paul's Mission*, 22–25, Ronald Hock argues that these rabbinic quotes reflect later tradition (after Paul) and thus do not substantiate this dominant view held by most New Testament scholars. However, Jeremias maintains that there is explicit evidence that rabbis were taught the Torah and a trade in Jerusalem at the time of Christ. See J. Jeremias, *Jerusalem in the Time of Jesus* (Philadelphia: Fortress, 1969).

[231] Aboth IV, 7, in C.G. Montefiore and H. Loewe, *A Rabbinic Anthology* (Schocken Books: New York, 1974), 127–128.

[232] Aboth II, 2, in Montefiore and Loewe, *A Rabbinic Anthology*, 175.

in different ways. Some begged, others charged fees, accepted patronage,[233] or supported themselves by working.[234]

Both his rabbinic background and models from the Greek world indicate that Paul practiced a seamless approach to ministry. He was trained in both secular and sacred work and saw life, work, and ministry as a seamless whole. Likewise, we should not *compartmentalize* our lives. "*Whatever you do*, in word or deed, do everything in the name of the Lord Jesus" (Colossians 3:17, emphasis added). For those in business, our business is mission, and mission is our business. Ministry is not just something we do; ministry is life itself, because modeling is a crucial part of ministry.

GUIDING PRINCIPLES FOR PAUL'S APOSTLESHIP AND TENTMAKING

Paul was apparently criticized at Corinth for working and not accepting financial support.[235] His unwillingness to accept patronage had been misinterpreted and used as an argument against him. Thus, in 1 Corinthians 9:3, Paul defends

---

[233]   Fee, *The First Epistle of Corinthians*, 399. See also J.M. Everts, "Financial Support," in *Dictionary of Paul and His Letters*, electronic ed., ed. Gerald F. Hawthorne, et al. (Downers Grove, IL: InterVarsity Press, 1993), s.v. Most philosophers either charged fees or accepted the patronage of a wealthy individual. The major criticism of this method of support was that it placed a philosopher under obligation to a patron and therefore jeopardized the philosopher's freedom to teach the truth. In Hellenistic society, the giving and receiving of benefactions was an extremely important component of the social structure. The wealthy expressed their power by becoming patrons, and since benefaction was the basis of friendship, refusing a gift was an act of enmity. Philosophers who wished to avoid this network of obligation could either beg, as the Cynics chose to do, or work. However, since most of Greek society looked down on those who worked at a trade or begged, not many philosophers chose Thessalonian methods of support. Those who did gained freedom at the expense of social status.

[234]   In *Reading Acts: A Literary and Theological Commentary on The Acts of the Apostles* (New York: The Crossroad Publishing Company, 1997), 167, Charles H. Talbert comments about Paul's tentmaking: "Such behavior reflects ...that of certain Cynic philosophers (Diogenes Laertius 7.168; Epictetus 3.26.23)." See also Ronald F. Hock, "Paul's Tentmaking and the Problem of his Social Class," *Journal of Biblical Literature* 97 (1978): 563. After giving numerous illustrations from well-known Greek writers such as Plutarch, Epictetus, Lucian, Musonius, and Dio, Hock concludes: "The case of Dio is especially significant ...he adopted the role of Cynic missionary; his combining missionary activity and self-support is thus a close parallel to the case of Paul."

[235]   Understanding the social-intellectual milieu of Paul's day helps clarify the issues. Philosophers debated regarding the means of support that was appropriate for a philosopher. Should he or she charge fees, enter the households of the rich, beg, or work? Working was the least popular option and the one that Paul chose. (See Hock, *The Social Context of Paul's Mission*, 52–59, for a detailed summary.) In *Application Commentary, New Testament: 1 Corinthians* (Grand Rapids: Zondervan, 1994), 173, Craig Blomberg notes: "They have come to doubt his apostolic authority (vs. 2–3), precisely because he is not charging them for his ministry (cf. 2 Cor 11:7). Itinerant Greco-Roman philosophers and religious teachers supported themselves in one of four ways: charging fees, staying in well-to-do households, begging, or working at a trade. The last of these was least common but generally acknowledged to give the philosopher the greatest freedom to teach however he liked. The powerful patrons in the Corinthian church doubtless would have preferred to have Paul accept their money but give them deference and political support in return. When he refused and continued to rely on tentmaking instead (cf. Acts 18:1–4), they charged that his unwillingness to go along with their patronage demonstrated that he did not have the same authority as other itinerant apostles or preachers."

his apostleship: "This is my defense to those who sit in judgment on me." In the rest of the chapter, Paul explains some of his guiding principles on apostleship and doing business as missions.

First, he argues for the "rights" of an apostle. In a series of cascading questions and multiple metaphors he drives home his point. Soldiers, farmers, shepherds, priests, and even oxen all receive remuneration for their labors. He clinches his argument by appealing to a word from Jesus: "the Lord has commanded that those who preach the Gospel should receive their living from the Gospel" (1 Corinthians 9:14, NIV).[236]

Nevertheless, Paul renounces this God-given right. Several times in this chapter he states emphatically:

If others have this right of support from you, shouldn't we have it all the more? But we did not use this right. On the contrary, we put up with anything rather than hinder the Gospel of Christ (1 Corinthians 9:12, NIV).[237]

What then is my reward? Just this: that in my proclamation I may make the Gospel free of charge, so as not to make full use of my rights in the Gospel (1 Corinthians 9:18–19).

Why did Paul work as a tentmaker and voluntarily relinquish his rights to be supported as an apostle? The historical context in which Paul worked gives us valuable insight. Paul's adamant refusal to accept support almost certainly stands in contrast to the practices of the itinerant philosophers who peddled their wisdom or religious instruction for monetary gain.[238]

---

236   Jesus' teaching on this subject is in the form of a proverb rather than a command ("the worker is worthy of his support," Matthew 10:10; Luke 10:7; see also 1 Timothy 5:18). But Paul clearly understood it as carrying the weight of a command.

237   The pronoun "we" implies that his teammates, Silas and Timothy, most likely worked at a trade as well.

238   See 2 Corinthians 2:17; 1 Thessalonians 2:5–10. See also P.W. Barnett, "Tentmaking," in *Dictionary of Paul and His Letters*, electronic ed., ed. Gerald F. Hawthorne, et al. (Downers Grove, IL: InterVarsity Press, 1993), s.v. According to Barnett, "Greco-Roman culture was accustomed to traveling philosophers (see Philosophy) and teachers who would be paid a fee for their efforts or, alternatively, given hospitality and other benefits by wealthy patrons, sometimes under circumstances that generated scandal (see Stumbling Block). It was not uncommon for itinerant lecturers to enjoy an evil reputation (Philostratus *Vit. Ap.* 1.13; Lucian *Herm.* 59; Dio Chrysostom *Disc.* 8.9). Paul certainly enjoyed the patronage of the wealthy and could easily have sought and received payment (e.g., Acts 17:4, 12; Rom 16:23; 1 Cor 1:14; Acts 19:31) ...[C]onscious that he may have been perceived as just one of many itinerant lecturers, some of whom were none too scrupulous, Paul may have worked to support himself out of concern lest his ministry and the message of the Gospel be associated with other traveling philosophers (cf. 1 Thes 1:5; 2:3–6; 1 Cor 9:12; Acts 20:33–35). Paul contrasts with

This much is clear about Paul's situation in Corinth: he felt that receiving support from those he was ministering to, instead of working to support himself, would adversely impact the work of the Gospel.[239] Thus, Paul did not accept the patronage of the Corinthians so that he could blamelessly proclaim the Gospel. It was an issue of credibility.

For Paul, tentmaking was a non-negotiable part of his apostolic calling.[240] The full-time ministry of the word was not Paul's highest ministry consideration. His greatest concern was to minister the word with integrity and credibility.

HE FELT THAT RECEIVING SUPPORT FROM THOSE HE WAS MINISTERING TO, INSTEAD OF WORKING TO SUPPORT HIMSELF, WOULD ADVERSELY IMPACT THE WORK OF THE GOSPEL. THUS, PAUL DID NOT ACCEPT THE PATRONAGE OF THE CORINTHIANS SO THAT HE COULD BLAMELESSLY PROCLAIM THE GOSPEL. IT WAS AN ISSUE OF CREDIBILITY.

INSIGHTS FROM PAUL'S EXPERIENCE

Paul worked as a tentmaker out of *necessity*. Though he was supported by some churches some of the time, he did not have the luxury of regular gifts from churches. Most of the time, he needed to work to support himself and his team.

Paul worked as a tentmaker for the sake of *credibility*. He was willing to labor for long hours at his trade rather than be accused of impure financial motives. He also worked hard as a tentmaker so that he could preach the Gospel without feeling obligated to a patron, thereby jeopardizing his freedom to teach the truth.

Paul the tentmaker-apostle modeled an *integrated identity*, for at least three reasons: 1) His training as a rabbi helped him embrace seamless ministry.

---

himself the newly arrived opponents in Corinth as 'those who peddle (*kap leuontes*) the word of God' (2 Cor 2:17), '[who] tamper (*dolountes*) with God's word' (2 Cor 4:2) and who 'prey upon' (*katesthiei*, literally 'devour') [you] (2 Cor 11:20). This vocabulary implies the receipt of improper payment, the watering down of the message and the exploitation of the hearers. For his part Paul was true to the message, working rather than accepting payment for his ministry, and caring for his congregations (cf. 1 Thessalonians 2:5–10). See also Fee, *The First Epistle of Corinthians*, 399, 411.

239   According to Blomberg, *Application Commentary, New Testament: 1 Corinthians*, 176–7: "Whenever requesting or even accepting payment could hinder the spread of the Gospel, 'tentmaking' must always take precedence. Bi-vocational ministry has numerous advantages—freedom from human "strings," not imposing a financial burden on any group of believers, and exemption from charges of mismanaging funds or ministering primarily for financial gain."

240   See Siemens, "Tentmakers Needed for World Evangelization," 738; Hock, *The Social Context of Paul's Mission*, 68.

2) For Paul, all of life was devoted to God. Hence, his theology was not confused by a secular–sacred dichotomy. 3) As a tentmaker, Paul was able to share his faith in the context of his work.[241] His job helped him live out an integrated identity as an apostle.

Paul's model of tentmaking is *reproducible.* Churches in most developing countries do not have the financial capacity to follow a Western model of donor-support. Even if they did, tentmaking would remain the model that can be imitated by the greatest number of new workers.

Paul's tentmaking enhanced his *church-planting effectiveness.* Paul's work as a tentmaker enabled him to share the Gospel freely in the context of his work. This is not true about all tentmaking. Some jobs facilitate the forming of communities of Jesus-followers and others do not. For example, when I (Rick) first lived in Indonesia, I taught English to ethnic Chinese young people. However, I was seeking to share about Jesus with Sundanese. If I were starting over today, I would look harder for a working environment that would put me in daily contact with Sundanese.

There are important *similarities* between Paul's tentmaking and ours today. Both Paul and today's workers are "tentmakers" for the sake of the Gospel. Both Paul and today's tentmakers do tentmaking out of necessity: Paul's need was financial; today's workers often need a legitimate visa. Like Paul, we seek credibility in the community and to integrate our faith in everything we do. Finally, both Paul and most tentmakers today also receive some financial support from churches.[242]

There are also significant *differences.* Motivation for modern tentmaking has been initially focused on procuring visas so the Gospel can be communicated in countries that do not issue missionary visas. Paul saw his business ministry and teaching ministry as one. Another major difference between Paul and modern apostles is cultural and linguistic distance. Paul did not have to learn another language. He could minister in Greek. While he faced different cultural contexts, they were more similar to his than most tentmakers face today. Practically, this means that modern tentmakers need to invest more time in one place working and ministering than Paul did. No other factor enhances a worker's ability to minister than language fluency. Research has shown that tentmakers who work

---

241 Hock, "The Workshop as a Social Setting," 450.

242 "You Philippians indeed know that in the early days of the Gospel, when I left Macedonia, no church shared with me in the matter of giving and receiving, except you alone" (Philippians 4:15).

and learn the language simultaneously do not learn the language well. So, during the intensive period of language and culture learning, today's apostles need outside financial support.[243]

DOUBLE VISION OR 20/20 VISION?

A score of 20/20 on an eye exam is considered excellent. In the twenty-first century, effective tentmakers need both viability and integrity in all we do. We need "20/20 vision," not "double vision." Let us illustrate with a true story.

Cary[244] and Ibrahim both manage local language schools. Cary's school specializes in teaching English, Ibrahim's teaches Arabic. Both Cary and Ibrahim have degrees in religious studies. Cary is a fundamental Baptist minister from small town, United States. Ibrahim is a fundamental imam from small town, Thailand. They became roommates, each hoping to win the other to his own faith. But in time, they learned to respect and even love one another. Cary knows all about Ibrahim, but Cary has hidden from Ibrahim several facts about his past and his relationship with his sending church. Though Ibrahim was antagonistic for months, he has started studying the Bible. Cary often visits the mosque when Ibrahim preaches. Recently, Cary's parents visited. Ibrahim went out of his way to show Cary's family a good time. At the end of their visit, Ibrahim expressed interest in visiting America and staying with Cary's family. Cary and his family did not know what to say, as everyone in Cary's hometown knows Cary as a missionary, not as a businessman. Ibrahim specifically requested that he could visit Cary's church. Is there a problem?

EFFECTIVE TENTMAKERS NEED BOTH VIABILITY AND INTEGRITY.

Jesus Christ remains the same (Hebrews 13:8), but the world is changing rapidly. The Internet, satellite communications, and air travel have all shrunk the world considerably. If we want to "turn the world upside down" for Jesus (Acts 17:6, RSV), we cannot continue doing things the same old ways, utilizing the same old strategies based upon the same old assumptions that guided us in the past. A paradigm shift needs to occur within the mission world.

---

243 Patrick Lai, *Tentmaking: Business as Missions* (Waynesboro, GA: Authentic Media, 2005), 29.
244 Although the stories are true, names and locations have been altered.

Examined in light of twentieth-century mission strategies, Paul's approach would be unconventional. If we wish to reach every tribe, language, people, and nation in the twenty-first century, we must break away from the accepted, the taken-for-granted, and the conventional. We need to distinguish human ideas from biblical principles. As both the church and mission agencies come to grips with Paul's holistic approach to ministry, we need to get into the Bible and out of our boxes. We need to prayerfully reevaluate how we send and train missionaries, even rethinking the foundations of how we do missions.

The first church my wife and I (Patrick) planted in Indonesia was on a rural undeveloped island called TK. One day as my wife was traveling to the island, she was stopped by the police and taken to the station for questioning. The local imam happened to stop by the police station while she was being questioned. The authorities were not pleased when my wife explained her purpose for visiting TK was to teach the Bible. The next question the policeman asked her was, "What does your husband do?" When she replied, "He's a businessman," and described our business, the imam interrupted and said, "Well, he's just like me: a businessman who teaches religion!"

To many Muslims, the word "missionary" is the equivalent of the word "terrorist." They see missionaries as outsiders who have entered Muslim communities against the will of the people and sought to change the people's religion, culture, and way of life—in some cases even converting children and kidnapping them to a distant city.

In Islam, many imams (like the apostle Paul) work regular jobs in the community. As a missionary, I would be perceived as a trained terrorist. As a Christian businessman, I am nothing noteworthy (1 Thessalonians 4:11; 1 Peter 5:5–6), simply a contributor to the community who is living and acting according to my beliefs.

Tentmakers who are Christians do not carry the history or stigma of being missionaries. No country on earth has outlawed our greatest witnessing tool (John 13:35)—love. By living and working a life of love, we are recognized as different by those around us. We are no longer perceived as professional Christians, but as foreign Christians who have become part of the local community. In time our love gives us the permission—even the respect—to speak of our faith (Romans 10:14).

Back home, Cary's church may feel their trust has been betrayed if he is anything other than a missionary. After all, the church commissions missionaries—not businessmen—to share the Gospel. How can Cary come to present himself as the same person to his differing audiences? To present himself to the church at home as a business person, he risks the rejection of his church—their financial support, prayers, and pastoral care. To present himself as a missionary to his local friends would bring rejection and possibly the cancellation of his visa. Cary's ability to maintain an integrated identity requires that both he and the church accept who he is and what he does without using the term "missionary." If Cary's life at home is one eye and his life in Southeast Asia is another eye, clearly Cary does not have a healthy 20/20 vision. He needs a corrective lens placed over his "life at home" eye, so that he may be "seen" correctly.

We need to encourage workers to present themselves to both their Muslim friends and church members at home as they are, whether that be as a business-woman, teacher, social worker, or something else. We need to develop a "seam-less identity" within our sending churches. For example, every time someone calls me a "missionary," I remind them that I am a businessman called to the "uttermost parts," and they are called to their "Jerusalem" or "Judea." When they praise me (or others) for being "full-time Christian workers," with a smile on my face I ask whether there are any part-time Christians. Correcting people will be a very slow process, but I know it will bear fruit if we do not lose heart.

PAUL TEACHES US THE VALUE OF BECOMING ALL THINGS TO ALL
PEOPLE THAT WE MIGHT SAVE SOME.

The world has gotten smaller. There is no hiding anything about our past anymore. The problem Cary has with communicating his identity can be seen as a vision problem—it lies in how he perceives himself and how his church and friends at home perceive him. Unless our vocations overseas are viable and real, and unless our churches understand and accept our vocations overseas, there will be distorted vision.

Paul teaches us the value of becoming all things to all people that we might save some (1 Corinthians 9:19–22). Cary needs to ensure he is not faking his job overseas, but working a real job that is making a real contribution, which is adding value to the community. Cary's home church needs to view Cary as a businessman who is serving God overseas, giving him the freedom to present himself in America just as he does in Southeast Asia.

Paul lived a seamless life. He integrated his life, work, play, and worship. He had one calling: to be an apostle. For him, that meant ministering the word and making tents. Everything he did he considered to be ministry. Making tents, being a passenger on a ship, speaking in the synagogue—whatever he did, Paul did for the glory of God (Colossians 3:23). If we are to bear witness to God in all we do, say, and think, then we need to move away from compartmentalizing our lives. We need to correct our "double vision."

A 'COVER'? OR REAL WORK?

In my (Patrick's) surveying of 450 tentmakers,[245] the majority of tentmakers did not initially intend to be in business when they moved overseas, but God and their circumstances either forced or led them into it. However, most of the tentmakers surveyed did not initially place a high value on integrity and viability. More than 20 percent of these overseas workers saw tentmaking as a "cover." They had a work visa but did little or no actual work.

The research showed these overseas workers are less effective in evangelism and church planting than tentmakers who actually perform the work they say they are doing. The way workers are identified and how their identities correlate with what they do has a real impact on their witness for Jesus. On the other hand, it is worth noting that tentmakers do not minister skillfully or fruitfully just because they are doing real work. According to the research, tentmakers need accountability to be fruitful in church planting.

---

[245]   Lai, *Tentmaking: Business as Missions*, 57.

As one who previously had a job which served merely as a "cover,"[246] I (Patrick) can bear witness to the importance of being credible. My friend Abdul knew me to be a businessman. After he believed in Jesus, I began discipling him, spending several hours a week with him. He soon discovered that my business was just a shell company. He discovered that I had neither an office nor employees, and I did very little real work for the company. In time, Abdul lost confidence in me and my two-faced life and stopped meeting with me. The ends do not justify the means (2 Corinthians 11:12). Whether we work in a business, school, or NGO, deceit in any aspect of our life and work will in time rob Jesus of his glory.

The Gospel is foolishness to Muslims (1 Corinthians 1:18, 23). Alone, it rarely draws people to Jesus. That is why we must be "doers of the word and not merely hearers" (James 1:22, NASB). Jesus often healed and fed those who came to him. He often ministered to people's physical needs before speaking of the Kingdom of God. When we work in the marketplace alongside those we are seeking to reach, the people both see and hear our faith, which makes the Gospel understandable and applicable to their daily lives.

---

[246] There are five types of tentmakers. T-1 tentmakers are individuals who are hired by companies in their home countries to do jobs they are uniquely qualified for in foreign countries. The companies pay their salary and often provide numerous benefits to entice these workers to work overseas. T-1 tentmakers are sincere Christians who are active witnesses for the Lord at home as well as abroad. However, T-1s usually are not overseas out of any special calling or desire to minister, but because they have been sent there by their companies. T-2 tentmakers are similar to T-1s in that T-2s also fulfill the commonly agreed upon criteria for tentmakers and are to a large percent (90 percent or more) supported through their job. However, T-2s differ from T-1s in that they do have a calling from the Lord to reach out to a specific people group. T-3 tentmakers differ greatly from T-1s, though they are similar to T-2s. Like T-2s, T-3s meet all the *commonly agreed upon criteria* for being a tentmaker and all or most of the *important but not essential criteria*. However, T-3s are partially and sometimes fully supported by their churches at home. Thus, back home T-3s are considered by at least some people to be missionaries, while overseas T-3s have non-religious identities. T-4 tentmakers are not tentmakers in the sense of working regular nine to five jobs for companies, but they are not regular missionaries either. T-4s are workers like missionary dentists, doctors, or social workers. T-4s have real jobs and do real work, but unlike T-3s who are involved in purely secular positions, T-4s usually work for a charity or non-government organization (NGO) and often among the poor. T-5 tentmakers are really regular missionaries, not tentmakers. However, as the peoples they are ministering to are in countries that do not grant missionary visas, T-5s have created an identity for themselves that is something other than a missionary or a religious professional. T-5s may have a title or position with a business, but by prior agreement they do not actually work for their company. Some T-5s create shell companies to enable them to reside legally in the country. Such companies, whether functioning or not, simply provide cover visas by which T-5s may enter and reside in the country.

IMPLICATIONS FOR THE TWENTY-FIRST CENTURY

Traditional Bible school or theological seminary models are not adequately training seamless disciple-makers with integrated identities, because their focus has been on training people for pastoral work or work among Christians. Sending churches exacerbate a sense of dual identity among tentmakers as they continue to work with old missionary paradigms (and terms) and in practice only understand the role of the classic, fully supported, non-tentmaking missionary. In other words, the identity of the ones sent from the church is missionary, no matter what their vocation may be.

Paul's 2,000-year-old paradigm of tentmaker-apostle offers surprising hope for new paradigms of ministry today. Training and sending workers like Paul—who have integrated identities and combine credible tentmaking with fruitful disciple making—is the challenge of the twenty-first century.[247]

---

[247] Some schools offer programs that equip students in both areas. Biola University presently offer both a TESOL degree and a business degree that includes cross-cultural training. The School of Intercultural Studies at Fuller Theological Seminary offers a joint program in TESOL with Azusa Pacific University and an MBA with Hope University.

Chapter 24

Recapturing the Role of Suffering

NIK RIPKEN

"Unless a kernel of wheat falls into the ground and dies,
it remains a single seed. But if it dies, it brings forth much fruit."
John 12:24

The call of God compels us to articulate and practice a biblical vision of our calling—a vision grounded in the Word of God and informed by the experience of God's people through the ages—a vision that transcends culture and reflects the very heart of God. Our common assumption is that our methodology and practice are sound and solid; we normally take that for granted. But wisdom demands that we listen to the voices of brothers and sisters in Christ whose experience is different from our own. We have much to learn and, in some cases, much to unlearn about what it means to live as God's people in the world.

THE TESTIMONY OF BELIEVERS LIVING IN PERSECUTION

The testimony of believers living in the midst of persecution challenges the church in the West, and its emissaries, to recapture a biblical missiology—a missiology that is mature enough to embrace suffering, persecution, and even martyrdom. Believers in settings of persecution, through numerous interviews, suggest that the church in the West has lost its missiological edge and that it has grown soft in the face of overt persecution. The story told by persecuted believers calls to mind God's people of old. The priests of the Old Testament could rightly interpret the Ten Commandments and parse the grammatical nuances of the law code. But the work of the priests was much broader and richer than merely that. These ancient carriers of God's Word could also place these commandments upon their shoulders and carry them into battle, through swollen rivers, across deserts, and over mountains. These messengers of God were courageous carriers of the Word, calloused of feet and hand, seasoned mentally and spiritually. These priests knew the Word, and they lived the Word. And they rightly understood that a life lived in the presence of God would be framed by suffering and persecution. In fact, for these ancient heroes of the faith, that is what it meant to share in the Kingdom of God.

THE CALL OF GOD COMPELS US TO ARTICULATE AND PRACTICE A
BIBLICAL VISION OF OUR CALLING.

Can the same be said of us? We are the modern carriers of this same Word. Do we understand the central place of suffering and persecution in the faith we claim? Or, in light of the freedom that has shaped us, have we written those troubling truths out of the story? Are suffering and persecution essential parts of the story—or are they relics from another time and place? Modern Western believers may revolt at the thought—but unless we find our identity as God's people in the midst of suffering and persecution, we will sadly discover that we have no identity.

In the former Soviet Union, believers understood that their heritage was one of suffering and persecution. To this day, believers growing out of that heritage claim that persecution is "normal," that it is as normal as the "sun coming up in the east." For decades, believers in the former U.S.S.R. and in neighboring China have lived victoriously in the midst of persecution. They have done this by incarnating a genealogy of faith that models from one generation to the next how a follower of Christ lives and how a follower of Christ dies. When these believers are asked, "Where did you learn to live like this? Where did you learn to die like this?" they answer, "I learned this from my mother and my father. I learned this from my grandfather and grandmother." Though enduring and excelling in the midst of persecution is never easy, these modern-day giants of the faith teach us through their flesh and souls that following Jesus involves a cross as well as a crown.

This is a seminal issue for first-generation believers who are emerging into faith from within Islam. Who is able to teach these new MBBs how to live in Christ? Who will teach these new MBBs how to die in Christ? These are especially critical questions in light of the fact that it is often their biological parents and grandparents who lead in their persecution. It is often immediate family members who beat the new MBBs, place them under house arrest, disinherit them, and then arrange marriages for their believing daughters to Muslim men thirty years their senior. It is often immediate family members who turn the new believers over to the religious authorities. Who will teach these new believers how to live in Christ—and, perhaps, even to die in him?

This will never happen without a genealogy of faith. But a genealogy of faith will likely not be found in the immediate family. If it is to be found at all, *it will originate from the very people who have shared with these new believers the Gospel story.* This precious responsibility falls on the shoulders of witnesses from outside the culture. They will be the ones to model for MBBs a genealogy of faith. This genealogy of faith will include at least two elements. First, the witnesses will model a genealogy of faith that is grounded in the story of God's people through the ages. They will build for these new believers, in literate and oral forms, a biblical genealogy of faith that spans no less than the sixty-six books of the Bible, Genesis to Revelation. Second, they will incarnate a living example of a genealogy of faith—one that both asks and answers this crucial question: "Do you want to know how to live and die in Christ? Then watch our lives as we live them out in your midst." Such was the admonition of the apostle Paul to believers in the early church. And God's people on mission, even today, will find the courage to say the very same thing.

Of course, making such a claim is both difficult and humbling. Entering into suffering is unspeakably painful. But even more terrifying is watching "our Joseph" begin to experience his or her own persecution. That's where most of us want to draw the line. How exactly do we react today when "our Joseph" is thrown into Pharaoh's prison unjustly? What do we do when our beloved "Joseph" begins to suffer for the faith? E-mails fly as we demand the immediate release of "our Joseph" who has been wrongly accused and imprisoned. We petition governments to intercede, and we bring political and military might to bear on the situation. We threaten the persecutors. We call the church to pray that the persecution might end. Many Western-based and well-meaning organizations have developed a protocol for responding to events of persecution, often adopting a four-fold agenda that aims to:

1. Stop the persecution;

2. Punish the persecutors;

3. Promote Western forms of government and democracy; and

4. Raise funds that will aid in the rescuing of believers from persecution.

Much to our amazement, a truly biblical vision would likely respond in a different way. How might we develop a spiritual, emotional, and physical toughness that, when Pharaoh throws "our Joseph" into prison unjustly, *we allow him or her to stay in jail?* Where does such strength and spiritual insight come? And, then, do we dare consider this thought: to rescue Joseph prematurely from prison, before he has the opportunity to interpret Pharaoh's dream, would lead to the starvation and destruction of both Egypt and Israel, the destruction of both persecutor and persecuted. How do we know when it is within God's will for Joseph to remain in jail for a season? For most of us, the answer is easy. We can allow that *as long as it is someone else's Joseph.* But when it is "our Joseph" undergoing persecution, there erupts an overwhelming desire to rescue this dear brother or sister from the prisons and crosses that necessarily accompany faith in the Messiah.

RESCUING BROTHERS AND SISTERS FROM PERSECUTION AND PLANTING CHURCHES MAY NOT BE COMPATIBLE.

Believers living in the midst of persecution call us to intervention and prayer. They call Western Christians who are not themselves in the midst of overt suffering to pray—to pray not that persecution for other believers might end, but that the persecuted would be obedient in the midst of their suffering. Obedient to what? Obedient to endure and to share, especially with their persecutors, the forgiveness and love that are found through the resurrection of Jesus Christ. Such a missiology does not quantify persecution as either good or bad. Persecution just "is." Whether persecution is a curse or a blessing depends ultimately on how believers respond to their suffering. If believers run in fear from persecution, then the faith community has a serious problem to confront. Conversely, if a believer enjoys persecution and seeks it out, then the faith community is dealing with someone with serious psychological sickness.

A biblical vision reminds us that believers should not fear the persecution that is inherent in following Christ, engaging in compulsive fleeing. But, at the same time, believers should not seek out persecution when God has determined that believers are allowed to live in a season of grace.

We can learn much from the response of MBBs to this telling question: "What do you learn from Western witnesses?" The initial answers are affirming and kind. MBBs express gratitude for the Gospel that witnesses have sacrificially carried to them. They marvel at the selflessness of witnesses as they meet human needs at great cost, both financially and personally. MBBs are typically in awe that Western missionary families have given up living in the rich West for the sake of the poor and lost among the nations. MBBs have many kind things to say about Western workers. But, eventually, other answers are offered. When confidences are won, and candidness appears, MBBs often share insights that are more difficult to hear and accept. "What do we learn from missionaries?" They often repeat back to us, *"Missionaries teach us to be afraid."*

MODELING FEAR IN THE FACE OF SUFFERING IS A
MISSIOLOGICAL ERROR. SADLY, IT IS MORE THAN THAT.
IT IS, QUITE SIMPLY, SIN.

What are Western missionaries afraid of? According to these gracious MBBs, they fear that their platform might be compromised, that they might be kicked out of a country, that they might lose their work permit or visa. They fear that their children might have to move with them to another country, that they might be uprooted from their schools and friends. They dread the thought of having to learn another language. Most of all, they fear that the fruit of their ministry will be targeted; that new believers might be persecuted, fired from their jobs, divorced from their families, and beaten. They fear most that "our Joseph" will go to jail or, worse, be martyred because of the faith that has been born because of their witness. Satan plays on this fear as they are accused by the secular media or even other mission partners of "getting this person harmed or killed." This fear tends to make them timid in their witness. When faith does break out, often they will extract "their believer" to another country of perceived safety, preferably in the West. Therefore, church planting is compromised. In fact, if this pattern is followed, the planting of a church will likely never happen.

Apparently, as far as we know, Jesus never extracted one follower to another country. He never guaranteed his followers personal safety—and consistently called for a clear witness to family, culture, and country—even when such a witness was certain to carry a high price. Jesus warned his followers that persecution was simply a part of following him. He told his followers to prepare for its coming. Jesus said in Matthew 10:23, "When you are persecuted in one place, flee to another. I tell you the truth, you will not finish going through the cities of Israel before the Son of Man comes" (NIV).

Believers living in settings of persecution offer another insightful piece of counsel. Missionaries most often, they point out, face persecution as a result of discipling, baptizing, and gathering MBBs together within the missionaries' living environment. The regular meeting of MBBs in their homes, or singling out MBBs and worshipping with them in their location, frequently leads to persecution. And, tragically, this is persecution for reasons other than for who Jesus is. Persecution that results from a personal relationship with a Western missionary—or persecution that grows out of employment, education, or worship—is different from persecution for who Jesus is. MBBs suggest, creatively, that missionaries were called by God to expend their lives among those who remain in lostness. MBBs suggest, conversely, that most missionaries get into trouble, not because they are leading lost people to Jesus, but because they are spending the bulk of their time among *those already added to the Kingdom of God.*

MBBs ask us to be a model for them. They want us to model how to witness to the landlord, the neighboring family, the corrupt policeman, and the suspicious immigration officer. They desire to watch our marriages and child rearing to see how families can reach families. They long to see us witnessing in culturally appropriate ways to the people we encounter through everyday living.

This is not to be seen as a blanket indictment of the Western worker. We have been persecuted, forcibly expelled from the people we love, refused visas, jailed, and martyred. Yet the words of our brothers and sisters who live in persecution carry the weight of truth. Often persecution is visited upon the MBB because of the Christian agency employing him. The very lives of MBBs are jeopardized by sharing in worship with foreigners, or accepting Bibles and other discipleship materials too bulky to hide. In many venues, some who are persecuted for possessing Christian literature cannot even read what they have been handed. Baptism for MBBs is a real testament of faith. Often persecution soars for the MBB at the time of his or her baptism. Yet the risk intensifies when the baptism is at the hands of foreigners or witnessed by outsiders. The accusation that Christianity is a foreign religion, just for Westerners, is heightened even more when a Western face leads in the pastoral duties among those already reborn into the Kingdom of God.

MBBs ASK US TO CONSIDER TAKING MOST OF OUR RISKS AMONG THOSE WHO ARE STILL LOST RATHER THAN TAKING MOST OF OUR RISKS AMONG THOSE ALREADY SAVED.

Believers living in persecution point to another telling observation in regard to the ministry of Jesus. Consider the environment in which Jesus fermented the coming Pentecost of Acts 2. His country was occupied by a foreign army and controlled by a severe dictatorship. Such was the brutality of the day that Herod slaughtered hundreds of innocent babies in response to the birth of the King of the Jews. The religious rulers of Jesus' day preferred to partner with the occupiers rather than lose their power, prestige, and authority to this new movement. Early in his ministry, these religious leaders sought to kill Jesus. He lived and ministered in an environment where the potential for persecution was endemic.

Yet for the entire three years of Jesus' ministry, and in spite of his overt challenges to the powers of his day, how many of his followers were beaten, tortured, imprisoned, and killed? Not a single one! Jesus was culturally astute and bold in his witness. Framing the Gospel by both words and deeds, he created a safe place for seekers and new followers to hear, understand, and believe within their social units. Prior to Pentecost, severe persecution was not visited upon those seeking and following Jesus. After Pentecost, believers were in the thousands and better equipped both to endure and excel through their sufferings for Christ.

Learning from the Persecutors

What is the goal of the persecutors? Perhaps a better way to ask this question is to ask, "What is the goal of Satan?" Many suggest that the goal of Satan is to have us kicked out of our homes, to take away our jobs, and to destroy our marriages. Evil itself, we are led to believe, prefers to beat, torture, imprison, and even kill followers of Jesus. Thus the reports that stir our hearts, move us emotionally, empty our pocketbooks, and motivate us into a rescuing mode highlight the loss of liberty, the bruising of the body, and the taking of life.

But if persecution, suffering, and martyrdom are defined in this way, then countries such as Saudi Arabia and Somalia would not even be included in a list of the world's top persecutors. Why not? By most accepted definitions, a country has to have a significant number of believers in order to persecute them. Saudi Arabia is so closed that it refuses to allow the Gospel a hearing at all. Therefore, the number of true believers to persecute is miniscule. For the same reason, Somalia has been removed from most of the lists denoting the top countries that persecute believers in Jesus. This is due to the simple fact that radicals in that country have either forced most MBBs out of their land or they have killed them. Has persecution ceased in Somalia because there are no Christians left to persecute? If persecution is to be measured only in terms of overt acts, what does one call countries, cultures, and people groups that are so resistant that they allow no hearing of the Gospel, no understanding, no accepting, and no gathering together?

But persecution does not always take that form. Believers living in the midst of persecution suggest strongly that the goal of Satan is not to beat, torture, or kill believers. The goal of Satan and his persecutors, suffering believers remind us, is to silence believers, to make believers lose (or give up) their voice, and to diminish witness. Also, the persecutors strive to silence witness as covertly as possible. The most successful persecution happens when an immediate family member, a boss, a spouse, or the culture in general, pressures the follower of Christ into remaining quiet, keeping faith "personal." The persecutors want to relegate faith to the environs of the Western world. Or they desire that faith be practiced only within the walls of a few church buildings that are closely monitored by the state or the local religious authorities.

PERSECUTION, AT ITS EVIL HEART AND ESSENCE, DENIES OTHERS
ACCESS TO JESUS.

Believers living in the midst of persecution suggest that, when they are rejected by their families, thrown into prison, beaten, and killed for their faith, then that is precisely the time for the global Church to rejoice and give God praise. Why would they make such an insane suggestion? It is these overt acts of persecution that reveal the persecutors' abject failure to silence witness, diminish faith, or slow Pentecost from arriving once more in the midst of a resistant culture. Overt persecution is a sign of the failure of the persecutors. Failure to keep believers quiet leads to overt persecution—so overt persecution is an indication that believers have refused to be quiet! Overt persecution authenticates the faith within resistant cultures. Overt persecution gives faith value in the eyes of those who watch believers and marvel at their willingness to suffer and die in Jesus' name.

What that means is that a radically different understanding of persecution, suffering, and martyrdom must be considered. In this light, countries such as Saudi Arabia and Somalia can be listed at the very pinnacle of those who persecute the faith and the faithful because, at their core, they seek to deny people access to the eternal life that is found only in Jesus. The implication for the Western church and her cross-cultural witnesses is huge. Every day, every follower of Jesus decides whether to side with the persecutors or the persecuted. Believers side with the persecutors when they withhold their witness—and they side with the persecuted when they are open in sharing their faith.

If persecution is defined by beatings, imprisonments, and martyrs alone, then the Western church is correct to pray "for" the persecuted. Persecution is about "those poor people and the terrible things happening to them." But if persecution is defined in terms of denying others access to Jesus, then perhaps praying "with" the persecuted will have a more intimate feel as we side with persecuted brothers and sisters by choosing to give our witness boldly.

WHAT, THEN, ARE WE TO DO?

What might a truly biblical missiology look like? What might we choose to learn—and unlearn—in light of this worldwide witness? And how might we live in response?

We begin with this startling word: the number one cause of persecution is people giving their lives to Jesus. We can reduce persecution, most easily, by reducing the number of those who come to salvation! Most Christians in the West have been taught to pray for persecution to end, to pray that suffering would cease, and to pray that martyrs would be only an historical reference. The only possible way for those things to happen is to stop people from accepting Jesus. The major cause of persecution is people giving their lives to Christ and, then, refusing to deny others access to the very same Savior. Salvation and witness inevitably result in persecution for Christian believers.

SALVATION AND WITNESS INEVITABLY RESULT IN PERSECUTION
FOR CHRISTIAN BELIEVERS.

Persecution, quite simply, is normal for Christians. Both the witness of Scripture and the testimony of history bear this out. How, then, are Western missionaries to react? Consider these simple words of counsel:

» Accept the hard truth that persecution is normal and prepare yourself and others for that reality.
» Become culturally astute. Strive to create a safe place and space of time for lost people to hear, understand, believe, and experience Pentecost before being visited by severe persecution.
» Lose your fear and claim your freedom to be a culturally wise and bold witness to the resurrection of Jesus Christ. Losing fear and claiming freedom have little to do with political environment. Followers of Christ are as free to share their faith in Afghanistan as they are in the United States or Europe. The issue is not whether we are free to share; the issue is whether we are willing to suffer the consequences of expressing our faith. We are all free—but not all of us are willing to bear the consequences of a free and bold witness.

» Be tough—emotionally, spiritually, and physically—for you will be the cause of an increasing amount of persecution as thousands of lost people hear and believe your witness. Persecution and response to the Gospel are the two sides of the same coin. Understand that bold witness will necessarily result in persecution—not because you are unwise in your practices, but simply because Satan detests faith and desires that no one become a child of God.

» Do not run from persecution—and do not seek it.

» Decide not to extract a believer. Decide not to rescue others from sharing in the sufferings of Christ.

» And never regret that others joyously received your witness, even if the cost of their faith carries the high cost of persecution. Remember that the resurrection came through crucifixion.

» Never lessen the price paid by believers in persecution. No matter how the persecution event is publicized, no matter what victory might be won, no matter the glorious finale—persecution is not fun, and it is not to be sought. It is blood, sweat, and tears. It is physical and psychological abuse. It is isolation and years of separation. It is growing up as a child with a father in prison. It is raising children without a mate, ostracized from the community. Never slight the price paid by believers in persecution and never become casual about the cost. Honor the suffering of brothers and sisters in Christ by telling the truth about the price they have paid.

» Determine to live out your genealogy of faith, modeling for first-generation, emerging believers, how a follower of Christ lives and dies. Have the courage to say, "Watch my life as it is lived out in your midst." And then live a life that is worthy of being copied.

» Through it all, become a risk taker among lost people so that they—every tongue and every tribe—might have opportunity to hear, understand, believe, and be gathered in the Body of Christ.

Never forget that Jesus is worth it.

Conclusion: Gathering around the Lord of the Harvest

"Pray ...the Lord of the harvest to send out laborers into the harvest."
Matthew 9:38, RSV

"There was a great multitude that no one could count,
from every nation, from all tribes and peoples and languages,
standing before the throne and before the Lamb ...with palm branches in
their hands. They cried out ...saying, 'Salvation belongs to our
God who is seated on the throne, and to the Lamb!'"
Revelation 7:9–10

The prayer, planning, and activities of which this book is a part were inspired by the vision of the Apostle John, described in the Foreword, of heavenly beings singing to the Lamb of God:

You were slain, and with your blood you purchased for God members of
every tribe and language and people and nation (Revelation 5:9, NIV).

That vision has led to our vision to see effective efforts to plant fellowships of followers of Jesus among all Muslim peoples by the grace of God.

Place in the Train of History

As has been noted in the Introduction, a century ago a General Conference for work among Muslims was held in Cairo in 1906, chaired by Samuel Zwemer. This was followed by the World Missionary Conference in Edinburgh in 1910, which gave a prominent place to the Muslim world, and the Lucknow Conference of 1911 devoted entirely to the work with Muslims. The Lausanne Congress of 1974 turned the Church's attention to unreached people groups. Then the Glen Eyrie Conference of 1978, recorded in *The Gospel and Islam*, applied the unreached people emphasis to Muslim peoples and suggested practices that might be fruitful. These emphases have been carried on by the Muslim track of the Lausanne Committee in subsequent consultations.

The research leading into and the analysis proceeding from the Consultation in Southeast Asia in the spring of 2007 is summarized in this book and its accompanying CD. As this consultation in some ways mirrors those of Cairo (1906) and Glen Eyrie (1978), there will need to be means to evaluate the progress toward the fulfilling of our vision, just as the Lucknow Conference in 1911 provided a century ago.

The Immediate Task

Between the book and the accompanying CD, the Global Trends track has provided up-to-date listings of Muslim people groups, their degree of engagement with Christian witness, and potential means of effective engagement. As indicated in chapter six, we should:

- » Continue to update our people groups lists, the extent to which they are engaged with Christian witness, and the resources for engaging those that are not;
- » Focus resources on regions like Sudan and India with their many unengaged peoples;
- » Increase efforts to mobilize and deploy resident disciple-makers;
- » Implement innovative means without abandoning proven principles, utilizing, for example, the Internet and other technologies;
- » Develop means of ongoing evaluation of practices and engagement;

» Carefully evaluate the types of individuals and teams that are required in each context; and
» Look for like-minded partners on every continent, and people from the North need to take a genuine supportive role in initiatives from the Global South.

With respect to the sharing of the Gospel:

» In contextualization, be sensitive to Muslim views while listening to the opinions of Muslim background believers;
» Challenge syncretism by discussing syncretistic elements as they arise; and
» Understand that conversion and growth in Christ are normally incremental as part of a process.

With respect to the Fruitful Practices track, far more data were collected in the Consultation surveys, small group discussions, case studies, interviews, and testimonies than have been able to be analyzed in the time since those meetings. This has led us not to share even some of the preliminary tentative conclusions for fear that they will not stand up to further scrutiny. The CD accompanying this volume, however, draws some further and more precise conclusions than were available for this written text.

The Knowledge Stewardship Team will meet in the fall of 2008 to seek to draw some more definitive conclusions that can be shared by an updated CD or other means. In particular, there is need to evaluate how results are affected by such variable factors as time, place, and social circumstances.

When my family and I went to Kabul, Afghanistan, to pastor a church in the 1970s, my brother gave us a picture of an Afghan farmer with the words, "In due season we shall reap if we faint not" (Galatians 6:9). As we look from the 'first fruits' to the full 'harvest,' this is certainly far more important than any analysis of people groups and fruitful practices, for as our Pauls may plant and our Apolloses may water, we are reminded that it is God, the Lord of the Harvest, that gives the growth (1 Corinthians 3:6). Our task is to be faithful and not faint.

THE FRUIT OF THE VINE

Our Lord at the Last Supper said that he would not eat of the fruit of the vine again until the Kingdom of God comes. Then he took the bread and broke it and said, "This is my body." He took the cup and said, "This ...is the new covenant in my blood" (Luke 22:16–20).

In both Glen Eyrie and Southeast Asia, when we broke the bread and drank the fruit of the vine, we looked ahead, as we do now, to the fulfillment of the original vision—a time when we shall sing with our Muslim friends who have followed the Lamb that was slain, "By your blood you purchased for God members of every tribe and language and people and nation" (Revelation 5:9, NIV).

Bibliography

Accad, Fouad Elias. *Building Bridges.* Colorado Springs: Navpress, 1997.

Al-Jawziyya, Ibn Qayyim. *Natural Healing with the Medicine of the Prophet.* Translated by Muhammad Al-Akili. Philadelphia, PA: Pearl Publishing House, 1993.

Al-Ashqar, Umar Sulaiman. *The World of the Jinn and Devils.* Translated by Jamaal al-Din M. Zarabozo. Boulder, CO: Al-Basheer Company, 1998.

Arnold, Clinton. *3 Crucial Questions Regarding Spiritual Warfare.* Grand Rapids, MI: Baker Books, 1997.

Anderson, John D.C. "The Missionary Approach to Islam: Christian or 'Cultic'?" *Missiology: An International Review* 4, no. 3 (1976): 258–99.

Azumah, John. *The Legacy of Arab-Islam in Africa.* Oxford: Oneworld, 2001.

Bailey, Kenneth E. *Poet and Peasant and Through Peasant Eyes: A Literary-Cultural Approach to the Parables in Luke.* Grand Rapids: William B. Eerdmans Publishing Company, 1983.

-----. *Jesus Through Middle Eastern Eyes: Cultural Studies in the Gospels.* Downers Grove: IVP Academic/InterVarsity Press, 2008.

Baker, Raymond William. *Islam Without Fear: Egypt and the New Islamists.* Cambridge, MA: Harvard University Press, 2003.

Barnett, P.W. "Tentmaking." In *Dictionary of Paul and His Letters*, electronic ed., edited by Gerald F. Hawthorne, Ralph P. Martin, and Daniel G. Reid. Downers Grove, IL: InterVarsity Press, 1993.

Barrett, David B., Todd M. Johnson, and Peter F. Crossing. "Missiometrics 2007: Creating Your Own Analysis of Global Data." *International Bulletin of Missionary Research* 31, no. 1 (January 2007): 25–32.

Barrett, David, George T. Kurian, and Todd M. Johnson. *World Christian Encyclopedia.* 2nd ed. New York: Oxford University Press, 2001.

Blincoe, Bob. "Honor and Shame: An Open Letter to Evangelical Leaders" *Mission Frontiers* 4 (2001).

Blomberg, Craig. *Application Commentary, New Testament: 1 Corinthians.* Grand Rapids: Zondervan, 1994.

Bongoyok, Moussa. "The Rise of Islamism among the Sedentary Fulbe of Northern Cameroon: Implications for Theological Responses." PhD diss., Fuller Theological Seminary, School of Intercultural Studies, 2006.

Bosch, David. *Transforming Mission.* Maryknoll, NY: Orbis Books, 1991.

Broomhall, B. *The Evangelisation of the World: a Missionary Band, a Record of Consecration, and an Appeal.* London: Morgan & Scott, 1889.

Brown, Rick. "Brother Jacob and Master Isaac: How One Insider Movement Began." *International Journal of Frontier Missions* 23, no. 3 (2007): 41–42.

-----. "Explaining the Biblical Term 'Son(s) of God' in Muslim Contexts." *International Journal of Frontier Missions* 22, no. 3 (2005): 91–96.

-----. "Selecting and Using Scripture Portions Effectively in Frontier Missions." *International Journal of Frontier Missions* 18, no. 4 (2002): 10–25.

-----. "Translating the Biblical Term 'Son(s) of God' in Muslim Contexts." *International Journal of Frontier Missions* 22, no. 4 (2005): 135–45.

Brown, Rick, and Christopher Samuel. "The meanings of κυριος 'Lord' in the New Testament." Unpublished paper, 2002.

Bruce, F.F. *Commentary on the Book of the Acts.* Grand Rapids: William B. Eerdmans Publishing Company, 1975.

Cate, Patrick O. "Gospel Communication From Within." *International Journal of Frontier Missions* 11, no. 2 (April 1994).

Cherif, Mustapha. "Ce que j'ai di au pape ...." *Le Nouvel Observateur*, no. 2195, November 30, 2006.

Claydon, David, ed. *The Impact on Global Mission of Religious Nationalism and 9/11 Realities.* Lausanne Occasional Paper, No. 50. Pattaya, Thailand: Lausanne Committee for World Evangelization, 2004.

Conn, Harvey M. "The Muslim Convert and his Culture." In *The Gospel and Islam: A Compendium,* edited by Don McCurry, abr. ed., 79–113. Monrovia, CA: MARC, 1979.

Corwin, Gary. "A Humble Appeal to C5/Insider Movement Muslim Ministry Advocates to Consider Ten Questions." *International Journal of Frontier Missiology* 24, no. 1 (2007): 5–20.

Cumming, Joseph. "Did Jesus Die on the Cross? Reflections in Muslim Commentaries." In *Muslim and Christian Reflections on Peace: Divine and Human Dimensions,* edited by J. Dudley Woodberry, Osman Zumrut, and Mustafa Koyles, 32–50. Lanham, MD: University Press of America, 2005.

de Heusch, Luc. *Why Marry Her? Society and Symbolic Structures.* Translated by Janet Lloyd. Cambridge, UK: Cambridge University Press, 1981.

Eddy, W.K. "Islam in Syria and Palestine." In *The Mohammedan World of To-day: Being Papers Read at the First Missionary Conference on Behalf of the Mohammedan World Held at Cairo April 4th–9th, 1906.* New York: Fleming H. Revell, 1906.

Eonè, M. Tadjé. *Et si le terrorism manipulait les media? [What if terrorism was manipulating the media?].* Chennevières-sur-Marne, France: Editions Dianoïa, 2005.

Everts, J.M. "Financial Support." In *Dictionary of Paul and his Letters,* electronic ed., edited by Gerald F. Hawthorne, Ralph P. Martin, and Daniel G. Reid. Downers Grove, IL: InterVarsity Press, 1993.

Fabian, Dapila N. "The Muslim Bible Translator in the Context of Today's African Christianity—A Dilemma for Missions." http://academic.sun.ac.za/as/cbta/Bible%20in%20 Africa_Sept2005/Table%20of%20conts%20The%20Bible%20in%20Africa_Papers.htm (accessed August 28, 2007).

Fee, Gordon D. *The First Epistle of Corinthians*. Grand Rapids: William B. Eerdmans Publishing Company, 1987.

Fourest, Carolyn, and Fiammeta Venner. *Tirs croisés*. Paris: Calmann-Levy, 2003.

Frizzell, Tabitha. "Christ Draws Young Muslims, in Spite of the Dangers." *IMB News Stories*, August 21, 2002.

Garrison, David. *Church Planting Movements—How God Is Redeeming a Lost World*. Bangalore, India: WIGTake Resources, 2004.

Gaudeul, Jean-Marie. *Called from Islam to Christ*. East Sussex, UK: Monarch Books, 1999.

-----. "Learning From God's Ways." In *From the Straight Path to the Narrow Way*, edited by David Greenlee, 81–92. Waynesboro, GA: Authentic, 2006.

Geertz, Clifford. *Islam Observed: Religious Development in Morocco and Indonesia*. Chicago: University of Chicago Press, 1971.

Glassé, Cyril. *The Concise Encyclopedia of Islam*. New York: HarperCollins Publishers, 1989.

Global Research Department, International Mission Board. "Complete List of People Groups Excel Spreadsheet.xls." http://www.peoplegroups.org/Downloads.aspx (accessed January 15, 2008).

Goldingay, John. *How to Read the Bible*. London: Triangle, 1997.

-----. *Models for Interpretation of Scripture*. Grand Rapids, MI: William B. Eerdmans Publishing Company, 1995.

Goldsmith, Martin. "Community and Controversy: Key Causes of Muslim Resistance." *Missiology: An International Review* 4, no. 3 (1976): 317–23.

Greenlee, David, ed. *From the Straight Path to the Narrow Way: Journeys of Faith*. Waynesboro, GA: Authentic, 2006.

Greenlee, David. "How Is the Gospel Good News for Muslims?" In *Rethinking Our Assumptions: Toward a New Christian Understanding of Muslims in the 21st Century*, edited by Evelyne Reisacher, Joseph Cumming, Dean S. Gilliland, and Charles Van Engen. Pasadena, CA: William Carey Library, forthcoming.

Greeson, Kevin. *The Camel: How Muslims Are Coming to Faith in Christ!* Arkadelphia, AR: WIGTake Resources, 2007.

Haney, Jim. "Abdul's Testimony." From an interview during a church-planting movement assessment, Asia, 2002.

Hess, J. Daniel. *The Whole World Guide to Language Learning*. Yarmouth, Maine: Intercultural Press, 1994.

Hiebert, Paul. *Anthropological Reflections on Missiological Issues*. Grand Rapids, MI: Baker Book House, 1994.

Hiebert, Paul, Daniel Shaw, and Tite Tiénou. *Understanding Folk Religion*. Grand Rapids, MI: Baker Books, 1999.

Higgins, Kevin. "Acts 15 and Insider Movements among Muslims: Questions, Process and Conclusions." *International Journal of Frontier Missiology* 24, no. 1 (2007): 29–40.

Hill, Harriet. *The Bible at Cultural Crossroads: From Translation to Communication.* Manchester: St. Jerome Publishing, 2006.

Hirsch, Alan. *The Forgotten Ways: Reactivating the Missional Church.* Grand Rapids: Brazos Press, 2006.

Hock, Ronald F. "Paul's Tentmaking and the Problem of His Social Class." *Journal of Biblical Literature 97* (1978): 555–64.

-----. *The Social Context of Paul's Mission.* Philadelphia: Fortress, 1980.

-----. "The Workshop as a Social Setting for Paul's Missionary Preaching." *The Catholic Biblical Quarterly* 41 (1979): 438–50.

Hubbard, David A. *Thessalonians: Life That's Radically Christian.* Dallas, TX: Word Books, 1977.

Huntington, Samuel P. *The Clash of Civilizations and the Remaking of World Order.* New York: Simon & Schuster, 1996.

Internet World Stats. "Internet Usage in the Middle East." http://www.internetworldstats.com/stats5.htm (accessed March 14, 2007).

James, Tim. "Working with Colleagues from Other Faith Traditions." *International Journal of Frontier Missions* 23, no. 2 (2006): 61–66.

Jenkins, Philip. *The New Faces of Christianity: Believing the Bible in the Global South.* Oxford: Oxford University Press, 2006.

-----. *The Next Christendom: The Coming of Global Christianity.* Oxford: Oxford University Press, 2002.

Jeremias, J. *Jerusalem in the Time of Jesus.* Philadelphia: Fortress, 1969.

Johnstone, Patrick. "Affinity Blocs and People Clusters: An Approach Toward Strategic Insight and Mission Partnership." *Mission Frontiers*, March–April 2007. http://www.missionfrontiers.org/archive.htm (accessed February 4, 2008).

Joshua Project. "All Peoples-by-Country (single file)," http://www.joshuaproject.net/download.php (February 13, 2008).

Kaiser, Walter C., Jr. *Preaching and Teaching from the Old Testament: A Guide for the Church.* Grand Rapids, MI: Baker Academic, 2003.

Kateregga, Badru D., and David W. Shenk. *A Muslim and Christian in Dialogue.* Scottsdale, PA: Herald Press, 1997.

Kathir, Ibn. *Tafsir Ibn Kathir.* Abr. ed. Translated by Safi al-Rahman Mubarakfuri. Vol. 1. Riyadh, Saudi Arabia: Darussalam, 2000.

Keener, Craig S. *The IVP Bible Background Commentary: New Testament.* Downers Grove, IL: InterVarsity Press, 1994.

Kim, Caleb. *Islam among the Swahili in East Africa.* Nairobi, Kenya: Acton Publishers, 2004.

Kistemaker, Simon J. New *Testament Commentary.* Grand Rapids: Baker Books, 1993.

Knowledge Stewardship Team. "Where Most Fellowships Are Planted." Presentation to Allegro Executive Planning Team, 2007.

Kraft, Charles. *Anthropology for Christian Witness.* Maryknoll, NY: Orbis Books, 1996.

-----. "Contextualization in Three Crucial Dimensions." In *Appropriate Christianity*, edited by Charles Kraft, 99–116. Pasadena, CA: William Carey Library, 2005.

-----. *Defeating Dark Angels: Breaking Demonic Oppression in a Believer's Life.* Ann Arbor, MI: Servant Publications, 1992.

-----. "Dynamic Equivalence Churches in Muslim Society." In *The Gospel and Islam: A Compendium,* edited by Don McCurry, abr. ed., 114–28. Monrovia, CA: MARC, 1979.

-----. "What Encounters Do We Need in Christian Witness." *Evangelical Missions Quarterly* 27 (1991): 258–65.

Kurtzman, Charles. *Liberal Islam: A Sourcebook.* New York: Oxford University Press, 1998.

Lai, Patrick. *Tentmaking: Business as Missions.* Waynesboro, GA: Authentic Media, 2005.

Larson, Warren Fredrick. *Islamic Ideology and Fundamentalism in Pakistan: Climate for Conversion to Christianity?* Lanham, MD: University Press of America, 1998.

-----. "Islamic Fundamentalism in Pakistan: Its Implications for Conversion to Christianity" Ph.D. diss. Fuller Theological Seminary, School of Intercultural Studies, 1996.

------. "Then and Now: New Challenges and New Breakthroughs." in *Understanding Muslims: Journal of the Zwemer Center for Muslim Studies.* Columbia International University posted on March 16, 2007. http://www.ciu.edu/muslimstudies/journal/modules/smart-section/item.php?itemid=3.

Lausanne Movement. The, http://www.lausanne.org/lausanne-1974/lausanne-1974.html (accessed February 13, 2008).

Lepsius, J.A. et al. *Methods of Mission Work among Moslems.* New York: Fleming H. Revell Co., 1906.

Lewis, Tim, and Bob Goldmann. "Saul's Armor and David's Sling: Innovative Sending in the Global South." *Mission Frontiers* 29, no. 3 (May–June 2007): 20.

Lewis, Rebecca. "Strategizing for Church Planting Movements in the Muslim world." *International Journal of Frontier Missions* 21, no. 2 (Summer 2004): 73–77.

Liverman, Jeff. "What Does It Mean to Effectively 'Engage' a People?" *Mission Frontiers,* November–December 2006. http://www.missionfrontiers.org/archive.htm (accessed January 21, 2008).

Lovejoy, Grant, Steve Evans, Annette Hall, David Payne, Sheila Ponraj, Mark Snowden, and Avery Willis, eds. *Making Disciples of Oral Learners.* Lausanne Occasional Paper, No. 54. Pattaya, Thailand: Lausanne Committee for World Evangelization, 2005.

Marsh, Charles. *Too Hard for God?* Carlisle: Paternoster Press, 2000.

Marshall, Paul, ed. *Radical Islam Rule's: The Worldwide Spread of Extreme Shari'a Law.* Lanham, MD: Roman & Littlefield Publishers, 2005.

Massey, Joshua. "God's Amazing Diversity in Drawing Muslims to Christ." *International Bulletin of Missionary Research* 17, no. 1 (2000): 3–12.

Matheny, Tim. *Reaching the Arabs: A Felt Need Approach.* Pasadena: William Carey Library, 1981.

Maurer, Andreas. "In Search of a New Life: Conversion Motives of Christians and Muslims." In *From the Straight Path to the Narrow Way,* edited by David Greenlee, 93–108. Waynesboro, GA: Authentic, 2006.

McCurry, Don. *The Gospel and Islam.* Monrovia, CA: MARC/World Vision International, 1979.

McCurry, Don. "A Time for New Beginnings." In *The Gospel and Islam: a 1978 Compendium,* edited by Don McCurry, 13–21. Monrovia, CA: MARC, 1979.

McGavran, Donald A. *The Bridges of God*. New York: Friendship Press, 1956.

-----. *Understanding Church Growth*. Grand Rapids, MI: William B. Eerdmans Publishing Company, 1970.

McVicker, Mary. "Experiencing Jesus: Reflections of South Asian Women." In *From the Straight Path to the Narrow Way*, edited by David Greenlee, 125–36. Waynesboro, GA: Authentic, 2006.

Melbourne, Colin. "Nozad: New Born in Christ," From a testimony (paraphrased in modern English), http://www.born-again-christian.info/nozad.htm (accessed February 10, 2008).

Metzger, Bruce M. *A Textual Commentary on the Greek New Testament*. 4th ed. New York: United Bible Societies, 2001.

Miller, William McElwee. *Ten Muslims Meet Christ*. Grand Rapids: William B. Eerdman's Publishing Company, 1969.

Moltmann, Jürgen. *The Crucified God: The Cross of Christ as the Foundation and Criticism of Christian Theology*. Translated by R.A. Wilson and John Bowden. Minneapolis, MN: Fortress Press, 1993.

Montefiore, C.G., and H. Loewe. *A Rabbinic Anthology*. Schocken Books: New York, 1974.

Mooneyham, W. Stanley. "Keynote Address." In The *Gospel and Islam: a 1978 Compendium*, edited by Don McCurry, 22–37. Monrovia, CA: MARC, 1979.

Müller, Roland. *Honor and Shame*. Philadelphia: Xlibris Corp., 2000.

-----. *The Messenger, the Message, the Community: Three Critical Issues for the Cross-Cultural Church Planter*. City, Turkey: Can Book, 2006.

Musk, Bill. *Touching the Soul of Islam*. Crowborough, UK: Monarch Publications, 1995.

-----. *The Unseen Face of Islam*. Kent, UK: MARC, 1989.

Naja, Ben. *Releasing the Workers of the Eleventh Hour*. Pasadena, CA: William Carey Library, 2007.

O'Dell, Carla, and C. Jackson Grayson. *If Only We Knew What We Know: The Transfer of Internal Knowledge and Best Practices*. New York: Free Press/Simon Schuster, 1998.

Parshall, Phil. *Beyond the Mosque*. Grand Rapids, MI: Baker Book House, 1985.

-----. "Danger! New Directions in Contextualization." *Evangelical Missions Quarterly* 43, no. 4 (1998): 404–6, 409–10.

-----. *New Paths in Muslim Evangelism*. Grand Rapids, MI: Baker Book House, 1980.

Patterson, George, and Richard Scoggins. *Church Multiplication Guide: The Miracle of Church Reproduction*. Pasadena, CA: William Carey Library, 2002.

Peace, Richard. *Conversion in the New Testament: Paul and the Twelve*. Grand Rapids and Cambridge: William B. Eerdmans Publishing Company, 1999.

Philips, Abu Ameenah Bilal. *The Exorcist Tradition in Islaam* (sic.). Sharjah, UAE: Dar al Fatah, 1997.

Quinn, Charlotte A., and Frederick Quinn. *Pride, Faith and Fear: Islam in Sub-Saharan Africa*. Oxford: Oxford University Press, 2003.

Reisacher, Evelyne. "North African Women and Conversion: Specifics of Female Faith and Experience." In *From the Straight Path to the Narrow Way*, edited by David Greenlee, 109–23. Waynesboro, GA: Authentic, 2006.

Sakr, Ahmad H. *Al-Jinn*. Lombard, IL: Foundation for Islamic Knowledge, 1994.

Sanneh, Lamin, *Translating the Message: The Missionary Impact on Culture*. Maryknoll: Orbis Books, 1989.

Scoggins, Richard. *Building Effective Church Planting Teams: A Handbook for Team Leaders and Mentors*. http://www.dickscoggins.com/books/teams.php.

Scudder, Samuel H. "The Student, the Fish and Agassiz." http://www.bethel.edu/~dhoward/resources/Agassizfish/Agassizfish.htm.

Shah, Idries. *The Pleasantries of the Incredible Mullah Nasrudin*. New York: Penguin Arkana, 1993.

-----. *The Subtleties of the Inimitable Mullah Nasrudin*. London: Octagon, 1983.

-----. *The Exploits of the Incomparable Mullah Nasrudin*. New York: E.P. Dutton, 1972.

Sheffield, Dan. "Assessing Intercultural Sensitivity in Mission Candidates and Personnel." *Evangelical Missions Quarterly* (January 2007): 22–28.

Siemens, Ruth E. "Tentmakers Needed for World Evangelization." In *Perspectives on the World Christian Movement*, edited by Ralph D. Winter and Steven C. Hawthorne, 733–41. Pasadena: William Carey Library, 1999.

St. John, Patricia. *Until the Day Breaks*. Carlisle: Authentic Media, 1994.

Stacey, Vivienne. "Practice of Exorcism and Healing." In *Muslims and Christians on the Emmaus Road*, edited by J. Dudley Woodberry, 291–303. Monrovia, CA: MARC Publications, 1989.

Stark, Rodney. "The Role of Women in Christian Growth." In *The Rise of Christianity: A Sociologist Reconsiders Christianity*, edited by Rodney Stark, 95–128. Princeton, NJ: Princeton University Press, 1996.

Steffen, Tom. *Connecting God's Story to Ministry*. La Mirada, CA: Center for Organizational and Ministry Development, 1996.

-----. *Passing the Baton: Church Planting That Empowers*. La Habra, CA: Center for Organizational & Ministry Development, 1997.

Strom, Kay Marshall, and Michele Rickett. *Daughters of Hope*. Downers Grove, Illinois: InterVarsity Press, 2003.

Talbert, Charles H. *Reading Acts: A Literary and Theological Commentary on The Acts of the Apostles*. New York: The Crossroad Publishing Company, 1997.

Tennent, Timothy. "Followers of Jesus (Isa) in Islamic Mosques: A Closer Examination of C-5 'High Spectrum' Contextualization." *International Journal of Frontier Missions* 23, no. 3 (2006): 101–15.

Terry, J. O. "Good News for Those with Stories of Grief: A Message for Women Who Share Stories of Personal Misfortune and Grief." Unpublished manuscript, Media Consultant for Asia and the Pacific, International Mission Board, Southern Baptist Convention, 2000.

Travis, John. "The C1–C6 Spectrum?" *Evangelical Missions Quarterly* 34, no. 4 (1998): 411–15.

-----. "Must All Muslims Leave Islam to Follow Jesus?" *Evangelical Missions Quarterly* 34, no. 4 (1998): 411–15.

-----. "Producing and Using Meaningful Translations of the Taurat, Zabur and Injil." *International Journal of Frontier Missions* 23, no. 2 (2006): 73–77.

Travis, John, and Anna Travis. "Appropriate Approaches in Muslim Contexts." In *Appropriate Christianity*, edited by Charles H. Kraft, 397–414. Pasadena: William Carey Library, 2005.

Turner, Victor. *The Ritual Process*. Ithaca, NY: Cornell University Press, 1969.

Weerstra, H.M., and J. Massey, eds. *International Journal of Frontier Missions: Muslim Contextualization* I 17, no. 1 (2000).

Wherry, E.M., et al. *Islam and Mission.* New York: Fleming H. Revell, 1912.

Wiher, Hannes. *Shame and Guilt: A Key to Cross-Cultural Ministry.* Bonn: Verlag für Kultur und Wissenschaft, 2003.

Wilder, John W. "Possibilities for People Movements Among Muslims." *Missiology: An International Review* 5, no. 3 (1977).

Williams, Brad. "The Emmaus–Medina Intertextual Connection: Contextualizing the Presentation of God's Word." *International Journal of Frontier Missions* 23, no. 2 (2006): 67–72.

Willis, Avery. *Indonesian Revival: Why Two Million Came to Christ.* Pasadena, CA: William Carey Library, 1977.

Wilson, J. Christy. *Apostle to Islam: A Biography of Samuel M. Zwemer.* Grand Rapids, MI: Baker Book House, 1952.

Winter, Ralph D. "The Editorial of Ralph D. Winter." *Mission Frontiers*, March–April 1996. http://www.missionfrontiers.org/archive.htm (accessed February 2, 2008).

-----. "The Two Structures of God's Redemptive Mission." In *Perspectives on the World Christian Movement* (Notebook Edition), edited by Steven Hawthorne and Ralph Winter, 131–33. Pasadena, CA: William Carey Library, 1999.

Woodberry, J. Dudley. "A Call to Evangelicals to Respond to a Significant Muslim Overture." http://www.christianitytoday.com/ct/2007/octoberweb-only/143-42.0.html, also on www.acommonword.com/mediaresources.

-----. "Contextualization among Muslims: Reusing Common Pillars." In *The Word among Us,* edited by Dean Gilliland, 282–312. Dallas, TX: Word Publishing, 1989.

-----. "Current Trends in Islam." MR552/562. Course syllabus. Fuller Theological Seminary, Pasadena, CA, 2002.

-----. "A Global Perspective on Muslims Coming to Faith in Christ." In *From the Straight Path to the Narrow Way,* edited by David Greenlee, 11–22. Waynesboro, GA: Authentic, 2006.

-----. "The Relevance of Power Ministries for Folk Muslims." In *Wrestling with Dark Angels,* edited by C. Peter Wagner and Douglas Pennoyer, 313–31. Ventura, CA: Regal Books, 1990.

-----. "To the Muslim I Became a Muslim?" In *Contextualization and Syncretism: Navigating Cultural Currents,* edited by Gailyn Van Rheenen, 143–57. Pasadena, CA: William Carey Library, 2006.

Woodberry, J. Dudley, and Russell G. Shubin. "Why I Chose Jesus." *Mission Frontiers* (March 2001): 31.

Woodberry, J. Dudley, Russell G. Shubin, and G. Marks. "Why Muslims Follow Jesus." *Christianity Today* 51, no. 10 (2007): 80–85.

Ye'or, Bat. *The Dhimmi: Jews and Christians Under Islam.* Rutherford, NJ: Fairleigh Dickinson University Press, 1985.

Zeidan, David. "The Problem of Alienation—Nibbling at the Fringes or Going for the Centre?" www.angelfire.com/az/rescon/alienation.html (accessed August 28, 2007).

Zwemer, S.M. et al., eds. *The Mohammedan World of Today.* New York: Fleming H. Revell, 1906.

Zwemer, Samuel M., and Annie Van Sommer. *Our Moslem Sisters.* New York: Fleming H. Revell, 1907.

About the Authors and Editors

Eric and Laura Adams have worked for twelve years in South Asia among Muslim peoples through development work and sharing the hope within them. Currently, they work in Europe in a mentoring and training capacity for those wanting to demonstrate the love of Jesus among Muslims.

Don Allen is in his fifteenth year as Director of Training for the U.S. office of an agency working among Muslims. He has also spent the past five years in Fruitful Practices research. He and his wife Karen spent several years working with Kurdish refugees in the Southwest United States. He holds an M.Div. in New Testament Studies and a D.Min. in Leadership Development.

Mike Barnett is Professor of Missionary Church Planting at Columbia International University. He and his wife, Cindy, served for twelve years with the International Mission Board focusing on work among least reached and unengaged peoples. Mike continues to serve as a strategy consultant, creative access advocate, and team coach for various missions and organizations. The Barnetts have two grown children, Michelle and Cole, both living in Texas.

John Becker was born and raised in the San Francisco Bay Area, where he met his wife, Maureen. In 1994 they joined Africa Inland Mission International (AIM) to serve in outreach to South Asian people living in Kenya. Since 2002, John has served as one of the directors on AIM's international office team. He is most content spending time with his wife and four children in the great outdoors.

John has a bachelor's degree in Social Science from San Francisco State University, and a Master of Arts of Exegetical Theology from Western Seminary.

Ted Bergman coordinated SIL's global research to discover and catalogue every language in the world and to assess its current state of development from 1983 to 2006. Presently, he is Sociolinguistics Coordinator for Asia and Editor-in-Chief for SIL Electronic Survey Reports. He also assists the International Language Assessment Coordinator, particularly with people profiles. Ted and his wife, Gwen, served across Africa from Nairobi from 1986 to 1998.

Moussa Bongoyok is the Academic Dean at Bangui Evangelical Graduate School of Theology. He holds a Ph.D. in Intercultural Studies (with a special focus on Islamic Studies) from Fuller Seminary. His wife Priscille and he have a long experience of ministry among Muslims in sub-Saharan Africa.

Andrew and Rachel Chard are from England and have been with Africa Inland Mission International as church planters since 1994. Their passion is for the unreached. Since 2003 Andrew and Rachel have been joint team leaders of an international church-planting team among a Muslim people group. Andrew studied theology and missiology in England and was later ordained in 1996. He gained his master's degree in Biblical Studies under Trinity Theological Seminary and is currently working on a doctoral program under Canterbury University, England. Rachel is by professional training a physical therapist, studied missiology pre-field, and has worked closely with Andrew in their church-planting and leadership roles. They continue to serve in Tanzania, East Africa, and have three teenage children.

Jack Colgate and his wife and children have lived in Asia as friends of Muslims and as Gospel planters since 1990. Jack and his wife also help to coach and to train other Gospel planters in fruitful ministry among Muslims. Jack was born and reared in Southeast Asia. He holds a D.Miss. from Fuller Seminary's School of Intercultural Studies.

Joseph Cumming is Director of the newly established Reconciliation Program at the Yale Center for Faith and Culture at Yale Divinity School. He also teaches courses in Islamic Studies at Fuller Theological Seminary, and is completing his Ph.D. in Islamic Studies and Christian Theology at Yale University. During his fifteen years in Mauritania, he served as Director of Doulos Community, a Christian humanitarian organization working in nutrition, public health, agriculture, microcredit, and emergency relief. Joseph and his wife Michele, a registered nurse, are parents of boy–girl twins born in June 1992.

Abraham Durán has served for fifteen years among Muslims. With his family, he was among the first generation of cross-cultural workers sent out from the Evangelical churches of Latin America. Abraham is one of the leaders of Frontiers (Fronteras), an international organization that sends teams of ordinary people to serve Muslims while inviting them, with love and respect, to follow Jesus.

Sue Eenigenburg, currently based in Reading, Pennsylvania, is the Director of Women's Ministry for Christar. She has been involved in missions for more than twenty years, with twelve of those years in the Middle East. Sue is married and has four children and one granddaughter.

David Garrison is the South Asia regional leader for the Southern Baptist International Mission Board. He is the author of several books on mission to unreached peoples, including *Church Planting Movements* (2004), *Strategic Directions for the 21st Century* (1998), and *The Nonresidential Missionary* (1990). Garrison has served as a missionary in Hong Kong, Egypt, Tunisia, and India.

Seneca Garrison is a high school student who has spent much of her life in the 10/40 Window as a student in Egypt, Tunisia, India, and Thailand. She has also been an active member of a house church in India that multiplied to more than 100 daughter churches. Thus, she writes about church-planting movements as an insider and practitioner. She currently lives with her family in Southeast Asia.

Andrea and Leith Gray work in Bible translation and consulting in West Asia, where Leith has lived and worked since 1988. They are involved in training local and cross-cultural co-workers on how to present the message of the Bible creatively and incarnationally in local contexts. They have particularly enjoyed partnering with colleagues from a Muslim background as they seek to make the message of the Bible clear and relevant to local people. Andrea and Leith have two young children.

David Greenlee has served for more than thirty years with Operation Mobilization, the last ten as International Research Associate. He holds a Ph.D. in Intercultural Studies from Trinity International University and is the editor of *From the Straight Path to the Narrow Way: Journeys of Faith* (2004).

Ahmed Haile was born and grew up in a camel-herding Muslim home in Somalia. Christ met Ahmed in his late teens. He completed high school in the United States, and went on to earn a bachelor's degree in Economics, a Master's of Peace Studies, and a Master's of Public Administration. He has done postgraduate studies as well. Ahmed and his wife Martha have been involved in a variety of ministries related to Somalia. He also lectures on peace and conflict transformation at Daystar University and serves as a key leader in the emerging Somali fellowships in the Nairobi area.

Jim Haney serves as Director of the Global Research Department of the International Mission Board, Richmond, Virginia, USA, and has been with the department since 1999. Before this, from 1981 to 1999, Jim served as a church planter among the Edo of Nigeria and the Bimoba, Mamprusi, Konkomba, and Frafra of Ghana in West Africa. During this time, he assisted with various research projects in that region of the world. Jim is married to Donna and has two grown children, Heather and Rachel.

Ramsay Harris has lived and worked in one of the poorest Muslim nations on earth for more than a dozen years, and he has also worked in or visited more than twenty other Muslim countries. He has been an effective church planter, and he has also been actively involved in humanitarian work. He has observed firsthand the problems that arise when Christians mix money and church planting in naïve ways.

Kevin Higgins has worked among Muslims in North America, East Africa, and two countries in South Asia. He is now the executive director of Global Teams, and continues to provide leadership for a growing movement among several Muslim people groups in South Asia. He is active in training international workers for ministry among Muslims and has authored articles and training materials available in several languages.

Scott Holste serves on the Overseas Leadership Team of the International Mission Board as Associate Vice President for Research and Strategic Services. Scott and his wife Janie formerly worked with unreached people groups in Southeast Asia and northern Africa. They have three children.

Patrick Johnstone served for sixteen years as a missionary evangelist in southern Africa. During that time, he wrote the first edition of *Operation World*, of which there have been now five further editions. He was for twenty-two years part of the leadership team of WEC International with a special brief for strategy and research to better enable the agency's church-planting vision among the least-reached peoples on earth. He is now writing a book on the future of world evangelization.

Caleb Chul-Soo Kim has been involved in sharing the Gospel with Muslims in East African regions since 1989. He holds a doctorate from Fuller Theological Seminary. He has been serving as a full-time lecturer at Nairobi Evangelical Graduate School of Theology in Nairobi, Kenya, since 2002, and authored *Islam among the Swahili in East Africa* (2004). Caleb lives in Nairobi with his wife, Manok, and their younger daughter.

Patrick Lai is a slave of Jesus Christ. He is the author of *Tentmaking: Business as Missions* (2005), as well as several articles on business as mission. During his twenty-four years in Asia, the Lord has enabled Patrick's team to plant two churches and two fellowships among Muslims and spawn five other teams in the region, while starting several profitable small businesses, which employ locals and expatriates. He is the founder of the OPEN Network, a network for tentmakers, and he coaches tentmakers throughout the 10/40 Window.

Jeff Liverman has been a student and servant of Muslims since 1985. He has lived and worked primarily in Central Asia and served in various roles. Presently, Jeff continues to serve with Frontiers in an international capacity. He and his wife, Cookie, have two adult children and two grandchildren.

Greg Livingstone and his wife, Sally, have been serving Christ among Muslims since 1963 in South Asia, Southeast Asia, the Middle East, and Europe. His roles have included overseeing fellowship formation, serving as a "team forming coach," and equipping workers for service. Greg has written and edited numerous chapters and articles, and specializes in the history of mission to Muslims. He and Sally have three sons and six grandchildren.

Rick Love has earned a D.Min. in Urban Studies from Westminster Theological Seminary and a Ph.D. in Intercultural Studies from Fuller Theological Seminary. His studies and leadership experience have enabled him to travel, lecture, and write extensively about Christian–Muslim relations. He loves coaching leaders and talking to Muslims about Jesus while drinking espresso.

Chris Maynard had a career in information technology for twenty-eight years, and is now a freelance consultant in information management. He uses his skills to facilitate better deployment of global church resources. Chris assisted the Global Trends team with organizing information about unreached people groups and currently leads a local homegroup. He and his wife Judy have two adult daughters.

J. R. Meydan has lived among Muslims since 1999. After graduating with a master's degree in Intercultural Studies from Wheaton College, she and her husband joined Pioneers to recruit and lead a multi-national team to minister among Muslims in South Asia. She has authored a number of articles presenting ethnographic research on their people group, and is currently editing a book entitled *Muslim Ministry and Foreign Funding: The Impact of External Funds on Indigenous Church-planting Movements in Muslim Lands.*

Phil Parshall and his wife, Julie, have lived among Muslim peoples since 1962, first with International Christian Fellowship (now SIM) in Bangladesh and then in the Philippines. Presently, he is Missionary at Large with SIM. He holds a doctorate from Fuller Seminary and authored nine books on Islam.

Nik Ripken is a mission veteran of twenty-five years with the International Mission Board of the Southern Baptist Church, having served in Malawi, South Africa, Kenya, Somalia, and Ethiopia. Dr. Ripken and his wife Beth serve as Strategy Associates in northern Africa and the Middle East with specific responsibilities for the Horn of Africa and some Gulf States.

Dwight Samuel has been in North Africa for many years in many capacities but mostly as a student of life. He has had the privilege of being the friend of many nationals and cross-cultural workers. In close encounters with communities of faith as well as from more distant observations, he has learned much about the dynamics of life together in new contexts.

Michael Schuler has lived and worked as a tentmaker in Central Asia for the last ten years. He has been involved with a church plant among a traditional segment of an unreached Muslim people group. He is currently setting up and running a business in another restricted-access country.

David W. Shenk grew up in East Africa and served for sixteen years with Eastern Mennonite Missions (EMM) in reaching out among Muslims in Somalia and Kenya. Then, for more than two decades, he served in missions and academic administration. Currently, he is Global Missions Consultant with EMM, with a special focus on the world of Islam.

Erik Simuyu was challenged to reach out to Muslims at the age of ten, and has been doing just that since 1991. Currently, Erik is the Director of Haradali Mission, an indigenous mission agency working among Muslims in East and Central Africa. He is also the host of a weekly program on Hope FM, and is involved in the care and discipleship of Jesus-followers in Nairobi.

Moses Sy and his family have been living in North Africa among Muslim peoples since 1996. They have seen house churches being planted that today are spreading all over the country. They moved in 2007 into another North African country to train nationals in church planting among the unreached tribes.

John and Anna Travis and their family have had the privilege of living in Muslim communities in Asia for the past twenty years. John frequently lectures on contextualization, Jesus-centered movements, power encounter, and Bible translation. His writings have been published in a number of books and journals and translated into a number of languages. John is presently completing a Ph.D. on the topic of healing and deliverance prayer in cross-cultural ministry.

Debora Viveza has been living in Southeast Asia with her husband, and their four children for the last eight years. Together with her husband she ran a company in Holland for fifteen years before they moved overseas. Now, they are running a new business in Southeast Asia. Before moving overseas, Debora earned her bachelor's degree in Missiology.

Annie Ward lives in Central Asia, where she has been ministering for eleven years among Muslims. For the past five years, she has been communicating the Gospel in oral ways by song, recitation, and telling Bible stories. She also trains others to do so. She is a linguist and an English teacher by profession, but now, primarily a housewife, she uses the opportunities in her neighborhood for evangelism and discipleship.

Pam Wilson has been working in West Asia in church midwifery for twenty-five years. She has a husband named Dave, a master's degree from Fuller Theological Seminary, and a pile of ironing on the floor.

J. Dudley Woodberry is Dean Emeritus and Senior Professor of Islamic Studies at the School of Intercultural Studies at Fuller Theological Seminary in Pasadena, California. He has served with his wife and three sons at the Christian Study Centre in Rawalpindi, Pakistan, and as a pastor in Kabul, Afghanistan, and Riyadh, Saudi Arabia.

Index

From Seed to Fruit
Supplemental Resources CD

The following are the requirements and instructions for viewing the Supplemental Resources CD enclosed in this book.

System Requirements:

PC compatible only; Windows XP or higher

Software Requirements:

Microsoft Word, PowerPoint and Excel; Acrobat Reader; Microsoft Internet Explorer 5.0 or higher; Microsoft .NET Framework 1.1 or higher (available on the CD)

Start Up:

1. Insert CD.
2. If a warning box appears, click Yes.
3. The CD should automatically launch to a green screen (if not, see Troubleshooting).
4. On the green screen, click on Launch Application.
5. Click on Run, and then Run again (do NOT click save).

Troubleshooting:

Start Up: The CD should automatically launch to a green screen. If not, open your My Computer folder and right click the CD drive. Select Open. Double click on default.htm to manually open.

Launch Application: If Launch Application does not open, click on <<click here to install>> at the bottom of the page to install .NET Framework.

If Launch Application still does not function after Framework is installed, open My Computer, right click the CD drive and select Open. Double click the App folder. Double click on Partnership.exe.

To replace defective CDs, contact our distributor Send the Light at 1-800-MISSION.